AF778729

PERSONAL FINANCIAL PLANNING

The Adviser's Guide

Second Edition

Rolf Auster

COMMERCE CLEARING HOUSE, INC.
4025 WEST PETERSON AVENUE CHICAGO, ILLINOIS 60646

This publication is designed to provide accurate and authoritative information in regard to the subject matter covered. It is sold with the understanding that the publisher is not engaged in rendering legal, accounting or other professional service and that the author is not offering such advice in this publication. If legal advice or other expert assistance is required, the services of a competent professional person should be sought.

ISBN 0-8080-0003-9

© 1993, Commerce Clearing House, Inc.

All Rights Reserved

Printed in the United States of America

Preface

The last few years have seen a phenomenal growth of personal financial planning as a specialty and as a full-fledged profession. As a result, there is a continual and increasing need for literature which specifically addresses the concerns of the financial adviser. Accordingly, this book is directed at the myriad of individuals whose livelihood includes the rendering of personal financial advice, including, among others, CPAs, attorneys, personal financial planners, stockbrokers, investment advisers, insurance agents, and trust officers.

Personal financial planning is a continuous process that takes place in a dynamic financial environment. Self-contained and up-to-date through the Revenue Reconciliation Act of 1993 (the RRA of 1993), *Personal Financial Planning: The Adviser's Guide* answers the majority of questions an adviser may have about a client's financial situation, including such issues as the client's home, insurance, savings, credit, and retirement and aspects of estate planning.

This book contains a wealth of information with state-of-the-art estate planning strategies and income tax advice. End materials include a set of tax tables and present value tables, as well as a detailed index. A user will find this book a highly valuable reference and financial planning tool.

Rolf Auster

November 1993

About the Author

Rolf Auster holds a Ph.D. in Finance from Northwestern University and is a tax lawyer (LL.M. in Taxation), a CPA, a Certified Financial Planner, and a Certified Fund Specialist.

His teaching career started in 1965 and, since then, he has taught Finance and Investments at the University of Illinois at Chicago, Accounting at DePaul University, and Taxation and Estate Planning at Florida International University in Miami.

He has authored a dozen books on tax planning and investments and hundreds of articles in finance, accounting, real estate, insurance, pension, and tax journals. His practical experience includes commercial banking and frequent consulting engagements for professional tax and financial advisers.

CONTENTS

Detailed Table of Contents begins at page vii.

TABLE OF CONTENTS

CHAPTER 1

INTRODUCTION: THE PERSONAL FINANCIAL PLANNING PROCESS

CHAPTER 2

TIME VALUE OF MONEY

CHAPTER 3

BUDGETING, SAVINGS, AND CHECKING

CHAPTER 6

PERSONAL LOANS AND CREDIT MANAGEMENT

Credit Cards

Main Sources of Loan

CHAPTER 9

EQUITY INVESTMENTS

Par.

Sales of Interest Coupons and Stripped Bonds

Municipal Bonds

CHAPTER 11

TAX-SHELTERED INVESTMENTS

Tax Shelter Characteristics

CHAPTER 14

TAX ASPECTS OF CASUALTY GAINS AND LOSSES

CHAPTER 17

ESTATE, GIFT, AND GENERATION-SKIPPING TRANSFER TAXES

Par.

APPENDIX

PRESENT VALUE TABLES AND TAX RATES

INDEX

CHAPTER 1

INTRODUCTION: THE PERSONAL FINANCIAL PLANNING PROCESS

¶ 101 FINANCIAL PLANNING EXPLOSION

The unusual growth in the number of financial planners is highlighted by increased membership in the International Association of Financial Planners ranging from 5,000 in 1979 to 25,000 in 1993. California, Texas and Florida have the greatest concentration of planners. Accounting for this increase are such factors as:

1. High inflation rates in the early '80s;
2. Constant changes in the tax law;
3. Increases in real income;
4. Proliferation in two-earner families;
5. Increases in college cost;
6. Increased life expectancies necessitating more careful retirement planning for more years; and
7. Introduction of new life insurance products, e.g., adjustable, variable, and universal policies.

¶ 102 PERSONAL FINANCIAL PLANNING SERVICE CLIENT

However, the typical client is hard to identify. The following situations indicate that the client is in need of Personal Financial Planning services:

1. Client's investment portfolio is limited to Certificates of Deposit or money market funds as the stock market is soaring.
2. Client has a successful business and wants to pass it on to children or grandchildren without paying substantial estate taxes.
3. Client has limited life insurance and does not know what kind or how much to buy.
4. Client is worried that the children's college education expenses will necessitate so much debt as to jeopardize the client's own retirement plans.
5. Client consistently spends more than he makes.

On the other hand, people with household income below $50,000 a year, without a significant net worth above and beyond the home equity, will generally have a limited need for professional financial planners. The modest need that may exist can rarely justify an initial fee of up to $1,500 to get started, plus renewals and review fees, from a simple cost-benefit analysis viewpoint.

Typical advice given to planners concerning prospective clients is as follows:

1. Make as much small talk as the client wishes.
2. Ask about the client's financial goals and concerns as well as related issues.
3. Explain how financial planning will help the client.
4. Bring up fees and time horizons.
5. Keep an eye open for clues relating to other services the client may need.

Literature, including the daily press, advises prospective clients to ask planners the following questions. The planner should be prepared.

1. *What is the planner's specialty?* If the answer is specific, such as insurance, mutual funds, real estate or shelters, the client is advised to look elsewhere.
2. *Is the planner affiliated with any other firm?* If yes, the possibility of a bias results again in a further search.
3. *Does the planner earn significant commissions?* An objective planner earns most income from fees.

4. *What is the planner's education and experience?* If the planner's background is specialized, e.g., insurance, or the planner has no experience, the search goes on.
5. *Will the planner give professional references?* If not, the search continues; if yes, the references are contacted.
6. *Can the planner answer technical questions?* Here the client studies a narrow area, such as Code Sec. 401(k) or salary reduction plans, and asks the planner specific questions to test the expertise. If the planner fails, the search goes on.
7. *What does the planner charge?* If a flat number is mentioned up front, the search goes on. The right answer is that the fee will depend on what the client needs and what the planner can do.

¶ 103 SIX OBJECTIVES OF FINANCIAL PLANNING

The goals of financial planning range from living a life in reasonable comfort to providing for survivors. Thus, in general terms, the objectives are:

1. To achieve and maintain a desired standard of living.
2. To provide protection for family and assets, e.g., life insurance, medical and disability insurance, home and auto insurance, etc., or even education for the spouse.
3. To save for short-term goals, e.g., vacation, emergency, cosmetic surgery.
4. To invest for the future, e.g., for the children's education, for long-term security, for specific goals, such as retirement at age 55.
5. To provide for retirement or for financial independence, which may come automatically (e.g., through working 40 years for the same employer that provides a good pension plan) or which may have to be homemade (e.g., a defined benefit Keogh Plan for the self-employed).
6. In addition, estate planning is necessary to carry out the client's wishes after death, and simultaneously reduce the wealth transfer tax. Estate planning should take place throughout the client's life, even if the assets are quite limited.

Clearly, the objectives are interrelated. For example, if objective one is paramount, i.e., the client wishes to maintain the highest possible lifestyle, the remaining five goals evaporate. Similarly, if the client is single or has no children, and a working spouse, goals 2 and 3 may be deemphasized.

¶ 104 THE FINANCIAL ACTIVITY HIERARCHY

The client's total financial picture may be broken down into four major groups of activities[1] as follows:

1. *Cash management activities* include checking, savings, and money market accounts.
2. *Investment activities* include stocks, bonds, partnership interests, and collectibles.
3. *Employment activities* include the net worth of one's own business, a pension or profit-sharing plan, or an Individual Retirement Account.
4. *Life-style activities* include the home, transportation (autos) and such items as jewelry, furs, and other valuables.

Under the activity approach, each activity is treated as an independent entity and accounted for separately in terms of cash flow, income and expense, assets and equities, and tax consequences and net worth. After being evaluated in isolation, all financial reports are consolidated into the client's total financial picture and evaluated by their impact on the bottom line.

¶ 105 THE PERSONAL FINANCIAL PLANNING PROCESS

The financial planning process may be broken down into six steps:

1. *Collect and study all relevant data.* The planner helps the client gather all financial records from wills and insurance policies, to brokerage statements and checking accounts.
2. *Define financial goals.* The client establishes goals such as foregoing retirement if necessary, accumulating $1 million in securities by age 50, financing a son's law school studies, etc.
3. *Find financial problems.* The client's problems may include excessive housing costs, inadequate insurance, high-risk investments, nonaggressive tax position, a compulsive-shopper spouse, etc.
4. *Establish a written financial plan.* The plan should provide recommendations for both specific and alternative suggestions of financial actions. These may include specific types and amounts of insurance to buy, a family budget, cash flow analysis, securities diversification strategies, etc.
5. *Plan implementation.* The planner may work with the client in carrying out recommendations or work with the client's

[1] David L. Unger, "The Activity Approach to Personal Financial Planning," *Journal of Accountancy,* April 1985.

other advisers, e.g., a broker, lawyer, CLU, banker, or tax adviser.

6. *Plan review.* Annually and/or upon change in circumstances, e.g., upon divorce, death of spouse, promotion, retirement, etc., the plan should be revised and updated.

¶ 106 PERSONAL FINANCIAL PLANNING SOFTWARE

Since 1985, there has been an explosion in personal finance software packages that are compatible with home computers. Some packages perform individual tasks, such as check writing, keeping track of family net worth, cash management, or sources and uses of funds. Other packages are more comprehensive and offer complete home financing systems, projections, budgeting and financial reports, including tax preparation, insurance needs, portfolio management, and planning the family's financial future.

The major PFP software packages are all compatible with the IBM PC and usually one or more of the following: Apple II, MacIntosh, Commodore 64, or Atari. Prices generally range from $60 to $245.

¶ 107 AMERICAN INSTITUTE OF CERTIFIED PUBLIC ACCOUNTANTS AND PERSONAL FINANCIAL PLANNING

The American Institute of Certified Public Accountants authorized a Personal Financial Planning division in May 1986. Membership is limited to CPA members of the AICPA, and the stated objectives for CPA personal financial planners include:

1. sharing their specialized knowledge,
2. expanding their competence,
3. enhancing their profitability,
4. exchanging experiences and ideas, and
5. communicating the competence of CPAs in the PFP field to the public.

A quarterly newsletter, "The Planner," is sent to members. The annual membership fee includes the newsletter and an amount earmarked for a public relations effort to convince the public that the CPA is a "competent, objective and trustworthy PFP professional."

Since 1988, the institute has been conferring the PFS (Personal Financial Specialist) designation on CPAs who pass an examination and meet a three-year experience requirement.

In September 1993, the AICPA issued the first of its *Statements on Responsibilities in Personal Financial Planning Practice.* Entitled *Basic Personal Financial Planning Engagement Functions and Responsi-*

bilities, it is advisory only and not enforceable under Rule 202 of the AICPA's Code of Professional Conduct. However, it provides useful guidance for CPAs who perform PFP engagements. The AICPA has issued exposure drafts of the next two statements, which deal with CPAs who use other advisers and CPAs who implement financial planning decisions.

CHAPTER 2

TIME VALUE OF MONEY

¶ 201 INTRODUCTION

Present value computations are necessary when the alternatives being compared involve payments to be made at different points in time. Unless the time value of money is taken into account, the payments, the cash flows, the different tax liabilities, etc., are not comparable. Reducing all future payments to their present value neutralizes the time factor through the use of a common denominator, e.g., the discount rate.

Since the present value of future payments depends on the discount rate, the decision maker should select the rate with some care. Theoretically, the discount rate is the cost of capital, or the minimum rate of return which is competitive with that on the best alternative investment available to the taxpayer. Since it is a measure of the opportunity cost, it is subjective and varies from time to time and from taxpayer to taxpayer. It is likely to be at least a percentage point or two above the rate of inflation. In most cases the discount rate will fall somewhere between 6% and 12%.

A LITTLE MATH

Is it "better" to receive $600 today or $1,000 five years from now? If the discount rate is 10%, a present value table furnishes the number .621. This means that $621 would grow to $1,000 in five years at 10%. Consequently, the present value of $1,000 in five years is $621, more than $600. However, if the required rate of return is 12%, the present value is only $567 and $600 today is "better."

Mathematical Examples

¶ 202 PRESENT VALUE OF A SINGLE AMOUNT

If an amount, A, is to be received n periods from now and the discount rate is r percent, the present value of A equals

$$A/(1+r)^n.$$

Thus, if $1,000 is to be received five years from now and the discount rate used is 10%, the present value is

$$\$1{,}000/1.10^5.$$

The present value of a single payment table shows the values of $1/(1+r)^n$. The discount factor at five years and 10% is .621. Therefore, .621 × $1,000, or $621, is the present value we are looking for.

¶ 203 FUTURE VALUE OF A SINGLE AMOUNT

If an amount, A, is invested today for n periods and the rate of return is r percent, the future value of A equals

$$A(1+r)^n.$$

Thus, the future value is computed by multiplying, while the present value is computed by dividing, i.e., the future value is compounded and the present value is discounted. Compounding and discounting are opposites, or reciprocals.

If $1,000 is to be invested for five years at 10%, the future value is

$$\$1{,}000 = 1.10^5.$$

Since the present value of \$1 in five years at 10% is .621, the future value of \$1 today is 1/.621 or 1.6103. Therefore, 1.6103 × \$1,000, or \$1,610, is the future value we are looking for.

¶ 204 PRESENT VALUE OF AN ANNUITY

As has been shown, the present value of one amount, A, to be received n years from now at r percent equals $A/(1+r)^n$. Similarly, if a given amount, A, is to be received each year for n years at r percent, the sum of the present values is

$$A/(1+r) + A/(1+r)^2 + A/(1+r)^3 + \ldots A/(1+r)^{n-1} + A/(1+r)^n$$

This is a geometric series that may be simplified to a short expression, a summation formula, in this case

$$A \times \frac{1 - 1/(1+r)^n}{r}.$$

Thus, if \$1,000 is to be received each year for five years, starting in one year, at a discount rate of 10% the payments are worth

$$\$1{,}000 \times \frac{1 - 1/1.10^5}{.10}.$$

According to the present-value-of-\$1-received-annually table, \$1 received at the end of each year for five years at 10% is 3.791. Therefore, 3.791 × \$1,000, or \$3,791, is the present value we are looking for.

¶ 205 FUTURE VALUE OF AN ANNUITY

As indicated at ¶ 204, above, the present value of an annuity of \$1 is

$$\frac{1 - 1/(1+r)^n}{r}.$$

Furthermore, a single payment will grow by a factor of $(1+r)^n$. Therefore, the future value of an annuity equals

$$\frac{1 - 1/(1+r)^n}{r} (1+r)^n \quad \text{or} \quad \frac{(1+r)^n - 1}{r}.$$

Thus, if \$1,000 is to be invested each year for five years at 10%, starting in one year, at the end of the fifth year the investor would have

$$\$1{,}000 \times \frac{1.10^5 - 1}{.10}.$$

This equals $\$1{,}000 \times \frac{1.6103 - 1}{.10} = \$1{,}000 \times 6.103 = \$6{,}103$.

Investing an annuity over the years is the same as investing its present value today.

Applications of Tables

¶ 210 PRESENT VALUE OF A FUTURE AMOUNT

Due to deferral techniques, a $10,000 tax liability is pushed five years into the future. If the taxpayer's discount rate is 10%, the tables show that the present value of $1 five years from now is .621. Thus, paying $10,000 in tax five years from now is comparable to paying $6,210 today. If the rate of return is 15%, today's value would be reduced to $4,970, and at 20% would only be $4,020. A deferral of 10 years at 10% would result in a present value of $3,860. Thus, the timing of a payment has a dramatic effect on the present value, as does the decision maker's rate of return. The longer the time horizon and/or the higher the rate, the lower the present value of a future payment.

¶ 211 FUTURE VALUE OF A PRESENT INVESTMENT

Future values are opposites of present values. Thus, .621 is the present value of $1 to be received five years from now, discounted at 10%, because $1 is the future value of .621 invested today and left to compound at 10% for five years. Once this is understood present value tables can be used to answer questions such as: *What after-tax return is required for an investment to triple in eight years?*

If the present value of $1 is .33, this means that .33 cents would grow to $1, i.e., an investment would triple at the applicable interest rate and over the applicable period. Thus, looking horizontally across from eight years in the present value table would yield the factor .33, and then reading off the applicable rate in the table would show that .327 is located under 15%. As a result, the money triples in eight years at 15%.

¶ 212 COMPUTING AVERAGE COMPOUNDED GROWTH RATE

The price of a stock grew from $20 to $50 in five years and the value of a house increased from $40,000 to $100,000 in five years. A natural question to ask is: *How fast did the price go up?* This is equivalent to asking for the internal rate of return, or the average compounded rate of return, or the growth rate. Again, the present value of a single payment table may be used: 20 is 40% of 50; 40 is 40% of 100. Therefore, the relevant discount factor is .4, i.e., if .4 is the present value of $1, it is because money grows by a factor of 2.5 at whatever term and rate combination looked at. Across from five years is .402 located under a rate of 20%. Thus, the stock price and house value both have increased by 20% a year.

¶ 213 USE OF INFINITY IN ANNUITY COMPUTATIONS

It is both fun and instructive to experiment with present value computations. Assuming a 10% interest rate, the discount factor for 40 $1 payments received at the end of each year is 9.779, which may be viewed from two vantage points:

1. The present value of $1,000 received at the end of each year for 40 years (a total of $40,000) is only $9,779 at 10%.
2. $9,779 is invested at 10%, compounded annually. At the end of each year $1,000 is withdrawn. After the 40th withdrawal the principal is gone.

If an additional $221 is invested the principal would never have to be touched, since $9,779 plus $221 is $10,000 and $10,000 invested at 10% will generate $1,000 in income forever. Thus, the difference between infinity and 40 years is only about 2% of principal at a 10% rate.

¶ 214 SINGLE PAYMENT AND ANNUITY TABLE INTERPLAY

The annuity table is merely a summation of the single payment table and is used for convenience. Thus, if a payment of $1,000 is to be received at the end of each year for four years and the discount rate is 10%, the present value may be found in two ways:

1. Using the annuity table, the annuity of $1,000 is simply multiplied by 3.17, the present value of $1 received at the end of each year for four years at 10%, resulting in a present value of $3,170.
2. Using the single payment table each payment is discounted and the results are added up.

Year		
1	$1,000 × .909 =	$ 909
2	$1,000 × .826 =	826
3	$1,000 × .751 =	751
4	$1,000 × .683 =	683
		$3,169

(Because of rounding, a $1 difference resulted.)

The annuity table can be used only under the following conditions:

1. The payments must be exactly equal.
2. Payments are made at equal time intervals, such as quarterly or annually.
3. The discount rate used is constant over the relevant term.

If any of the three conditions is not met, each payment must be handled separately and the single payment table must be used.

¶ 215 FINDING THE INTERNAL RATE OF RETURN

By investing $120,000 today the investor expects to receive $40,000 a year for five years. What is the expected rate of return? The numbers must be standardized so that the annuity table may be used. If $120,000 yields $40,000, $3 must be invested to yield $1 per year. Therefore, the discount factor to look for under five years is three. Note that the number 2.991 is under 20%. $40,000 a year for five years then represents a yield of 20% or so on $120,000. 20% is the average compounded rate of return.

¶ 216 PRESENT AND FUTURE VALUES OF AN ANNUITY

A lucky bettor wins $300,000 in the State Lottery, payable at the rate of $20,000 a year for 15 years. This annuity is also known as a term interest and clearly has a present value far less than $300,000. For example, a winner who can assign the winning ticket to a bank using a 10% discount rate will collect $152,120. This is because the discount factor corresponding to 15 years and 10% is 7.606 and $20,000 × 7.606 = $152,120. Thus, $152,120 is the present value of $20,000 a year for 15 years at 10%.

What is the *future* value of $20,000 a year for 15 years at 10%? Since the present value of $20,000 a year for 15 years at 10% is $152,120, one point must be clearly understood. *Investing $152,120 today at 10% for 15 years is equivalent to investing $20,000 a year at 10% for 15 years.* Therefore, the future value of this annuity is simply $152,120 × 1.10^{15}. The single payment table shows the value of $1/1.10^{15}$ as being .239. The future value of $20,000 a year for 15 years at 10% is therefore $152,120 × 1/.239 or $634,485. In this example the present value of the annuity is approximately one-half of the actual payment and one-fourth of its future value.

Additional Applications: Mortgages, Bonds, and Taxes

¶ 220 15- AND 30-YEAR MORTGAGE COMPARISON

The following is a 15- and 30-year mortgage comparison. Consider a fixed rate, 10% level payment mortgage. According to the annuity table, the present value of $1 a year for 15 years at 10% is $7.606 and for 30 years it is $9.427. This means that a loan of $7,606 at 10% will require the annual payment of $1,000 for 15 years and that a $9,427 loan will require an annual payment of $1,000 for 30 years at 10%. An interesting question is: By what percentage should the payment for a 30-year loan be increased if it is to be paid off over 15 years at 10%? The answer can be found by taking the ratio 9.427/7.606 or 1.2394, meaning that a 23.94% increase is required.

Example: A homeowner takes out a $100,000 mortgage for 30 years at 10% with no prepayment penalties. Since $1 a year will pay off a loan of $9.427, the annual payment required is $100,000/9.427 or $10,608. This represents a monthly payment of $884 and total payment of $318,240, of which $218,240 is interest.

If the annual payment is stepped up to $10,608 ×9.427/7.606, or $13,148, the monthly payment is $1,096. By paying this $212 extra a month, the loan is paid off in 15 years and total payments equal $197,220, of which $97,220 is interest. $121,020 in interest is saved.

To summarize:

	Annual Pmt.	*Monthly Pmt.*	*Total Pmt.*	*Total Int.*
15-year loan	$ 13,148	$ 1,096	$197,220	$ 97,220
30-year loan	10,608	884	318,240	218,240
Difference	$ 2,540	$ 212	$121,020	$121,020

Thus, disregarding taxes, an annual payment of $2,540 for 15 years resulted in a lump-sum savings of $121,020. This is, of course, a 10% return on investment.

To turn the numbers around: If $2,540 was invested each year at 10% for 15 years, the future value of this annuity would be equal to the present value of $10,608 a year for the next 15 years.

Proof

$ 2,540 × 7.606 × 1/.239	=	$81,000
$10,608 × 7,608	=	$81,000

¶ 221 BOND VALUES

The market value of a bond is simply the present value of the interest payments and the principal, discounted at the "market rate of return" for a bond with its risk characteristics.

Example: A $1,000 face value bond pays 8% interest a year and matures in 20 years. If the market rate is 10%, the value of the bond is found in two steps:

Present value of interest payments	
$80 × 8.514 (from the annuity table, 10%, 20 years)	$681.12
Present value of principal	
$1,000 × .149 (from the single payment table, 10%, 20 years)	149.00
Market value of bond	$830.12

More typically, the investor looks up the price, maturity and coupon rate and computes the discount rate. Thus, if an 8%, 20-year bond is selling for $830, the *yield to maturity* is 10%. The yield to maturity is the same as the internal rate of return or the average compounded growth rate. These are all names for that discount rate which will reduce future cash flows to a present value equal to the investment.

¶ 222 PRESENT VALUE OF FUTURE TAX LIABILITIES

In some cases a taxpayer has a choice between paying a tax immediately or deferring and increasing the tax payment.

> ***Example:*** A lump-sum distribution of $100,000 may be taxed immediately at 14% and be invested at 10% before taxes. Alternatively, the full $100,000 may be rolled over into an Individual Retirement Account and yield 10% tax deferred. If the tax bracket is a constant 28%, which alternative would maximize after-tax proceeds after 10 years at a discount rate of 10%? (It is assumed that the age $59\frac{1}{2}$ requirement will be met.)

No tax deferral		
$86,000 × 1.072^{10}	= $86,000 × 2.0 =	$172,000
Rollover		
$100,000 × 1.10^{10}	= $100,000 × 1/.386	
$100,000 × 2.5967 =		$259,067
Less 28% tax		−72,539
After-tax withdrawal		$186,528

> Thus, the deferral of the tax payment resulted in higher after-tax cash, despite a significant increase in the tax itself.

The concepts discussed here will prove useful throughout the book. Incidentally, in lieu of using the present value tables in the Appendix, all calculations may be performed on a pocket calculator.

CHAPTER 3

BUDGETING, SAVINGS, AND CHECKING

¶ 301 INTRODUCTION

This chapter serves as an introduction and a setting for further readings of the chapters on credit, investments and tax shelters. Inflation led to unprecedented interest rates and new forms of savings certificates and money market funds. In addition to personal budgeting, the discussion covers types of savings accounts, types of savings institutions, safe deposit boxes, and the intelligent use of checking, including some less-known facts.

Personal Budgeting

¶ 302 WHY A BUDGET?

A budget is a future plan of sources and uses of funds. Since no one can be forced to stick to planned expenses, a budget is an application of willpower. It is *not* merely a record of expenditures, although bookkeeping is necessary to implement the plan. A budget is a financial tool that is most useful to people with low salaries. Here are three famous quotes from literature, and if any one of them applies to the client, a budget is definitely needed:

"I never waste money; I always spend it all."

"I can resist anything except temptation."

"Give me the luxuries and I can dispense with the necessities."

Due to inflation, the need for a budget is greater than ever. In 1939 a two-child family earning $25,000 paid $1,700 in federal income tax and could live comfortably. Today the tax liability on $25,000 is closer to $4,000. The cost of living has gone up at least 300%. This means that some $75,000 *after taxes* is needed to maintain the same life-style as the $25,000 the family had in 1939. Before-taxes income from all sources must, therefore, be closer to $150,000. Under the current tax structure, nontaxable fringe benefits are more attractive than cash.

Here are *three good reasons* to implement a budget:

1. *Maintain a solvent life-style.* Some one million American families a year file personal bankruptcy. Quite a few of them have a history of high earnings. People tend to adjust their life-style to their earnings. Regardless of their income level, they com-

mit themselves to regular expenses which may even exceed their take-home pay. They buy bigger houses, additional and more expensive cars (and replace these cars for newer models more often), and private boats, and send their children to private schools. The average family is broke within months if unemployment strikes. The reasons are that the higher the salary, the greater the gap between the salary, and the unemployment compensation (since 1979, unemployment benefits may be taxable in part) and the longer it typically takes to obtain a suitable position elsewhere.

There are two kinds of insolvencies:

(a) Insolvency in the equity sense is defined as the inability to meet financial obligations when due. The basic job of a budget is to keep cash inflows at least equal to cash outflows, preferably with some margin for safety and savings, i.e., to ensure liquidity.

(b) Insolvency in *the bankruptcy sense* refers to the simple and common phenomenon that liabilities exceed assets. Because the present value of future earnings is *not* an asset, although the client easily can obtain unsecured personal loans on the basis of it, this situation is common indeed.

2. *Achieve financial goals.* Without a long-term financial plan, it is difficult to reach major goals, such as providing for retirement, early disability or death, a new house, children's college education, etc.

3. *Preserve peace of mind.* A client whose assets, earnings and disposable income are known will not suddenly one day wind up in the red. Many highly paid individuals are quite naive about their own financial affairs, considering their often sophisticated knowledge of their business affairs. On the other hand, there are several things a budget is *not* designed to do:

(a) Its purpose is *not* to make a miser of the user.

(b) It is *not* designed to make a family miserable by having to account for and prove every expense or deviation from the budget.

(c) The budget should *not* result in transporting money from one envelope or fund to another.

HOW TO BUDGET

A budget should ideally be *definite, workable, realistic,* and *viable.* It should contribute to the following:

1. The budget should show where the money is coming from and where it is going.
2. The cash outflow should cover the following in order of importance: necessities, comforts, self-improvements, and luxuries.
3. The budget should supply the means for saving.
4. It should help build good spending habits.

These objectives can be accomplished if the budget is kept simple and the family works together, even if no one has to account for every dollar.

Personal financial planning is similar to corporate financial planning:

1. A family needs a financial policy.
2. Financial statements, such as a balance sheet, income statement and cash-flow budgets should be prepared.
3. The family should plan for the present, five years ahead, and for life.
4. Major spending goals should be established.

If these things are done, at best the client has good planning; at worst, ample warning. The plan developed should have the following three main components:

PROJECTED INCOME

Projected income includes the client's and other family members' salaries, plus investment income. It may be necessary to assess the outlook of employers and their industries.

SPENDING PLANS

Spending plans should be both short- and long-term. Review what was done last year; budget for next year and predict any potentially large expenditures (a daughter's wedding, a new home, college education, etc.).

INVESTMENT PROGRAM

Should the client's investments be changed? Perhaps money should be committed to a conservative option writing program or commercial real estate. Keeping money in the bank beyond a point is like keeping a race horse in a closet.

To get started it is useful to set up a personal balance sheet, consisting of assets and liabilities. The assets should be valued at market values, not cost. Included should be the car, furniture, jewelry, cash value of life insurance, the home, etc., as well as bank deposits and securities. Then all debts are subtracted, including the mortgage, credit card balances, etc. The result is the *net worth.* If it is positive, fine, however, the following questions should be asked:

1. If the client's salary stopped today, how long can the current lifestyle be maintained without liquidating assets?
2. Is the client saving at 3% while paying 18% on personal debts, such as charge accounts?
3. How much money can be raised on assets without selling some that the family would rather keep (the home, the car, a favorite collection or securities, etc.).
4. Once unemployed, it suddenly becomes hard to raise cash. If savings are limited, has the client established credit lines with banks and executive finance companies just in case?
5. Include unpaid taxes as part of the liabilities. If the client has interest and dividend income, withholding may fall short of eventual tax liability.
6. Salaries are *not* assets, even if funds may be borrowed on the strength of them.

¶ 303 CASH INFLOWS

Once a family has formulated an idea of its current financial position through the use of a personal balance sheet, it is ready for a plan of action, the budget itself. The two main components of a budget are cash inflows and cash outflows, which are not necessarily the same as income and expenses. Anyone who lives beyond one's means is "poor" in the budget sense and perhaps insolvent in the equity sense. Even someone with a good income may not be able to buy new cars, go on vacations, send children to college, buy a vacation home, and still save for retirement. The first thing to do is to buy a pocket calculator to speed up calculations. Then expected cash inflows over the next 12 months may be added up. These are comprised of:

1. *Take-home salaries.* Gross income is reduced by federal, state and local taxes, social security taxes, contributions to pension plans, etc.
2. *Interest, dividends, royalties and rent.* An allowance must be made for the tax. If due declarations of estimated tax are not filed and the employer is not withholding additional tax on salaries, there may be an extra tax to pay come April 15 next year *plus penalties.* The penalty is computed as interest but is nondeductible.

3. *Inheritances.* Inheritances from relatives or friends still in *probate* but expected to be paid within a year. Provisions must be made for local death, succession, or inheritance taxes.

4. *Sales of Assets.* Cash from projected sales of assets, from securities to personal property, such as cars, boats, etc. Capital gain taxes reduce such proceeds. The trick is to have these cash inflows exceed cash outflows *in the long run.* Particular care must be taken not to adjust expenses upward because of nonrecurring cash inflows.

¶ 304 CASH OUTFLOWS

Controlling cash outflows should ideally enable the client to accomplish the following:

1. To own a home and have sufficient life insurance;
2. To keep at least six months' salary in a savings account or savings certificates;
3. To keep borrowing, exclusive of mortgage, down to two months' salary, but remember: It is undesirable to borrow at 18% while savings earn 3%-5%;
4. To keep housing costs at 35% or less of take-home pay; and
5. To save 5%-10% of salaries monthly.

CASH FLOW STATEMENT (ANNUAL)

CASH INFLOWS		*CASH OUTFLOWS*	
Take-home pay		Mortgage or rent	
Interest		Property taxes	
Dividends		Income taxes, other than withholding	
Investment income		Groceries	
Social Security		Clothes	
Pensions		Utilities	
Tax refunds		Home repairs and maintenance	
Inheritances		Transportation and auto	
Miscellaneous	________	Insurance premiums	
TOTAL	________	Medical and dental	
		Education	
		Restaurants and entertainment	
		Vacations and leisure	
		Charitable contributions	
		Incidentals	________
		TOTAL	________

Financial growth is impossible unless more is earned than spent, and more is saved and invested than borrowed. If cash inflows fall short of cash outflows, assets must be liquidated and/or funds must be borrowed.

How does the client control expenses? Spending will *vary in two dimensions:*

1. *Expenses will vary with family size, tastes, priorities and personal preferences.* Some people will rather spend more money on a bigger house and a bigger car than on vacations, for example. Large families tend to eat more at home than out to avoid astronomical restaurant bills. However, they spend more money on clothes, groceries, medical care and tuition.
2. *The spending pattern will display a certain life-cycle variation.* Housing costs as a percentage of income go down with age because the mortgage payments are fixed and therefore lower due to inflation. Eventually they disappear altogether.

Medical care tends to go up with age, but food costs tend to remain about the same until children are leaving home. Tax bills tend to go up for several reasons:

1. When children leave home, the dependency exemptions are lost. This typically happens many years before the increased age-65 standard deduction becomes available.
2. Itemized expenses go down because a smaller and smaller fraction of the mortgage payment will represent interest. This is magnified by the fact that the absolute payment goes down compared to income, due to inflation.
3. The client's earning power is likely to reach a peak at age 40 to 60, resulting in higher tax brackets.
4. If savings have accumulated, more taxable dividends and interest will be collected.

Here are typical percentages of take-home pay spent by the average American family on major items:

Housing and household operations	30%
Food, alcohol and tobacco	25%
Transportation	15%
Clothing	10%
Recreation	7%
Medical care	7%
TOTAL	94%

The above-listed six items alone cost the average family almost all its income. If a seventh item, "miscellaneous," is thrown in, there is not much room for savings, except indirectly through home ownership, Social Security, and pension plans. Lower income families tend to spend a higher percentage on food and housing. Higher income families tend to spend more on recreation, such as country club fees, golf and vacations.

¶ 305 HOW TO CUT SPENDING

Here is a useful tool in determining and controlling a client's spending habits. Create a pay cut on paper. Assume that as of next month the salary is reduced by 10%. Figure out how to live on the new salary and what the client would have to be without. Then try it again with a 20% paycut. Maybe the client simply has to omit savings or amend some personal habits, such as cocktails, smoking, or expensive restaurants. Some of the factors most likely to cause excessive spending are discussed below:

IMPULSE BUYING

The higher a salary, the more expensive the items bought on the spur of the moment. Even a mink coat or a car may be purchased this way.

CONSPICUOUS CONSUMPTION

Most people who have any money to spend like to proudly display the fruit of their labors, rather than just have some "boring" saving certificates or municipal bonds.

EASY CREDIT

Credit cards have been distributed around the country like confetti the last few decades. Diners Club started around 1950, American Express at the end of the fifties and Carte Blanche in the early sixties, to name the leading "travel and entertainment cards." In the seventies, bank cards, like Master Card and Visa, took off, if not over. It is quite common to have at least half a dozen major cards. At the minimum, this leads to higher restaurant bills, since the client cannot run out of spending money in the short run.

PLANNED PSYCHOLOGICAL OBSOLESCENCE

The economy would doubtless suffer if everyone kept using everything for the full physical life, but for the individual it does lead to higher spending. New styles and fashions are designed to cause the customer to discard perfectly useful items and buy new ones to "stay with it."

Cash outflows can be classified in two broad categories, according to how easy it is to cut down on them. To use cost accounting terminology, they may be labeled fixed or variable costs. The fixed costs are regular or committed expenses, while the variable costs are discretionary, flexible, controllable, or postponable expenses. In the long run, even the fixed expenses may become at least partly controllable.

FIXED EXPENSES

Most of these are hard to reduce overnight, such as mortgage payments, insurance payments and property taxes. In the long run, the client's house can be sold, if necessary or desirable, but living quarters must still be rented. Some fixed expenses are temporary, such as installment payments on loans, pledged charitable contributions, child support and alimony, and tuition. Others may seem fixed in that the client may automatically pay them, but the following may be reduced: charitable contributions, subscriptions, membership dues, term insurance premiums, utilities (the extra phone, the installation of insulation), food bills (through wise shopping), transportation (buy a cheaper car), medical care (by keeping in shape), etc.

VARIABLE EXPENSES

These are expenses that everyone could do without if necessary. If they are paid for regularly, it is through force of habit, not because of being billed for them on a regular basis. In this category are included liquor, tobacco, restaurants, recreation, self-improvement courses, movies, records, books, papers, magazines, personal appearance, vacations, and travel, as well as entertainment in general. A pay cut is most likely to affect these first.

¶ 306 TYPICAL SAVINGS OPPORTUNITIES

In a 28% tax bracket, a nondeductible dollar saved is equivalent to $1.39 dollars earned. Here are some of the easiest ways to save after-tax dollars:

1. *Groceries.* Eat before going to the store, check supplies before going, keep to the shopping list, avoid pre-cooked products, buy on sale, use private labels, and buy economy sizes. Substantial savings are often possible with a minimum of extra inconvenience.
2. *Stop smoking.* If the client smokes two packs a day and buys them individually, this may cost over $1,400 a year, or over $1,900 of pre-tax income.
3. *Keep in shape.* This saves on medical bills, food and drink (due to dieting), and clothes (smaller sizes and less elaborate camouflage are needed).
4. *Use cheaper transportation.* This ranges from buying a compact car or not owning a car to flying nightcoach.

5. *Cut down on restaurants.* Sunday brunches may be bargains, but if a couple goes out to a restaurant for dinner, they may easily spend $40 with tax and tips as compared to $5 if the couple had eaten at home.
6. *Save on utilities.* If the client owns a house, the cost of installing insulation may return as much as 50% on investment, tax free, year after year. A solar water heater may cost $1,200 to install, but if it saves $240 a year, that's 20%, tax free.

ILLUSTRATIONS OF SPECIFIC CASH FLOW IMPROVEMENT OPPORTUNITIES

There are almost always ways to save money or increase cash flow. Here are a few:

1. *Prepay high interest mortgages.* Paying off a 30-year mortgage of $100,000 at 12% results in a monthly payment of $1,029 and total interest of $270,000. If instead, $514.50 is paid every two weeks (one-half of $1,029) the mortgage is paid off in 19 years at a total interest cost of $154,000. The reason is simple: there are 4⅓ weeks in a month.
2. *Switch passbook savings* to Certificates of Deposit (CDs) or government bonds. The yield may almost double.
3. *Reduce the tax refund* to a minimum since no interest is paid on amounts overwithheld. The *employee* decides how much the employer is to withhold by claiming withholding exemptions on Form W-4.
4. *Borrow on life insurance policies.* Old policies permit borrowing at 6% or less. The funds may then be invested at a higher rate elsewhere.
5. *Pay property taxes directly.* Property taxes are paid once or twice a year. The mortgagee (bank) typically requires advance monthly payments to save up for the tax, but pays no interest on the average balance.

¶ 307 GET MORE FORMAL EDUCATION

Here is a final tip which will increase the client's job security, earnings and chances for promotion, as well as the opportunity to change jobs or get a new one if laid off: Go back to school. The most generally useful degrees and designations for business people are the following:

Certified Public Accountant (CPA), Certified Management Accountant (CMA) (no additional schooling may be necessary), or a law degree (JD).

MASTER OF BUSINESS ADMINISTRATION

The MBA designation is so established and recognized that many schools even offer MBAs in taxation as an alternative to an MST. Most programs are part-time. Executive MBAs are offered one full day a week, such as alternate Fridays and Saturdays for two years. The most popular majors are finance and management.

OTHER GRADUATE BUSINESS DEGREES

These include Master of Management (MM), Master of Science in Management (MSM) and more specialized degrees, such as Master of Accounting and Master of Science in Taxation. (Some 125 Masters programs currently offer a tax option under various names.)

All of the above can be acquired on a part-time basis, often with financial assistance from the employer.

¶ 308 DETERMINING THE SAVINGS LEVEL

For $5, everyone can open a savings account, and everyone should. There are four basic considerations in selecting one's investments: (1) *safety,* (2) *liquidity,* (3) *return,* and (4) *purchasing power protection.* Some 60% of all adults in the U.S. have some type of savings account. An account does provide the ultimate in safety and liquidity, but the return is low and there is no protection against inflation. A depositor gives up potential capital gains for the certainty of receiving interest and principal. A savings account is boring, but safe, liquid, and insured. The interest rate less tax and inflation may result in a negative net yield, but at least the client cuts the loss which would have resulted from keeping money in cash, checking accounts or mattresses. Typical investments, such as stocks and bonds, are discussed in the next several chapters.

At what point does savings stop and investing start? Typical definitions range from two months' to one year's salary, depending on the following factors:

1. Is the depositor saving for a specific purpose or purposes?
2. Is there any chance that large sums may be needed overnight? The following will reduce such contingencies:
   (a) Life insurance,
   (b) Medical insurance,
   (c) Disability and accident insurance, and
   (d) Employee benefits, particularly pension and profit-sharing plans, and death benefits.
3. Is there any other way the client can raise cash quickly?

4. If the client suddenly became unemployed, how long would it take to find another job?
5. Does the spouse have marketable skills so as to quickly be able to get a good job?
6. How many fixed expenses are there?
7. How much savings does the client need for peace of mind?

¶ 309 HOW TO SAVE

Here is some basic advice to help one add to savings with a minimum of discomfort:

1. Take a pay cut on paper, i.e., establish an automatic savings program. A 10% payroll deduction is reasonable, and the wage earner will soon become accustomed to it.
2. Bank any extra money that comes along. Examples include interest, dividends, inheritances, gifts, gambling winnings, and bonuses.
3. Do not overpay income tax. If the IRS owes a taxpayer money on April 15, no interest is paid on that refund.

TYPES OF SAVINGS ACCOUNTS

Here is a brief rundown of the most common types of savings accounts and some practical aspects of each:

1. *Individual account.* Anyone with a Social Security number may have a savings account. Only the owner can draw money from the account and the passbook is required.
2. *Joint account.* A joint account with a right of survivorship is most commonly used by spouses because either party may withdraw funds from the account without the consent of the other. Upon the death of one co-owner the survivor automatically becomes the sole owner of the account by operation of law.
3. *Trust account.* A trust account is an individual account, with a named beneficiary. The advantage of a trust account is that the beneficiary, like a joint owner, receives the account upon the death of the owner by operation of law but cannot touch the account during the life of the owner.
4. *Custodial account.* Custodial accounts are typically opened in the names of children under the Uniform Transfers to Minors Act. Subject to rules under which unearned income in excess of $1,200 of a child under age 14 is taxed at the parents' rate, the interest is taxed to the child at a low or zero rate of tax. The transfer is irrevocable and becomes the property of the child

upon reaching the age of majority. At that time the beneficiary can either withdraw the balance or leave it on deposit.

5. *Fiduciary account.* If the client is appointed executor or trustee, a fiduciary account is needed to avoid commingling of funds.
6. *Organization account.* This type of account is opened by a club, group, lodge, or other organization.

¶ 310 SAVINGS INSURANCE

A savings account is insured up to $100,000, i.e., if the financial institution goes under, the depositor has a claim for the deposit plus accrued interest, or $100,000, whichever is less, against a federal insurance company.

¶ 311 FACTORS INFLUENCING THE RETURN ON SAVINGS

The rate of interest earned on savings depends on three main factors:

1. *The size of the investment,* i.e., volume. If nothing else, the client at least saves commissions in the securities markets. In the savings market, a higher rate of interest is received, due to the economics of scale.
2. *The investment horizon,* i.e., the saver's patience. In the savings market the interest received is higher the longer the depositor is willing to tie up the funds. This attractive feature is, however, coupled with certain penalties for early withdrawals.
3. *The degree of risk assumed.* It is generally believed that the average person would prefer to take a low rather than a high risk. If this is true, it follows that a higher return must be offered to compensate an investor for assuming a higher degree of risk. An example can easily be found in the bond market. The lower the quality rating of a bond with a given maturity, the higher the yield to maturity.

When the focus is on savings instruments in banks and savings and loan associations, it is discovered that the interest rate will vary drastically depending on the following factors:

1. *Type of institution.* Generally, commercial banks, by law, must pay a lower maximum rate than Savings and Loan Associations.
2. *Size of deposit.* A minimum deposit of $1,000 to $10,000 may be required if the interest is going to be substantially higher than on a regular passbook account.

3. *Length of time.* To get the highest interest rate possible, the savings may have to be committed for several years.

¶ 312 THE POWER OF COMPOUNDING INTEREST

One thousand dollars will grow to $4,180 in 15 years at 10% compounded annually. In fact, if $1,000 *a year* is invested at 10%, the depositor would have some $160,000 after 30 years. Thus, any systematic savings program, particularly if within the framework of a tax-sheltered retirement plan, will result in a large absolute sum at retirement. It remains to be seen what the purchasing power of this high absolute number will be.

Here is a simple rule of thumb that quickly enables anyone to estimate how fast a sum will grow: Take the number *72* and divide it by the interest rate. The result is the number of years required for the original investment to double. Alternatively, if the constant *72* is divided by the number of years in which the money is required to double, the return necessary to accomplish this is obtained.

> ***Example:*** At 8%, money doubles in $72/8 = 9$ years, at 12% money doubles in $72/12 = 6$ years, etc. This means that at 12% an investment of $10,000 would grow to $20,000 after 6 years, $40,000 after 12 years, $80,000 after 18 years, $160,000 after 24 years, etc. This procedure is not mathematically accurate, but provides a remarkably close approximation for "normal" interest rates, say from 4-18%.

If the client only has $1,000 to save, a rate of 5 to 6% may be available, but only if the funds are tied up for several years. Once $10,000 or more is available, the depositor may receive as much as 8% and above and only have to make a one-year commitment.

¶ 313 SAVINGS CERTIFICATES

Since 1978, savings certificates have been offered with a yield tied to the six-month Treasury bill rate which varies on a daily basis. But once the certificate is purchased the interest is guaranteed until maturity. Unfortunately, federal regulations now prohibit both compounding of the rate and the payment of the extra 1/4% initially offered by banks, savings and loan associations and mutual savings banks. Since July 1, 1979, four-year certificates tied to Treasury notes have also been sold.

If $10,000 or more is available, the client should consider the direct purchase of Treasury Bills as an alternative to a savings account because:

1. Treasury bills are not subject to state and local taxes because they are issued by the U.S. Government. If the depositor lives

in a high tax state, such as New York, the local tax may be as high as 15%.

> *Example:* Someone is in the 15% local tax bracket and in the 30% federal tax bracket. If this investor purchases two $10,000 Treasury Bills for $19,000 maturing in six months, the return is $700 after taxes. In contrast, $19,000 invested in a savings certificate at 10% would yield $950. After all taxes the investor only has $584 left. Because of the local tax the Treasury bill would yield about 12% more earnings.

2. T-bills can be used to meet margin requirements for security purchases or commodity futures transactions, whereas savings certificates cannot.

3. Savings certificates are subject to steep penalties in the event of premature withdrawals; T-bills are not. If the investor buys T-bills directly from a district office of the Federal Reserve Bank, no purchase commissions are incurred. If they are sold early, a commission of $25 per $10,000 is incurred.

¶ 314 PENALTIES FOR EARLY WITHDRAWALS

It is important to realize that a depositor can withdraw the savings at any time, regardless of what type of account or what certificates are involved. While the interest may always be cashed in without any penalty, if the principal is touched prior to maturity, the depositor loses three months' interest on six-month certificates and six months' interest on one-year or longer certificates.

One way of decreasing the risk of losing interest is by buying multiple certificates in the lowest denomination allowed. In this way the depositor can cash in a few of the accounts without forfeiting the interest on all of them. If cash is needed just prior to maturity, a loan should be considered.

¶ 315 MONEY MARKET FUNDS

Regulation Q, now defunct, historically limited the interest rate on small deposits to some 5%-5½%. Large investors, on the other hand, were able to earn from 9%-15% in the 1980s on Certificates of Deposit and other short-term instruments by investing at least $100,000. Money market funds were started in 1972 to close this gap and have been remarkably successful with assets always above the $100 billion mark. Most of these funds are no-load funds, taking their fees from the gross yield on their portfolios. By the early 1990s, interest rate levels had dropped markedly.

Money market funds are a type of mutual fund, except that, instead of investing in stocks and bonds, they invest in short-term money market instruments, such as:

1. Soon-to-mature *government agency bonds.*
2. *Treasury bills,* which have a maturity date not beyond a year after issuance.
3. *Commercial paper,* which are unsecured, negotiable promissory notes issued by large corporations for up to 270 days in units of $100,000 or more on a discount basis.
4. *Certificates of deposit,* which are issued by banks in high denominations, typically $100,000 minimum. The interest is relatively high, the certificates are negotiable, and for very high amounts, they may be issued for extremely short periods, even one day. The most common maturity is six months, and because they are negotiable, they may be sold to third parties rather than be redeemed, unlike the typical savings account.
5. *Banker's acceptances,* which are drafts that banks promise to honor at maturity.

The initial deposit in a money market fund varies from $1,000 to $10,000, the interest earned varies daily with fluctuations in the money market, and the depositor can even write checks against the investment. A typical fund yields no more than what can be earned directly if the depositor has at least $10,000 to invest in savings certificates. There are some arguments against these investments:

1. Someone who is going to invest in a fund may be better off with a tax-exempt municipal bond fund. Such funds commonly yield from 3% to 5%, which corresponds to 4.5% to 7% in a 30% tax bracket. After taxes a money market fund may hardly keep up with inflation.
2. When interest rates fall, prices of bonds and stocks move up. Short-term money market instruments, by their very nature, will not go up significantly, leading to opportunity costs.
3. When interest rates rise, market values of the money funds fall and/or yields go down. This would make high-yielding savings certificates more attractive, since both the yield and the principal are fixed.
4. There are yield complexities in money funds. Mutual funds fluctuate more, but short-term instruments fluctuate as well. The yield is not guaranteed and the fund managers cannot predict it. In fact, the yield has sometimes dropped below the passbook rate. When market values change because of interest

rate variations, the funds keep the asset values constant, but instead adjust the yield. This results in greater fluctuations the shorter the shares are held. Thus, even in short-term money market funds a depositor should plan to hold the shares for at least a year. The most reliable yield indicator is probably the 30-day average yield and is readily available from the fund. If the interest rate rises immediately after a deposit, the value of the fund's asset decreases. This decrease is deducted from the yield immediately. In the long run, gains tend to offset losses. If a withdrawal is made early, however, the effective yield may be substantially less than what was "promised."

On the average, the typical instrument held by a fund matures in 41 days. The annual yield required to be quoted by the SEC is an annualization of the last seven-day yield, omitting capital gains and losses. This omission may substantially overstate or understate the true yield. The savings are typically *not* insured. Whenever redemptions exceed new savings, the funds have to liquidate, perhaps leading to capital losses.

Here are some factors to consider before choosing a specific money market fund:

1. *The type of fund.* Some invest exclusively in government instruments, others in tax-free municipals, others sell variable annuities, but most carry a balanced portfolio of treasury bills, CDs and commercial paper.
2. *Convenience.* The initial investment may be a minimum of \$500 or \$10,000. Subsequent investments may be a minimum of \$25 or \$1,000. Check cashing may be provided for a minimum amount of \$50 or \$10,000. Make sure the office can be reached easily, at least by phone.
3. *The yield.* The depositor should understand how the yield is computed and the impact capital gains and losses have had and may have on it.

Despite the availability of interest-bearing checking accounts since January 1, 1981, the return of short-term rates to more traditional levels, and the availability of money market accounts in brokerage houses, banks and "savings and loans," money market funds' assets seem to have settled near the all-time high of some \$200 billion.

¶ 316 CREDIT UNIONS

Credit unions are nonprofit associations owned by their members. To be a member, a person must purchase at least one share, typically worth $5. Savings is done by purchasing additional shares. The members may also be eligible for personal loans for any purpose, often at rates below finance company and credit card rates. Most credit unions give its savers a passbook but pay interest above the passbook rate on savings accounts. Some have checking accounts. Credit unions are typically formed as a service to a group of employees, fraternal, or religious organizations. Large corporations often encourage the establishment of such an organization and may offer a free office on the corporate premises. The savings are insured for up to $100,000 under the Federal Credit Union Act of 1970. State-chartered organizations may join.

¶ 317 COMMERCIAL BANKS—A FINANCIAL DISNEYLAND

The average person thinks of a commercial bank as the place for a checking account and a car loan; it may, in fact, be a financial Disneyland. All of the following services are available in commercial banks, and most of them are available at any large bank.

Automatic savings

Credit cards (Visa and MasterCard)

Financial and investment counseling

Personal financial planning

Automatic loan repayments

Banking by mail

Business and collateral loans

Collection services (interest coupons, letters of credit, etc.)

Safe-deposit boxes

Foreign exchange

Home improvement loans

Investment services, such as U.S. savings bonds

Savings accounts

Travelers' checks

Trust departments

Night deposits

Personal loans

Money orders, cashiers' checks and bank drafts

¶ 318 HOW TO USE SAFE-DEPOSIT BOXES

The client should rent a safe-deposit box in case the home is burglarized or destroyed by fire or other natural catastrophe. The box should contain items which are difficult, costly, or impossible to replace. Here is a list of the most common items kept in a safe-deposit box:

1. *Personal documents,* including birth certificates, marriage certificates, divorce decrees, citizenship papers, passports, diplomas, adoption papers, military discharge papers, trust agreements, diaries, family records, letters, Social Security cards, and photographs.

2. *Insurance policies,* such as the homeowner's policy, but *not* the life insurance policy. Upon death the box is sealed, which is exactly the time the policy is needed.

3. *The will,* but only a copy. The original should be kept with the law firm or other safe place for the same reason the life insurance policy should be kept elsewhere.

4. *Property records,* such as deeds, mortgages, bills of sale and leases.

5. *Investments,* ranging from coins, gold, heirlooms, medals and stamps to bank books and stocks and bonds. Securities may be kept at the broker, and since the introduction of the Securities Investors Protection Corporation, they are insured within limits.

6. *Tax records,* ranging from important cancelled checks to books and records and copies of past returns.

   Business records, such as articles of partnership, corporate charters, blueprints, drawings, surety bonds, pension certificates and trademark papers.

7. *Miscellaneous documents,* such as abstracts, contracts, legal documents, receipts, etc.

8. *Inventories.* A list of valuables in the household should be kept in case of theft or destruction. Include photographs, serial numbers, etc. Also keep a list of the items in a safe-deposit box at home.

A small, free safe-deposit box may be available where the client has a checking or savings account. The annual rental price list of a major commercial bank ranges from \$13 for a 2″ × 5″ and up to \$700 for a 51″ × 32″. All are 23″ long. The fee is deductible if income-producing securities are kept in the box, but not to the extent they are tax-exempt municipal bonds.[1]

Because the box is sealed upon the death of the owner, the question of how to provide access to the box arises. A joint box may lead to arguments about who owns what. In addition, a lawsuit against one may tie up the property of both parties. This problem may be solved by authorizing the spouse or other party to open the box as an agent. Nevertheless, the box is sealed upon the owner's death until a tax clearance is obtained. Consider this alternative: Keep all the client's papers in the spouse's box and all the spouse's papers in the client's box. The survivor then has immediate access to the other's papers and property.

¶ 319 HOW TO COMPUTE INTEREST

There are numerous books on how to maximize savings interest by utilizing several savings institutions simultaneously. Here are some typical gimmicks:

IN BY THE 10TH EARNS FROM THE FIRST

Thus, a depositor can earn interest on the same money from two banks for 10 days each month.

EARN INTEREST TWICE OVER WEEKENDS

Some banks cut off earlier than others. Thus, if one cuts off at 2 p.m. Fridays and another cuts off at 3 p.m., the depositor withdraws funds from the first bank and makes a deposit in the other between 2 and 3 p.m. Withdrawals made after cut off are not counted until Monday, and deposits made prior to cut off start earning immediately.

TAKE ADVANTAGE OF GIFTS

Many banks give away free gifts to attract depositors. By moving deposits around, diligent depositors can accumulate quite a collection of toys and household appliances. There are reasons why few depositors do this:

1. Most depositors want a permanent relationship with a bank so as to utilize other services from mortgages to travelers' checks and safe-deposit boxes.
2. In the case of small savings, getting a few extra dollars in interest each month is not worth the inconvenience, split-second timing, etc. When large amounts are at stake ($10,000 and up), the depositor can qualify for interest rates substantially higher than the passbook rate merely by buying savings

[1] Code Sec. 265.

certificates or Certificates of Deposit and making a one-time, one-place commitment.

3. The fair market value of gifts as well as all interest earned are fully taxable.

4. Most banks charge a fee for closing an account.

CONTINUOUS INTEREST

The more often interest is compounded, the higher the effective rate. With semiannual compounding, the depositor gets interest on the first six months' interest the next six months, rather than one year's interest at the end of the year on the opening balance with annual compounding. Many banks have gone so far as to compound the interest continuously, but, as the following table shows, most of the benefit is achieved once the interest is compounded at least quarterly.

EQUIVALENT ANNUAL RATE						
annually	*semiannually*	*quarterly*	*monthly*	*weekly*	*daily*	*continuously*
6%	6.09	6.156	6.168	6.18	6.183	6.185

It is readily apparent that at low interest rates, such as 5% or 6%, even continuous compounding will add only some 3% to interest income compared to annual compounding, while the difference between quarterly and continuous compounding is negligible.

¶ 320 WAYS OF COMPOUNDING INTEREST

The effective rate may differ from a given nominal rate since the way the letter is applied varies greatly. Here are four common ways to compute interest on a savings account from the most to the least attractive.

FROM DAY OF DEPOSIT TO DAY OF WITHDRAWAL

Introduced by the Chase Manhattan Bank in 1962, this method pays interest every day on every dollar of deposit. The depositor need not worry about when during the quarter a withdrawal is made.

LAST-IN, FIRST-OUT (LIFO)

Under this method a withdrawal is deducted from the most recent deposit. If, for example, a depositor had $5,000 in the bank from the beginning of the year, then deposited $1,000 on November 1 and withdrew $600 on December 20, the $600 is deducted from the $1,000 deposit, not the $5,000 opening balance. Consequently interest is received December 31 on $5,000 the whole year and on $400 the last two months.

FIRST-IN, FIRST-OUT (FIFO)

If, again, a depositor had $5,000 in the account from the beginning of the year, deposited $1,000 on November 1 and withdrew $600 on December 20, the following happens: On December 31 interest is received on $4,400 from January 1 to November 1, on $6,000 from November 1 to December 20, and on $5,400 from December 20 to December 31.

LOWEST BALANCE

If the account balance varies from $500 to $5,000 during the year, the depositor receives interest on $500. The use of such an account should be avoided unless the account is frozen anyway for a rainy day.

Although savings accounts theoretically require advance notice of withdrawals, as a practical matter any sum within reason will be available any time. But beware of penalties. With regular pass-book accounts the only common penalty is the loss of interest on the amount withdrawn for the quarter during which the withdrawal loss was made. There are two ways to deal with this penalty:

1. Make any withdrawal on one of the first days of a new calendar quarter, i.e., in January, April, July, or October.
2. If the money is urgently needed just before the end of a quarter, the depositor should get a passbook loan for a few days. On the first business day of the new quarter a withdrawal can be made and the loan can be paid off. Even if the loan carries a rate of 12% for example, for 10 days, and the passbook rate is 5%, the depositor is still ahead. If the loan is $1,000 for 10 days, interest income for a quarter is $12.50 and interest expense for 10 days is $3.33. The depositor therefore saves over $9 per thousand if the loan is for 10 days, more if the loan period is shorter.

Checking Accounts

¶ 325 CHOOSING AND OPENING A CHECKING ACCOUNT

Anyone can open a checking account by mail or in person. In person a few minutes is sufficient. The customer fills out a form and makes a deposit. A checking account is a *demand deposit* account, traditionally paying no interest and charging service fees. The modern trend is to pay the passbook rate on the average balance, e.g., 3%.

There are several advantages of having a checking account:

1. The customer establishes a bank relationship and a credit reference.

2. Checks and bank statements are useful tools in personal budgeting. A monthly record is provided of income and expenses, which makes it easier to substantiate tax deductions.

3. Many accounts come with credit lines or bank credit cards, free travelers' checks, safe-deposit boxes, etc.

The customer almost always pays something, directly or indirectly, for a checking account, but occasionally banks offer free checking to attract new customers. The alternatives described below are common, and the typical bank gives the customer a choice:

1. *Activity plan.* A nominal monthly fee is paid, such as 50 cents plus a fee of 10 or 15 cents per check. This is attractive if only approximately six checks a month are written.

2. *Minimum balance plan.* Nothing is paid if the customer keeps either a minimum balance at all times or a minimum average monthly balance. The latter is more attractive than the former, but in both cases the return on investment is lost on the extra funds kept in the account to meet the requirements.

3. *Flat fee.* Here the given monthly fee, typically \$5-\$10, is independent of the number of checks written and the balance in the account. This is attractive if the customer writes numerous checks *and* keeps a low balance.

4. *Two-way checking.* Under this plan, the customer is not charged for the checking account *and* never keeps a balance in the checking account. On the other hand, a passbook savings account paying low interest must be maintained in the same bank. Typically, at least \$2,500 must be on deposit in the savings account, and funds are transferred to the checking account automatically as checks are presented. A monthly fee is paid if the savings balance drops below the minimum. The main disadvantage of such a plan is the loss of control of the savings since "overdrafts" automatically eat them up. The advantage is free checking with all deposits earning interest.

Cost is an important factor in choosing the type of account, but when it comes to choosing the bank itself, the client should be concerned primarily by location, convenience, and the range of services available.

¶ 326 WHAT IS A CHECK?

A check is a bank draft, a negotiable instrument, and can be written on anything. The IRS, for example, sometimes receives checks written on shirts from taxpayers claiming they take the shirts off their backs. Such checks are routinely cashed. The drawer is, however, typically charged a fee by the bank for writing unconventional checks.

A check can be defined as follows: A check is an unconditional order to a financial institution (in the "old days" commercial bank only), to pay a specific amount of money on demand to a legal person or persons (individual, partnership, corporation, etc.), or to a bearer as of a specified date and is authorized by the account holder. Thus, the check must have five items written on its face to be legally valid:

1. The name of the bank (drawee) and the account number.
2. The person to be paid (could be "bearer" or "cash") called the payee.
3. The amount to be paid.
4. The date as of which it is payable on demand.
5. The signature of the maker.

The following is a look at what could happen to a check if any of the above requirements is tampered with.

OMISSION OF THE NAME OF PAYEE

This has the same effect as making the check payable to bearer, because anyone in physical possession of the check can fill in the missing name or write "cash."

OMISSION OF AMOUNT

Writing a "blank" check is dangerous and can prove to be expensive. The maker is liable for any amount filled in as long as the check is clean on its face. After the check is honored, the maker may have a lawsuit against the party who exaggerated the amount.

OMISSION OF DATE

This is not risky, but again, anyone can write in a current date. Negotiation will not be prevented.

OMISSION OF SIGNATURE

Without the drawer's signature the check is invalid and does not legally have to be paid. It is a favorite stalling device to "forget" to sign. But even then, the bank's computer may erroneously accept it. In addition, many banks will accept it if the payee guarantees the lack of signature.

CONFLICTING AMOUNTS

The amount is written both in numbers and in longhand on the face of the check. Some banks do not accept checks with different amounts, but most will simply follow the longhand.

OLD DATES

It is very easy to write "old" checks. During the month of January, thousands of people write year-old checks from force of habit. Although a check is valid for six years (the statute of limitations), most banks will refuse checks that are more than 90 days old.

POSTDATING

Creditors do not like post-dated checks because they must be saved up for the future. The check is perfectly valid, but the payor may die or the check may get lost in the meantime. If the check is presented by mistake prior to the written date, the bank may bounce it and charge its usual fee.

UNCONVENTIONAL CHECKS

If the maker writes a check on odd-sized paper, such as letters or telegrams, or nonpaper, etc., the drawee will charge extra. But blank checks, available in any stationery store, are perfectly acceptable. Lawyers, real estate brokers, insurance agents, and other professionals keep blank checks handy so that a client's typical excuse, "I forgot my checkbook," is rendered null and void.

PENCIL-WRITTEN CHECKS

Writing in pencil does not invalidate a check, but the payee may be tempted to erase the amount and substitute a higher number. A check showing evidence of erasure or corrections is legally valid, but will generally be returned anyway, to protect the drawer.

OUT-OF-TOWN CHECKS

The client may have a checking account anywhere in the country, or, for that matter, dollar accounts abroad. The only advantage of such accounts is that it will take considerably longer for a check to clear. But the "float" is paid for by the inconvenience of location. If delays are desirable, they can typically be achieved simply by the use of suburban checking accounts.

¶ 327 HOW TO WRITE AND USE CHECKS

Here are some tips to keep in mind when writing checks:

1. Fill in the register or stub first. Make sure to have a record of the date, the check number, the amount, the payee and the item paid. This is useful if the client wants to stop payment or deduct the amount for tax purposes, the check is lost, or the payee claims no payment has been received.

2. Date the check the day it is written, even if it is a week-end or holiday. A postdated check may be presented anyway and may bounce.
3. Spell the name of the payee correctly. If the name is misspelled, the bank may want a double endorsement.
4. Use lines or waves to fill in unused spaces both after the handwritten amount and payee's name.
5. Write the amounts in figures and in words as far to the left as possible to prevent easy alterations. Make sure the amount is the same both in numbers and words. Banks will honor the handwritten one.
6. Sign only after everything else is filled out. Never sign a blank check.
7. Use the memo section in the lower left corner for the account number, invoice number, description of reason for payment, etc. In addition to ensuring a correct credit, it is more convincing for tax purposes.
8. Never change or cross out written items on a check. If a mistake is made, destroy the check and write a new one.
9. If possible, arrange for direct deposits of checks to be received, such as paychecks or social security checks. This avoids delays and the risk of loss.
10. If checks are written and deposited the same day, the checks written may bounce. The drawee is entitled to clear the deposit before giving a credit. This may take several days, particularly if the drawee bank is out of state. Since October 1988, the institution must make the funds available within three business days of deposit (seven for out-of-state checks) under federal law.
11. If a check is needed for a closing of a real estate or similar transaction, the seller needs to know that the buyer's check is good. There are two ways to handle this:
    (a) A *certified check.* The teller stamps a personal check "certified", a bank officer signs it, and the balance is deducted from the maker's account.
    (b) A *cashier's check.* The customer purchases and pays for a check drawn against the bank's own funds.
12. Avoid overdrafts. Banks charge $15-$25 per overdraft and this fee is nondeductible.

13. If a joint checking account is used the parties should keep each other informed to avoid surprises on the monthly statement and bounced checks.

¶ 328 ENDORSING CHECKS

Anyone who receives a check for value in good faith and without notice of any dishonor or defense is a *Holder in Due Course* (HDC). An HDC takes the check free of personal defenses, subject only to real defenses. This means that if the client signed a check for worthless merchandise, the recourse is against the *seller,* not against whoever is holding the check. Even if payment were stopped on the check, the maker would still have to pay a third-party HDC. There are four types of endorsements or combinations thereof:

1. *Blank endorsement.* Only the payee's name is signed on the back. Whether the check was originally payable to bearer or order, the instrument is now payable to bearer. A payee should therefore be named above the payee's signature. Otherwise, anybody in possession can cash it.
2. *Special endorsement.* The name of the new payee is written above the signature. Only the named payee can cash it.
3. *Restrictive endorsement.* The purpose for which the check is endorsed is specified, i.e.,

   Order the Dollar Bank

   For Deposit Only

   Signature
4. *Qualified endorsement.* The term "without recourse" is added before signing. As a practical matter no one wants a check if liability is disclaimed.

Whenever a check is payable to bearer (to "cash"), no endorsement is needed. A special endorsement will convert it to "order paper." An endorsement makes the signer a guarantor. Thus, if the check is dishonored, an endorser is liable to anyone following after on the check. The endorser in turn has recourse against anyone in front including the drawer. If the bank deposits a check in someone's account, it is authorized to fill in the necessary endorsement if it is missing.

¶ 329 DIFFERENCE BETWEEN "NOT SUFFICIENT FUNDS" AND "UNCOLLECTED FUNDS"

If the maker writes a check in excess of the bank balance, the check will bounce and the drawee will charge $15-$25 for doing it.

If the maker wrote a bad check knowingly, there may also be criminal liability for fraud. Distinguish this from the following situation: Someone receives a check for $500 from a client, deposits it in the bank and writes a check for $300 to a third party. The check deposited bounces, causing the check written to bounce as well. In this case the depositor is in the "Uncollected Funds" rather than in a "Not Sufficient Funds" situation. The account holder may have to pay the same fee, but is *not* guilty of fraud, assuming good faith.

¶ 330 HOW TO STOP PAYMENT

The typical situations when the client needs to enter a stop order are: the loss of a check or the checkbook, whether through negligence or theft, the receipt of substandard merchandise, or a creditor claiming not to have received the check. Where a checkbook is lost, the client should consider closing the account. In situations where a new check is written and issued, payment is stopped on the old check.

The stop order should be specific, i.e., it should include name and account number as well as the payee, amount, date and check number. An oral stop order, i.e., a phone call, is good for two weeks. Within this period, the maker will receive and return a confirmation form. Once confirmed, the stop order runs for six months. Needless to say, any liability to pay is not affected by a stop order. In fact, the use of a stop order without good reason may make the client liable for fraud.

¶ 331 CHECKING ACCOUNTS WITH CREDIT LINES

More and more financial institutions now offer a pre-established line of credit with checking accounts. The credit line typically is limited to one month's salary and ranges from $1,000 to $10,000. A loan is automatically granted when a check is written above the balance in the account and is advanced in $100 units. Many banks provide a separate set of checks which can be written directly against the credit line. The customer may pay off the credit line, in full or in part, any time without prepayment penalties. The interest rate typically ranges from 10% to 15% annually, and the loan is often covered by credit life insurance. Interest is debited monthly based on the average monthly balance.

There is one trap. For example, assume that the client starts from ground zero, depositing one $1,000 check and writing another. If the check written comes to the bank before the deposit is cleared, a loan of $1,000 is granted immediately, on which 15% is charged. A day or two later $1,000 is deposited in the checking account when the deposit clears. The two transactions do not cancel each other out. Even though the client has a zero balance overall, technically there is a $1,000 loan and a $1,000 demand deposit. It is, therefore, important to keep track of both balances.

Proper monitoring will signal when to pay off all or part of the loan balance by writing a check to the bank. Any repayments must be initiated by the customer.

¶ 332 CHECKS AND TAXES

A checking account properly used will give the client records needed for budgeting and taxes. The memo portion of the check in the lower left corner should be utilized to specify what is being paid for. Many expenses paid will be tax deductible, such as some interest payments, local taxes, charitable contributions, professional dues and subscriptions, medical care, etc. All such checks should be kept in an annual file to help when filing the tax return and to substantiate deductions. A check mailed on the last day of the year is deductible in the year mailed for income tax purposes, even if cashed the following year, but only if it is honored. But beware of gifts. A gift is not completed until the check is cashed. To ensure that the donor qualifies for the $10,000 exclusion each year, a check should be written well before year-end, or alternatively, a cashier's check or certified personal check might be used. The IRS is very strict in regard to this area.

¶ 333 PRIVACY AND THE BANK SECURITY ACT OF 1973

U.S. banks do not provide their customer with much privacy. A person may, however, have bank accounts in any name desired, but must register such name with the Secretary of State, which involves a small fee and some constructive notice to the public through advertising. It is easy for the IRS and other governmental agencies to obtain bank records through so-called "third-party summonses." Here are some of the requirements imposed upon a bank by federal law:

1. Any transaction within the U.S. involving $10,000 or more must be recorded.
2. Any transaction involving the U.S. and another country and at least $5,000 must be recorded.
3. Copies must be kept of all checks amounting to at least $100.
4. Cash transactions involving $10,000 or more must be reported to the IRS. Since 1985, this requirement is imposed on all businesses.

¶ 334 RECONCILING THE BANK STATEMENT

The balance shown in the bank statement is commonly called the *bank balance* and the "stub" balance shown in the depositor's own records the *cash balance.* Unless an account is inactive, these two numbers will invariably be different. Here is how to reconcile them:

1. *Outstanding checks.* When the maker writes a check, immediately deduct the amount from the cash balance. If the bank has not yet recorded it, it must be deducted from the bank balance.
2. *Unrecorded deposits.* Unrecorded deposits must be added to the bank balance.
3. *Service charges.* These have reduced the bank balance and must also be deducted from the cash balance.
4. *Errors.* If the depositor has made a mistake, the cash balance must be adjusted. If the *bank* has made the error, it must be brought to the attention of the bank and the bank balance must be adjusted. For a joint checking account, the procedure may be more cumbersome, but it works the same way.

CHAPTER 4

THE PRINCIPAL RESIDENCE

¶ 401 INTRODUCTION

Whether to rent or buy a home is both a financial and personal decision, i.e., both quantitative and qualitative. It is one of the most important personal financial decisions the average individual makes, but it is a decision which typically must be made several times in a lifetime, due to the mobile nature of our society. Most people wind up both renting and buying at various points in their lives. The decision most often must be made at the time of marriage, after a divorce and when the family moves. See ¶ 402 for discussion of the advantages of renting and ¶ 403 for a discussion of the advantages of buying.

Renting vs. Buying

¶ 402 ADVANTAGES OF RENTING

There are many advantages to renting a residence.

FLEXIBILITY

A tenant can leave on short notice. The typical lease is only for one year and if the property is attractive and in demand, it is not hard to sublet the residence and move out early. The more frequently an individual moves, particularly if more often than every three years, the more attractive renting becomes. Financing, selling, and closing costs can be very high, unless spread over several years.

LACK OF DOWN PAYMENT

The typical down payment on a residence is 20% of the purchase price. Even if the purchaser has the cash, the return on it is lost and money doubles every nine years at 8% and every six years at 12%. Thus the opportunity cost of tying up the money can be substantial. At the minimum renting may give someone a chance to save up for the down payment.

REPAIRS AND MAINTENANCE

If the client does not like manual work or prefers not to engage in maintenance chores, e.g., snow shoveling and the like, such client may be better off renting (or at least buying a condominium apartment). Generally, repairs, maintenance, landscaping, property taxes, etc., are the responsibility of the landlord.

TESTING THE NEIGHBORHOOD

By renting, the client has ample time to observe the neighborhood and the community without making a major commitment. Leasing with an option to buy may allow the client to have it both ways. If the experience is enjoyable, a purchase is indicated; if not, space is rented elsewhere.

RENT UPON RETIREMENT

Many couples find upon retirement that they own a valuable asset in their home, by then fully paid for. They can sell it, often tax free, and use the proceeds to travel and maintain or increase their standard of living, assuming they become renters. And why not? At that time the children have moved and a pleasant, problem-free city apartment without the need for a car may be just the right thing for them.

LACK OF INDEBTEDNESS

Some people would rather not be $100,000 in debt, even if the home value far exceeds it. One thing is sure: if one is a tenant, there can be no foreclosure, only an eviction.

LESS SPACE

This is an advantage in the sense that a tenant is less likely to need household help. And if there are no children, a large house may be more of a burden than a blessing.

ALTERNATIVE INVESTMENTS

At least in the short run, less money need be tied up in rental property. This leaves the tenant with a substantial sum to invest in more liquid assets, assuming the existence of a down payment in the first place. A home may prove a good investment, but it is *not* liquid.

WAIT FOR HIGHER INCOME LEVEL

Generally, someone can qualify for a more expensive home if renting rather than buying. It is easier to convince a landlord with a vacancy that someone is good for a year's rent than to convince a lender that the same person can pay off a mortgage with the same monthly payments. This is particularly true if the credit rating is not the best. If the client is optimistic about dramatic increases in the income level in the near future, the purchase decision may be deferred until a more desirable home can be afforded.

¶ 403 ADVANTAGES OF BUYING

For the average person, particularly one in a high tax bracket, the advantages of home ownership typically exceed any benefits derived from renting for the following reasons:

1. Owning a home with a mortgage on it provides an excellent "forced savings" plan. In fact, equity is built two ways: through *paying off principal* and through *increases in market values*. In the long run home values should at least keep up with inflation.

2. Owning a home fulfills the basic desire to own real estate and can provide the pride of ownership as well as stability, security and social status. It can also give a family "roots."
3. Owning a home typically cuts down on many restrictions common in the rental market, e.g., homeowners are free to have children, pets, cultivate noisy hobbies, etc.
4. Once people own a home, they become less hesitant about spending money and effort in improving the residence. They add a garage, energy-saving equipment, a recreation room, etc., without feeling that they are doing it for someone else.
5. Some people enjoy gardening, minor chores and the like, around the house. It does provide recreation and a change of pace, particularly for people with desk jobs.
6. Owning a home provides *privacy*. No landlord comes around to collect rent or inspect the premises. There is no need to worry about whether the lease is going to be renewed.
7. Owning makes it possible to acquire more space. Generally, renting is more expensive than owning the same property in a normal market. After all, the landlord wants a markup to cover management and expected vacancies, and earn a reasonable profit. The larger a family, the more likely that it must own, rather than rent, to get the space needed.
8. A home is not liquid, but at least it is possible to build a substantial equity and there are several ways to cash in on it. (See below.) In addition to refinancing the first mortgage or adding a second mortgage, substantial cash may be available on sale. This may be so *even if a new residence is purchased at the same price.*

Example: Hilda bought her home for $50,000 10 years ago with a 20% down payment. Today she sells it for $150,000 and pays off the mortgage, perhaps $37,000 at that point. If she buys a new home for $150,000 and puts up 20%, she only ties up $30,000 of the $113,000 she had left from the sale, leaving her with $83,000 in cash. And no tax is due because of the roll-over provisions. She may, of course, choose to put up a higher down payment, particularly if the mortgage interest is higher than the return she can reasonably expect on her alternative investments.

9. Mortgage payments are often fixed over the term of the mortgage, typically 25 or 30 years (but see below). In contrast, the rent will normally go up annually. On the other hand, property taxes and maintenance expenses will go up over the years.

10. The longer a home is owned and the higher the home owner's tax bracket, the more attractive owning becomes. Studies have shown that the cost of ownership in the long run constitutes only some 15% of annual income as opposed to approximately 25% for renters. In a high tax bracket, the mere fact that mortgage interest and property taxes are deductible puts the home buyer way ahead of a renter who can deduct nothing.

When comparing the cost of renting with that of buying, the following table may be helpful:

	Monthly Expenses	
	Buy	*Rent*
Fixed Costs		
Basic payment	principal & interest (after taxes)	rent
Property tax (after tax)	X	
Insurance	X	X
Variable Costs		
Maintenance	X	
Utilities (heating, cooling, cooking, etc.)	X	X
Miscellaneous	X	X

Even if the monthly after-tax cash flow in the beginning may be similar, the annual comparison becomes more and more stacked in favor of owning as the rent goes up and the mortgage payments stay the same. In addition, the equity build-up is frosting on the cake.

¶ 404 SHOPPING FOR A HOME

There are really only two main questions when it comes to shopping for a home:

1. How much can the client afford to pay?

2. Is the home worth what the seller wants? Historically most advisors claimed that the price should not exceed 2½ times the buyer's gross income, meaning that if the purchaser's salary was $50,000 the home should be below $125,000 in price. But consider the following:

   (a) The higher the down payment the more expensive the affordable home. The client *can* afford a much higher down payment if a greatly appreciated home is being sold.

   (b) As a practical matter an individual can afford whatever price the lender (mortgagee) will grant a mortgage on. Most lenders do, however, use a formula based on annual income.

(c) The more optimistic the client is about future income, the more likely a current overextension.

(d) In a time of increasing prices and mortgage rates someone may be willing to buy a home that may seem expensive today, but is likely to become reasonable, comparatively speaking, in the foreseeable future.

Having determined the price range, the time has come to find the best value. Here is a rundown on what to do:

1. *Decide what is wanted.* Does the client want to live in the city, the suburbs, or the country? How many rooms, bathrooms, and acres are desired? Does the client want one or two stories, wood or brick, conventional or ranch-style, garden or patio? What about purchasing an old, spacious house which needs fixing up? Is a separate dining room for entertainment needed? Do the family members need privacy? The list is endless.

2. *Shop around.* Don't be in a hurry. The homeowner may live in the home for years, even decades. The average family looking for a newer home is likely to spend some three months looking and actually visiting about a dozen houses. Everyone should do this unless that "dream house" is found right away.

3. *Decide where to look.* The obvious places include the real estate section of a newspaper for the relevant area. Some people even drive through desirable neighborhoods looking for "for sale" signs, or the home shopper can contact real estate brokers in the area of his choice. They have listings and the *seller* pays the commission. Many buyers assume that the seller will pass on the 5-7% real estate commission, but these rumors are exaggerated. A $150,000 house is a $150,000 house. Its value does not depend on whether it is for sale by owner or not but on comparable sales and what the traffic will bear. The mere fact that an increasing number of homes are for sale "by owner" testifies that the sellers do not believe they can pass on the commission. Otherwise, why would they do the work themselves for nothing? If looking for bargains, consider foreclosure and estate sales. At the minimum, find out *why* the house is on the market.

4. *Be aware that housing needs change.* By the time a client reaches the early forties, children are still at home who frequently have friends over. A four-bedroom house in the suburbs may be desired. By the time the client reaches the fifties, the children will have probably left. It may be time to sell the four-bedroom house and buy a two-bedroom house or a condo-

minium. In addition, a vacation home, which will eventually serve as a retirement home, may be desired.

5. *Pricing the home.* Homes are generally valued per square foot. The average home on the market today, new or old, averages approximately 1,300 square feet while the average new home contains about 1,500 square feet of improved floor space. If the home is newly constructed, the price is generally not subject to negotiation. The builder simply charges cost plus a profit margin. But the price charged must, of course, be compared with other prices for older homes. One way to start the appraisal process is to get a price per square foot in the neighborhood from a realtor or a mortgagee. If this is $40, for example, it must be multiplied by the number of square feet of developed floor space in the home being looked at, even if the client has to measure it personally. From this "construction cost" any needed repairs are deducted. This basic figure must be adjusted for the following factors:

   (a) *Functional obsolescence,* i.e., how old-fashioned is the home?

   (b) *Economic obsolescence,* i.e., is the neighborhood declining?

   (c) The *condition of the lot,* i.e., is there a front or side yard, a garden, landscaping, walls, trees, a drive, etc.

   (d) The *exterior* of the house, i.e., the porch, steps, doors, windows, screens, gutters, siding, roof, paint, chimney, etc.

   (e) The *interior* of the house, i.e., the bathroom, fixtures, painting and plaster, locks, fireplace, basement, attic, closets, electric wiring and plumbing, heating, air conditioning, floors, carpeting, kitchen appliances, etc.

   (f) Any notable *improvements,* i.e., a pool, a garage, a patio, a barbecue pit, a family room, etc.

The only way to get everything one desires is to build a house. This is a lot of bother and is also time consuming. On the other hand, if an old house is purchased, the buyer has no recourse against the seller if the house turns out to be a lemon, i.e., there are few, if any, warranties. The seller can be guilty of fraud, but only if the buyer can prove that the seller intentionally misrepresented a material fact, which caused damages.

¶ 405 TYPES OF DEEDS

A deed must be in writing and must convey title to an interest in real estate from the grantor to the grantee. There are two kinds of deeds:

A *warranty* deed, where the grantor guarantees the grantee good title and can be sued successfully if the title is defective, even if nobody knew it, and

A *quit-claim* deed, which only conveys that interest which the grantor has or may have. The seller does not claim any ownership interest but merely that if there is one, such interest is conveyed. Often such a deed is conveyed for a nominal price to guarantee the grantee that the grantor has no possible future claim.

¶ 406 TITLE INSURANCE

The homeowner cannot generally obtain a mortgage without title insurance, but everyone should have it, in any event, because it protects against possible claims not readily apparent from the record of deeds, such as:

1. missing heirs,
2. forged deeds,
3. defects in the record,
4. mechanics liens, and
5. obligations of the previous owner, such as unpaid taxes.

¶ 407 REAL ESTATE CONTRACT

Whether one is buying or selling real estate, an individual is well advised to use a lawyer who is experienced in real estate transactions. If someone is not using a lawyer when buying or selling property worth over $100,000, when would such a person ever use one? Here are some main points to watch out for:

1. *Mortgage contingency clauses.* The buyer should have at least 30 days to obtain a mortgage commitment. When money is scarce, lenders are busy. The typical contract provides for a return of the deposit ("earnest money") if the purchaser, after a reasonable effort, is unable to obtain a mortgage and notifies the seller by the deadline of this fact. The buyer is better off if the contract is automatically canceled if the buyer cannot get a mortgage. The seller prefers the former, which increases the likelihood of keeping the deposit as "liquidated damages" to compensate for lost time. (Any forfeiture is ordinary income for tax purposes.)

2. *Mortgage assumptions.* If an existing mortgage at a low rate can be assumed by the buyer, both parties are better off; the seller is better off because the home is easier to sell, and the buyer is better off because a cheap mortgage is obtained. The typical mortgage contains a "due on sale" clause. Thus, the mortgage balance is accelerated unless the lender gives consent, and, even if consent is granted, the seller remains liable unless the lender grants a release. Any mortgage assumption agreement must be in the sales contract.
3. *Surveys.* Surveys often cause delays. The contract should spell out the type and the nature of the survey and how recent it should be.
4. *Possession.* The contract should provide for the money penalties per day if the seller fails to make the premises available as well as a substantial withholding in escrow to guarantee possession.
5. *Remedies for breach.* Real estate is one of the few examples in contract law where *specific performance* is available. Thus, if the seller has a change of mind, the buyer can sue for specific performance, i.e., the seller can be compelled to convey. If the contract is not performed due to the fault of the buyer, it is commonly provided that the seller can keep the earnest money deposit, often 10%, as "liquidated damages," i.e., the seller covers expenses, including brokerage commissions, if any, and keeps the rest. This remedy is exclusive of other remedies, such as the right to sue for consequential damages.
6. *Miscellaneous.* The contract should spell out the price, how it is to be paid, a legal description of the property, a bill of sale covering personal property, such as rugs, drapes, and furniture, how property taxes are to be prorated, as well as insurance, water and utility bills, when possession is available, the seller's title, when the deposit is to be returned, any other agreement, such as promises to repair, and the seller's signature, including all co-owners.

¶ 408 PRESENT AND FUTURE INTERESTS IN REAL ESTATE

The following are the main interests that can be owned in a piece of real estate:

1. If property is owned outright, the owner has a *fee simple* interest.
2. If property is transferred "to A for life," A has a *life estate;* A is a life tenant.

3. If property is transferred "to A for life," the grantor has a *reversion* since when A dies, the property will revert to the grantor or the grantor's heirs.
4. If property is transferred "to A for life, then to B," B has a vested *remainder;* B is the remainderman. Even if B does not survive A, B's heirs will own the property in fee simple when A dies.
5. If property is transferred "to A for life, and if B survives A, then to B," A has a life estate and B has a *contingent remainder.* If B dies before A, the property goes back to the grantor, who therefore has a reversion.
6. If property is transferred "to A for life, and if B survives A, then to B, otherwise to C," C has a future interest called an *executory* interest, a form of remainder.

¶ 409 CO-OWNERSHIP OF HOMES

There are four types of co-ownership recognized in the United States: joint tenancy with right of survivorship, tenancy by the entirety, tenancy in common, and community property. Because the house is the most commonly co-owned asset, these forms of ownership are discussed at ¶ 410-416.

¶ 410 JOINT TENANCIES

Most couples own their homes in joint tenancies. To qualify for a joint tenancy a couple must satisfy the four unities of *time, title, interest* and *possession:*

1. The interests must be created at the same time. For example, if someone owns a house, gets married, and gives the spouse one-half of it, only a tenancy in common results because the new interest came later. Thus, it is necessary to deed the property to a third party, typically a lawyer, who would deed it back to the couple as joint tenants.
2. The title must be the same, i.e., conveyed in the same transaction and held by each party identically. Thus, if one spouse holds her interest as a trust beneficiary and the other spouse holds his interest directly in his name, they do not qualify.
3. The co-owners must hold the same fractional undivided interest. Thus, two joint tenants must own one-half each, three joint tenants must hold one-third each, etc.
4. They both have the right to 100% possession of the property, subject only to the other's equal right.

The reasons most couples use the joint tenancy form of ownership are convenience and family protection, i.e., the survivor automatically becomes the sole owner by operation of law, will or no will, which also means no probate. But look out for the following disadvantages:

1. The whole property is included in the taxable estate of the first one to die (one-half if they are married) unless, and to the extent, the survivor can prove contributions. Only the portion includible in the estate receives a new, fair market value basis.[1]
2. Control over the property is lost. For example: the husband dies, and his widow becomes the owner; she remarries and puts the house in joint tenancy with her new husband; she dies, he owns the house, and the children have nothing.
3. Both spouses may die in an accident. Where the property goes depends on the wills, if any; otherwise it will depend on the laws of interstate succession.

¶ 411 TENANCIES BY THE ENTIRETY

This is a special joint tenancy with right of survivorship between spouses only and is recognized in a decreasing number of states. In some states a couple can only own real estate this way; in other states personal property can be owned by this way as well. Husband and wife are regarded as *one,* and one spouse, therefore, cannot convey the property without the consent of the other.

¶ 412 TENANCIES IN COMMON

Unless it is spelled out that the property is held with right of survivorship, co-owners are presumed to be tenants in common. Tenants in common differ from joint tenants in the following respects:

1. They may own different interests, i.e., one person may own three quarters while the other owns only one quarter, for example.
2. The interests need not be created at the same time.
3. There is no right of survivorship, i.e., each owner disposes of the shares owned by will and does *not* avoid probate.
4. Only the share actually owned by a co-owner is taxed for estate tax purposes regardless of who contributed what.

¶ 413 COMMUNITY PROPERTY

Community property is similar to a tenancy in common but is enforced under local law between married couples whether they want it

---

[1] Code Sec. 1014(a).

or not. Everything earned or acquired during marriage, from income to property, is presumed to be earned and owned equally by both spouses. There is no right of survivorship. Nine states are community property states: Arizona, California, Idaho, Louisiana, Nevada, New Mexico, Texas, Washington, and Wisconsin. (For estate and gift tax aspects of co-ownership, see separate chapters on estate and gift tax and estate planning.)

¶ 414 SHARED EQUITY PLANS

Shared equity plans work as follows:

1. A financially poor family who wishes to live in a home it cannot afford gets together with a financially rich investor looking for a tax shelter.
2. The two parties purchase the home together and must both own an undivided interest therein. The investor puts up all or part of the down payment and some or none of the monthly expenses, but lives elsewhere.
3. The ownership percentages may be any numbers the parties agree on, such as 50/50 or 80/20 and the resident rents the investor's share for a fair market value rent.
4. The investor gets to claim depreciation as well as a deduction for taxes and interest paid, which could more than shelter the rental income.[2]
5. Upon sale, the proceeds are split according to the contract initially signed.

¶ 415 CONDOMINIUMS

A condominium means a "fee simple in the sky," i.e., a condo apartment owner owns the apartment itself and the appliances and fixtures therein, plus an undivided share of the common areas, such as the lobby, the pool, and perhaps even the stores. Instead of rent, the homeowner pays "assessments," the monthly maintenance charges. And just like rent, they tend to go up each year with inflation.

There are three basic reasons for the popularity of condos:

1. In large cities, population pressures have led to skyrocketing rents and the lack of rental units.
2. Landlords faced with higher property taxes and maintenance and utility expenses are looking for ways to sell their buildings at high prices.

---

[2] Code Sec. 280A(d)(3).

3. People like to own their own home, not only for the tax deductions and to build equity, but for the satisfaction, pride and commitment that owning a home provides.

Converting a building amounts to little more than buying a building *wholesale,* fixing it up a little, then selling the individual units *retail,* say at a 50%-100% mark-up.

When buying a condo, unlike a co-op, the purchaser is in a very similar situation as when buying a conventional home. The homeowner gets legal title to real estate, puts up a down payment, qualifies for a traditional mortgage, and pays property taxes, etc. However, the monthly assessment in luxury buildings may run several hundred dollars a month.

Condos can be purchased in every price range and size. The size runs from studios to multiple bedrooms. A three-bedroom condo in a large metropolitan area may thus fall in the range of $80,000-$300,000, depending on the address and amenities provided. The condo owner can typically sell to anyone, subject only to the homeowners' association's right of first refusal. Some buildings have restrictions on children and pets.

The advantages of owning a condo rather than renting the same apartment are several:

1. The owner builds equity through partially tax deductible payments.
2. The building will be better kept up if everyone owns and cares for a unit.
3. The building will be operated and managed by the homeowners' association. The representatives, themselves homeowners, will supervise the building.
4. People achieve a higher social status and satisfaction from knowing that they own the apartment and, in most cases, they derive happiness from knowing they make out better financially than if they were renting. It is not uncommon for the after-tax monthly payments to amount to less than rent, while the property appreciates.
5. If the condo owner should later decide to buy a house, the gain on the condo may be deferred by reducing the cost basis in the house (see below).

In the '80s, the most common reasons cited for stable or falling condo prices were poor construction, lack of privacy and fights with homeowners' associations. In addition, here are *some condo pitfalls* to watch out for:

1. If the building is just going condo, watch out for unrealistically low estimates of utilities, maintenance and property tax figures.
2. If the units are not sold within a reasonable time, the developer may rent them out. Even if they are sold, the owners may rent them out as an investment. In any case, tenants are less careful and messier than owners because their incentive to behave is lower.
3. Unless the condo ownership includes a share of all common areas, such as the health club, pool and garage, the residents may find themselves paying exorbitant rent for these on top of the regular assessments.
4. Even if not satisfied with the management company, the condo owners may find themselves locked into a multiyear contract.
5. The homeowners' association may have an option on the apartments (a "right of first refusal"), but it is rarely exercised.
6. The board of directors of the homeowners' association may pass numerous rules and regulations which the individual unit owner does not agree with, from restrictions on children and pets to the opening hours of the pool and the stores. But, at least, since 1976, the homeowners' association may enjoy the status of a tax-exempt organization.

What if an apartment building is being converted? The good news is that the tenants get an option to buy below the market, which is fine if they wish to buy and the building is a hit. The bad news is that those who do *not* want to buy must move (but are entitled to at least 90 days' notice). Many people are either unable or unwilling to buy their units. For example, a retired couple pays $500 in rent. One day they are told: "You have 90 days to either move out or buy your apartment for $60,000, including a down payment of $12,000. You will then pay $100 a month in property taxes, $200 in assessments and $400 for the mortgage." Even if they had the down payment, they probably would not qualify for the mortgage. And, even if they did, they have little or no taxable income to deduct interest and property taxes from.

The core document in a condo is the *declaration.* This piece of paper contains the conditions, convenants and restrictions governing the sale, ownership, use and disposition of condo units within local condo law. Potential buyers should note the absence of federal condo law. Each jurisdiction, i.e., the 50 states and the District of Columbia, has its own local condo law. The declaration gives authority and power through its bylaws to the Board of Directors of the Association to regulate and administer the affairs of the condo, as well as authority to assess and collect the maintenance fees.

It generally requires at least 75% of the owners' votes to amend the declaration.

¶ 416 CO-OPERATIVE APARTMENTS (CO-OPS)

It is probably safe to say that co-ops are on their way out as condos conquer the land. Strictly speaking, the individual apartment dweller does not own the co-op apartment. A corporation does, and the individual owns stock in the corporation which provides the right to an apartment. When investing in a co-op, the purchaser pays the full value of the apartment, but can only mortgage the shares. Unless the buyer has other collateral, the owner may have to pay cash for any excess of the value over the share of the "blanket" mortgage on the building. The owner must pay a share of the mortgage on the building as well as the property taxes. The monthly assessments would be similar to those of a condo. The basic disadvantage of a co-op is that the buyer has no title to the unit and cannot obtain a traditional mortgage. Because of this, co-ops are harder to sell. One advantage is that the interest rate on the "blanket" mortgage may be quite low, due to the sheer size of the loan and because it is likely to be an old one. What it boils down to is that a condo is somewhere in the middle between a co-op and a conventional home.

Financing the Home

¶ 420 ADVANTAGES OF OBTAINING A MORTGAGE

The average family in the U.S. is paying off a mortgage. It is probably the "happiest" debt they have for several reasons:

1. It does not even count as consumer debt because it is a payment in lieu of rent, building equity for the owner.
2. The interest is lower than on most other loans, except life insurance policy loans and passbook loans through which the debtors "borrow their own money."
3. Because of the size of the interest payments and the property tax, it is the prime reason people itemize their deductions. This in turn enables people to deduct all kinds of miscellaneous deductions which otherwise would be "wasted," such as charitable contributions, medical expenses, professional fees, etc.
4. The fixed payments become easier to make as inflation reduces the real dollars paid. At the same time, and for the

same reasons, the mortgagor builds equity while the payments become cheaper and cheaper compared to rent.

5. Real income is likely to increase over the life of the mortgage.

It is necessary to keep in mind that obtaining a mortgage is not based on need. Therefore, someone may finance a home to obtain funds for any purpose, such as a business.

¶ 421 TYPES OF MORTGAGES

By far the most common mortgage is the *conventional* mortgage. Only two parties are involved, the homeowner and the lender (the mortgagor and the mortgagee). It is not uncommon to purchase decreasing term life insurance to cover the mortgage balance. More than 90% of all home mortgages are of this type and the borrower may be able to finance up to 95% of the appraised value. The trend, however, is to require a larger down payment, say 10%-20%, due to the general reluctance of real estate prices to increase since 1980. There are three functional variations of the mortgage:

1. The so-called *budget* mortgage whereby the monthly payments to the lender include not only principal and interest, but also a pro rata payment to cover property taxes and home insurance.
2. The *package* mortgage through which the homeowner can throw in major appliances and the like and get a loan to cover the purchase of these included in the regular, long-term mortgage.
3. The *open-end* mortgage, which provides for a "reborrowing" feature, i.e., once the principal has been reduced by $5,000; for example, the mortgagor is entitled to borrow it again and add it to the outstanding balance.

Mortgages can also be broken down into categories based on how repayments are made:

The most common by far is the *direct reduction plan.* The payments are fixed over the term. The term is up to 30 years for two reasons:

1. The owner should finish the payments before retirement, and
2. The life of the house should be considerably longer than the term. Each fixed payment is applied first to interest on the remaining balance, the remainder to principal. Obviously, almost all is interest in the beginning, and almost all is principal towards the end.

The *fund plan* is fortunately uncommon. Here, the payment goes first towards the interest, but instead of repaying the principal, the remainder is put in a savings account with interest until the balance equals the principal. Because the mortgage rate exceeds the savings interest, this is a poor deal.

Variable (adjustable) mortgages provide for periodic changes in the interest as the money market rates change. The interest is often linked to the prime rate and changed annually or semiannually. This is a bad deal for the homeowner if interest rates go up, good if they go down, but in any event certainty is lost. One advantage is that the initial rate is lower than the fixed rate on a traditional mortgage. Another variation on variable mortgages is the *graduated* or *flexible payment plan,* i.e., the payment is low in the beginning and higher later. This is an advantage for young people whose income is expected to grow rapidly.

GUARANTEED MORTGAGES

Mortgages are sometimes guaranteed by the government subject to restrictions and limitations. There are two kinds:

Federal Housing Administration loan guarantees, established by Congress in 1934 to alleviate the fears of lenders during the depression. The loans may require smaller down payments due to the lower risk and the loans may be used for improvements, vacation homes and low-income housing. The disadvantages include the small size of loans eligible and the insurance premium of 0.5% of the unpaid loan which is paid by the borrower.

Veterans Administration guarantees have been available since 1970 to all veterans honorably discharged with at least 181 days of active duty. No down payment is required, but the loans available are small, limited to 60% of the appraised value, and the lending institution has no duty to write such mortgages.

¶ 422 DEDUCTING MORTGAGE INTEREST AFTER TAX REFORM

The mortgage interest deduction was, as a practical matter, largely untouched by the otherwise sweeping Tax Reform Act of 1986 and Revenue Act of 1987. The mortgage interest rules are as follows:

1. Interest on loans secured by the principal residence plus one second home is deductible as "qualified residence interest" under two sets of circumstances:

   (a) the loan is "acquisition indebtedness," i.e., the loan proceeds are used to purchase, improve, reconstruct, or construct one or both of the two homes. The limitation is $1 million.

(b) "home equity loans" up to $100,000 are allowed without regard to their purpose in addition to acquisition indebtedness.

2. Pre-October 13, 1987, loans are grandfathered in, i.e., they are treated as acquisition indebtedness, but reduce the over-all limitations. Once qualifying as acquisition indebtedness the balance may be refinanced at any time without adverse consequences. The first $100,000 of excess refinancing automatically qualifies as a home equity loan.[3]

Interest on mortgages above the limits is subject to the limitations on deductibility of personal interest, investment interest, or passive activity losses, etc., as the case may be.

¶ 423 WHO ARE THE LENDERS?

There are several sources of home mortgages:

In addition to specialized *mortgage companies,* which are a recent phenomenon, *savings and loan associations and savings banks* are the only institutions that specialize almost exclusively in mortgages. In a sense, all savers historically subsidized the mortgage industry due to Regulation Q of the Federal Reserve Board, which finally has been phased out. Regulation Q prohibited commercial banks from paying even the same interest which could be paid by savings and loan associations. As a consequence, availability of mortgage funds was made more likely. Up to 95% of the funds of a Savings and Loan association are tied up in mortgages. In many cases, savings and loan associations simply collect the points and sell the mortgages in the secondary market. The interest charged is often the lowest available and the terms the longest.

Commercial banks also write mortgages, but they generally require a larger down payment and a shorter repayment period.

Life insurance companies deal in large amounts of money, but do occasionally write mortgages on expensive homes.

¶ 424 ASSUMPTIONS

The homeowner may be able to *assume an existing mortgage.* Although an old loan often carries a low interest rate, due to inflation, it is unlikely to be sufficient unless the buyer comes up with a sizeable down payment or a second mortgage. The seller may be unwilling to assume an exisiting mortgage because of paying "points," i.e., a service

---

[3] Code Sec. 163(h).

charge expressed as a percentage of the loan to the lender (mortgagee) for the privilege. In addition, the seller remains liable for the mortgage unless the lender agrees to a release. Most mortgages are "due on sale" and not assumable.

¶ 425 SELLER FINANCING

The seller may grant a mortgage directly. When the seller and mortgagee are one and the same, the loan is a *purchase money* mortgage. There are several reasons why the seller might grant one:

1. A quick sale is denied and the buyer may not be able to obtain a standard mortgage within a reasonable time.
2. The mortgage interest charged is so high that the seller would rather collect, for example, 14% from the buyer on a secured loan than try to invest elsewhere.
3. By granting a loan, the seller can postpone the gain on the sale until the payments are collected by employing the installment method for tax purposes.

The advantages to the buyer are:

1. The several-week process normally required in a lending institution is bypassed.
2. The terms are less rigid than in an institution offering a standardized product.
3. The seller will rarely charge points.
4. The buyer's credit rating may be poor so as to limit available alternatives.

On the other hand, the seller may charge a higher interest rate, require a higher down payment, and desire a shorter repayment period.

¶ 426 DOWN PAYMENT

When selling an appreciated home for cash, the seller has an ample down payment available for the next home after the mortgage is paid off. Although not generally required to put up more than 5%-20% of the appraised value, a buyer should consider putting up more for the following reasons:

1. The higher the down payment, the lower the interest rate the lender will charge, but within narrow limits. 1 to 1½ percentage points may be saved.
2. The higher the interest rate, the less likely it is that the extra cash may be invested elsewhere at a higher rate of return. Should interest rates decline by a meaningful percentage, the homeowner can always refinance. As a rule of thumb, refinanc-

ing should be considered only if the interest rate is reduced by at least two percentage points *and* payments are to be continued for at least three years.

3. The buyer will be able to acquire a more expensive home because the salary is compared to the monthly payments, not only to the total selling price.

On the other hand, the buyer should not commit to such a high down payment that funds for moving expenses, closing costs, remodeling, furnishing, drapes and the like may be short.

¶ 427 LOAN TERM

The typical mortgage has a life from 15 to 30 years with 25- and 29-year mortgages the most common. Because of inflation, many advisors feel that the mortgage should be the largest loan obtainable for the longest period possible. If feasible, the mortgage should have no prepayment penalties in case of sale, early pay-off, or refinancing. The longer the term, the lower the monthly payments, but the higher the total interest paid.

The following table shows the monthly payment and the aggregate interest paid on a 10%, $100,000 mortgage:

Loan Term	*Monthly Payment*	*Total Payments*	*Total Interest*
15	$1,075	$193,500	$ 93,500
20	965	231,600	131,600
25	909	272,700	172,700
30	878	316,080	216,800

Ideally, the mortgagor should time the mortgage so as to deduct the bulk of the interest at the highest possible tax bracket. Because the interest constitutes most of the payments in the early years, a person should not even buy a home unless located in a high bracket. Conversely, the loan term should not extend into the retirement years when the tax bracket is likely to drop.

From the above table, it is clear that a mere $87 extra a month will pay off a $100,000 mortgage in 20 years rather than 30. The mortgagor will own the home free and clear 10 years sooner. In addition, the homeowner saves $84,480 in interest before taxes.

ILLUSTRATION OF TWO WEEKS VS. A MONTH

A 30-year, $100,000, 12% traditional mortgage would carry a monthly payment of $1,028.60. If, instead, one-half of $1,028.60, or $514.30, was paid every two weeks, the mortgage would be paid off in less than 19 years, more than 11 years earlier. This, in turn, means a reduction in total interest cost from $270,000 to $154,000. This is made possible due to the fact that there are $4\frac{1}{3}$ weeks in a month, resulting in two extra biweekly payments a year.

If the homeowner did acquire a long-term loan and comes into extra cash, extra payments should be considered if the after-tax mortgage interest exceeds the after-tax return to be obtained by investing the money elsewhere. Some mortgages have restrictions on prepayments. Sometimes no prepayments can be made the first five years and/or prepayment penalties may be assessed.

¶ 428 IMPORTANCE OF LOW-INTEREST LOANS

Mortgage rates have fluctuated widely in recent years. As a rule of thumb, each one-half percentage point is worth approximately $4 per $1,000 per year for a 30-year mortgage. For a $100,000, 30-year mortgage, the monthly payments for various interest rates are:

8%	9%	10%	11%	12%
$734	$805	$875	$952	$1,029

Thus, someone who borrowed at 8% winds up paying $734, or $141 less per month for 30 years, than if paying 10%. This amounts to $50,760 over the life of the mortgage.

POINTS

There are three kinds of "points" that can be involved in the purchase or sale of a home:

1. The typical lump-sum fee, generally from 1%-3% of the loan, charged by the lender as additional interest at the time the proceeds are made available. This is deductible immediately as interest and need not be amortized over the life of the mortgage if:
   (a) the mortgage is to purchase or improve a principal residence,
   (b) it is secured by the home,
   (c) charging points is customary in the area,
   (d) the charge is in line with what is charged by other lenders in the area, and
   (e) the debtor has sufficient funds available to pay the points. Otherwise the three points paid on a $100,000, 30-year mortgage must be deducted in increments of $100 a year for 30 years, rather than $3,000 immediately.[4]
2. Loan service fees and other closing costs may also be expressed as points. These are not deductible as interest, but must be

[4] Code Sec. 461(g).

added to the cost basis. To be deductible as interest, points must be paid for the use or forbearance of money.

3. If a lender consents to letting a buyer assume the seller's mortgage, it often charges points for the privilege. Any such points paid by the seller merely reduce the selling price. This is far less attractive than a deduction because it will simply reduce a capital gain or the amount postponed or excluded anyway.

¶ 429 SPECIAL TERMS

No two lending institutions will offer the exact same terms. Here are some variations to look out for:

1. The extent of prepayment penalties.
2. Does the borrower have to make monthly payments in escrow to provide for home insurance and property tax? If so, is interest paid on the funds? Note also that the property tax payments are not deductible until paid by the lender to the taxing authorities.
3. May the life of the mortgage be extended during the term?
4. Would it be possible to have a future buyer assume the mortgage?
5. Is it an "open-end" mortgage so as to enable the homeowner to borrow any repayment of principal already made ("reborrowing" feature)?
6. How much and what type of homeowner's insurance is required?
7. Does the lending institution count both spouses' income when considering the borrowing limit? The trend is definitely in this direction.

¶ 430 ADJUSTABLE INTEREST MORTGAGE PLANS

On April 3, 1980, the Federal Home Loan Bank Board unanimously approved the adjustable interest mortgage plan. As an alternative to the traditional, up to 30-year fixed rate mortgage, the interest rate can be adjusted every year and is typically linked to Treasury note yields. The rate can be dropped without limit, but can go up a maximum of two percentage points per year for a maximum of five percentage points over the life of the mortgage.

The objective was to make mortgage money more readily available by not locking the approximately 2,000 federally chartered savings and loan associations into a given rate for decades. The Federal Home Loan Bank will keep an index of market mortgage rates for previously owned homes to which changes will be linked. Although the mortgage is technically renewable every three, four, or five years, it must be renewed by the lender despite late payments by the borrower. The borrower may repay without penalties upon 90 days' written notice ahead of the renewal date. By 1985, the adjustable mortgage was offered by virtually all lending institutions in all parts of the country.

¶ 431 CONVERTIBLE MORTGAGES

A convertible mortgage is an adjustable rate mortgage that may be changed to a fixed rate mortgage for a slight conversion fee. The advantage of this is an effective refinancing option, without title searches and closing costs. The conversion fee is typically 1% of the loan balance. Ideally, the homeowner will have the following experience:

1. By agreeing to an adjustable rate, the borrower is able to obtain a short-term rate of, for example, 8%, when the fixed, long-term rate is 10%.
2. A few years later, the fixed rate is down to 8%, at which time the homeowner converts and locks in the new 8% rate permanently.

The Home: A Tax-Sheltered Investment

¶ 435 INTRODUCTION

The home is probably the largest purchase the average person ever makes and is often the largest investment and most valuable asset. It is also the most common tax shelter, since property taxes and mortgage interest are deductible each year, while the appreciation is taxable, if at all, only upon later sale and then as a capital gain. Since most mortgages are for 30 years or less, they are usually paid off completely by the time retirement comes. This is, of course, the way the lenders want it. A substantial nest egg is built two ways:

1. By paying off the mortgage plus interest on a monthly basis.
2. Through increases in the price of the property. The latter is due both to increases in real value of real property and inflation. (On the other hand, property taxes may also increase drastically.)

¶ 436 "BASIS" IN THE HOME

For tax purposes, the word "basis" means the investment in property, typically cost. This is the amount deductible from the selling price to arrive at gain or loss. The cost basis in a residence equals the purchase price, regardless of whether all or part of it was borrowed and whether or not the lender has legal title during the repayment period.

It also includes various purchase expenses, such as legal fees or other closing costs. Expenses of purchase are added to the cost only if they were not otherwise deducted, for example, as moving expenses or interest.

The cost also includes improvements made that, unlike ordinary repairs and maintenance, increase the value of or extend the life of the property. Painting the house would be maintenance, while adding a garage, a terrace or a room, foı example, would constitute improvements.

Furniture, appliances, carpeting, etc., are *not* part of the cost, unless they are fixtures. The cost of fixtures are added to the cost basis, however. A fixture is under typical state law, something that cannot be removed without damage to the house. Therefore, a stove, carpeting, panelling, etc., may be considered part of the residence and the cost included in the basis.

Tax Deferral on Replacing a Residence

¶ 440 GENERAL RULE IN A NUTSHELL

If a homeowner sells a principal residence at a gain and replaces it with another home within 24 months, all or part of the gain on the sale is postponed.[5] Postponement, rather than outright forgiveness, is accomplished by reducing the cost of the replacement residence by the gain allowed to be postponed. To put it simply, if all the proceeds from the sale are reinvested, no part of the gain is taxable. If less than the proceeds are reinvested, all or part of the gain is taxed.

If the requirements are met, the rules apply automatically. Inflation in recent times has made this rule almost a social necessity in our mobile society. Statistics show that some 65% of American families own their own home and move every seven years on the average.

ILLUSTRATION: THE RULE IN OPERATION

Here is a numerical example that illustrates how the rule works:

The old home has a cost basis of $50,000, and it is sold for $100,000. Selling expenses are $6,000 and the seller spent $1,000 on "fixing-up" expenses. If the seller does *not* replace the home, and the over-age-55 benefit discussed below does *not* apply, a long-term capital gain of $44,000 results. (Installment reporting may, of course, be used if applicable.)

Assume that another house was purchased for $95,000. This is how it would work:

---

[5] Code Sec. 1034.

Gross sales price	$100,000
less selling expenses	6,000
Net sales price	$ 94,000
less "fixing-up" expenses	1,000
Adjusted selling price	$ 93,000
less cost of new home	95,000
Money not invested	—0—

Since at least $93,000 is invested, the whole $44,000 is postponed. This is always the case if the seller reinvests the whole adjusted selling price. The cost of the replacement residence is simply what was paid for it, less the postponed gain, or $95,000 − $44,000 = $51,000. Note that the adjusted selling price was reduced by the "fixing-up" expenses. This is solely for the purpose of computing the amount of the selling price that must be reinvested to postpone the tax on the gain on the old residence. "Fixing-up" expenses do *not* count to reduce the gain the seller is trying to postpone.

The sales price less the selling expenses equals the net selling price, and the net selling price less "fixing-up" expenses equals the adjusted sales price. These concepts can be defined further:

Selling expenses include real estate commissions, advertising, legal fees and other expenses incurred in connection with the sale. *"Fixing-up"* expenses mean expenses incurred *only* to assist in the sale, such as painting, minor repairs, etc. These can be deducted solely to determine the adjusted selling price if:

1. The work was performed during the 90 days prior to the date on the sales contract,
2. It was paid for within 30 days of *the closing* (which typically takes place many weeks after the contract was signed), and
3. The expenses cannot be otherwise deductible or added to cost.

By using the last example but varying the cost of the replacement residence, the following table emerges. Column one recapitulates the previous example:

	1	*2*	*3*
Adjusted selling price	$93,000	$93,000	$93,000
Cost of new residence	95,000	70,000	40,000
Money not invested	0	23,000	53,000
Gain for tax purposes	0	23,000	44,000
Gain postponed	44,000	21,000	0
Basis of new residence	51,000	49,000	40,000

To reinforce the above: The gain on the previous residence is taxed if the cost of the new residence falls short of the adjusted selling price of the old, but only to the extent of the lesser of the gain or the amount not reinvested.

¶ 441 HOW TO REPORT GAIN OR LOSS TO THE IRS

If the seller has a *gain or loss* on the sale of a home, Form 2119, "Sale or Exchange of Your Home," is required to be filed, whether the home is replaced or not. Form 2119 contains the worksheet needed to make the calculations and is also used for the age 55 benefit discussed at ¶ 450 and following.

The Replacement Period

¶ 445 PURCHASE

If the homeowner purchases a replacement residence, the deal must be closed within 24 months before or after the closing of the sale of the old residence. In addition, the new residence must be used as a home within the same 48-month time period. Improvements made within the replacement period count as amounts reinvested. If an old residence is swapped for another home, such an exchange qualifies as a purchase. The replacement residence must be *owned* by the seller (and/or the spouse, as discussed below). Therefore, if someone sells a home, gives the money to a daughter, for example, and *she* buys a house and the seller lives in it with her, the rule does *not* apply.

A gift or inheritance is *not* a purchase. The *old* residence may have been a gift or inheritance, however.

¶ 446 CONSTRUCTION

If the seller builds a replacement residence, construction can start *any time prior to* the sale of the old residence. But the seller can only count the construction costs incurred prior to the sale that were incurred the last 24 months as part of the replacement costs.

In addition, construction must have started within 18 months *after* the sale and the homeowner must move in physically within 24 months after the sale. Furnishing the home is not sufficient. The IRS is serious about the deadline.

It was noted at ¶ 445, above, that a gift or inheritance does not constitute a purchase. Neither do improvements to property thus acquired. However, *reconstruction* of a gift or inheritance qualifies as construction. Thus, if a complete reconstruction is entered into (not mere improvements) *the costs of such reconstruction* only count as replacement costs and the 48-month, 18-month and 24-month rules apply.

¶ 447 DUAL-PURPOSE HOMES

A homeowner can have only one principal residence. Thus, a summer home sold at a gain is taxable even if the proceeds are used to buy a principal residence or to make improvements on a home.

If part of a home is used for a business purpose, such part does not qualify.

Business purposes include:

1. Renting out part of a house.
2. Taking deductions for an office at home.

Thus, if 1/6th of a home is treated for tax purposes as a home office, only the gain on 5/6th of the home can be postponed.

If the seller owned only part of the home (unless the other part is owned by the spouse), only such part actually owned is the principal residence, even if living alone.

If the seller moves out prior to sale and rents the home out until it is sold, the home still may qualify if the time limitations are met. There is no requirement that the home be idle in the interval between sale and replacement.

¶ 448 HOW MARRIAGE AFFECTS THE RULES

The postponement of gains works for a married couple the same as it works for a single taxpayer. The married couple are, in effect, viewed as one. Thus, whether one spouse owns the principal residence, or they own it as joint tenants, tenants by the entirety, or as tenants in common, or as community property, and whether the replacement home is owned by either or both, they qualify. If, however, the ratio of ownership changes, they must both consent in writing. Thus, if a *husband* owns the home they both live in, sells it at a gain, and the *wife* buys another house with her independent funds, the transactions qualify as long as the properties, old and new, were used as the principal residence of both, and they consented. The gain postponed reduces the cost of the replacement property in proportion to the ownership ratio of the replacement residence. Thus, if the husband owned the old home, and a new home is purchased jointly, they both reduce the cost of their share by one-half of the postponed gain.

The rules are more flexible than generally known. For example, if two single individuals each, own a home get married, sell the homes and purchase a new residence as co-owners, both gains may qualify for postponement. Should a couple get divorced and sell their co-owned home and subsequently both buy replacement residences, the gain on the sale is prorated to both, so that both benefit from the rule.

The law is flexible enough to allow a surviving spouse to roll over the gain if the other spouse died after the sale of the old home but before the purchase of the new one.

The Age 55 Gain Exclusion

¶ 450 HISTORICAL BACKGROUND

Starting in 1964, a taxpayer who disposed of a home after age 65 could, by election, exclude any realized gain attributable to the first $20,000 of the "adjusted selling price".[6]

For taxable years beginning after 1976, the $20,000 limitation was increased to $35,000.[7]

For sales and exchanges after July 26, 1978, the variable exclusion became a flat maximum of $100,000 of any realized gain and the taxpayer's age requirement was reduced significantly from age 65 to age 55. The new election was made available notwithstanding any election in effect under prior law. The ownership and use requirement was also liberalized from five of the last eight years prior to sale to three of the last five years.[8] For dispositions prior to July 26, 1981, the seller could elect to use the old ownership and use requirement.

Finally, for sales and exchanges after July 20, 1981, the flat exclusion was increased to $125,000.[9]

A mentally or physically incapacitated taxpayer over age 55 only needs to have owned and occupied a home for one (rather than three) year during the last five years prior to sale if the taxpayer is placed in a nursing home.

¶ 451 SUMMARY OF CURRENT REQUIREMENTS

The basic rules for electing the $125,000 exclusion are as follows:

1. The reason for the sale is irrelevant and includes involuntary conversions, such as those caused by fire, flood and condemnation.
2. The seller must have attained age 55 no later than the date of sale or exchange, i.e., at "closing."
3. The seller must have owned and used the home as a principal residence for at least three years in the aggregate during the last five years prior to sale. The home could therefore have been rented out the last two years, for example.

---

[6] Code Sec. 121 as introduced in P.L. 88-272, § 206(a).

[7] Code Sec. 121(b) as amended by P.L. 92-455, § 1404.

[8] P.L. 95-600, § 404(d).

[9] Code Sec. 121(b)(1), P.L. 97-34, § 123.

4. Neither the seller nor the other spouse may previously have elected the $100,000 or $125,000 exclusion.
5. If the seller is married on the date of sale, the other spouse must join in the election.
6. If the home is owned jointly, as community property, in a tenancy by the entirety, or in a joint tenancy, but *not* in a tenancy in common, it is sufficient that one spouse meets the age, use and ownership requirements.
7. If a deceased spouse met the *ownership and use requirements,* the surviving spouse may make the election if the latter meets the *age requirements.*

¶ 452 MARITAL STATUS AND THE ELECTION

One insidious trap for the unwary is brought about by two rules in Code Sec. 121:

1. If the seller is married at the time of sale, the spouse must join in the election, and
2. Once having made the election, no new election may be made by the seller or the spouse.

Example: H_1 owns a home and is married to W. H_1 sells his house and makes the Code Sec. 121 election joined by W. H_1 dies and, years later, W marries H_2. Neither W nor H_2 can make a new election. If W and H_2 are just living together, however, then H_2's election is intact. Should W and H_2 divorce, H_2's election is restored.

¶ 453 SEPARATE RETURNS

The maximum exclusion is the same $125,000 for a married couple as for a single taxpayer. Thus, if a couple owns their home as joint tenants, tenants by the entity, tenants in common, or as community property the exclusion is limited to $125,000 on a joint return or $62,500 each on separate returns. If they are not legally married, both are eligible for up to $125,000 each.

If the home is owned in the name of one spouse only and the spouses file separately, the nonowner spouse is not entitled to the other half of the exclusion, since only the owner realizes a gain from the sale.

¶ 454 EXCLUSION AND DEFERRAL INTERPLAY

As indicated at ¶ 440 above,[10] the seller of a house must exclude all or part of the gain if a replacement residence is purchased within 24 months before or after the sale. A gain is recognized only to the extent

[10] Code Sec. 1034.

the cost of the new home falls short of the "adjusted selling price" of the old home.

The excluded gain, which is always 100% of the realized gain, up to the maximum of $125,000, simply reduces the "adjusted selling price" of the old residence. Thus, the exclusion reduces the amount required reinvested to postpone any remaining gain.

> ***Example:*** Hilda sells her home with a $50,000 basis for $300,000. Without an exclusion election she must reinvest the full $300,000 to defer all gain. With the exclusion she needs only invest $175,000. Furthermore, the exclusion does not reduce the basis in the replacement residence.

¶ 455 DECISION SITUATIONS

When a residence is sold at a gain, it is not always obvious whether to elect the exclusion or not. In any event, the seller has the full, three-year statute of limitations to change the decision, whether the election was made or not.[11]

The following are some situations that may confront the seller:

SITUATION A

The full gain on sale is deferred because a new residence is purchased for the proceeds. Here the exclusion election should *not* be made. Since no tax is due whether the gain is excluded rather than postponed, the only effect of the election is to step up the basis in the replacement residence. During ownership, however, the basis in a residence is largely irrelevant, since the property is nondepreciable. On a subsequent sale the exclusion election may then be made with two possible advantages:

1. The gain is likely to be greater so that the exclusion may be utilized to a greater extent.
2. The exclusion may be higher (it has already been increased three times).

Thus, the seller has little to gain if any, but something to lose, by making the election.

SITUATION B

The gain is $125,000 or above and the seller is not contemplating the purchase of a new home. The election should be made to avoid tax on a considerable gain, even if the seller is not sure about buying another home. Should the situation change within three years, the election may be revoked.

---

[11] Code Sec. 121(b)(3).

SITUATION C

The seller knows "for sure" another residence will never be acquired. Here the election should be made regardless of how small the gain may be. The smaller the gain the more certain the seller should be about never buying another home.

SITUATION D

The seller is to recognize a gain of less than $125,000 because of partial deferral under Code Sec. 1034 or because the realized gain is small. Because the portion of the exclusion not used evaporates once the election is made, this is the only difficult decision situation. Unless no replacement residence is ever to be purchased (Situation C, above) the seller has to ask the following: *Is the tax savings today greater than the present value of estimated future tax savings?* The answer is difficult since there are several unknowns, i.e., the future gain, the future exclusion, the future tax rate, the discount rate and the time until sale. However, both the future gain and the exclusion will most likely increase, and if tax rates are relatively stable, trade-offs between time and money can be considered.

For example, the "Rule of 72" shows that money doubles every r years, where r is the discount rate. Thus, money doubles in nine years at 8%, six at 12%, and four years at 18%. In other words, if the present tax savings are $10,000, a future tax savings of $20,000 will have to be generated within six years at a discount rate of 12%, or within four years at 18%, etc. If this is unlikely in the seller's subjective opinion, the election should be made currently.

¶ 456 ADVANTAGES AND DISADVANTAGES OF INSTALLMENT SALES

If the seller of a home "takes back" a mortgage, the home is disposed of in an installment sale. Both a buyer and seller must weigh the advantages and disadvantages of an installment sale.

Advantages:

1. The seller postpones taxation until collection.
2. It is easier for the buyer (who may be a relative) to make the purchase.
3. By spreading the gain over several years, the seller may lower the average tax bracket.
4. The seller still qualifies for the deferral and exclusion rules.

Disadvantages:

1. The buyer may be unwilling or unable to pay.

2. The installments will lose purchasing power due to inflation.
3. There will be significant taxable interest income.

In order to compute the tax liability under the installment method, several concepts must be explained.[12]

¶ 457 SELLING PRICE

This is the gross selling price without reduction for commissions or other selling expenses and including mortgages assumed by the buyer (or purchased subject to). It also includes the face amount of the installment obligations.

NET SELLING PRICE

This is the selling price less selling expenses.

GROSS PROFIT

The gross profit is the gain or net selling price less the cost basis in the property transferred.

¶ 458 CONTRACT PRICE

This is what the buyer is going to actually *pay,* or the selling price less liabilities assumed or purchased subject to (such liabilities are only deducted to the extent they do not exceed the basis as explained below). Thus, if the seller owned the property free and clear, the contract price equals the selling price.

GROSS PROFIT PERCENTAGE

This is computed thus:

$$\frac{\text{Gross profit} \times 100}{\text{Contract price}}$$

This percentage is applied to principal payments made to compute the taxable amount.

¶ 459 PAYMENTS IN THE YEAR OF SALE

The following are *included* as payments made in the year of sale:

1. The down payment, including any deposit ("earnest money") made prior to closing, even if in a prior taxable year, if credited towards the down payment. No selling expenses can be offset against the down payment. If an option had been sold to the buyer, it is part of the down payment if the buyer gets credit for it. If not, it is part of the selling price.

---

[12] Code Sec. 453.

2. Liabilities assumed by the buyer (or purchased subject to) to the extent they exceed the cost basis.
3. Payments and prepayments on the installment obligation.
4. Notes, if payable on demand.
5. Obligations of the seller assumed by the buyer and paid in the year of sale, e.g., commissions, interest expenses, real estate taxes, etc.

The following are *excluded* from payment:

1. The installment obligation itself.
2. Interest payments on the obligation.
3. Mortgages assumed (or subject to) up to basis. This is true even if the seller took out the mortgage recently, as long as it was a "reasonable time" prior to the sale.
4. Any payments made by the buyer on the mortgage assumed or bought subject to *after* the sale.

The seller may dispose of the deferred obligation, but this is a taxable sale and the basis is the face amount less the gross profit percentage.

Example: Hilda sells her house for $100,000 (cost $40,000) to be paid at the rate of $10,000 a year plus interest starting in the year of sale.

The gross profit equals $100,000 less $40,000, or $60,000. Note that the gross profit is reduced by both the age 55 exclusion and/or the gain deferred due to replacement, if applicable.

The gross profit percentage equals

$$\frac{\$60,000}{\$100,000} \times 100 \text{ or } 60\%.$$

Thus, $6,000 a year for 10 years is taxable (total gain $60,000). Each installment is considered to include a proportionate part of the gain. If the property was mortgaged at $20,000 and the buyer assumed it, the contract price is reduced to $80,000 and the gross profit percentage is increased to

$$\frac{\$60,000}{\$80,000} \times 100 \text{ or } 75\%.$$

Thus, $7,500 will be taxable each year for eight years for a total of $60,000. Notice that the mortgage is *not* counted as payment in the year of sale, but it does reduce the contract price.

Assume, instead, that the buyer bought the property subject to a $60,000 mortgage. Liabilities in excess of basis, or $20,000

($60,000 less $40,000), are counted as a payment in the year of sale. The first installment is due in the year after sale.

The gross profit is still $60,000. The contract price is $60,000 ($40,000 deferred plus liabilities in excess of basis). The gross profit percentage is 100% applied to four payments of $10,000 and to the $20,000 of mortgage assumed in excess of basis in the year of sale. Counting liabilities in excess of basis both as a payment *and* as part of the contract price has the effect of limiting the gross profit percentage to 100% in all cases.

¶ 460 HOW TO INCREASE CAPITAL GAIN BY REDUCING INTEREST INCOME

When selling a capital asset on the installment plan, it is a temptation not to charge interest and increase the price correspondingly. This would have the effect of converting interest income to capital gain. It would also have the effect of denying the buyer an interest deduction and providing a higher basis.

The rule is that the IRS will impute interest and recalculate the selling price and the installments due, unless the seller charges at least 9% simple interest, or, if less, the applicable federal rate. This would increase the seller's interest income and the buyer's interest expense.[13]

The rule only applies if at least one payment is due more than a year after sale and then only to payments due more than six months after sale. Furthermore, it only applies if the selling price exceeds $3,000 and the asset sold is a capital asset.

To increase the capital gain to the greatest extent, the seller should charge only the minimum required simple interest and increase the price accordingly.

Office-at-Home Expenses

¶ 465 INTRODUCTION

A taxpayer may be able to deduct a portion of home expenses as business expenses, including depreciation or rent, even if only the family uses the home. To do it, the taxpayer must meet the requirements for an office at home.[14] See ¶ 466.

¶ 466 HOW TO QUALIFY

The following requirements must be met:

1. The homeowner must operate a trade or business from the home. This does not have to be a main business. A person may have any number of businesses, such as real estate sales,

[13] Code Sec. 483.

[14] Code Sec. 280A.

writing books and articles, consulting, personal financial planning services, etc. A sideline is sufficient.

2. One or more areas in the home must be used exclusively for business. This does not mean it has to be used more than an hour or two a day, but it does mean that it cannot be used for personal reasons at all with two exceptions:
   (a) storing inventory in part of the home, or
   (b) running a regular day-care service for children or others who cannot take care of themselves.
3. The room must be used for business on a regular basis.
4. If the homeowner is employed, the home office must be used for the *employer's* convenience, but may also be for the employee's own comfort.
5. One of the following must be met:
   (a) it is the principal place of a trade or business,
   (b) it is where the taxpayer regularly meets patients, clients and customers, or
   (c) it is a separate structure used exclusively for business, such as a studio for an artist or a greenhouse for a florist shop owner.

These requirements can be met by various individuals. The office-at-home deduction cannot exceed the net income reported from the trade or business giving rise to the deductions. The excess is carried forward.

¶ 467 WHAT TO DEDUCT

There are three types of deductions that may be claimed:

1. *Deductions to be taken in full:*
   (a) Painting or repairs done to the home office.
   (b) Repairs to typewriters, calculators and other office equipment.
   (c) Business long-distance phone calls.
   (d) Depreciation on office furniture and equipment. If acquired after 1986, a seven-year life generally applies.
   (e) Business publications.
2. *Deductions to be allocated in part according to office space:*
   (a) Rent or mortgage interest.
   (b) Real estate taxes.
   (c) Heating.
   (d) Cleaning services.

(e) Insurance premiums (fire, theft, etc.).

(f) General home repairs, such as roof and plumbing, painting the exterior, etc.

(g) Depreciation of the home, exclusive of land cost, as well as improvements.

3. *Deductions to be allocated to business use:*

(a) Electricity.

(b) Gas, other than heating.

(c) Telephone. (The law denies a deduction for the monthly base charge of the first telephone in a home.)

(d) Garbage collection.

The office at home deduction is available only to the extent of net income generated by such office (gross income, less allocable expenses other than office at home deductions). To the extent such expenses exceed the net income limitation, they are carried forward to the following year and aggregated, subject to the same limit, with that year's office at home expenses. Furthermore, if the taxpayer is an employee, the office at home deduction is a "miscellaneous itemized deduction" and the sum of such expenses is only deductible to the extent they exceed 2% of adjusted gross income.

This income limitation also applies to the partial use of a home. Thus, if the taxpayer rents out the second floor of the home, rental expenses, including expenses allocable to the second floor such as interest and taxes in excess of rental income, must be carried forward.[14a]

¶ 468 AVOIDING A TAX TRAP ON SALE

The portion of a home, such as one-fourth or one-sixth, used for business, is no longer part of the residence. Therefore, the seller cannot roll over the gain on that portion upon sale and repurchase and does not qualify for the age-55 exclusion of up to $125,000 on that portion. The gain is also going to be proportionally greater because the cost basis is reduced by depreciation claimed. If the seller used straight-line depreciation, there can be no depreciation recapture. However, if accelerated cost recovery was used, the gain is depreciation recapture to the extent of depreciation claimed. Furthermore, for installment sales after June 6, 1984, there is no deferral of the tax on depreciation recapture, even if it exceeds the down payment.[15]

By claiming the home office deduction, the homeowner has:

1. sheltered income with ordinary deductions,

[14a] Code Sec. 280A(c)(5).

[15] Code Sec. 453(i).

2. had the interest and tax-free use of income, perhaps for many years, and
3. converted some or all of the deductions into capital gains, perhaps indefinitely postponed.

The IRS concedes that, if the seller *did not qualify* for the office-at-home deduction in the year of sale, the office is converted to a residence retroactively, the slate is wiped clean and *all* gains may be excluded or deferred.[16] The simplest way not to qualify is to fail the exclusive use test by reading a book or watching TV on occasion in the business area.

¶ 469 CASHING IN ON THE HOME EQUITY

As noted in previous material, the principal residence can be the largest investment the average person makes. It possesses a number of tax shelter characteristics, including the deductibility of mortgage interest and property taxes, deferral of gain on replacement within two years and/or gain exclusion of up to $125,000 for owners over age 55. Over the years great appreciation is likely, which on sale is taxed as a long-term capital gain. The maximum capital gains rate is 28%, even for taxpayers in the 36% and 39.6% tax brackets introduced in 1993. If the owners live in the home for the rest of their lives, the cost basis is stepped up to fair market value.[17]

On the other hand, many older homeowners are faced with the following situation. The children have moved, the mortgage is paid off, and property taxes are increasing, as are repairs and maintenance. Due to low retirement income, such as nontaxable social security benefits, these homeowners are caught on the horns of a dilemma: They can ill afford to keep the home, but they are often reluctant to sell and move out for personal reasons. Because of the significant equity in the home, however, several alternatives exist whereby cash can be generated without a move.

¶ 470 CASH-GENERATING ALTERNATIVES

1. Retention of Ownership Strategies:
   (a) Partial rental (income only);
   (b) Borrowing;
   (c) Refinancing first mortgage (lump-sum);
   (d) First or second mortgage (lump-sum); and
   (e) Reverse mortgage (income only).
2. Relinquishing Ownership Strategies:
   (a) Outright sale and lease-back (lump-sum);

---

[16] Rev. Rul. 83-26, 1983-1 CB 234.

[17] Code Sec. 1014(a).

(b) Deferred payment sale and lease-back (lump-sum and income or income only);

(c) Installment sale;

(d) Private annuity sale;

(e) Gift of remainder to charity (deduction only); and

(f) Part sale/part gift and lease-back (lump sum and/or income).

PARTIAL RENTAL

Renting out a portion of one's home has several advantages: cash is generated; ownership is retained; and if the tenant is carefully selected, good companionship is possible. A widow, for example, may rent to another widow who cannot afford to rent an apartment by herself.

TAX ASPECTS OF BEING A LANDLORD

When the taxpayer is a landlord, rent paid is gross income when received, even if paid in advance.[18] It is reportable on Schedule E with Form 1040. Landlords may offset the tax to be paid on the rental income because of the following: Social security payments escape tax in part or in full; if age 65 or over, an increased standard deduction is allowed; the general standard deduction is available; and if one-half of the home is rented out, one-half of the mortgage interest and property tax is transformed from itemized expenses to rental expenses. As such, these factors reduce gross income directly ("above the line"); and rental expenses, such as maintenance, insurance, utilities, advertising and depreciation, are also deductible from gross income (to the extent allocable to the rental portion).

Security deposits are not income, unless stipulated as "last month's rent."

A TAX TRAP

The portion rented out is no longer part of the "principal residence." Therefore, on a later sale, the special tax benefits on the sale of a residence do not apply. Thus, the gain on the rental portion is taxable, even if a new residence is purchased within 24 months and even if the age 55 exclusion is elected. The gain may even be ordinary income in part, to the extent accelerated depreciation has been claimed in excess of straight-line (on a cumulative basis).

¶ 471 RENTING TO RELATIVES

If a fair market value rent is charged, *all* deductions are allowed, even to the extent of creating a deductible tax loss, regardless of who

[18] Code Sec. 451(a).

the tenant is.[19] As seen above, however, losses from the partial rental of a home are carried forward and are limited to rental income.[20] Should the rent charged be less than full value, no losses are allowed even as a deferral. Deductions are only allowed up to the amount of the rental income. Taxes and interest are applied first, miscellaneous rental expenses second and depreciation last.

¶ 472 BORROWING

Refinancing is the *only way* to cash in on the equity in a home *without* sharing the space or giving up ownership. Typically, a total of 70%-80% of appraised value may be borrowed. (For a detailed discussion of when to refinance or prepay a mortgage, see the next chapter.)

Borrowed money is not income, even if the loan exceeds the cost basis of the residence. Interest paid, however, is deductible, but only if the homeowner itemizes deductions.

Refinancing means borrowing subsequent to the original purchase and giving the lender (mortgagee) security in the home. If there is no mortgage currently, a first mortgage will be given. Should there be a remaining balance on the original first mortgage, a decision must be made:

1. Should the money be borrowed on a second mortgage, or
2. Should the first mortgage be paid off and a new first mortgage be given?

The trade-off typically is between keeping a low interest first mortgage and paying a high rate on a second, versus paying one rate on a new first mortgage which is likely to be between the original first and a new second. Ideally, the homeowner will pick the alternative which minimizes the present value of after-tax payments to be made. If cash flow is the main concern, the new first mortgage route is often best, since the repayment period is normally much shorter for a second mortgage (5-15 years versus 20-30 years).

Prepayment penalties and other costs, such as points, title insurance, recording fees, appraisal, survey, etc., must be taken into account.

¶ 473 REFINANCING AND THE OLDER HOMEOWNER

An elderly homeowner is unlikely to qualify for a 30-year mortgage. This problem may be approached in several ways:

1. A short-term loan may be taken out, such as a three-, five- or seven-year loan, and subsequently be refinanced;

---

[19] Code Sec. 280A(d)(3).

[20] Code Sec. 469(l).

2. A long-term loan is possible if additional collateral is put up, such as life insurance, or if a co-signer is found, perhaps a relative or friend; or
3. A "reverse mortgage" specifically designed for retired persons may be available.

¶ 474 REVERSE MORTGAGES—FIXED TERM

In 1977, the Federal Home Bank Board, which regulates 86% of the Savings and Loan Associations, endorsed reverse mortgages for the retired. The objective was to enable retirees to borrow against their home equities so that they could afford to keep their homes without giving up ownership or space. The first reverse mortgage granted offered the following terms:

1. A loan of up to 80% of appraised value was granted.
2. The loan amount was paid to the homeowner in installments, e.g., the loan balance went up each month, but the monthly proceeds went down, being reduced by the interest on the increasing loan balance.
3. The loan itself was not repaid, but came due, in full, after the term agreed on, e.g., five, seven or ten years.
4. At the end of the term the loan had to be repaid or negotiated, but an extension was not guaranteed. If the homeowner could not pay, the home was sold, the loan repaid and the net proceeds paid to the homeowner.

Clearly, this type of loan does not guarantee that the homeowner will be able to stay in his home for life, unlike the reverse annuity mortgage.

¶ 475 REVERSE ANNUITY MORTGAGES

The *reverse annuity mortgage* works as follows:

1. A savings and loan association grants a mortgage guaranteed by the U.S. government.
2. The proceeds are used to buy an annuity for the retiree from an insurance company.
3. A fixed monthly annuity is paid to the homeowner. The mortgage balance is increased each month, but no tax is due since the annuity is all borrowed funds.
4. When the retiree moves or dies, the house is sold and the principal mortgage amount is paid. Any leftover proceeds go to the retiree or the retiree's estate.

This approach guarantees a home and an income for life and the loan is not due until the homeowner's death (or previous move).

¶ 476 ADVANTAGES OF PRIVATE ANNUITIES OVER REVERSE MORTGAGE ANNUITIES

If a homeowner sells the remainder in the house to the children for a private annuity, the following advantages are possible:

1. The homeowner owns the life estate and need not pay rent.
2. If the present value of the annuity according to Treasury tables equals the value of the remainder, the home is not subject to gift or estate tax.
3. Payments will be based on full market value of the remainder, not on a percentage of appraised value.
4. No interest is paid since the annuity constitutes sales proceeds.
5. The age-55-or-over gain exclusion can be used.
6. The home can stay in the family with less difficulty.
7. One or more installments may be forgiven as part of a gift program.

¶ 477 SALE AND LEASEBACKS

A sale and leaseback results in relinquishment of ownership. The homeowner becomes a tenant, but at least on an outright sale, the seller may become cash rich, since the gain of up to $125,000 from sales proceeds will be excluded from gross income if the taxpayer qualifies for the age 55 exclusion. On the other hand, rental payments are nondeductible. The buyer has acquired a tax shelter, deducting interest and taxes in a higher tax bracket, as well as repairs, maintenance and depreciation. The buyer can use 27.5 year cost recovery on a straight-line basis.[21]

¶ 478 SALE TO UNRELATED BUYER/LESSOR

When there is a sale to an unrelated buyer/lessor, the advantages include:

1. The property may be sold at close to full value.
2. Normally, the buyer obtains financing from a source other than the seller.
3. The buyer can use cost recovery and maximize his tax losses with less scrutiny from the IRS.

Disadvantages include:

---

[21] Code Sec. 168.

1. Full rent will be charged and increases may be made at each renewal.
2. The buyer may refuse to renew the lease or may sell the property or wish to live in the house.
3. Full expenses of sale will be incurred, e.g., a 6% brokerage commission and legal fees.

¶ 479 SALE TO A RELATIVE

When there is a sale to a relative, the advantages include:

1. Less than maximum rent may be charged. The buyer must charge "fair" rent to generate tax losses, but there is still some leeway.
2. A long-term lease, even for life, is more probably attainable.
3. No real estate broker is needed, thus no broker's fee.
4. Estate planning objectives may be accomplished through reducing the price, forgiving one or more installments, etc.

Corresponding disadvantages include:

1. It may be difficult to sell for full value and collect, particularly from a child who is going to inherit anyway.
2. A lump-sum outright sale is unlikely. A sale for a private annuity or an installment sale is more likely to be the norm. This is usually attractive, primarily for estate planning reasons.

If the seller wishes to be assured of a lifetime use, a life estate is retained and a remainder is sold. Since a remainderman is not entitled to depreciation,[22] it is virtually impossible to sell to an unrelated party and ill-advised to sell to a relative. To preserve the depreciation deduction the home should, if sold to a relative, be sold in full, but the lease should be renewable at the seller's option. If only the remainder is sold, the buyer receives no rent and gets no depreciation.

SETTING THE SELLING PRICE

If the sale is to a relative, the following considerations on setting the selling price should be made:

1. If the gain is within the $125,000 exclusion, a price increase will result in tax-free income to the seller and a step-up in depreciable basis to the buyer; and
2. There is a trade-off between price and terms. Thus, if the sale is for an installment obligation, the price may be reduced and

[22] Code Sec. 167(d).

the interest rate increased. If the buyer is in a higher income bracket, income-splitting results.

However, the advantage of income-splitting is reduced to the extent the seller is taxed on the interest and the buyer loses depreciation deductions.

JOINT OCCUPANCY

If the buyer is a relative or friend, the buyer and the seller may wish to live together. A buyer who purchases all, but rents back one-half of the residence, will have rental income and depreciation deductions reduced by one-half. If the buyer only buys half, there will not be any depreciation to deduct. Taxes and interest are always deductible, but only as itemized expenses, if allocable to personal living space. Structured appropriately, a sale and partial-lease back will give the seller funds and a companion with a minor adjustment in life style. The buyer receives an investment, a tax-shelter, and a social life.

¶ 480 DEFERRED PAYMENT SALES

If the buyer is a close relative so that the sale is part of an estate plan or the mortgage market is tight, the seller may help finance the purchase. There are two main types of deferred payment plans with variiations. They are: an installment sale, where the buyer pays a fixed price in installments, with or without a down payment, secured or unsecured, typically at even intervals; and a private annuity sale, whereby the buyer pays a fixed amount periodically for the life of the seller. The payments may be secured or unsecured and there may be a down payment.

The present value of the annuity, based on the seller's life expectancy (using Treasury tables), is set equal to the value of the home at the time of sale, but the buyer's total payments may be more or less, depending on how long the seller actually lives. This technique is predominantly used in a family setting. A lease-back may be entered into in both payment plans.

INSTALLMENT SALES

Advantages:

1. Taxation is deferred until collection;
2. It is easier to effect the purchase for the buyer;
3. If the buyer is a relative, one or more installments may be forgiven without gift tax (up to $10,000 a year);
4. The gain still may be excluded under the "over-55 rule" (up to $125,000); and

5. The buyer's basis in the home equals the full face value of the notes.

Disadvantages:

1. The buyer may default;
2. Inflation may erode the purchasing power of future collections; and
3. If the forgiveness of an installment is a gift, the seller must nevertheless recognize gain on the unpaid note.[23]

PRIVATE ANNUITIES

Advantages:

1. Same as one through four, under advantages of installment sales;
2. No income is recognized by the seller upon forgiveness of one or more payments;
3. No "notes" are included in the seller's estate; and
4. An immediate gain is recognized if the annuity is secured.[24]

Disadvantages:

1. Same as one and two under disadvantages of installment sales;
2. The buyer only counts payments actually made as the purchase price (basis); and
3. The buyer gets no interest deductions, but the seller still recognizes income upon collection.[25]

¶ 481 CHARITABLE CONTRIBUTIONS OF REMAINDER INTEREST

A remainder interest in a residence, vacation home, ranch or farm may be gifted currently to charity, resulting in a present income tax deduction.[26] Thus, the homeowner makes a current gift of a future interest. The life estate is retained, i.e., the right to live in the home for life, whereupon the charitable organization receives the home outright.

The deduction is an actuarially determined fraction of the current value of the home based on the life expectancy of the homeowner. The older the homeowner, the larger the deduction. Unisex Treasury tables, adjusted monthly, are used for this purpose.[27] The estate of the homeowner includes the residence,[28] but an offsetting charitable contribution deduction is allowed.[29] If the homeowner is well off, it is possible to

[23] Code Sec. 453B(f).
[24] *Estate of Lloyd G. Bell,* CCH Dec. 32,025, 60 TC 469 (1973).
[25] Rev. Rul. 69-74, 1969-1 CB 43.
[26] Code Sec. 170(f)(3).
[27] Code Sec. 7520 and Notice 89-60, 1989-1 CB 700.
[28] Code Sec. 2036.
[29] Code Sec. 2055.

save on two taxes with the same gift; income tax currently and estate taxes later.

> ***Example:*** An individual deeds the remainder in a home, worth $100,000 and expected to appreciate, to a public charity. Depending on the donor's age the deduction is as follows, assuming a 10% discount rate:

Age	*55*	*60*	*65*	*70*	*75*	*80*	*85*
Deduction	$19,954	25,509	32,030	39,478	47,851	56,341	64,641

The deduction is limited a 30% of adjusted gross income with a five year carryover.[30]

Advantages:

The following are some of the advantages of a charitable contribution:

1. The homeowner can benefit a favored institution, such as a university or a church.
2. Immediate and future tax savings may be realized.
3. The homeowner has a legal life estate.

Disadvantages:

The following are some of the disadvantages:

1. Unless the homeowner has taxable income and considerable wealth, the tax savings are limited.
2. Ownership after death is irrevocably relinquished.

CONCLUSION

The financially poor homeowner need not sell the home to generate cash. Several strategies exist which will enable the homeowner to retain use of the home while raising funds. Sometimes either title or space must be given up. Tax consequences must always be considered before any alternative is selected.

¶ 482 SELLING A HOME TO A CLOSE CORPORATION

By selling a home to a closely held entity the seller may be able to get funds out without the necessity of a taxable distribution. This is best illustrated by an example.

> ***Example:*** Assume Hilda purchased her home for $50,000, but that it is currently worth $150,000. If she sells it to the corporation for $150,000, the following will happen:

1. Hilda receives $150,000 in cash as proceeds from the sale and not as a dividend;

[30] Code Sec. 170(b)(1)(C)(i).

2. Unless Hilda and her spouse own 50% or more of the value of the stock *and* the home is depreciable to the corporation, the $100,000 gain is a capital gain. Otherwise it is ordinary income;[31]
3. If Hilda is age 55 or over, she may exclude up to $125,000 of gain in full by election.[32] She must also have owned and used the home for at least three of the last five years. The gain is excludable whether ordinary or capital in nature;
4. The corporation's cost basis in the home is $150,000. If it is sold right away, there should be no gain or loss;
5. If Hilda still wishes to live in the home, the corporation may rent it to her and claim depreciation;
6. If Hilda is under 55 and her gain (see 3, above) is ordinary income, she might consider the following:
   (a) Have the corporation rent out the house to a third party;
   (b) Roll over the gain by purchasing a replacement residence;
   (c) Depending on how these transactions are financed she may still have substantial funds left over; if Hilda had a small mortgage, the corporation paid cash, but she got "seller financing" on her replacement residence.

¶ 483 THE MAGIC OF A SALE TO AN S CORPORATION

There are alternatives to an ordinary sale. Here is a tax strategy with some unique advantages:

Hilda moved to another state and purchased a new residence. She is considering selling her old house, but the market is weak. The rental market is strong, but she will not be able to defer her substantial gain unless she sells it within two years of her new home purchase. Hilda can have it both ways by selling her old residence to a Subchapter S (S) corporation, which may be 100% owned by her, then having the corporation rent it out indefinitely. Consider the advantages:

1. Since the corporation is a separate legal person, Hilda has *sold* her old residence and will be able to defer the gain on it. The S corporation will sign installment notes and make payments later;
2. The S corporation will have a stepped-up, fair market value basis, tax-free to Hilda, who rolled over her gain;
3. When the S corporation rents out the house, it can do so indefinitely and depreciate the new, higher basis; and

[31] Code Sec. 1239.

[32] Code Sec. 121.

4. Being a nontaxable flow-through entity, the S corporation's deductions for depreciation, interest and property taxes wind up on Hilda's tax return, perhaps to more than offset the rental income. The result is a homemade tax shelter.

Any net rental loss is deductible to the extent of $25,000, notwithstanding the passive activity loss deferral rules, discussed in Chapter 11.

By 1993, interest rates were at a 20-year low, resulting in unprecedented mortgage prepayments and refinancing. Due to the importance of this topic, the next chapter treats it in more detail.

CHAPTER 5

WHEN TO REFINANCE OR PREPAY A HOME MORTGAGE

When to Refinance a Home Mortgage

¶ 501 INTRODUCTION

By 1993, home mortgage rates had reached a 23-year low and homeowners were refinancing their mortgages to an unprecedented extent. A decision to refinance must take into account several factors, such as

1. The reduction in the mortgage interest rate;
2. "Points" charged by the new mortgagee;
3. Prepayment penalties on the old mortgage;
4. Closing costs, such as appraisal fees, inspections, title insurance, legal fees, and mortgage insurance premiums;
5. Whether the homeowner itemizes expenses or takes the standard deduction; and
6. How long the taxpayer intends to retain the mortgage, e.g., how likely is it that the taxpayer will move within three to five years?

Discussed below is a set of rules developed to assist a homeowner to make a rational refinancing decision.

¶ 502 DEDUCTIBLE AND NONDEDUCTIBLE ITEMS

The following items are deductible:

1. The mortgage interest itself;
2. Prepayment penalties on the old mortgage are deductible as "qualified residence interest"; and
3. "Points" paid on the new mortgage are deductible ratably over the life of the new mortgage. To the extent the proceeds are used for improvements or reconstruction, an allocable share of the points is currently deductible.

The following items are nondeductible:

1. Closing costs, such as appraisals, inspections, legal fees, title insurance, and mortgage insurance. These costs cannot be added to the homeowner's basis in the home or in the loan either.
2. "Points" paid purely to refinance an existing mortgage, but they may be amortized over the new mortgage term.

In any event, a homeowner will derive no tax benefits, even from deductible items, if the standard deduction is claimed ($6,200 on a joint return in 1993).

¶ 503 CHOOSING THE NEW MORTGAGE TERM

The term of a new mortgage will almost always differ from the remaining term of the old mortgage. However, the homeowner may typically select a term from 10 to 30 years. If there are no prepayment penalties, the homeowner may consider the maximum available term to retain flexibility, since any desired amortization schedule may be adopted at any given time, subject only to the minimum payment due. This is particularly attractive at a time when the interest rate is exceptionally low.

> ***Example:*** A homeowner is replacing an existing first mortgage with a new $100,000, 7½%, 30-year mortgage. The monthly payment is $699.21. To amortize the mortgage over 15 years, the monthly payment must be increased to $927.01. In other words, if a 15-year mortgage is taken out, the homeowner *must* pay at least $927.01 a month or be in default. By selecting a 30-year mortgage, the homeowner *may* pay $927.01 or more, but is only obligated to pay $699.21. Thus, with a long-term mortgage, the homeowner may, at any time, convert to a shorter-term mortgage without closing costs.

¶ 504 REFINANCING AN ADJUSTABLE RATE MORTGAGE

An increasing number of homeowners have Adjustable Rate Mortgages (ARMs). The rate typically starts low, but may be increased annually, for example, by a maximum of two percentage points, subject to an overall maximum over the whole term, for example, six percentage points. Such mortgages often provide that the homeowner may convert to a fixed rate mortgage for the remaining term. Even though a small conversion fee may be payable, no closing costs need be incurred. Therefore, if the homeowner plans to remain in the home indefinitely *and* the fixed rate is exceptionally low, historically speaking, the homeowner may be well advised to convert to lock in the current low long-term rate. Since future rates cannot be predicted, the decision is a matter of judgment.

¶ 505 REFINANCING DECISION RULES

In the following situations, the homeowner should generally refinance:

1. There are no closing costs and the new mortgage interest rate is lower than the old rate.

2. The remaining mortgage balance is refinanced for the remaining term and the monthly payment is reduced.

3. The homeowner needs extra cash and the mortgage rate is lower than the interest rate on alternative loans, including home equity loans.
4. The new mortgage rate is at least two percentage points lower than the old rate and the homeowner has no plans to sell the home for at least three years.

In other cases, a further analysis is required, taking into account the time value of money (present value analysis) as shown below.

¶ 506 MAKING PRACTICAL REFINANCING DECISIONS

In practice, the homeowner must take into consideration different mortgage rates and terms, taxes, closing costs and points to make a rational decision.

> ***Example:*** The homeowner currently carries a 30-year, 9% mortgage with 12 years remaining and a loan balance of $60,000. The monthly payment is $682.82. If the mortgage is refinanced, the new mortgage will require $2,000 in nondeductible closing costs and one point to be added to the mortgage balance. At 7% and a 15-year term, the new $60,000 mortgage requires a monthly payment of $544.69. The homeowner is *not* saving the reduction in the monthly payment of $138.13. To make a valid comparison, a 12-year amortization schedule must be assumed. The monthly payment required to pay $60,000 over 12 years equals $633.20. The question therefore becomes: Is it worth paying $2,000 upfront in nondeductible closing costs to cut the monthly payment by $59.62? Two common decision rules are the *payback method* and the *net present value method.*

THE PAYBACK METHOD

Here, the homeowner computes the number of months it will take to recoup the closing costs. If the standard deduction is claimed, the homeowner saves $59.62 before *and* after taxes. Since $2,000/$59.62 equals 33.5 months, it will take close to three years to repay the closing costs. This is not unreasonable, and the homeowner may very well choose to refinance. If the homeowner itemizes deductions, the decrease in the monthly payment must be reduced by the tax benefit lost, for example, 28%, to $42.93. At that level, it will take $2,000/$42.93 or 46.6 months, or almost four years, to repay the closing costs and the homeowner may be less inclined to refinance.

THE NET PRESENT VALUE METHOD

Under this method, the homeowner computes the present value of the after-tax monthly payment reduction and refinances if it exceeds the closing costs. The payment reduction must be based on and amortization schedule equal to the remaining term of the *old* mortgage. Since the opportunity cost is the cost of retaining the old mortgage, it makes sense to use a discount rate equal to the old mortgage rate. Using the example above, the present value of a monthly annuity of $59.62 for 144 months at 9% equals $5,238.87. Since this is far in excess of the $2,000 of closing costs incurred, refinancing is indicated.

If the homeowner itemizes expenses at a 28% tax rate, the present value of a monthly annuity of $42.93 for 144 months at 9% should be computed. This number is only $3,772.31, but still in excess of $2,000, again indicating that refinancing should take place.

The opposite decision would probably be reached if only a one-point reduction in the mortgage rate is possible and/or the homeowner may move within the next few years.

When to Prepay a Home Mortgage

¶ 510 INTRODUCTION

A homeowner with a mortgage may typically prepay all or some of the mortgage principal without prepayment penalties. Whether this should be done depends on alternative investments available. In general, a mortgage prepayment should only be made if the after-tax mortgage rate exceeds the after-tax rate of return on available investment vehicles. The decision is complicated by many factors, such as whether the homeowner claims the standard deduction and the availability of deductible Individual Retirement Arrangement (IRA) contributions and salary reduction plans, such as Code Sec. 401(k) or 403(b) plans.

Below, three approaches to making the mortgage prepayment decision are explained and illustrated with practical examples. The mathematics are kept at a minimum and none of the computations require more than a pocket calculator.

¶ 511 THE FINANCIAL CONSEQUENCES OF MAKING EXTRA MORTGAGE PAYMENTS

When a homeowner adds to the regular monthly mortgage payment, the following occurs:

1. The extra amount paid reduces the principal balance directly.
2. Since less principal and interest will be payable in the future, the remaining mortgage term is lessened.
3. The required minimum monthly mortgage payment remains the same.

As a result, the homeowner's near-term obligation is unaffected, but the mortgage will be paid off sooner. By making prepayments, the homeowner/mortgagor can adopt a customized amortization schedule. Thus, by varying the mortgage payment (subject to the monthly minimum), a mortgage may be paid off over any desired term shorter than the original maximum payment period contracted for.

> ***Example:*** *The effect of lump-sum prepayment.* Donald originally borrowed $100,000 at 8% payable in equal monthly amounts over 30 years. His minimum monthly payment is $733.76. After 14 years (168 payments), the unpaid principal balance is $79,332.33 and 16 years remain of the original term. If Donald makes an extra $10,000 payment at this point, the principal balance is reduced to $69,332.33. The minimum required monthly payment is still $733.76. However, the remaining term is reduced from 192 (16 × 12) to 149.6 or approximately 3½ years.
>
> By way of comparison, if Donald had refinanced his old $79,332.33 mortgage with a new $69,332.33 mortgage, also at 8% with a 16-year term, his monthly payment would have fallen from $733.76 to $641.27.
>
> ***Example:*** *Converting a 30-year mortgage to a 15-year mortgage.* Donald enters into a $100,000, 8%, 30-year mortgage, requiring a monthly payment of $733.76. He would like to pay it off in 15 years but does not want to be committed to do so. The monthly payment required to amortize the mortgage over 15 years equals $995.65.
>
> ***Example:*** *Decreasing the remaining mortgage term.* Same as the previous example, but Donald made only his minimum payment the first 10 years, leaving him with a principal balance of $87,725. At this point, his financial circumstances have improved, and he wishes to pay off the remaining mortgage over 12 years rather than in 20. A fixed monthly payment of $949.58 will accomplish the goal of shortening the mortgage term from 30 to 22 years.

¶ 512 THE DISAPPEARING INTEREST PHENOMENON

In the case of a fixed monthly payment mortgage, the interest portion decreases each month (as the principal balance is reduced) with an offsetting increase in the principal payment portion. Thus, with the mere passage of time, the homeowner derives less tax benefits from the "qualified residence interest" deduction. In fact, because the standard deduction is indexed for inflation each year, the older the mortgage, the more unlikely it becomes that the homeowner will itemize deductions at all!

Example: *Principal and interest payment pattern.* A 15-year, 8%, $100,000 mortgage is amortized at the rate of $955.65 a month, or $11,468 a year. The interest portion decreases each year while the principal repayment increases. The interest and principal pattern may be demonstrated by the following numbers from individual years:

Year	*Principal*	*Interest*
1	$ 3,598	$7,870
5	4,949	6,518
7	5,805	5,663
10	7,374	4,094
12	8,649	2,819
15	10,986	482

Clearly, the homeowner is more likely to itemize deductions in the early years of the mortgage and to claim the standard deduction in later years. This tendency is exacerbated by the fact that the standard deduction is indexed for inflation.

¶ 513 WHY FEWER TAXPAYERS ITEMIZE THEIR DEDUCTIONS

Whether a taxpayer itemizes deductions or not, no tax benefit is reaped to the extent of the standard deduction. The number of taxpayers claiming the standard deduction is on the increase for two main reasons:

1. The standard deduction has become more generous in recent years. By 1993, it had reached $6,200 on a joint return and is increased annually for inflation.
2. A number of traditional deductions are subject to percentage floors, are deferred, or have become nondeductible. For example:
   (a) "Miscellaneous itemized deductions," such as investment expenses, have to be reduced by two percent of Adjusted Gross Income (AGI), medical expenses by 7½% of AGI and personal casualty losses by 10% of AGI.
   (b) Investment interest expenses must be deferred to the extent they exceed "net investment income."
   (c) Personal interest expenses and state and local sales taxes are nondeductible altogether.

A homeowner who does not itemize has more to gain by prepaying a mortgage than an itemizer, since the before-tax mortgage interest is saved in full.

¶ 514 MORTGAGE PREPAYMENT CONSIDERATIONS

The following factors *favor mortgage prepayments:*

1. The mortgage interest rate is high.
2. The taxpayer claims the standard deduction.
3. No deductible investment opportunities are available with tax-deferred yields, e.g., the homeowner is not covered by a Code Sec. 401(k) plan or is ineligible for a Code Sec. 403(b) plan or to make deductible contributions to an Individual Retirement Arrangement (IRA).

The following factors *favor alternative investments:*

1. The mortgage interest rate is low.
2. The mortgage contains a prepayment penalty clause.
3. The taxpayer itemizes deductions.
4. Deductible investment opportunities are available with tax-deferred yields, such as Code Sec. 401(k) and/or 403(b) plans and/or IRAs.
5. The employer makes matching contributions to an available salary-reduction plan, such as a Code Sec. 401(k) plan.
6. Favorable tax treatment is expected to be available upon the liquidation of the investment, e.g., 5-year forward averaging of a lump-sum distribution from a Code Sec. 401(k) plan after age 59½.

From the above, it may be concluded that the homeowner is *most likely to prepay* the mortgage if the mortgage interest rate is high, the standard deduction is claimed and only nondeductible investments with currently taxable yields are available. Conversely, the homeowner is *least likely to prepay* a mortgage if the mortgage rate is low, itemized deductions are claimed and deductible investments with tax-deferred yields are available (particularly if the employer makes matching contributions and/or forward averaging is possible).

¶ 515 MORTGAGE PREPAYMENTS VS. TAXABLE INVESTMENTS

Prepaying mortgage principal should be viewed as making an investment. The rate of return equals the mortgage interest rate less the mortgagee's tax bracket if the mortgagee itemizes deductions. If the standard deduction is claimed, the rate of return simply equals the mortgage interest saved. A homeowner with an outstanding mortgage who makes an alternative investment indirectly finances that investment with the home mortgage, since the mortgage could have been prepaid instead. As a result, a mortgage should only be prepaid if the after-tax mortgage rate exceeds the after-tax return available from other investments.

In the simple case where the alternative investment offers no tax advantages, such as tax deferral, the after-tax rates may be compared directly.

***Example:** Mortgage prepayments and taxable investments compared.* Paul has an 8% home mortgage which may be prepaid, in whole or in part, without penalties and is in the 28% tax bracket. If he claims the standard deduction, he earns an after-tax rate of return of 8% by prepaying mortgage principal. An alternative taxable investment would have to yield more than 11.11% to provide Paul with a higher after-tax return (11.11% – 28% = 8%).

If Paul deducts his mortgage interest, his after-tax mortgage rate is only 5.76% (8% – 28%). Thus, he is better off with an alternative taxable investment as long as the before-tax rate of return exceeds 8%. If the return is tax free, e.g., interest on municipal bonds, the rate of return need only exceed 5.76%, since this is the equivalent of a taxable return of 8%.

¶ 516 MORTGAGE PREPAYMENTS VS. TAX-DEFERRED INVESTMENTS

Investments considered as alternatives to mortgage prepayments may offer special tax advantages. Thus, contributions to IRAs may be deductible or nondeductible, but the earnings are not taxed until distributed. Contributions to Code Sec. 401(k) or 403(b) plans (salary reduction plans) are deductible *and* the earnings accumulate on a tax-deferred basis. Even though withdrawals of both principal and accumulated income are taxable, a lump-sum distribution may qualify for forward averaging, resulting in lower taxes.

To compare such investments with mortgage prepayments, the time value of money must be considered. Two approaches are discussed below:

1. The comparison of future or terminal after-tax values which is most appropriate when a series of payments are made.
2. The comparison of the after-tax internal rate of return for the tax-deferred investment with the after-tax mortgage rate.

Applications of the future value approach will be illustrated first.

***Example:** Mortgage prepayments and Code Sec. 401(k) contributions compared.* Corinne has a home mortgage with no prepayment penalties at eight percent with more than 12 years remaining, is in the 28% tax bracket, but claims the standard deduction. She wishes to save $100 a month before taxes and wonders if she should make an extra monthly mortgage payment of $72 ($100 – 28% tax) or make a monthly contribution of $100 to her employer's

Code Sec. 401(k) plan (salary reduction plan), also expected to yield 8% on a tax-deferred basis. If her investment horizon is 12 years, for example, the numbers work out as follows:

After 12 years, her mortgage balance would be reduced by the future value of an annuity of $72 a month, or $17,317. Alternatively, her Code Sec. 401(k) account balance would grow to the future value of an annuity of $100 a month, or $24,051. However, if Corinne withdraws the $24,051 and pays 28% tax, she is left with the same $17,317. She would therefore be indifferent between the two investment options. However, the Code Sec. 401(k) alternative would be *more* attractive if Corinne itemizes her deductions (since she would not forfeit the tax savings generated by the mortgage interest deduction), and/or the Code Sec. 401(k) plan earns a higher rate of return, and/or the distribution qualifies for forward averaging, or she leaves her account balance to grow on a tax-deferred basis.

Example: *The effect of itemizing deductions and forward averaging on the Code Sec. 401(k) plan alternative.* Bernadette wishes to save $100 a month for 10 years. She is in the 28% tax bracket, has an 8% mortgage with at least 10 years remaining and itemizes her deductions. The alternatives she is considering are to either pay off $72 a month of mortgage principal or to contribute $100 a month to her employer's Code Sec. 401(k) plan, expected to earn 5%. Using terminal value comparisons, the calculations are as follows:

Mortgage prepayment. Prepaying $72 a month of mortgage principal is like investing at an after-tax rate of return of 5.76% (8% – 28%). The future value of an annuity of $72 growing at an annual rate of 5.76% equals $11,647.

Section 401(k) plan contributions. The future value of $100 a month growing at 5% annually is $15,528. If this amount is distributed after 10 years and is subject to only 15 percent tax because of forward averaging, Bernadette would be left with $13,199. This is more than if she prepaid the mortgage even though her mortgage interest rate was 8% and the plan only earned 5%! However, if her tax rate on withdrawal was 28%, she would be left with only $11,180, making the mortgage repayment the best option.

If a taxpayer makes nondeductible IRA contributions, the earnings still grow on a tax-deferred basis and upon withdrawal the portion representing principal is not taxable. The following example shows the necessary calculations.

Example: *Mortgage prepayments and nondeductible IRA contributions compared.* Howard invests $166.77 per month ($2,000 a year) for 15 years in a nondeductible IRA yielding 8%. At the end of 15 years, his account balance equals the future value of an annuity of $166.77, compounded at 2/3 of 1% a month for 180 months, or $57,674. Of this sum, $27,674 represents the accumulated income and $30,000 the nondeductible contributions. If Howard withdraws the full amount, is in the 28% tax bracket and is over age 59½ (so that no penalties apply), he is left with $49,925 ($57,674 – $7,749, the 28% tax on $27,674).

If, instead, Howard prepaid mortgage principal of $166.67 per month and his mortgage rate is 7%, his principal balance would be reduced by $52,828 after 15 years. Thus, Howard would be better off prepaying his mortgage *if he takes the standard deduction.* If Howard were able to deduct all mortgage interest expenses associated with the amounts that were invested instead in the IRA, he would really earn only 7% less taxes, or 5.83% a year (.486 percent monthly) by prepaying the mortgage. The future value of an annuity of $166.67 per month for 180 months at .486% is only $47,787. In other words, if Howard itemizes, the nondeductible IRA becomes more attractive than the mortgage prepayment.

¶ 517 MAKING LUMP-SUM TAX-DEFERRED INVESTMENTS VS. MORTGAGE PREPAYMENTS

A prepayment of mortgage principal is nondeductible and the interest saved may or may not have been deductible, depending on whether the homeowner itemizes or claims the standard deduction. On the other hand, the alternative investment may be deductible up front, e.g., a contribution to a deductible IRA or a Code Sec. 401(k) plan. In addition, the yield is not taxed currently, allowing for tax-free compounding. However, all withdrawals are taxable, principal as well as accumulated income. In the case of a Code Sec. 401(k) plan, a lump-sum withdrawal may be eligible for forward averaging at favorable tax rates.

To allow a comparison of such investment vehicles with mortgage prepayments, one approach is to compute the *after-tax internal rate of return* on the investment and compare it with the after-tax mortgage rate. The internal rate of return is the average compounded growth rate, i.e., the discount rate which reduces future cash flows to a present value equal to the investment. Thus, once the investment and the future cash flows are known (or assumed known), the decision maker "solves for" the discount rate.

¶ 518 COMPUTING THE INTERNAL RATE OF RETURN FOR TAX-DEFERRED INVESTMENTS

Prepayment of mortgage principal must be made with after-tax dollars. However, amounts contributed to deductible IRAs or Code Sec. 401(k) plans constitute before-tax dollars. Thus, $1 used to prepay a mortgage must be compared with contributing $\frac{\$1}{1 - T}$ to a tax-deductible plan, where T is the taxpayer's marginal rate. If the tax rate is 28 percent, for example, $1.39 of pre-tax dollars may be contributed to a tax-deductible plan ($1.39 – 28% = $1) as compared with $1 of mortgage principal reduction.

If the plan earns a rate of return, r, annually, the account balance equals $\frac{(1 + r)^n}{1 - T}$ after n years.

At this point, if the plan participant withdraws the account balance in full and pays a tax rate T_w, the after-tax distribution equals

$$\frac{(1 + r)^n (1 - T_w)}{1 - T}.$$

To find the after-tax compounded growth rate, k, it is merely necessary to solve for k in the equation

$$(1 + k)^n = \frac{(1 + r)^n (1 - T_w)}{1 - T}.$$

In the case of an IRA which does not qualify for forward averaging on the distribution of a lump-sum, the tax rates on contribution and withdrawal may very well be the same, e.g., 28 percent. In this case, $(1 + k)^n$ *simply equals* $(1 + r)^n$ *and* $k = r$. Thus, the internal rate of return on the IRA simply equals its constant annual yield.

However, if the tax rate on withdrawal differs from the tax rate at the time of contribution, e.g., the plan is a Code Sec. 401(k) plan and the taxpayer qualifies for 5-year forward averaging

$$k = \left[\frac{(1 + r)^n (1 - T_w)}{1 - T}\right]^{1/n} - 1.$$

This is still a simple enough formula to be promptly calculable on a pocket calculator as shown in the example below.

> ***Example:*** *Computing the internal rate of return on a Code Sec. 401(k) plan contribution.* Donald's employer offers a Code Sec. 401(k) plan expected to yield 6%. If Donald invests in the plan, he expects to take a lump-sum distribution in 15 years and qualify for a 15% tax rate due to forward averaging. He is currently in the

28% bracket. The after-tax internal rate of return on a plan contribution (salary reduction) is computed as follows:

$$\left[\frac{1.06^{15}(1 - .15)}{1 - .28}\right]^{1/15} - 1$$

$$= \left(\frac{2.397\ x\ .85}{.72}\right)^{1/15} - 1$$

$$= 2.829^{1/15} - 1$$

$$= .07179.$$

As a result, Donald should prepay his mortgage if his after-tax mortgage rate is in excess of 7.18%, e.g., his mortgage interest rate is 7.25% and he claims the standard deduction. If Donald itemizes his deductions, the salary reduction plan offers a higher return unless his mortgage rate is at least 10 percent (10% − 28% = 7.2%).

Example: *Making deductible IRA contributions.* If the facts are the same as in the previous example except that Donald makes deductible contributions to an IRA in lieu of the Code Sec. 401(k) plan, the internal rate of return on the IRA is simply 6%, assuming that the lump-sum withdrawal is taxed at 28%. Thus, Donald should prepay his mortgage if the mortgage interest rate is above 6% if he takes the standard deduction or above 8.33% if he itemizes his deductions (8.33% − 28% = 6%).

¶ 519 ADVANTAGES OF MAKING THE MORTGAGE PREPAYMENT DECISIONS ANNUALLY

Most decisions as to whether to prepay a mortgage or make alternative investments may be made annually or even more often. Thus, the typical taxpayer is not committed to making contributions to an IRA or even to a Code Sec. 401(k) plan every year.

There are several advantages to making an annual decision.

1. The homeowner may choose not to make *any* investment one year because of personal expenses, such as a vacation or the purchase of appliances and furniture.
2. An increasing number of mortgagors carry adjustable rate mortgages (ARMs). Thus, the applicable mortgage interest rate may vary from year to year.
3. A homeowner may itemize deductions for many years, then switch to the standard deduction or even itemize every other

year! Taking the standard deduction substantially increases the attractiveness of prepaying the mortgage.

4. Every year provides the plan participant with another year's earnings performance of the plan. If the rate of return is lower than anticipated, the homeowner may switch to a mortgage prepayment program.

¶ 520 CONCLUSIONS

When prepaying a mortgage, a homeowner is making an investment yielding a rate of return equal to the after-tax mortgage interest rate. As a result, this should not be done if alternative investments are available which offer a higher after-tax rate of return. When comparing a mortgage prepayment with making a nondeductible and currently taxable investment, the after-tax rates of return may be compared directly. However, if the alternative investment offers tax-deferral features, the time value of money must be considered. One approach to making a valid comparison is to compare the after-tax terminal values of the alternatives, i.e., to compare the reduction in the mortgage balance at the end of the investment horizon with the accumulated alternative investment at that time. Another approach is to compute the after-tax internal rate of return on the alternative investment and compare it with the after-tax mortgage rate. Proceeding in this fashion the homeowner is better equipped to make a rational decision as to when to prepay mortgage principal. Ideally the decision is an annual one based on up to date information.

CHAPTER 6

PERSONAL LOANS AND CREDIT MANAGEMENT

¶ 601 INTRODUCTION

This chapter surveys personal loans and credit management, from credit cards to finance companies, from checking account credit lines to secured loans. It discusses how to establish and maintain credit, how to preserve a good credit rating, considerations when cosigning a loan, and how interest and finance charges are computed. Home mortgages are discussed at ¶ 420 and following.

¶ 602 TYPES OF LOANS

In the United States today, approximately 50% of all retail sales are made on credit, more than 90% of manufacturer's and wholesale sales are on credit, and close to 100% of home purchases are on credit. It is a world of credit cards, revolving credit, installment purchases, consumer loans, pledges, mortgages, conditional sales, liens, and credit lines. The client most likely has three types of loans outstanding at any given time:

1. *Consumer credit.* In a consumer credit situation, since the seller and the creditor is one and the same, the loan is also called a purchase-money loan. Examples include department store credit cards and installment purchases. Many department stores only accept their own card to save costs, earn interest, and encourage customer loyalty.

2. *Consumer loans.* As to consumer loans, the seller and creditor are two different persons. An example is the multipurpose credit card on which the client borrows money from the card issuer to purchase goods and services from others.

3. *Home mortgages.* Home mortgages fall outside the scope of consumer loans and were covered in Chapter 4, being long term, and an alternative to rent.

4. Managing the debt load.

The monthly payments on all the client's loans, other than the home mortgage, should, as a general rule of thumb, not exceed 20% of available cash flow. If it does not exceed 10% the client is considered to be in a good credit position.

The following checklist may be used to assess the client's debt situation:

	MONTHLY PAYMENT	*BALANCE*
Auto loans	$	$
Tuition loans		
Installment loans		
Credit cards		
bank		
gas		
store		
airline		
Credit lines		
home equity line		
overdraft line		
personal credit line		
Margin account/broker		
Unpaid taxes		
Informal debts		
	$	$

As people get older and/or their income increases, they tend to decrease short-term borrowing, except for credit card charges resulting from convenience buying. Debts incurred after reaching a certain age and position tend to be for major purchases, such as a boat, a car, a vacation home or for investments.

¶ 603 REASONS FOR BORROWING

On the one hand, the average person probably has less *need* to borrow now than ever, due to the existence of the following:

1. Social Security benefits.
2. Working spouses.
3. Life, health, accident and disability insurance.
4. Fringe benefits, not mentioned above, such as pension and profit-sharing plans, employee savings and thrift plans, medical reimbursement plans and death benefits.

On the other hand, with all these reasons to feel financially secure people hesitate less to go into debt. The main reasons for the increased borrowing appear to be the following:

1. *Impatience.* Life is short. Why not live now and pay later? Most people can enjoy a product or a vacation without having saved up the money first. There is a prevalent hunger to acquire and enjoy currently.

2. Owing money can provide an *incentive to work* harder. It is like forced savings. Buying on credit, then having to pay off the loan is *safer* than saving for it. In the latter case the goal, i.e., the purchase, may be put off indefinitely.
3. The combination of *inflation and taxation* may reduce the real, after-tax cost of borrowing below zero. See ¶ 604.
4. Sometimes no real choice exists because of an *emergency,* e.g., medical bills, or the inability to pay cash for something necessary and expensive, e.g., a car.

There are good and bad reasons for borrowing.

Some of the good reasons are:

1. Purchase of major items, such as a car, appliances, furniture, establishing a business, etc.
2. Establishment of a household, including the standard household items, but also the wedding, honeymoon, etc.
3. Emergencies of a medical or dental nature, accidents, funeral expenses for a parent, etc.
4. Education for the borrower, spouse or children. The future payoffs in both money and psychic income may more than justify a loan.
5. Bargains and special opportunities, e.g., borrowing to buy before prices go up, to make a deductible IRA contribution, or to get in on the ground floor of a business opportunity.

Some of the bad times and reasons to borrow include:

1. To alleviate the hardship in making repayments.
2. To buy on impulse products not really needed.
3. To acquire items merely for an ego trip or a spree.
4. To buy status symbols merely because they are such.
5. To borrow because of overoptimism about the future.
6. To gamble or speculate. This includes not only casino gambling, but certain tax shelters, speculative stocks, and commodity futures.
7. To pay living expenses.

¶ 604 PRE-BORROWING PLANNING

Prior to signing on the dotted line for a loan, the client should consider the following:

1. Has the spouse been consulted? A major loan may even require both spouses' signatures. It is a good idea to discuss a loan

before entering into it. Keeping financial secrets from each other may lead to domestic disputes.

2. Is the loan really needed? Why borrow at 18% while saving at 4%? The client may be better off selling low-yielding securities, bonds or stocks, rather than going into debt. Few investments yield more than what has to be paid for unsecured, personal loans.

3. Is the client using the cheapest form of financing? Commercial banks or credit unions may charge less than the seller or a finance company, a secured loan is cheaper than an unsecured loan, etc. It is easy to compare interest charges these days because the lender must disclose the effective rate under the "Truth in Lending Act."

4. Is the product or service purchased really necessary? If necessary, is it worth the price, including finance charges? It is depressing to make car payments, for example, long after the car has been sold or traded in.

5. Can the client afford to add new debts to the ones currently being paid off?

6. Is borrowing used as an alternative to savings? It is always cheaper to have savings for a rainy day than credit lines. However, if no savings are available, credit lines do provide emergency cash and should be maintained. As savings grow, there is less need for personal loan sources, although credit cards may be used for convenience.

7. Is the client borrowing to take advantage of an opportunity? If so, it may be easier to justify going into debt. Borrowing to buy anything of value is always more attractive than borrowing for consumption.

8. The loan contract must be read. There may be "hidden" charges or conditions. Take the word "default," for example. Most people think they are only in default if they are late with a payment. But the following may also constitute default:

   (a) Death, incapacity, or insolvency of the debtor.

   (b) Sale of collateral.

   (c) Reduction in value of collateral.

   (d) Borrowing more money on the collateral.

   (e) Moving out of state.

In the absence of any default clauses, default occurs only with failure to pay.

Before signing on the dotted line, there are two kinds of preparations the borrower should make:

1. *Gathering information.* This includes figuring out how much is needed and collecting anticipated required information such as copies of tax returns, reasons for the loan, net worth and income figures, outstanding debt, credit history, account numbers, and employment history (a resume is helpful).
2. *Comparison shopping.* Various lines of creditors exist, ranging from banks, savings and loan associations and credit unions to finance companies, including executive loan services and perhaps the employer. The reason for shopping is the bewildering array of interest rates, credit limits, repayment schedules, prepayment penalties, and collateral requirements.

¶ 605 HOW TO REDUCE BORROWING COSTS

Here are some tips to help the client keep borrowing costs at a minimum:

If many small loans are outstanding at high rates, a second mortgage or debt consolidation loan at lower rates may be considered.

It is easy and convenient to charge cash on credit cards, but the charge may be up to 24% annually as opposed to perhaps 12% on traditional executive loans through finance companies. Often a phone call may be sufficient to get a loan, but even if an application must be filled out, it may be worth it.

If possible, collateral should be used. Secured loans are cheaper.

A "free" credit available should be used first, such as the typical 30-day charge accounts which charge no interest if the balance is paid currently.

The lower the down payment and the longer the repayment period, the more the interest adds up. Low monthly payments are deceptive.

Old loans, including the mortgage, which carry low interest rates should be paid off last.

An eye must be kept on prepayment penalties on long-term loans.

¶ 606 INTEREST AND FINANCE CHARGES

Interest is the price paid for the forbearance of money. Under the "Truth in Lending Act" (real name Consumer Credit Protection Act of 1969), the effective rate charged on all consumer borrowing transactions up to $25,000 must be disclosed. Knowing the annual percentage rate, it is easy to compare sources of credit.

The *finance charge* should not be confused with the *interest charge*. In addition to the interest, it includes all payments required to get credit, such as loan fees and service charges, points, finder's fees, investigation fees, credit insurance charges, etc.

With a major item, such as a home, many fees are *not* part of the finance charge. These are the fees which would not go away even in a cash purchase, and include taxes, license fees, appraisal fees, title insurance, closing costs, legal fees, etc. Here are some of the main ways interest is computed:

SIMPLE INTEREST

Example: $1,000 in cash is borrowed. One year later, $1,120 is repaid in a lump sum. The interest rate was 12% simple, but nobody, except friends and relatives, lends money this way.

DISCOUNT RATES

The finance charge is deducted from the face amount up front. *Example:* $1,000 is to be paid off in monthly installments over one year. If 8%, or $80, is deducted immediately, the *effective* interest is almost doubled and is 15.68%. The reason is that only about half of the loan, or approximately $460 is available on the average during the year. In fact, whenever a loan is paid in installments, the borrower only has half of the proceeds available, on the average. The only time the average loan balance equals the proceeds is when the loan is repayable in a lump sum ("balloon payment") at the end of the term. This does not mean, however, that interest charges are less in the latter case. The discount would simply be increased.

"ADD-ON" RATE

Under this method the finance charge is added to the amount of the loan. The borrower receives the full amount requested but must pay back the sum of the two. If the annual add-on rate is 10% a year, for example, the true rate is 18.5%. Again, the true rate is almost twice the rate used because the loan is being paid off during the period the interest is charged.

SIMPLE MONTHLY RATE

On bank credit cards and revolving credit accounts, the interest is commonly expressed as a percentage of the average daily balance per month. Thus, 1½% means 18% annually, 2% means 24%, etc.

¶ 607 REBATES

When a loan is paid off early, the borrower is entitled to a rebate on the interest. But if the client expects to receive a two-thirds reduction if the loan is paid off after one-third of the repayment period, a cruel awakening is required. The reason is that in the early months, most of the payment is interest, while towards the end, it is mostly principal. In many cases, finance companies and other lenders rebate interest based on the "Rule of 78." The number 78 refers to the sum of the numbers 1 through 12. Thus the number 78 is only correct when dealing with a 12-month loan.

> ***Example:*** The client borrows $1,000 for one year, paying an add-on rate of 8%, meaning that the interest charge is $148. If the balance is paid off after four months, the refund is (8+7+6+5+4+3+2+1)/78 of the interest which is 18/39 of $148, or about $69. Thus, even though two-thirds of the term remained, less than half the interest was returned to the borrower. Again, this is because most of the principal was available in the early months. If the loan is a two-year loan, the denominator is the sum of the numbers 1 through 24, or 300. The numerator is still the sum of the remaining months. Thus, if the balance of a two-year loan is paid off five months ahead of time, the fraction of the total interest rebated is (5+4+3+2+1)/300 or 15/300, which is only 5% of the interest.

THE IMPACT OF INFLATION AND TAXATION

Interest and finance charges are deductible, if at all, as itemized expenses. The taxpayer needs to show that the debt is bona fide and that the interest was paid and not prepaid.[1] The limitations on the deductibility of interest are severe for personal interest:

1. No deduction is allowed for interest on loans used to purchase or carry tax-free income-producing property, such as municipal bonds.[2]
2. No deduction is allowed for interest on loans to buy cash-value life insurance, since cash-value increases are tax free, unless at least four of the first seven annual premiums are paid for first.[3]
3. A deduction is allowed for current or past due interest, but prepaid interest is not deductible until the year incurred.[4]
4. Even if the hurdles above are cleared, no consumer interest is deductible after 1990.[5]
5. There are limitations on investment interest deductions, i.e., interest on loans incurred to buy stocks, bonds and the like. The annual limit is equal to net investment income, generally

[1] Code Sec. 163.
[2] Code Sec. 165.
[3] Code Sec. 164.
[4] Code Secs. 163 and 463(g).
[5] Code Sec. 163(h).

including long- or short-term capital gains. Starting in 1993, long-term gains only count to the extent taxed at the same rate as other income. Any excess is carried forward to the next year, subject to the same limit.[6]

Inflation is a good reason for being in debt. The borrower pays back the loan with cheaper dollars. Assuming an inflation rate of 4%, for example, a 10% mortgage loan is almost *free* in real terms to a 28% taxpayer. This is because inflation reduces the 10% nominal rate to a 6% real rate, but the full nominal rate is tax deductible, reducing the real rate to 3.2% after taxes. Most people do not borrow *because* of taxes and inflation, but these factors make it easier to be a debtor.

Credit Cards

¶ 610 CREDIT CARD BOOM

The first credit cards reared their heads around the turn of the century. A typical card is made of plastic, has the holder's name and signature on it and is 2 inches by 3½ inches long. Even though the "Truth in Lending Act" forbids the sending out of unsolicited credit cards, they have nevertheless been distributed like confetti. It is a rare person today who does not have at least some credit cards of the 3,200 types being issued. Currently, some 300 million credit cards are outstanding, and many individuals possess in excess of 20 cards. Seventy-five percent of all adults have at least one card, and the average person has over five. The best known cards are of relatively recent origin. Although, the first bank card was issued by Franklin National Bank of New York in 1951, it was not until the 1970s that Visa and BankAmericard (now Master Card) were issued in record numbers.

Individual banks do not offer their own credit cards. In effect, the credit card issuers franchise their cards to the nation's banks for a fee. The bank cards currently generate some $20 billion a year in billings, one-third of which is outstanding at any given time. The individual issuers set the interest rate, credit limit, annual fee, and other terms.

Travel and entertainment cards are also of recent origin. Diners Club was formed in 1950, American Express in 1958, and Carte Blanche in the early '60s. Bank cards are more popular than travel and entertainment cards for two reasons:

1. No substantial income is needed to obtain one. An income of $6,000 a year may do it. As a general rule, the more "prestigious" cards require an annual income of $25,000 or more.

[6] Code Sec. 163(d).

2. If the holder does not plan to use the cards but wishes credit references, the low fee is attractive. Some institutions charge no fees to their regular customers.

The use of cards goes up with income because the type of items most frequently purchased with cards historically have tended to be luxuries requiring discretionary income.

Easy credit, notably credit cards, is the main reason for personal bankruptcies, which have now reached about one million a year in the U.S.

TYPES OF CARDS

All credit cards may be broken down into two broad categories:

1. *Single-purpose cards.* These include cards issued by sellers of goods and services, i.e., airlines, motel chains, car-rental agencies, phone companies, oil companies, and department stores. There are two trends here:
   (a) The cards tend to be valid for more and more extras. Airline cards may be used to buy merchandise, pay hotel and restaurant bills, etc.
   (b) The multipurpose cards have gained more and more acceptance, making single-purpose cards gradually obsolete despite (a) above. In other words, why keep a department store card if the store accepts VISA?
2. *Multipurpose cards.* These include the above-mentioned bank cards as well as the travel and entertainment ("T&E") cards. They are accepted at literally a million places around the world, but traditionally they have been used mostly in bars, restaurants, hotels and expensive shops.

CHARACTERISTICS OF MAJOR CREDIT CARDS

	VISA	*PREMIER VISA*	*MASTER CARD*	*MASTER CARD GOLD*	*AMERICAN EXPRESS GREEN*	*AMERICAN EXPRESS GOLD*	*AMERICAN EXPRESS PLATINUM*	*DINERS CLUB*	*CARTE BLANCHE*
Annual Fee	Variable, from zero to $30, decided by the issuing bank				$35	$65	$250	$45	$45
Credit Limit	$600-10,000	$5,000-50,000	$600-10,000	$5,000	$NONE	$2,000 and up	$NONE	$NONE	$NONE
Eligibility	Variable, set by issuing bank				$25,000 income	$40,000 income	$100,000 income	$25,000 income	$25,000 income
Minimum Payment	Variable, set by issuing bank, subject to State regulations, typically at least 5% of balance				BALANCE	BALANCE	BALANCE	BALANCE	BALANCE
Check Cashing	NO	NO	NO	NO	$1,000	$2,000	$10,000	$1,000	NO
Traveler's Checks	YES	YES	YES	YES	YES	YES	YES	YES	NO
Free Traveler's Checks	NO	YES	NO	YES	NO	NO	NO	YES	NO
Individual Receipts	NO	NO	NO	NO	YES	YES	YES	YES	YES
Guaranteed Hotel Reservations	NO	YES	NO	YES	YES	YES	YES	YES	NO

In addition, most cards offer travel insurance and provide cash through automatic tellers.

¶ 611 WHAT CAN BE CHARGED

Since the '70s, the range of goods and services available on a charge basis has reached truly staggering proportions, limited only by the ingenuity of man. Thus, the cardholder can charge not only dinners, transportation and hotels, but charitable contributions, tuition, massage parlors, dentists', physicians' and lawyers' bills, driving lessons, rent, theater tickets, etc. By 1985, all bank and T&E cards also granted cash advances through national, automatic, 24-hour teller machines.

¶ 612 ADVANTAGES OF HAVING MAJOR CREDIT CARDS

There are many advantages of having credit cards, apart from the simple slogan: "Buy now, pay later":

1. *Security and convenience.* The cardholder is never broke as plastic cards provide funds almost anywhere. The cards are safer than cash because of the $50 limited liability on charges made by unauthorized users even prior to reporting the card lost.

The holder may shop by phone or mail by simply providing the seller with the card number, name, and expiration date.

Major cards have worldwide recognition and can be used anywhere in any currency, which are then translated into dollars.

2. *Recordkeeping.* Expenses charged are itemized in monthly statements. If used for business, these records are invaluable in claiming deductions and/or in seeking reimbursements from an employer.

For small additional fees or no fees, *other family members* may be issued their own cards.

Many cards provide *cash advances,* often several thousand dollars on short notice, even to the extent of giving the holder personal checks for any purpose.

Many cards provide *emergency check cashing* or allow the purchase of travelers' checks on the card at home and abroad.

Some cards provide *low-cost insurance,* such as flight insurance, and group health or accident insurance.

Some cards provide *emergency card replacement* in major cities around the world.

Major credit cards, even if rarely used, provide excellent *credit references* for other loan purposes.

¶ 613 IMPORTANCE OF SELF-CONTROL

Most people can use credit cards intelligently; others cannot. "Buy now, pay later" is probably the largest reason for personal bankruptcies. With credit cards the consumer has an almost unlimited spending power in the *short* run. In the *long* run, all bills must be paid with the high interest which accompanies unsecured, personal loans. Despite the often-touted advantage of "one monthly check," studies show that people who use general-purpose credit cards write *more* checks than people who do not. The reasons for this include the use of several credit cards and charging small items which would otherwise have been paid in cash.

Two reasons why credit card charges may get out of control are:

1. Credit card ceilings cannot be supervised in practice. The limit on a bank card may be $1,000 or $2,000, but the individual merchant, hotel, restaurant, etc., is not necessarily going to check an individual's balance. At the most, the number on the card is going to be compared against a list of cancelled cards, unless the purchase is a major one.
2. There is no limit on the number of credit cards one person may use. Some people have run up $100,000 or more on their combined credit cards before throwing in the towel.

A cardholder's right and means of self-defense include:

When purchasing goods and services, the customer has more rights, consumer protection, etc., than in a cash loan transaction. As soon as the card is accepted, the title to the merchandise passes to the buyer and cannot be repossessed.

SAFETY VALVE

The basic safety valve in all indebtedness is: Separate assets from liabilities. In the simplest case, all assets are held by the spouse, but all indebtedness is the client's name or vice versa. A spouse is not responsible for the other spouse's debts, thus sheltering the former's assets. Under the current gift tax law, unlimited gifts by one spouse to the other are free of gift tax.[7] Corporations, partnerships, and trusts can often be used for the same purpose of isolating assets from an individual's creditors.

The client should establish as much credit as possible when it is needed the least. It does not hurt to have a collection of bank cards and other credit lines, particularly if little or no fees are involved, absent usage. Creditors do *not* review the client's financial situation periodi-

[7] Code Sec. 2523.

cally. They care at the time of application, not thereafter. In fact, even after a personal bankruptcy, cards *not* involved in the proceeding are not going to be cancelled.

¶ 614 EQUAL CREDIT OPPORTUNITY ACT OF 1975

It has traditionally been difficult for women to obtain credit, including credit cards, on their own without a husband "sponsor." A step in the right direction was the Equal Credit Opportunity Act of 1975. The main provisions of the Act are:

1. Creditors cannot discriminate on the basis of gender or marital status.
2. The application cannot require specific information on gender or marital status.
3. A co-signer or sponsor can no longer be required.
4. The past earnings history must be taken into account.
5. If rejected, the applicant must be given the reasons within 60 days, if requested.
6. A creditor who does discriminate is liable for actual damages, plus up to $10,000 in punitive damages.

Many women do inadvertently make problems for themselves by notifying their creditors and credit card issuers of their name change upon marriage. Frequently, creditors go so far as to cancel the account, or at least to demand a reapplication. There are two ways to handle this problem:

1. Omitting to notify creditors of the change, or
2. Failing to change the name.

In every state, except Hawaii, a woman is *not* required to adopt her husband's name.

¶ 615 INTEREST AND PRINCIPAL PAYMENTS

If credit card bills are paid on time, there may never have to be any interest charges, assuming no cash advances. However, if the client uses a travel and entertainment card and pays $50 a year in fees, this could work out to be the equivalent of a significant "interest" charge. For example, if the average debit balance is $250 due to miscellaneous personal spending, the cardholder is effectively paying 20% a year in nondeductible interest.

The consumer should beware of any card which mentions the phrases "loan," "credit limit," or "line of credit." The trend is towards charging interest on the *average monthly balance,* even if only services and merchandise have been charged. This means that the cardholder is charged interest from the date of purchase, without having a free ride for weeks, even months, as previously.

The most attractive cards in this regard are the 30-day open balance department store cards, gasoline cards, and travel and entertainment cards. With these cards, the customer typically has 25 days to pay before interest is charged from the billing date. As a practical matter, it takes another week or two before a finance charge is added. By knowing the billing dates, a customer may charge major purchases on or immediately after the billing date. Since the purchase will not be on the next statement, the customer has an interest-free loan for about two months.

Often, any balance due can be paid in installments, except on most travel and entertainment cards. A typical minimum installment may be $1/24$ of the highest monthly balance. At this rate, it would take six years to pay off the balance. But since the debtor can always charge up any remaining balance, in effect, the loan *never* has to be paid off.

The interest rates vary from state to state, due to local usury laws, but the range is from 10% to as high as 24% on cash advances, with the most common rate being 18%.

¶ 616 LIABILITY ON LOST OR STOLEN CREDIT CARDS

The typical adult possesses at least six credit cards. They should be kept at home unless needed. In most cases, a person only needs one, if any, on a typical day. If the cardholder wishes to use them all, the card carried may be rotated. This limits the number of cards that may be lost or stolen. On extended trips, the traveler may wish to bring more than one card. But even on vacations, the round-trip airfare and hotel may have been paid in advance (by credit card). Travelers' checks and one universal card may therefore suffice. If a traveler loses travelers' checks, there is no personal liability whatsoever.

Here are some additional ways to protect the credit card holder:

1. Only cards really needed, wanted, and which will be used regularly should be kept. This is particularly true for cards which do not even grant cash advances if needed. All unneeded cards should be destroyed. The average person may find that the only cards needed are one travel and entertainment card and one bank card.
2. A *list* should be kept of all credit cards retained, including name, address, and phone number of the issuers and the card numbers. Large issuers have 24-hour-a-day toll-free numbers so that the holder immediately can report any loss and have the card cancelled. The call must be followed up with a letter.

3. A new card should be signed upon receipt and *not* in pencil.
4. The card should never be loaned to anyone else.
5. Cards should not be left where someone else can get them.
6. If the card should be lost or stolen, the cardholder has no liability whatsoever if the loss is reported prior to fraudulent use. This is true even if thousands of dollars are charged by a thief subsequently.

The liability is a maximum of $50 per card even if the loss is not discovered for months or it was not reported, regardless of the amount of unauthorized charges. This compares favorably with losing cash.

Even this limited liability cannot be imposed unless the issuer of the card complies with the following rules under the Federal Credit Card Protection Law (an amendment to the "Truth in Lending Act"):

1. The cardholder must have accepted the card by signing and/or using it,
2. The cardholder must have been informed of any potential liability,
3. The cardholder must have been supplied with a stamped, self-addressed envelope so as to conveniently report any loss,
4. The card must identify the holder through signature and photograph of fingerprint.

The bad news is that the cardholder has unlimited liability if the card is used for business purposes. Also, if someone loses a card three times, some issuers will cancel the card. Even if the liability is limited to $50, it may temporarily ruin the customer's credit rating if current charges are not paid in full.

¶ 617 THE HOLDER-IN-DUE-COURSE PROBLEM

Whenever money is borrowed from an independent third party, i.e., the credit card issuer, to purchase goods or services from a second party, the general rule is that the finance company is a *holder in due course* (HDC). No personal defenses, such as defective or shoddy merchandise, can be asserted against the credit card company. The client's recourse is against the *seller*. Fortunately, a law became effective in 1975, that created an exception to this rule. The consumer can now withhold payment from the credit card issuer as well as the seller if:

1. The purchase price exceeded $50.
2. The transaction took place within 100 miles of the cardholder's residence.

3. The purchase was charged to a *bank* card (Visa, MasterCard, American Express Gold).
4. The cardholder can prove an attempt to obtain satisfaction, such as by retaining a copy of the letter of complaint.

¶ 618 JOINT ACCOUNTS

A joint credit card is one used by two persons, typically spouses. If a joint account is used, both parties are liable for the charges, even if each person has a separate card. Another disadvantage of a joint account is that it is easy to lose track of the aggregate charges, making the monthly statement an unwelcome surprise on occasion. Thus, overcharges may more easily occur than if each person has a separate account.

¶ 619 DISCOUNTS FOR PAYING CASH

When making a major purchase from a business accepting credit cards, a cardholder may be able to obtain discounts by showing the credit card, then offering to pay cash. A seller who accepts a bank card typically gives up 3%-5% to the issuer but receives the funds as soon as the credit card slip is deposited in the bank. But if a travel and entertainment card is used, the merchant may give up 7% and may have to wait many weeks before being paid the 93%. Thus, the best result can be achieved by "threatening" to use a universal nonbank card. Discounts cannot be granted on items such as airfares because the prices are not negotiable.

¶ 620 HOME EQUITY CARDS

Since consumer interest deductions were phased out, it makes sense to use credit cards secured by the client's home, or to take out a home equity loan to pay off and cancel all credit cards. The advantages of a home equity loan are:

1. The interest is deductible on loans up to $100,000.[8]
2. Annual fees on numerous credit cards are saved.
3. The interest rate is lower.

However, there are disadvantages of home equity credit:

1. The closing costs are considerable and may not be deductible. Points may have to be amortized over the loan term.
2. The homeowner may go overboard on personal spending with a credit line of $50,000 and up and never pay off the mortgage.

---

[8] Code Sec. 163(h).

3. If monthly charges are paid off currently on credit cards, there are no interest expenses to save or convert to deductible "qualified residence interest."

Main Sources of Loans

¶ 625 CREDIT UNIONS

To get a loan, the client must be a member and shareholder. Most employees or members of a fraternal or religious organization have access to a credit union. Credit unions often render credit counseling services and provide insurance as well as grant emergency loans and "any purpose" loans.

The *advantages* of borrowing from a credit union include:

1. They are sympathetic because they are the borrower's associates.
2. They conduct no credit investigations.
3. The interest rate is low, typically up to 12% on unsecured loans and as low as 8% on secured loans.

The *disadvantages* include:

1. The maximum amount to be borrowed will rarely be above $10,000 and it is often lower.
2. The loan must be paid back quickly, typically over two years, but rarely more than five.
3. It is difficult to keep the loan confidential because the borrower is, in effect, dealing with an organization consisting of associates or fellow members.

On the balance, however, the client can get a cheap, small loan with a minimum of red tape.

¶ 626 FINANCE COMPANIES

In the 1980s, there were finance company offices almost on every block in every city in the country. How did they grow so fast? At the risk of oversimplifying, they rent an office and lend out $1,000. The customer signs a note for $1,250, including interest. They take the note to their bank and borrow $1,000 on it, and the ball starts rolling.

To get a loan, their credit requirements must be met, but they are stringent. Because of that and the low limit on the amount (the average loan is under $2,000), the interest rate is high, normally from 12%-36%, with 18% being typical. The repayment term is from one to five years, with two years being most common. People often prefer to go to finance companies rather than banks because they are less formal.

Because of credit card cash availability, personal finance companies have declined in importance.

Different states have different limits on interest and unsecured loan amounts. Thus, there are many executive loan services located in other states that the borrower can deal with. Many of these advertise in the financial pages. Some of these provide unsecured signature loans of up to $25,000 and may even take the application on the phone (toll-free). They then mail the customer the note, who signs it and mails it back, whereupon they send the check. What could be less personal?

By dealing with out-of-state firms, the lender beats the low credit limits but not the high interest or the credit investigation.

¶ 627 BANKS

There are several *advantages* of dealing with banks:

1. Because banks are quite conservative and risk-averse, a good rating with a bank is particularly beneficial in the quest for more and better credit.
2. Banks will consider a loan of any size and type from personal to business, secured or unsecured.
3. Banks have many other financial services and loans available, from credit cards and lines of credit with checking, to safe-deposit boxes.
4. The interest charged is often lower than what finance companies charge and is negotiable, except on small consumer loans.
5. Maturity dates are flexible. In fact, if the money is needed for six months or less, the borrower may obtain a *single payment loan,* i.e., the loan is due in full with interest at the end of the term. If the loan is for more than six months, it will be a conventional installment loan.
6. Automatic loan repayment may be arranged from a checking account. In fact, this is always done if the customer utilized a checking account credit line.

Here are some *disadvantages* when borrowing from banks:

1. Their credit standards are higher than for finance companies. But this is why they can charge less interest.
2. The payback requirements are quite rigid in terms of dates and amounts.
3. Banks do not like to bother with small loans, but the client may always borrow more than is needed, then make payments ahead of schedule.

¶ 628 SAVINGS AND LOAN ASSOCIATIONS

Up to 1972, savings banks only offered one type of loan, the passbook loan. To get a loan the customer simply pledged the passbook. Obviously, these loans were only available to account holders. They would typically lend 90%-100% of the deposit at an interest rate from 1%-2½% above the passbook interest rate. This appears to be reasonable, unless the following is considered:

1. The loan is riskless to the bank, since they already have the customer's savings as security. For the same reason, the credit rating will not be investigated.

2. The borrower's own funds are being borrowed. Why does not the customer simply borrow the funds directly, i.e., make a withdrawal? Money is saved that way. The only people who should take out passbook loans are those who are either psychologically unable to touch their savings, or are going to take it out anyway, but need a loan to avoid penalties for early withdrawals.

The typical payment schedule is from one to three years. In mid-1972, the federal authorities permitted savings and loan associations to get more involved in extensive consumer lending. Today, people not only have their conventional mortgage with their savings and loan associations, but also borrow for vacations, mobile homes, home improvements and appliances, etc. Home improvement loans in particular have enjoyed a rapid increase.

¶ 629 SECOND MORTGAGES

Anybody with significant equity in the home probably qualifies for a second mortgage. This is a common loan to take out for debt consolidation or for a business opportunity, for the following reasons:

1. The interest is lower than what finance companies charge but adds up to more due to low monthly payments and long payment terms.

2. Substantial amounts may be borrowed, perhaps up to 80% of the equity.

3. The payment term may be 10 years or more, even indefinite, if accessed through a credit line, with or without a credit card. If the first mortgage is small, the borrower should consider refinancing to get a new first mortgage at a lower rate and with a longer repayment period.

¶ 630 LIFE INSURANCE LOANS

If the client carries a so-called straight life, ordinary life, or whole life policy, which builds cash values, and wishes to raise cash on the policy, the cash value may either be surrendered for the cash surrender value, or it may be borrowed against. The latter is generally more attractive, because the insurance coverage is continued. Term insurance has no cash value. Note that it typically takes two to three years before even a straight life policy has *any* cash value and several more years before the value is of any substance compared with the face value. (Cash value equals face value at age 100.) Here are the *advantages* of borrowing against the policy:

1. The policy holder is entitled by contract to borrow up to 90-100% of the amount of the cash value, plus any dividends and interest. Thus, the borrower's credit rating, purpose of loan, other loans outstanding, etc., are all irrelevant. This is because the loan is virtually riskless to the insurance company. The policyholders are, in effect, borrowing their own money, not unlike obtaining a passbook loan.
2. The interest rate is the lowest obtainable anywhere in a business setting, commonly 8%-10%.

   Insurance premiums are based on the assumption that the money is reinvested by the company. If it lends it to the policy holder instead, it must be compensated. The rate is specified in the policy.
3. Interest is only paid on the remaining loan balance.
4. The repayment schedule is flexible. In fact, the borrower never needs to pay back the loan at all. If the loan is paid in installments the borrower may make payments together with regular premiums.

If this sounds too good to be true, here are some of the drawbacks:

1. The face amount is decreased by any loan outstanding, plus accrued interest. This decrease in coverage can, however, be offset by the purchase of term insurance for the life of the loan.
2. Because the loan need never be repaid, it is a temptation to let it ride and, at the most, pay interest only year after year. This is sound if the policy holder has other loans outstanding at higher rates to be paid off first.
3. If the insured systematically borrows to pay premiums, the interest is only tax deductible if at least four of the first seven

annual premiums were paid first.[9] In any case, interest must actually be paid, not just accrued, to be deductible and not constitute consumer interest.

4. Life insurance companies move carefully. The policy holder must write or call to get their loan application, fill it out, send it back, then wait for the check. The whole process may easily take several weeks.

¶ 631 LOANS ON SECURITIES

If an investor buys listed stock for $100,000 through a broker on margin, then one-half, or $50,000 may be borrowed (margin loan). In contrast, if the securities are initially paid for in full, the investor may borrow from a bank, using the securities as collateral. The percentage to be borrowed will depend on the safety of the stock and may vary from 40% to 80%. This fact has led some investors to pyramid their holdings in the following way:

1. Buy stock for $100,000 in cash.
2. Borrow $80,000 from a bank.
3. Buy stock for $80,000.
4. Borrow $64,000 from another bank.
5. Buy stock for $64,000.
6. Borrow $51,200 from a third bank.

In this fashion, they end up with approximately $500,000 of stock on which they owe $400,000. The problem is that the stock yields will rarely keep up with interest payments, thus necessitating appreciation. A 20% drop in price will reduce the equity to zero. This type of investment behavior is highly risky. If the client wishes to take advantage of high leverage, it makes more sense to buy or sell commodity futures contracts in amounts of $500,000. A trader may be able to put up less than $100,000 for the same action, there is no interest charge on the remaining balance (no indebtedness), and Treasury bills may be used to meet the margin requirements.

¶ 632 SECURED LOANS

If the loan is large because of the amount of money needed or because the product is expensive, the seller/lender or lender may want collateral. A collateralized loan is a secured loan. Article 9 of the Uniform Commercial Code governs the so-called "secured transactions," but in no way covers all secured loans. Excluded are such loans as passbook loans, life insurance policy loans, mortgages on real estate, etc. However, Article 9 covers almost all loans on personal property

[9] Code Sec. 264.

under whatever name called, as long as the parties intended to enter into a secured transaction, such as pledges, assignments, chattel mortgages, factor's liens, leases, consignments, and conditional sales contracts.

For the security interest to be asserted against the borrower, it must *attach.* There are three requirements:

1. The borrower must receive value;
2. The borrower must have an interest in the collateral; and
3. There must be a security agreement.

The creditor also wants to prevail over the borrower's other creditors. For this to happen, the attached security interest must be *perfected.* There are three main ways a creditor may perfect a security interest:

1. Being in *possession of the collateral,* i.e., the borrower pledges securities, a coin collection, etc., until the last payment is made.
2. *Filing a financing statement* with the Secretary of State, containing a reasonable description of the collateral, names and addresses of the parties, and the signature of the debtor.
3. If the seller is the creditor, it has a *purchase-money security interest in consumer goods.* Thus, if consumer goods, such as a television set, furniture, or appliances are purchased "on time" from a department store, the store has a perfected loan without possession or filing.

Upon default, the creditor can repossess the collateral and sell it. Proceeds are applied in this order:

1. The costs of repossession, storage, and sale.
2. The amount owed, plus interest, and legal fees.

Any excess belongs to the debtor. More likely there will be a deficit, for which personal liability exists.

¶ 633 NO PRINCIPAL PAYMENT ON CAR LOANS

Some cars, such as Rolls Royces, BMWs, and large Mercedes, may keep most of their value for years. To finance such a car, an increasing number of banks grant loans for up to 100% of the purchase price with little or no principal payment. Thus, with no down payment, all payments made, being interest only, may be tax deductible (if secured by a residence, for example). In contrast, *no* part of a *lease* payment is deductible, except to the extent that the car is used for business. At the end of the loan term, the borrower has three options:

1. Pay off the "balloon," i.e., the loan balance, and keep the car.

2. Turn in the car and cancel the loan (subject to mileage and "reasonable condition" clauses).
3. Trade in the car and refinance (a fee of $200 or more is charged for a trade-in).

Because of low monthly payments (all of which are deductible), such a car loan enables the client to purchase bigger, more expensive cars at lower after-tax cost. However, since 1991, personal interest is not deductible unless the lender obtains security in the customer's home or the loan is a business loan.

¶ 634 CREDIT LIFE INSURANCE

When applying for an unsecured personal loan, the client is typically offered credit insurance. Some lenders even require it, e.g., to cover a credit line with a checking account. Credit life insurance simply means that the loan balance, plus accrued interest, will be paid off upon the death of the debtor/insured. The cost of the insurance must be disclosed under "Truth in Lending."

Generally, credit insurance is not a good deal for the average person because:

1. The rates are often above group-term insurance rates usually readily available.
2. The typical loan is small and the amount of insurance cannot exceed the loan, rendering the increase in insurance coverage less meaningful.
3. There is no need to make an insurance decision merely because of a new, small loan. In any event, the client should consider the overall need for insurance in light of net worth, liquidity and total insurance carried, before adding less expensive insurance.

¶ 635 CO-SIGNING FOR OTHERS

Co-signers go under many names, e.g., sureties, guarantors, endorsers, accommodation makers, and conditional guarantors. In terms of liability, the following distinctions should be understood.

SURETY

Being a surety on a loan means being *primarily* liable. The creditor may choose to go to the surety directly and bypass the debtor. If this happens, the surety must seek reimbursement from the borrower.

GUARANTOR

A guarantor is *secondarily* liable. Thus, the lender must at least try to collect from the debtor first. As soon as the debtor refuses to pay, the guarantor must. No collection efforts are necessary. An endorser is in this position as well.

CONDITIONAL GUARANTOR

In this situation, the creditor must exhaust all reasonable collection efforts before seeking payment from the co-signer. This is the best situation a co-signer can be in.

In effect, being a co-signer is like borrowing money, then lending it to another party. As a general rule, it should not be done. Exceptions include helping out a good friend or relative, particularly one's children.

Co-signers are rarely compensated, so they have nothing to gain and much to lose. If the borrower's credit is good, no co-signer should be needed in the first place. Even if the debtor's financial position was fair at the time of co-signing, either party's ability to pay may deteriorate during the loan term. Once having paid after default, the co-signer is subrogated to the creditor's claim, i.e., the debtor can be sued for reimbursement. This may be costly, inconvenient, embarrassing and time consuming. If collection efforts fail, the co-signer is allowed a short-term capital loss for tax purposes.[10]

The fact that the debtor files personal bankruptcy or misrepresented the factual situation does not let the co-signer off the hook. However, the following acts may release the co-signer:

1. *Modifications* in the contract between the creditor and debtor, if material, and without the co-signer's consent.
2. *Release of collateral,* to the extent of the value, if the co-signer's position is materially affected.
3. *Expiration* of the statute of limitations.

Credit Rating

¶ 640 CREDIT RATING

An adverse credit rating can be a severe liability taking many years to improve. It can prevent the client from obtaining needed credit, from credit cards to a home mortgage. It can also make it harder to obtain insurance or standard insurance rates. Sometimes, it may even be more difficult to secure employment.

¶ 641 HOW THE CREDIT RATING IS COMMUNICATED

There are some 2,500 credit bureaus in the United States, and they keep records on almost all adults who are buyers, borrowers, or applicants for employment or insurance. This covers virtually everybody.

[10] Code Sec. 166(d).

The credit agencies belong to the Associated Credit Bureaus of America, Inc. and are linked together by toll-free phone numbers with access to computer banks. Not only do they exchange information but also *sell* it to stores, banks, merchants, finance companies, and anybody interested in the rating. Some 150 million credit reports are processed each year.

A file will include such information as name, address, age, marital status, profession, earnings, education, job history, moves, repayments, and court proceedings. The information is grouped under three headings, referred to as the three C's:

1. *Character.* Reputation in general.
2. *Capacity.* Education, other loans and earnings.
3. *Capital.* Ownership of a home, car, furniture, or other valuables.

Three main ways to establish and maintain a good rating are:

1. Borrow money, establish credit, and have credit cards. Create a track record of repayment, but do not have too many loans outstanding.
2. Never simply ignore bills. If you have a complaint, communicate it. If more time is needed to repay, ask for it and work it out.
3. Avoid default, repossessions, collection agencies, litigation, judgments, attachments, garnishment and, if possible, bankruptcy.

¶ 642 RIGHTS UNDER THE FAIR CREDIT REPORTING ACT

To the distress of many creditors, the debtor's rights have increased markedly over the last few years. For example, there are now a number of laws making creditors liable for harassment, invasion of privacy, libel or slander, extortion, coercion, grand larceny, criminal impersonation, etc., should they be too anxious to collect. Under the Fair Credit Reporting Act, the debtor's rights include the following:

If credit is denied, or the cost of credit is increased, the applicant has the right to demand the name and address of the credit agency responsible for the report.

The credit applicant can demand information about the nature, substance, and sources of personal data held by any consumer reporting agency. Such information is free if requested within 30 days of the credit application.

The debtor can be informed of which creditors have received a consumer report within the last six months.

Incomplete or erroneous information must be removed from a debtor's file; if, *after* the debtor insists on an investigation, it is discovered that certain information is inaccurate or unverifiable. In that case, the agency must also notify whoever has received the wrong information.

A debtor who cannot settle a dispute with the credit agency nevertheless has the right to put the debtor's version on file to be included in future reports. For a nominal fee, the agency is also required to send the debtor's version to creditors requested.

Bankruptcies stay on the credit report for 10 years, but other adverse information cannot be reported for more than seven years.

The credit bureau may be sued for damages and, in addition, the debtor may collect lawyer's fees and court costs if successful. It must be shown that the agency wilfully or negligently broke the law.

There are some *limitations* on the loan applicant's rights:

1. The Fair Credit Reporting Act does not apply to commercial credit or business insurance.
2. An individual cannot obtain a personal report. Even if personally appearing at the agency, the individual cannot physically handle the file or receive a copy.
3. The Act does not give the applicant the right to compel someone else to do business with the applicant.

¶ 643 WHAT A CREDITOR LOOKS FOR

Lenders are in the business of lending money. When someone borrows money, such a person is buying their product. Getting a loan is therefore simple in most instances. The following are some of the main factors considered before granting an unsecured personal loan:

1. *Ability to repay.* This includes the applicant's past earnings history, current earning power, other loans outstanding, stability of earnings, and net worth.
2. *Assets.* Does the client have assets that can be easily reached by a creditor, such as a home, a car, securities, or other valuables?
3. *Credit history.* Ideally, the client has established credit over the years and demonstrated the ability to handle it. In other words, there should be a consistent history of paying rent, credit card charges, etc., on time.
4. *Time on the job.* In general, creditors like to see that the debtor has worked for the same employer for several years.

However, if it was an upward move, a recent switch is not regarded unfavorably.

5. *Time at present address.* Creditors like to have someone living at the same address, or at least in the same city or state, for some time. But again, an upward move, such as purchasing a home rather than renting, may not be a negative factor.
6. *Home ownership.* Because of increasing home prices, homeowners have become better risks than tenants. Not only is it likely that there is a substantial equity in the home, but the debtor cannot as readily just pick up and leave. A listed phone in the debtor's own name is also a plus.
7. *Marital status.* A married person with children tends to be relatively stable, at least compared to a single individual. Such a person tends to be more financially conservative and has more to lose. On the other hand, the cost of living for a family may be substantially higher than that for a single person, and the increased costs may or may not be offset by the extra tax exemptions and a working spouse.

Here are some additional hints which will make it easier to obtain a loan or to increase the amount of a loan:

1. *Personal behavior.* If a loan is applied for in person, the client should dress nicely, be polite and not seem nervous. The applicant should be on time and fill out the application carefully, completely, and accurately.
2. *Income.* Report the *highest possible income* which can be justified. Include spouse's salary, part-time consulting income, dividends, interest, rent, and royalties.
3. *Special purpose.* If the articulated purpose of the loan is to pay the rent, buy groceries, etc., it will not be granted. Finance companies favor the following purposes: medical, dental and funeral expenses, vacations, furniture, education, auto and home repairs and improvements, and emergencies. The old saying that the applicant gets a loan only if it is not needed may be an exaggeration, but if it is needed *too* badly, it will be denied.

CHAPTER 7

LIFE INSURANCE

¶ 701 INTRODUCTION

In this chapter all major aspects of a client's life insurance program are discussed. The need for insurance, how to compute needed coverage, what to do if turned down, types of policies, insurance jargon, how to manage insurance, and how to protect it from creditors, etc. are evaluated. A thorough evaluation of term versus whole life policies is provided, as well as recent developments, such as variable, adjustable, and universal life insurance. Tax aspects are also important, in view of the fact that life insurance is one of the few tax shelters which, up to now, has been left largely untouched by legislation.

¶ 702 LIFE INSURANCE INDUSTRY

About 80% of the adult population in the United States carries at least some life insurance, and more than 90% of all two-parent families do. More than two *trillion* dollars of life insurance is in force with annual premiums of some $35 billion being collected.

There are about 1,800 life insurance companies in the United States which fall into two categories:

1. Stock companies owned by the shareholders, and
2. Mutual insurance companies owned by the policyholders.

Only about 150 of the 1,800 are mutual companies, but they account for more than half of all life insurance written. Mutual policies are *participating,* i.e., they pay dividends which simply represent a refund of part of the premium. The level of dividends depends on the amount of investment returns compared to the number of claims filed. Premiums vary greatly, but due to the considerable variety of policies available, it is not easy to compare policies by simply looking at the premiums.

¶ 703 WHY INSURANCE COMPANIES ARE PROFITABLE

Insurance companies have proliferated and become so profitable that quite a few people probably wish they had purchased life insurance *stock,* rather than a policy. The following are three basic and general reasons the insurance industry makes at least a small profit *regardless* of the policy sold:

1. Because of the increasing longevity of man, the typical mortality tables are at least somewhat behind the times.
2. Premiums are based on the average life expectancies of all members of the population, even though individuals with adverse risks have already been screened out, such as those with a history of cancer or heart trouble, alcoholics, criminals, and people with promiscuous lifestyles or in hazardous professions.
3. It invariably takes a while after death before the claim is filed and paid. Moreover, the beneficiary often elects a settlement option, such as an annuity or deferred payments. In addition, there is the customary profit margin added to the pure cost of the risk.

Even after specific policies are studied, opinions are divided, particularly with respect to comparisons between whole life and term insurance (discussed below). The adversaries of whole life argue that the insurance company keeps half of the premiums as profits, regardless of what happens, because:

1. If the insured dies with the insurance in force, the beneficiary collects the face amount, i.e., the same as if the insured had carried term only. The accumulated savings, the cash value, is forfeited to the company.
2. If the insured lives for decades and wants to cash in the policy, even though having paid for the risk all those years, only the cash value is returned, i.e., the savings part plus interest, often at low rates. Thus, regardless of what happens to the policyholder, on the average, the company keeps a good portion of the premiums. This, however, does not take away the need for life insurance or the need to compare different types of policies, a task to which we now turn.

¶ 704 NEED FOR LIFE INSURANCE

Most families would be broke within a few months after losing the salary of the breadwinner if they did not have life insurance. This is particularly true in the early years of a family. When the parents are young, they typically have small children, limited savings, and many debts, including a mortgage. Without a regular salary coming in, the financial structure collapses. Thus, a young breadwinner's prime concern is to arrange to keep the family's standard of living reasonably intact after death. The problem is that the policyholder cannot afford the premiums for the coverage needed on a whole life policy. The short-term solution is, of course, term insurance, because the same premium can typically buy three to five times the coverage in the early years. At the other extreme, at retirement, the children are gone, the mortgage and other debts are paid off, and investments have hopefully accumulated. At this point, if insurance is needed at all, it is to pay medical bills, funeral expenses and death taxes.

A cautious person with a family will always assume the likelihood of dying tomorrow and will annually review the probable consequences of a sudden death. Life insurance, almost by definition, therefore, becomes a necessity in most cases to provide an instant estate. It is a vital element in providing family security and a keystone to wise personal money management and estate planning. For example:

1. Life insurance provides the spouse with a feeling of security.
2. Life insurance can provide retirement income.
3. Life insurance proceeds provide the estate with instant liquidity, free of income tax.
4. Life insurance can provide a business with desired continuity of ownership through a program to buy out or retire shareholders and partners.
5. Through life insurance the insured can add to the coverage, change beneficiaries, borrow money, etc., without having to change the will.
6. Whole life insurance is a forced savings plan, the interest on which is accumulating tax free.
7. Policy loans are available regardless of credit ratings.
8. Through a spendthrift clause in the policy, neither the insured's nor the beneficiary's creditors can reach the policy or the cash value.
9. Settlement options provide the beneficiary with numerous ways of cashing in the policy, from lump-sum payments to installments or annuities.

¶ 705 FACTORS REDUCING THE NEED FOR LIFE INSURANCE

The following factors may reduce, or even eliminate, the need for life insurance:

1. The client is single or has no children.
2. The spouse is working or has marketable skills.
3. The mortgage is paid off.
4. The surviving spouse is eligible for a comfortable pension or other death benefit and is in the maximum social security bracket.

5. The client has considerable investments with a high yield and/or appreciation potential.

As a practical matter, very few people have all the above, and even if they eventually do, they need life insurance in the meantime. Until the children have grown up, until investments have accumulated, until the spouse dies, etc., the client should have insurance. The questions are: What kind? How much? For how long?

¶ 706 HOW MUCH INSURANCE IS NEEDED: TWO APPROACHES

A human life is, of course, irreplaceable and incapable of exact valuation. But the *economic* value of a life is susceptible to measurement. There are two fundamental approaches:

1. *The present value of future earning power approach.* Under this method, the client's earnings are projected for life, typically at an assumed growth rate, using a mortality table. This payment stream is then adjusted for income taxes and discounted back to the present through the use of a reasonable discount rate. This approach is widely used in wrongful death actions but often results in an amount far in excess of what the client would be willing to insure, even if the family could afford it.
2. *The needs approach.* The goal here is to become self-insured, i.e., if the family can maintain its standard of living without the client and without insurance, none should be purchased. Again, determine the need as if the client will die tomorrow and review the situation annually. Life insurance should really be viewed as death insurance. Life insurance is for dying, investment is for living. The two should not automatically be combined. A whole life policy can return 5%-6% tax free, not a poor return, but life insurance should not be used for investment purposes. Determine the basic coverage that is needed. A young family with children probably needs so much insurance that the income generated from all sources after the death of the breadwinner will amount to 60%-75% of present after-tax earnings. Once the children are grown, this figure will probably drop to below 40% and may even be zero, given sufficient investments.

Here is a methodology to compute the amount of insurance needed:

1. Compute the annual income that the family, excluding the insured, requires for housing, food, education, debts, vacations, clothes, etc.

2. Subtract all income received from all sources upon death of the insured. Include social security payments, pension and profit-sharing plans, the surviving spouse's income, investment income, etc.
3. If (1) exceeds (2), there is a gap which can be filled by insurance.

Assuming a family needs $40,000 a year to live on and would receive $25,000 a year without insurance, the client needs a policy with a face amount that would generate $15,000 a year after tax. If the proceeds can be invested at 5%, the amount needed is $300,000, at 7.5% $200,000, at 10% $150,000, etc. The coverage is very sensitive to the return obtainable. In fact, the coverage needed will change almost continuously with taxes, inflation, return on investment, income levels, asset values, etc. But the above framework should at least enable someone to come up with an approximate figure.

¶ 707 "WIFE INSURANCE"

Traditionally, life insurance was purchased only on the life of the breadwinner, ordinarily the male of the species. Today, three out of four wives are insured and not only because half of them work. Today the wife may well be the major breadwinner. Consider the following:

1. A housewife cooks, cleans, takes care of children, acts as a chauffeur, etc. Replacing those services may easily cost $10,000 or more a year.
2. There will be final expenses related to death.
3. A client making $60,000 a year, filing a joint return and claiming a spouse as an exemption saves more than $3,000 a year in after-tax cash. In other words, absent remarriage, the surviving spouse loses thousands a year just in taxes.

If there are no children, the need for "wife insurance" will be less. Even with children, the client should consider term insurance only, to be dropped when the last child no longer needs a mother's care.

In terms of priority, insure the breadwinner first. If the couple both work and the family counts on the wife's earnings, by all means take out insurance on her life for that reason. But even a nonworking wife is easily worth in excess of $100,000. The cheapest coverage can probably be obtained through a family rider on the client's own policy. Children constitute the last priority. It is hard to think of any reason why anyone should buy insurance on the life of a child. The death of a child is not likely to impose a financial burden on the family and the parent cannot insure against emotional distress. However, the client might consider paying for an "insurance option" to ensure that the children are guaranteed insurable up to a given amount when they grow up.

¶ 708 TYPES OF POLICIES

There are really just two general groups of life insurance, *term* and *whole life,* or "pure" and "permanent" insurance, and combinations thereof. They can be classified as follows:

1. *Endowment policies.* This is a permanent policy which reaches a cash value equal to the face value during the insured's expected lifetime, typically after a 20-30 year term. As a consequence, the premiums are high. When the value equals face, the insured has paid-up insurance. When no more premiums are due, the insured may cash in the policy or take installments or an annuity. This policy is unlikely to meet the needs of the average family.
2. *Whole life policies.* Whole life, straight life, ordinary life, permanent insurance, all refer to the same policy. A whole life policy solves the problem of term insurance by averaging the premiums over a lifetime. Both the face amount and the annual premium stay constant, regardless of how long the insured keeps the policy, up to age 100. At age 100, built-up cash value would equal the face value. Cash values are built, but the insured pays for it. If someone buys whole life at a young age, the initial premium may be 10 times the premium on a term policy with the same coverage. But eventually, by the time the insured reaches the late forties or early fifties, the constant premium will be less than the sharply increasing term premiums. The only way to buy insurance for an entire lifetime is by buying some type of whole life insurance. But, then again, who needs life insurance after age 65 or 70? Because the cash value builds up, the coverage (face less cash value) decreases annually. This is why the company can charge the same premium over the years. Unless the client plans to keep the insurance for decades, term insurance will generally make more sense, particularly if convertible to whole life. If a whole life policy is dropped after only a few years, most of the premiums are wasted. The basic advantages of whole life are the forced, tax-free savings (at up to 6%-8% in some companies if the policy is kept in force long enough), the liquidity to the estate, creditor-proof spendthrift clauses, the safety, the loan values, and the level annual premium.
3. *Term insurance,* also called "pure" insurance. Here the insured pays only for the risk of death and this, in many people's

view, is exactly what insurance is all about. "What does investing have to do with insurance?" they ask. Buy exactly the coverage needed, invest excess funds, and drop or reduce the insurance as it is no longer needed. Were it only that simple (see below). Someone at a young age with small children can obtain a much higher coverage with term than with whole life, but only for a limited period. However, that may be all many people need. The risk of dying increases gradually with age. The rise is slow until age 45 or so. After that, the risk and therefore the premiums increases sharply. Almost anyone can afford a $100,000 term policy in their twenties. It may cost less than $150. By the age of 60, the premium has gone up many times, to about $2,000 a year.

There are two basic ways to buy term coverage with variations:

1. Level term, on which the coverage stays constant, but the premium goes up every year, every five years, etc.
2. Level premium, on which the premium stays the same, but the amount of coverage goes down periodically.

Either policy may be automatically renewable, at the policyholder's option, and/or convertible into whole life. As a general rule, the informed buyer will probably find the five-year renewable and convertible level term policy the most practical and useful. The premium goes up every five years, but so may the ability to pay. Due to inflation the level term policy is, in effect, equivalent to a decreasing term policy with level premiums.

In other words, premiums go up, but in real dollars, they may remain relatively stable for many years. The coverage is constant, but in real dollars it is declining. The fact that the coverage goes down in real terms is unlikely to matter much. As time goes by, children become self-sustaining. Even if there would be a surviving spouse, less money is needed as the mortgage is paid off and investments, including deferred compensation and pension and profit-sharing plans, grow. And it is needed for less time.

A client who decides to buy term should buy group term if available. Ideally, the employer provides at least the first $50,000 on a tax-free basis.[1] If more is needed it should be purchased through a club or association the client belongs to. The premiums are lower than on individual policies and ordinarily no medical exams are needed. Everyone belongs to at least one group offering group term life insurance: a trade organization, an alumnus association, a credit card issuer, etc.

---

[1] Code Sec. 79.

¶ 709 COMPARING WHOLE LIFE WITH TERM INSURANCE

The most commonly encountered argument in favor of term insurance is that one can buy term and invest the difference. To evaluate term insurance, the following table is reproduced which shows the annual premium for $1,000 of term insurance for a random policy from ages 25 to 69.

Age	Premium	Age	Premium	Age	Premium	Age	Premium
25	$1.93	37	$2.80	48	$ 6.95	59	$18.59
26	1.96	38	3.01	49	7.60	60	20.34
27	1.99	39	3.25	50	8.32	61	22.24
28	2.03	40	3.53	51	9.11	62	24.31
29	2.08	41	3.84	52	9.96	63	26.57
30	2.13	42	4.17	53	10.89	64	29.04
31	2.19	43	4.53	54	11.90	65	31.75
32	2.25	44	4.92	55	13.00	66	34.74
33	2.32	45	5.35	56	14.21	67	38.04
34	2.40	46	5.83	57	15.54	68	41.68
35	2.51	47	6.36	58	17.00	69	45.61
36	2.64						

The premium multiplies 15 times from age 25 to age 64. At age 25 it takes 16 years before the premium doubles, but then it doubles about every eight years. The annual increase becomes steepest after age 45. Ideally, the client does not need insurance after 50. Again, the goal is to become self-insured early in life so that the "instant estate" is no longer needed.

One way to compare premium costs is to use the "Interest-Adjusted Index," published by the National Underwriter Company, 420 E. 4th St., Cincinnati, OH 45202. This book shows 10- and 20-year costs for insurance policies sold by all major U.S. insurance companies. If the policy is held less than 10 years, the client would invariably have been better off with term, due to the start-up costs of a whole life policy, e.g., the agent's commission and the prepayment of premiums necessary to keep them level.

Example: The client wishes to buy insurance for 20 years, from ages 40 to 59. According to the table the term insurance premiums would go up from $3.53 to $18.59. Using the "Interest-Adjusted Index," the following steps are taken:

1. Assume an interest rate, such as 5%.
2. Accumulate the 20 premiums at 5%.
3. Divide this "future value" by the 20-year discount factor in the table. The result is an interest-adjusted annual cost of $34.72, considerably above the typical annual premium on a whole life policy. At higher interest rates, however, whole life tends to suffer compared to a "buy term, invest the difference" strategy.

WHOLE LIFE VS. TERM

The following summarizes the main arguments in favor of whole life on one hand and term on the other:

1. *Cash values.* Whole life builds cash values, term does not. A frequently encountered argument against term insurance is: "Why pay for 20 years and have nothing to show for it?" There are several rebuttals to this:

   (a) Why pay much more and have little to show?

   (b) Why is 20 years of protection worthless?

   (c) Cash values merely represent the client's own savings.

   (d) A whole life policy is similar to a small term policy coupled with savings account. However, the insured can never have both the insurance and the savings. Upon death the company keeps the savings and pays the same proceeds as if the client had paid only for term insurance. If the policy is cashed in the insurance is canceled. If the insured borrows the cash value, interest is charged, and the proceeds will be reduced by any loan outstanding.

   Example: If an insured buys a $100,000 policy today and dies in a year, the beneficiary collects $100,000 whether the deceased had paid $2,000 for a whole life policy or $200 for term. After 20 years, the insured would have a cash value, which he paid for, of perhaps $35,000 so that the actual coverage is reduced to $65,000.

   The arguments from the other side are:

   (a) Whole life offers protection, for life, for a flat premium.

   (b) Some companies pay up to 6% interest in the long run on cash values, tax free. As a guaranteed safe and tax-free return, this may be hard to beat.

   (c) Many people would never save unless forced to. Thus, whole life insurance plus paying off a mortgage may represent the only realistic ways to save something for retirement, other than Social Security and pension plans.

   (d) The cash values may be borrowed at low interest without a credit check, any time, and without cancelling the policy. (Reminder: The consumer interest deduction has been eliminated.)

   (e) In a high tax bracket whole life can be cheaper than term insurance in the long run. The interest obtainable on other savings after taxes may be lower than the build-up rate in cash values. As long as at least four of the first seven years' premiums are not borrowed, the policy owner can borrow the cash values at low rates and deduct the interest if the proceeds are invested.[2]

(f) The cash values can be shielded from creditors.

2. *The time horizon.* Generally, the shorter the time the insured plans to keep the policy, e.g., the more optimistic the insured is about future investment accumulations, the less attractive a whole life policy. Cash values build slowly. If the client wants to hedge the bet, the client can buy convertible term, so that if it is later found that a long-term insurance program is desirable, a switch may be made. In the meantime, the insured enjoys good coverage at a low cost. When the policy owner can afford the premiums on whole life, it is time to convert. People who cannot afford the premiums need the most coverage at the least cost.

The disadvantages of term insurance are:

1. There is no tax-free, forced savings feature.
2. The premiums increase until they become almost prohibitive in later years.
3. It has no loan values.
4. Because of the limited incentive for the agent to sell term insurance, the seller is unlikely to render thorough advice on the client's personal financial and estate planning needs.
5. It only provides coverage for the term of the contract, not for the insured's entire life.

¶ 710 SINGLE PREMIUM WHOLE LIFE

Single premium life insurance is based on one fundamental idea: Instead of paying $2,000 a year for life for a $100,000 face value whole life policy, pay $20,000 up front for a paid-up policy in one or very few installments.

Example: The proposed insured, age 45, has a life expectancy of 30 years. At 8% the present value of $1 a year for 30 years is $11.258. Therefore the present value of a $2,000 per year premium is $2,000 × 11.258, or $22,516. At 8%, therefore, $22,516 paid as a single premium is equivalent to an annual premium of $2,000. In addition, due to administrative savings and lack of renewal selling efforts, etc., the insurance company may settle for a one-time $20,000 payment.

The characteristics of an instantly paid-up policy are:

---

[2] Code Secs. 264 and 163(d).

1. The emphasis is on investment, not insurance.
2. The commission is low and the whole premium, including the amount "allocable to term insurance," earns a guaranteed minimum yield.
3. Because the policy is designed as insurance, the cash value builds up tax free and it can be borrowed back, also tax free.
4. Under the Technical and Miscellaneous Revenue Act of 1988, some distributions (including loans) on "modified endowment policies" are taxed under Code Sec. 7702A. Thus, a distribution on such policies purchased after June 20, 1988, constitutes gross income to the extent the cash value exceeds the total premiums paid if the latter exceeds the premiums which *would have been paid* thus far, if the policy had been paid for in full in seven equal annual payments. A 10% excise tax on the income is applicable as well, unless the insured is 59½ years old or older, is disabled, or receives an annuity. The amount not taxed reduces the investment in the contract.
5. The build-up rate is a *net* interest rate after deducting insurance and administrative expenses, and it fluctuates with the rate earned on the underlying investment portfolio.
6. The accumulated interest may be borrowed back at no extra cost, but the premium itself (principal) may only be borrowed back at 2%-3.5% above the net rate earned.
7. Incentives to keep the policy include:
   (a) Surrender charges of up to 10% are charged initially, but gradually disappear.
   (b) If the policyholder borrows all the principal and then fails to pay the interest, the policy lapses. All accumulated interest then becomes taxable.
8. Although life insurance policies may be exchanged tax free (see below), there may be an exchange fee. Also, the amount borrowed, if not repaid before the swap, may be taxable in whole or in part.
9. As an alternative to a trust, a single premium policy has lower setup costs, provides tax-free earnings and necessitates no transfer of principal. (A final word of truth: a term insurance policy still provides far more pure insurance coverage per dollar invested.)

¶ 711 ADJUSTABLE LIFE

Adjustable life is designed for someone who cannot decide between term or whole life insurance. With adjustable life the client may annually change the death benefit and the premium. The cash value depends on the premium/death benefit mix. A minimum interest is guaranteed and the cash value may be borrowed. Because of this flexibility, the client needs only one policy ever. However, less flexible policies are cheaper. Adjustable life is suitable for people who do not know how much term or whole life they might want in the future, and for people who want to start off with mostly term and then gradually change to whole life.

¶ 712 VARIABLE INSURANCE

Variable insurance policies were introduced to offset inflation. The insurance company invests the premiums in common stock in the hope that these will constitute an inflation hedge. Both the premium and the benefits paid will vary with the yield on the underlying portfolio, but at a minimum the proceeds paid will equal the face value. The possible advantage is that the proceeds may far exceed the face value, but there are several disadvantages:

1. The premiums tend to be higher than those on a regular policy.
2. It is not possible to calculate the future loan and cash value of the policy. There is *no* surrender value.
3. It is uncertain what the coverage will be, which makes it harder to incorporate the policy in overall financial and estate planning.

While the insured may have a choice of two or more funds, such as a bond fund, a high income fund, a capital growth fund, or even a real estate fund, there are numerous expenses, including sales loads, annual administrative fees, policy issue expenses, brokerage commissions and state premium taxes. Switching from one fund to another can be done tax free.

Obvious alternatives to variable insurance are "buy term-invest-the difference" and universal life.

¶ 713 UNIVERSAL LIFE

By the mid-1980s, universal life accounted for 75% of premiums on new life insurance policies and comprised 38% of all new life policies. This new and very popular nonterm policy includes the following characteristics:

1. The investment portion of the policy is separately accounted for.
2. The amount of coverage can be increased or decreased.
3. The insurance premium may be even less than for term.

4. The premium can be increased or decreased.
5. The coverage can be tied to cost-of-living increases to offset inflation.
6. The policy has a cash surrender value and loan value.

The above will eliminate or reduce the need to choose between term and permanent insurance.

When the policy is written, it will obviously be geared to the client's needs at that time. But circumstances change, often rapidly. Should a change be requested, this can be done on the same policy format, within reason. This development has been heralded as the most important life insurance development of the century. The policies are available in all states, but, as expected, something extra has to be paid for this flexibility.

With *variable universal life* the insured selects the underlying investment vehicle, e.g., a bond fund or some type of stock fund, or both. These may be changed twice a year.

There are two types of death benefits:

1. *The type A death benefit* equals the face amount, *including* cash value, except that the death benefit increases as the cash value approaches the initial face amount.
2. *The type B death benefit* equals face amount, *plus* cash value.

In both cases, the death benefit ultimately increases as the cash value builds, in contrast with the traditional whole life policy.

To be regarded as tax-free life insurance, the "pure" insurance must be at least 140% of the cash value until the insured reaches age 40. The 140% amount may be reduced by one percentage point each year thereafter, but cannot go below 105%.

Once labeled "insurance," withdrawals up to the amount of total premiums may be made tax free, subject to the "modified endowment policy" rules, discussed above.

¶ 714 INSURANCE "RIDERS"

For additions to the premium, several "extras" may be added to an insurance policy, such as:

1. *Waiver of premiums* upon mental or physical disability.
2. *Multiple proceeds* upon accidental death. Everyone has heard of "double indemnity" clauses, but the insured may purchase triple or quadruple indemnity as well. These are not expensive because only approximately 7% of those insured actually die in accidents. For executives who make frequent airline trips, this

option provides less costly, year-round coverage than flight insurance. One should keep in mind, however, that the manner in which the client dies rarely affects how much insurance is needed.

3. *Accidental dismemberment clauses.* Here the insured collects for the loss of an arm, a leg, an eye, etc., without dying.
4. *Guaranteed insurability clauses.* This means that the insured may periodically increase the coverage without medical evidence.
5. *Disability income riders.* If the insured becomes disabled, the policy will pay income during disability.
6. *Additional term insurance riders* permit the insured to supplement the whole life policy through the purchase of term insurance in given amounts without a medical exam.

¶ 715 COMMON INSURANCE CLAUSES AND CONCEPTS

The policy will lapse unless the premium is paid within 31 days of the due date. If the insured dies during the grace period, the proceeds will be reduced by the unpaid premium. If the premium was prepaid, any payment allocable to the time after the month of death is refunded.

EXTENDED INSURANCE COVERAGE

Even if the premium is unpaid at the expiration of the grace period, a whole life policy does not expire immediately. The cash value will commonly be used to continue the coverage as a term policy. As an alternative, loans may be taken out for the purpose of paying the delinquent premiums.

REINSTATEMENT

Once the cash value is exhausted, the extended insurance coverage expires. Even then, the insured may reinstate the policy by paying the past due premiums plus interest. A new medical examination is then required.

INCONTESTABILITY CLAUSES

Once the policy has been in force for two years, the insurance company is precluded from contesting it due to erroneous information in the application. If the wrong age was given, the beneficiary will only receive the proceeds that the premiums paid would have purchased (if the insured was older) or the overpayments will be refunded (if the insured was younger).

SUICIDE CLAUSE

To prevent a person from buying insurance just prior to committing suicide, premiums will merely be refunded if the insured commits suicide within two years (sometimes one year) of purchasing the coverage.

PAID-UP INSURANCE

If the insured surrenders a whole life policy, the policyholder may elect to receive paid-up insurance, good for life, with a face value equal to what the cash value will buy at that time.

DIVIDEND OPTIONS

Dividends received on a participating policy may be taken in cash, may be left at interest, or may be used to buy additional paid-up insurance, one-year term insurance, or simply to pay part of next year's premium.

ASSIGNMENTS

The policy owner may assign ownership of the policy as a gift or for consideration, including as collateral for a loan, but the insurer must be notified in writing; otherwise the company will not recognize it under the law.

JOINT LIFE INSURANCE

Typically entered into by married couples or business partners, this type of policy pays off the survivor upon the death of the other policyholder. This policy makes sense if the survivor would have no further need for insurance coverage. The policy is cancelled as soon as one party dies.

¶ 716 LIFE INSURANCE AGENTS

The typical training program for agents focuses on sales techniques rather than technical knowledge. As a consequence, the public may rank an agent on a level with used car salesmen. Life insurance, particularly whole life, is sold, not purchased, and more sales are made at the kitchen table than anywhere else. An occasional agent is one of the 40,000 Chartered Life Underwriters (CLUs) with a demonstrated minimum knowledge in estate planning, personal financial planning, taxes, and the like. These tend to be the most professional agents, with technical knowledge to better serve the financial needs of the client.

The agent earns a much higher commission on whole life than term insurance, resulting from a higher percentage of a higher premium, typically 50% to 100% of the first year's premium, 5% to 15% for several years thereafter. An agent must be highly qualified, indeed, before the time, expertise and service extended is worth such remuneration.

¶ 717 LIFE INSURANCE OWNERS

The owner of a life insurance policy must at least have had an insurable interest in the insured at the time the policy was purchased. A spouse may insure the other spouse and the children; an employer, the employees; a partner, the other partners; and a creditor, the debtor (up to the loan amount). The insured can name anyone a beneficiary, and the policy can be assigned by notifying the company. Without the requirement that the owner have a reasonable expectation of financial benefit if the insured lives and, therefore, will suffer a financial detriment upon the insured's death, the whole field would be wide open for gamblers and even murderers. The owner also typically needs the insured's consent. Note that the relationship need only exist initially. A policy on a spouse's life does not become invalid merely because of divorce, for example. In many states the insured must have reached majority and be of sound mind, except that parents can take out insurance on their children.

¶ 718 HOW TO CHOOSE A BENEFICIARY

A beneficiary has no vested interest in the policy, unless irrevocably designated, for example, pursuant to a divorce decree. This means that by simply filling out a "Change of Beneficiary" form, a new beneficiary, whether related to the insured or not, can be appointed. Insurance proceeds pass directly to a named beneficiary. No will is needed. Even if the client has a will leaving everything to someone else, the beneficiary still gets the proceeds. Here are some considerations to keep in mind:

1. If the client names the estate as beneficiary, the proceeds will be subject to the claims of creditors, as well as estate tax. The will then governs the distribution from the estate. The estate will receive the proceeds if either no beneficiary is named or the ones designated are no longer living.

2. A beneficiary spouse should be referred to by name in case of remarriage after divorce. The beneficiary should be reconsidered after a divorce in any case.

3. If the children are designated as beneficiaries, they should *not* be named. The phrase "my children" is adequate, unless the client wishes to limit the beneficiaries to fewer than all the children. People often buy insurance when their first child is born, naming "Eva Jones" the beneficiary. Later they forget

to fill out a change form when additional children are born. Result: The first child receives the full proceeds.

4. Name *contingent* beneficiaries. If a beneficiary predeceases the insured and the latter has not named a contingent (secondary) beneficiary, the proceeds go to the estate. In the absence of a will, the proceeds will pass pursuant to the laws of intestate succession. Control is lost. In many situations "to Mary Jones, my wife, if living, otherwise to my children," will meet the case. Another reason that designation of contingent beneficiaries is important is the possibility that the beneficiary will elect a long-term settlement option and die before collecting all installments.
5. If the client possesses any "incidents of ownership" in the policy on his life, the proceeds are subject to estate tax.[3] The details are discussed in the chapter on estate and gift taxes. The client may be well advised to irrevocably assign the policy to the beneficiary or an insurance trust. Commonly, the spouse is both the owner and the beneficiary.

¶ 719 PROTECTION FROM CREDITORS

There are two parties in particular who should be concerned with whether the life insurance (cash values or proceeds) can be reached by their creditors: the insured and the beneficiary.

For the insured, the laws of most states allow the cash values to stay immune from the claim of creditors, even in the event of a personal bankruptcy. The same tends to be true for proceeds of life insurance, but only to a limited extent. In some states the proceeds must be paid to the surviving spouse or children to enjoy full exemptions.

The creditor of a beneficiary cannot reach the cash value, because the latter has no vested rights in it due to the fact that the beneficiary usually can be changed any time. If the beneficiary is irrevocably designated, the creditors in some states may be able to reach the cash value. Once the proceeds are paid, however, they are subject to the claims of creditors. To prevent this, many policies contain a *spendthrift* clause.

¶ 720 HOW TO SAVE ON INSURANCE PREMIUMS

People do not like to think about their own death. As a result, they often do not plan for it and never really learn about life insurance. Then one day, an agent comes, and they often buy whatever the agent wants to sell, invariably whole life, without a true understanding of

[3] Code Sec. 2042.

either the coverage or the cost. Apart from the obvious dilemma of buying whole life or term, discussed in depth above, there are several ways to keep the cost of insurance down:

1. *Purchasing preferred risk policies.* Many companies issue policies at less than normal premiums to people of certain professions with good habits. A nonsmoker in a "safe" profession may qualify for these low rates.
2. *Purchasing group-term insurance.* Everybody belongs to at least one group. Various clubs, unions, religious organizations, professional associations, alumni clubs, etc., offer reasonable term insurance, as well as health, accident, and disability insurance. The rates may be as much as 50% lower than on individual policies, and a medical examination is rarely necessary. Unfortunately, only a limited amount of insurance can be purchased in this fashion.
3. *Reducing the coverage* each time a child grows up, leaves the home, gets married, etc.
4. *Dropping the insurance* if a beneficiary dies.
5. *Reducing or cancelling* the insurance if the client has no debts, the home is paid for, and the policyholder has a reasonable nest egg built up, particularly if liquid.
6. *Paying the premium annually* is cheaper than paying it quarterly or monthly.
7. If a higher premium is paid because of a health problem or a hazardous occupation, notify the agent if the client's health or job has changed for the better.
8. If expanded coverage is desired, it is usually less expensive to add to a current policy than to buy a new one.
9. Upon retirement, the life insurance coverage should be reviewed. It may no longer be needed. If the coverage is no longer worth the premiums, the policy should be cashed in.
10. If the client is divorced and the former spouse is the beneficiary, the insurance may be dropped, unless there are children the client wants to name as beneficiaries instead.

¶ 721 MANAGING LIFE INSURANCE

The job is not over once the insured has purchased a policy, but most people simply lock the policy in a drawer or a safe-deposit box (policies should not be kept here) and forget about it. The client should ask the following questions periodically:

1. What am I covered for? Death only, or disability, accidents, dismemberment, etc.?
2. What is the amount of coverage? Do I have decreasing term insurance, double indemnity, etc.? Has the coverage kept up with inflation?
3. Have my circumstances changed? The business, income, investment, or family situation may have changed sufficiently to merit adjustments in the insurance program.
4. Do I have an agent? Do I have the name and address? Do I know *when* to seek advice? If I do not have one, do I know how to select one?
5. Do I know how to file a claim, how to increase or adjust coverage, change beneficiary, etc.?

¶ 722 SWITCHING INSURANCE

It makes sense to replace a term policy with cheaper, equivalent group insurance. It may also make sense to drop a relatively new whole life policy for a term policy. However, the client should think long and hard before dropping a whole life policy in favor of another whole life policy. The agent is obligated to spell out the differences between the current policy and the replacement policy, but a change is rarely advantageous because:

1. The client must submit to a new medical examination and may no longer be insurable.
2. The client has to pay the front-end costs again.
3. There will be a new incontestability clause, meaning the new policy can be contested by the insurer for two years.
4. The annual premium will be higher because the insured is older.
5. The client must try to avoid a time interval between the time the old policy lapses and the new becomes effective. Also, if both policies are effective simultaneously, there is some overlap of coverage and double premiums for this unneeded privilege.

¶ 723 SETTLEMENT OPTIONS

Upon the death of the insured, the policy typically gives the beneficiary several choices as to how the proceeds are to be paid:

1. Collecting a lump sum immediately.
2. Leaving the proceeds with the company and collecting interest only for one or more years.

3. An annuity for single or joint lives with a guaranteed minimum term, if desired, e.g., 10 or 20 years.
4. Time installments, where each installment includes interest on the remaining balance and therefore decreases over time.
5. Fixed amount installments, where each installment, including interest, is equal in amount.
6. A combination of the above, such as lump-sum installments or an annuity.

Under any deferred payment plan the beneficiary may receive monthly, quarterly, semiannual, or annual payments.

Insurance for Business Reasons

¶ 725 BUSINESS CONTINUATION INSURANCE

The owner of a small business needs life insurance for two reasons:

1. To protect dependents against losses resulting from premature death.
2. To assure the continuation of the business.

Cash will be needed to retire the interest of a partner or sole proprietor, or to buy the stock of a shareholder in a closely held corporation. Life insurance is invariably the most convenient way to provide funds for this purpose. With ample liquidity, the business can continue without interference from heirs and without the need to sell the business or its assets to pay estate taxes.

¶ 726 LIFE INSURANCE AND BUY/SELL AGREEMENTS

A buy/sell agreement is commonly used in closely held businesses to ensure the continuity of the business and to keep the business in the family. A buy/sell agreement is a contract providing for the sale of corporate stock upon the death, retirement, or disability of a shareholder. In addition, the proceeds paid will fix the value of the stock for estate tax purposes and will provide liquidity to the deceased shareholder's estate to pay debts and taxes.

There are two types of buy/sell agreements that will provide a ready buyer, instant liquidity, and continuity of business:

1. The *cross-purchase* agreement, which provides that the other partners or shareholders will buy the stock.
2. The *stock redemption* agreement which provides that the corporation will buy (redeem) the stock.

In either plan, life insurance is commonly used to provide funds to buy the stock. If the cross-purchase contract is used, all shareholders own a policy on the life of every other shareholder. Under a redemption plan, the corporation carries insurance on the life of the shareholders. When a shareholder dies, the proceeds are paid to the owner/beneficiary of the policy, who then uses the cash to buy the stock. As usual the premiums paid are nondeductible and the proceeds nontaxable. But if the policy was acquired from another shareholder, any excess of proceeds over premiums and consideration paid *is* taxable.

¶ 727 KEY EMPLOYEE COVERAGE

The loss of a key employee may result in a substantial economic loss to a firm, since experience and managerial skills are considerable assets, although not found on the balance sheet.

To determine needed coverage the basic approach is to estimate the economic loss from the death of a key employee and capitalize it at a reasonable rate. The relevant economic loss includes:

1. Lost profits for the replacement period after salary, taxes, costs of doing business, etc.
2. Executive search costs.
3. Training costs.
4. Lost sales to important customers.

A firm may find that the needed coverage may run into several hundred thousand dollars for just *one* key executive. Some executives may even be irreplaceable, economically speaking. Disability insurance should not be forgotten, either. In fact, the coverage needed for long-term disability will exceed the life insurance coverage due to the desirability of providing disability income to the executive.

¶ 728 SPLIT-DOLLAR LIFE INSURANCE: A FORM OF "KEY EMPLOYEE" INSURANCE

The typical split-dollar life insurance works like this: The corporate employer buys a whole life policy on the employee's life and owns the policy. The corporation pays a premium equal to the annual increase in cash value and the employee pays the rest. Because cash values soon start mounting, the premium is higher in the beginning. The corporation's balance sheet is, in effect, unchanged, because in lieu of cash, the cash value of the policy is listed as an asset.

There are two beneficiaries: one whom the employee designates and the employer. Whether the employee quits, retires, or dies, the cash value belongs to the corporation. When the employee dies, the beneficiary collects the proceeds less the cash value. Sometimes dividends on a participating policy are used to provide additional term insurance. The employee ends up with more insurance than can otherwise be justified. Each year the employee will receive taxable income, however. The income equals the cost of one year's term insurance for the net amount of coverage less the premium paid. In most cases, this will amount to a few hundred dollars on a $100,000 policy. The employee contribution will typically drop sharply after the first year and disappear altogether after nine or ten years.

Tax Aspects of Life Insurance and Death Benefits

¶ 730 EMPLOYEE DEATH BENEFITS

When a death benefit is paid to the beneficiaries of an employee, the first $5,000 paid is tax free.[4] Note the following:

1. The exclusion is generally unavailable to self-employed individuals, but it *is* available to employees of partnerships and sole proprietorships.
2. If there is more than one beneficiary, they must share the $5,000 exclusion.
3. The $5,000 exclusion is available to every employee without limit.
4. The nature of the beneficiary is irrelevant, e.g., the beneficiary can be the surviving spouse and/or children, a partnership, a corporation or a trust.
5. The exclusion is unavailable if the decedent could have cashed in the benefit prior to death.
6. A bonus, accrued vacation pay, uncollected salaries, etc., do *not* qualify. There must be a true death benefit.
7. If the benefit is left at interest, the interest is fully taxable.

¶ 731 DEATH BENEFITS AS GIFTS

When a surviving spouse and/or children receive a cash payment on account of an employee's death, the recipient will want to argue that the amount is a nontaxable gift. The employer, on the other hand, will want to deduct the payment as a business expense. If the amount does not exceed $5,000, it is automatically excluded from income but is still deductible. However, if the amount is substantial, the beneficiary will argue that all of it is tax free.

Although it is difficult to find a gift in an employer-employee setting, the taxpayer may prevail if the following criteria are met:

1. The payments were made directly to the beneficiaries, not to the estate of the decedent.
2. No direct benefit is received by the employer in return.

---

[4] Code Sec. 101(b).

3. The employer made the payment voluntarily and not pursuant to an enforceable agreement.
4. The recipients render no services.
5. The employee had been fully compensated.
6. The payment bears no relationship to the salary and is based on the financial needs of the family.

¶ 732 PROCEEDS OF LIFE INSURANCE

Life insurance proceeds are generally not taxed to the beneficiary, whether paid in a lump sum or in installments.[5] There are two reasons for this:

1. Premiums paid are nondeductible, except to the extent that they represent compensation.
2. Social policy has dictated favoring the dependents of a deceased breadwinner.

Proceeds received as a policy loan are often also tax free (subject to the "modified endowment contract" rules, discussed above). The tax-free nature of insurance proceeds applies whether the payment is made on an ordinary life policy, term insurance, workmen's compensation insurance, labor union death benefits, accident or health life insurance, or an endowment policy. Dividends paid are not taxable either, since they merely represent refunds of nondeductible premiums.

It makes no difference who the beneficiary is, whether or not related to the insured, an estate, trust, partnership, or corporation, with a few exceptions:

1. In the case of credit insurance, the creditor must include any excess proceeds over the principal owed as income.
2. If someone buys a policy and collects proceeds in excess of the purchase price, the gain is taxable as ordinary income.

The following transactions and transfers of policies are tax free:

1. Changing the beneficiary.
2. Transferring the policy to a partnership in which the insured is a partner or to a corporation in which the insured is an officer and/or shareholder.
3. Transfers covered by a nonrecognition provision, such as gifts, tax-free formations of partnerships or corporations, and corporate reorganizations.

---

[5] Code Sec. 101(a)(1).

¶ 733 SURRENDER OF POLICIES

If the insured surrenders a life or endowment policy, the company will pay the cash-surrender value. If the amount received exceeds the premiums paid, such excess is ordinary income. On the other hand, if less is received, the "loss" is a nondeductible personal expense.

¶ 734 EXCHANGES OF INSURANCE POLICIES

If an insurance policy is exchanged for another, the exchange may or may not be taxable. The following exchanges are tax free:[6]

1. The exchange of a whole life policy for another or for an endowment or annuity contract, including a variable annuity. The reason is that since the proceeds would have been excludible in the first place, no tax is avoided or postponed.
2. The exchange of an endowment policy for another (if the payments from the new policy do not start later than under the old policy) and the exchange of an endowment policy for an annuity contract.
3. The exchange of one annuity contract for another, if the annuity is for the life of the same individual.

TAXABLE TRANSACTIONS

The following transactions are taxable:

1. If cash is received in an otherwise tax-free exchange, any gain is taxable to the extent of the cash received. The gain is simply equal to the fair market value of what was received (policy plus cash) less what was paid for the contract surrendered (reduced by dividends, if any).

Example: Helga paid $10,000 in premiums for an ordinary life policy before exchanging it for an annuity contract worth $9,000 and $2,000 in cash. Because she realized a gain of only $1,000 ($11,000 less $10,000), this is all she must declare. But because she got $2,000 in cash, which is $1,000 more than what she declared, her cost basis in the annuity is reduced from the $10,000 cost in the old policy to $9,000.

2. The exchange of an endowment policy or annuity contract for an ordinary life insurance policy is taxable. Otherwise the policy owner could easily avoid the tax on these policies by substituting a policy, the proceeds of which are not taxable.
3. The exchange of an annuity contract for an endowment policy is also taxable. In this case the tax on the annuity payments

[6] Code Sec. 1035.

would be postponed until the maturity of the endowment policy, in the absence of a taxable exchange.

If an annuity is sold at a gain, the gain is taxable. Furthermore, a loss is *deductible* because an annuity is always deemed to be entered into with a profit motive. The loss is ordinary as opposed to a capital loss. However, if the insured cashes in an endowment policy for more than the premiums paid, ordinary income results. Any loss is nondeductible.

¶ 735 EMPLOYER-PAID LIFE INSURANCE

If an employer pays the premiums on an employee's life insurance policy, the tax consequences are as follows:

1. If the employer is the beneficiary, there are no tax consequences to the employee. The employer cannot deduct the premiums and the proceeds will be tax free.
2. An employee who can name the beneficiary is taxed on the premiums paid as compensation (except for premiums paid on the first $50,000 of group term life insurance). As a result, the employer corporation can deduct the premiums paid as compensation expenses.

¶ 736 DEDUCTING INTEREST ON LIFE INSURANCE LOANS

Millions of people have historically deducted interest on policy loans, or interest on loans to purchase (or that are secured by) life insurance. However, there are several traps to be aware of:

1. Interest paid on a loan to buy a single premium policy is nondeductible.[7] Also, none of four of the first seven annual premiums may be borrowed. This is because of the tax-free buildup in cash values.
2. The cash-basis policyholder receives no deduction unless the interest is actually paid and not just added to principal.[8]
3. A policyholder who makes an irrevocable assignment of the policy can no longer deduct interest paid after the assignment. Additional gifts are being made to the assignee.[9]
4. An assignee cannot deduct interest paid after the assignment, to the extent accrued before the assignment.[10]
5. Extra amounts paid because premiums are paid more frequently than yearly are nondeductible fees, not interest.[11]

---

[7] Code Sec. 264.

[8] *E.L. Cheeseman*, CCH Dec. 29,859(M), 28 TCM 1334 (1969) and Rev. Rul. 73-482, 1973-2 CB 44.

[9] *J.S. Dean*, CCH Dec. 24,742, 35 TC 1083 (1937).

[10] *A.I. Fox*, 43 BTA 895 (1941).

[11] Rev. Rul. 79-187, 1979-1 CB 95.

6. Accrued interest deducted from the proceeds paid to a beneficiary is rarely deductible, unless it qualifies as "deduction in respect of a decedent." This means that it would have been deductible if paid by the decedent prior to his death.[12]
7. Personal interest paid after 1990 is nondeductible.[13] If the loan is used for investment purposes, the interest paid is deductible to the extent of net investment income with a carryover.[14]

[12] Code Sec. 691 and *Hooks,* CCH Dec. 20,374, 22 TC 502 (1954).

[13] Code Sec. 163(h).

[14] Code Sec. 163(d).

CHAPTER 8

Nonlife Insurance

¶ 801 MEDICAL INSURANCE

The cost of a semiprivate room in a hospital is over $200 a day, an appendectomy may cost over $800, and a hysterectomy over $2,000. Life insurance is relatively straightforward. The insured is covered only for death and the beneficiary collects a given amount. Medical needs due to illnesses and accidents, on the other hand, are unpredictable. The insured may never be hospitalized, but if it comes about, the cost may range anywhere from a few hundred to hundreds of thousands of dollars. It is impossible to plan for it, which is the main reason to insure against it. Due to the myriad of causes of illnesses, the complexities of medical insurance policies are numerous. This makes it particularly difficult to understand a policy, notably, in regard to the exclusions. Mail order policies, for example, may sound simple in an ad, but collecting is a different matter.

The client can, to some extent, reduce the need for medical care by following basic but often unheeded advice: keeping weight down, cutting down on drinking or smoking, getting regular sleep and exercise, eating fruits and vegetables, drinking water, etc. But even so, medical insurance is still needed in case of illness or accident. The upper-middle-class client needs coverage primarily for large bills. This simplifies matters in addition to keeping premiums down. The better the insured's income and the greater the resources, the less the concern with co-insurance clauses and high deductibles. On the other hand, because no one wants to lose what is owned, the client must be insured against catastrophic expenses. Paradoxically, it is relatively cheap to buy policies with high limits when compared to the high cost of buying policies with low deductibles.

¶ 802 TYPES OF MEDICAL PLANS

The following headings are a capsule summary of several types of medical plans with specific recommendations.

HOSPITAL EXPENSE PLANS

Hospital expense plans are the most popular of all plans; they cover the cost of hospitalization (less a deductible and a coinsurance clause) and are renewable to age 65. For an increased premium the client can include coverage for a spouse and dependent children, for example, children under age 18 or full-time students. These plans only cover hospital room and board, which incidentally is more expensive than a luxury hotel.

SURGICAL EXPENSE PLANS

Surgical expense plans cover the cost of specific operations up to a maximum and are the second most popular plans.

GENERAL MEDICAL EXPENSE PLANS

General medical expense plans cover incidentals such as garden variety office visits, and they are of interest primarily to low-income people.

MAJOR MEDICAL PLANS

Major medical plans pay all expenses in the hospital, including treatment. Typically, there is a deductible and a co-insurance clause, e.g., the insured pays the first $1,000 plus 20% of the excess. "Catastrophic loss" insurances should be added. A $1,000,000 maximum is recommended. As in the area of personal liability insurance, it is more important to have a high upper limit than a low deductible.

COMPREHENSIVE PLANS

Comprehensive plans pick up the deductible and increase the percentage of expenses covered. They are *not* recommended if the client can afford the possible expenses of not being covered.

¶ 803 GROUP PLANS

If at all possible, group medical coverage should be obtained. An employer may provide the client with it; otherwise, the client can join a fraternal or professional organization offering such a plan. Employment plans may be paid for by the employee, the employer or both. In any event, there are several advantages of a group plan:

1. The cost is probably 15%-40% below that of individual policies.
2. The coverage cannot be cancelled while the insured is employed.
3. Preexisting conditions are usually not excluded, although there may be a waiting period for maternity benefits.
4. Dependent family members may be included at a reasonable cost.
5. No medical exam is required.
6. The maximum limit may be quite high, e.g., $250,000 or even $1 million.

One disadvantage of the employer plan is that the policy lapses 30 days after the employment ends. However, the employee may frequently convert group coverage to individual coverage during this 30-day period.

¶ 804 HEALTH MAINTENANCE ORGANIZATIONS (HMOs)

The most significant development in the delivery of medical services since the '70s has been the growth of Health Maintenance Organizations (HMOs). Their characteristics are:

1. They operate under the Federal HMO Act of 1973.
2. They provide a prepaid comprehensive system of medical care.
3. They encourage early detection and treatment through coverage for annual checkups and other preventive measures.
4. They are both the insurer and the actual provider of medical services.
5. There is no paperwork for the patient who only makes a small fixed payment per office visit such as $5. Generally, 100% of hospitalization is covered.
6. They have contracts for volume discounts with its affiliated physicians, hospitals, and laboratories.
7. Being both the provider *and* the insurer, they encourage cost effective treatments, e.g., no unnecessary hospital stays, maximum outpatient treatment, etc.
8. Each member must select one and only one primary care physician who is affiliated with the HMO. The primary care physician is responsible for *all* the patient's health care and will refer the patient to specialists as needed. The insured may change the primary care physician as often as once a month.
9. Out-of-the-area treatments are covered in emergency situations.

More and more employers are using HMOs for their group plans and typically pay from 50% to 100% of the cost. The employee may be offered a choice of HMOs and must be given the opportunity to opt out of the HMO or change provider annually during a short enrollment period. The annual cost for family coverage (two adults and two children) may run as high as $3,500 or more.

¶ 805 PREFERRED PROVIDER ORGANIZATIONS (PPOs)

The PPOs are a network of private physicians, dentists, and hospitals who agree to charge fixed, below average fees to groups hiring them, i.e., a volume discount. Most such groups are employers. The employer's only added cost is an annual fee for administration, e.g., 1% of annual claims.

The PPO offers advantages similar to those of an HMO, notably low fixed fees for office visits, no deductibles, no paperwork, and no high outlays subject to reimbursement. The choice of physician is limited, although it is wider than with an HMO.

¶ 806 BLUE CROSS/BLUE SHIELD

In general, commercial insurers are more reluctant to pay claims than Blue Cross/Blue Shield. Thus, while 40% of premiums are paid out in benefits by mail order firms, 92% is paid out under Blue Cross. Blue Cross is, in effect, controlled by hospitals and physicians who are happy to pay their own bills and pass on the cost to their patients. Nevertheless, the coverage is better per premium dollar than for commercial firms that are in business for themselves and not for the health care industry.

Blue Cross was created in 1929 to guarantee hospitals that their bills would be paid. Blue Shield, formed in 1946, covers surgical and general medical expenses and is also a nonprofit organization. They pay the hospital directly, while commercial carriers often pay the insured. The federal government has even delegated Medicare claim review to Blue Cross. Blue Cross also offers HMO and "Medigap" insurance.

¶ 807 MEDICAL REIMBURSEMENT PLANS

The main reason for selecting medical reimbursement plans is the tax benefit. An individual can only deduct medical expenses in excess of 7.5% of Adjusted Gross Income (AGI). This means that if the AGI is $50,000, the taxpayer gets no tax benefit from the first $2,250 of the family's annual medical expenses. If reimbursed by the employer, however, the employer gets a full deduction *without* the amount received being taxed to the employee. Economically, one can, of course, argue that the employee pays indirectly because the more fringe benefits received, the lower the salary. However, the employee still comes out ahead after taxes. It is a sound principle to receive as much compensation as possible in the form of nontaxable benefits.

¶ 808 HOW TO SAVE ON MEDICAL INSURANCE

There are many ways to save on medical insurance. The following are some ways to save:

1. Purchase the policy before having a history of illness.
2. Do not buy specific policies, such as cancer or leukemia policies. Select broad coverage.

3. The cost of a policy is a function of age, health, the deductible, length of the term, renewal clauses, types and amounts to be paid. Use a high deductible and a high maximum limit. Pay for an automatic renewal clause.
4. Use only one policy, such as major medical plus catastrophic losses. Drop any medical coverage in the auto or homeowner's policy.
5. Add a disability rider. Remember, if the client has exorbitant medical expenses, chances are that the earning power is lost as well.
6. Cover mental illness, alcoholism, and dependents.
7. Convert any employer group policy to individual coverage when the employee leaves the job, unless covered at the new job. Also convert upon retirement to supplement Medicare.
8. Keep any old disability policy. It is generally better to add to the existing coverage than to replace it.
9. Avoid duplication in policies.
10. Consider income insurance for both spouses if the couple depends on each other's income.
11. Pay the premium annually. (The IRS does not allow the added cost of paying frequently as an interest deduction.)
12. Consider excluding the following coverage:
    (a) Dental insurance. (Dental care is rarely very expensive. A few hundred dollars typically meets the cost.)
    (b) Maternity insurance. (Most people only have one or two children and the coverage is expensive. However, the client should be covered for possible complications. Also, coverage should be obtained if the client plans to have several children in rapid succession.)
13. Exercise caution with mail order insurance. Only about 40% of the premiums are paid out in benefits. Read the policy before signing up. Group insurance usually affords a better and more economical coverage.
14. Cosmetic surgery, such as hair transplants and face lifts, is not covered.

In addition to the above, here is some general advice: The client should have a family physician who knows the family's habits and medical history personally and who keeps a permanent record.

The client should exercise some preventive care, have regular checkups, call the physician if there is no need for an actual office visit, follow the doctor's advice, and exercise moderation in terms of smoking, drinking and eating.

¶ 809 CLAUSES TO BE AWARE OF

The clauses to watch for are the following:

Deductibles. The client should use as high a deductible as possible, such as $1,000. In any case, the actual amount of the deductible should be known.

Coinsurance. If the client can afford to pay 20% of the expenses beyond the deductible, an 80% coinsurance clause should be requested. 100% coverage is too expensive, and it is rarely needed.

Exclusion. Know the policy exclusions. The most common exclusions are mental illness, maternity, alcoholism, preexisting conditions, cosmetic surgery, and war. If the insured wishes to cover some of these contingencies, a rider may be purchased.

Waiting period. The average hospital stay is about eight days. Therefore, a common waiting period is a week.

In general, the typical policy excludes what is most likely to happen, e.g., short stays in the hospital, pregnancies, and preexisting conditions.

¶ 810 MEDICARE

The typical client is too young for Medicare and too well off for Medicaid. A person's potential Medicare is paid partly with *nondeductible* Social Security contributions, partly with *deductible* Part B premiums and voluntary Part A payments. Although people are eligible for Medicare at the age of 65 whether or not they retire, there are advantages to working past age 65:

1. Chances are the client stays healthier if engaging in systematic activities.
2. An employee keeps the group medical policy, typically providing better coverage than Medicare.

Once someone is both 65 years of age and retired, it may be discovered that Medicare covers less than 40% of medical expenses. As a result, many people are likely to need supplemental insurance. The House Select Committee on Aging found that $1 billion a year is spent on worthless or unnecessary insurance that does not cover the gaps and/or that duplicate Medicare. There is a bewildering array of policies, terms and conditions.

Medicare has two parts:

1. *Part A* is hospital insurance for the first 90 days for each "spell of illness" less a $676 deductible (in 1993) plus up to 100 days nursing home services for "spell of illness."
2. *Part B* covers physicians' fees, outpatient costs, etc., less an annual deductible of $100 (in 1993). But only 80% of "reasonable charges" are covered. Some physicians' charges far exceed what is defined as reasonable, in which case the patient pays 20% of the reasonable charge plus *100%* of the excess. As a practical matter the patient would therefore pay more than half the expense. If possible, a physician should be used who "accepts assignment," i.e., agrees to limit fees to Medicare coverage amounts.

THE MEDICARE CATASTROPHIC COVERAGE ACT OF 1988

From 1989, Medicare recipients have received expanded coverage, summarized below, financed in part by increased Part B monthly premiums—$36.60 in 1993.

SUMMARY OF MEDICARE BENEFITS

Hospitalization

Up to 60 days: No copayment required

61—90 days: Copayment $169 per day (1993)

91—150 days: Copayment $338 per day (1993) (Lifetime reserve days)

90 days allowed per "spell of illness"

No coverage after 90 days plus remaining lifetime reserve days

Nursing Home

Up to 20 days: No copayment required

21—100 days: $84.50 per day (1993)

100 days allowed per "spell of illness" after 3 or more days of hospitalization

Doctor (Part B coverage, only applicable if $36.60 monthly premium (in 1993) is paid)

$100 annual deductible (in 1993) plus 20% copayment

No coverage for fees charged in excess of Medicare guidelines.

(Lesson: Make sure physician "accepts assignment.")

Prescription Drugs

There is *no* coverage for prescription or self-administered drugs.

Under the new law, Medigap insurance is still very much needed, since the increased coverage merely reduces the out-of-pocket cost of medical services; it far from eliminates it.

¶ 811 DISABILITY INSURANCE

The younger the client, the greater the chance of serious disability as compared to death. Thus, at age 25, a person is seven times more likely to suffer a serious disability for at least three months than to die. A more frightening statistic is that one out of three 35-year-olds will experience a serious disability before age 65. The need for disability insurance is, therefore, vast.

The average worker's only protection against long-term disability, or the loss of income resulting therefrom, is Social Security Disability and Workers Compensation. This may *not* suffice for two reasons:

1. The maximum benefits may be a small percentage of salary.
2. Many clients, such as executives and professionals, are unlikely to have a work-related accident. Thus, disability is more likely to occur as a result of car accidents and leisure time activities.

To collect Social Security, mental or physical disability payments, the disability must be expected to last at least 12 months and there is a waiting period of five months. In addition, the client must be unable to work. Workers Compensation, which is state controlled and employer contributed, only pays for job-related injuries. Therefore, additional coverage is needed.

¶ 812 HOW TO DETERMINE NEEDED COVERAGE

Medical insurance only covers part of the economic loss sustained while ill. Depending on the employer's salary continuation plan, if any, loss of income may be the greatest expense during a prolonged illness or disability. The coverage needed is primarily a function of available income and assets. Here is a procedure to determine the required coverage:

1. Add up the family's annual living expenses.
2. Subtract expenses which go away if the client becomes disabled, such as
   (a) taxes (disability benefits may be partly or fully tax free),
   (b) transportation expenses,
   (c) entertainment, travel, etc., and
   (d) insurance premiums covered by "waiver of premium" riders.

3. Subtract the spouse's after-tax income if any.
4. Subtract Social Security benefits payable.
5. Subtract income (dividends and interest) on savings and investments, which would normally be reinvested rather than spent.
6. The net constitutes needed income, assuming no liquidations of assets.

Because the insurance premium is lower the longer the waiting period, a waiting period as far in the future as possible should be selected, commensurate with the extent to which the client is willing to deplete assets. The insured typically has a choice of 7, 15, 30, 90, 180, or 365 days after becoming disabled. The above procedure should be repeated whenever the client's needs and/or assets substantially increase or decline.

¶ 813 INCOME LOSS COVERAGE

If disability is defined in the strictest sense, payments will only be made if the insured is unable to perform any gainful employment whatsoever. Disability can also be defined in an income/loss coverage policy as the inability to perform all functions of the customary occupation. The premium will obviously reflect the definition used. Payments made for a disability caused by an illness normally cease upon attainment of age 65.

Women are often discriminated against when purchasing disability insurance. They may face low dollar limitations and short payment durations, e.g., a five-year maximum. However, lifetime coverage is more available if she is deemed to hold an executive position.

¶ 814 TYPES OF POLICIES

The typical commercial contract, also called the *basic* contract, can cover the insured for loss of income whether the disability is total or partial, temporary or permanent, and whether it is caused by accident or illness. Payments are typically made for two years, but only if the insured is unable to keep the old job. Payments may stop as soon as the insured works *any* job. For example, if five-year coverage is desired, the premium is likely to be $700 to $800 a year for benefits of $500 a week. Executives pay smaller premiums than workers.

Of special interest is the so-called *"residual"* policy. Like other policies the maximum benefit which can be paid is two-thirds of income or $5,000 (or $4,000 or $3,000) a month, whichever is smaller. Unlike under other policies, the benefit is not discontinued if the insured works, but is simply reduced by the percentage of normal salary earned. Thus, if the salary drops from $5,000 to $2,000 a month when the insured becomes partially disabled, the benefit paid is 40% less than with no income.

Clauses to be aware of:

1. *Presumptive disability.* Presumptive disability goes to the definition of disability and varies from policy to policy. It is the most important clause because it determines eligibility for benefits. Common exclusions are disability resulting from war or pregnancy. Dismemberments may result in lump-sum benefits.
2. *Double indemnity.* The insured collects twice the benefit for certain accidents. The client should not purchase this coverage. The need for income is rarely related to the cause of disability.
3. *Prorating.* This clause contains two elements:
   (a) The premium is subject to change if the occupation changes or the insured misstates age. In addition, benefits may be integrated with Social Security and Workers Compensation.
   (b) Total benefits from all insurance cannot exceed the salary. Thus, the client may be wasting premiums if buying multiple policies.
4. *Waiting period.* Again, the client should select the longest waiting period resources permit, one year if possible. Why insure against having to make withdrawals from a savings account? It makes sense to start off early in life with a short waiting period, such as 30 days, then later to increase it as the savings grow.

As is true for other types of insurance, such as life and health insurance, group disability insurance rates are lower. In fact, it is a popular fringe benefit and a most attractive one, since premiums are not tax deductible to the insured, not even as medical insurance. This is because the insured is protected against loss of income, not against medical expenses. For materials on how to shop for disability insurance, contact: National Insurance Consumer Organization, 121 No. Payne Street, Alexandria, VA 22314, (703) 549-8050.

Homeowners Insurance

¶ 820 OVERVIEW

A home buyer should inquire of the previous owners about the kind of coverage they had and with what insurer. If the client does not have a reputable insurance agent, a bank or lawyer may be consulted.

The home may be the largest investment most people ever make. It should be insured against full or partial loss. There are only two kinds of property in this world, real and personal. Land cannot be insured, but personal property can and should be. If the client has gathered earthly goods, it may be possible that collections of art, books, stamps, coins, comic books, etc., are worth more than the house.

Unlike life insurance where the buyer must have an insurable interest at the time of *purchase* to collect, property insurance law requires that the claimant have an insurable interest at the time of the *loss.* Homeowners buy insurance to achieve some peace of mind to meet the lender's requirements. Homeowners insurance can be broken down into three kinds. *Property insurance* and *liability insurance* refer to coverage for the owner's losses; *third-party insurance* refers to insurance for losses and injuries sustained by others for which the homeowner may be liable.

A homeowners policy is needed even if the client rents. The policy will cover personal property and liability just as with homeowners insurance.

If the client owns a condominium apartment, the building is covered by a "blanket" insurance policy through the homeowners association. This is all that is needed to obtain a mortgage, but the client still requires a homeowners policy unless

1. personal belongings are negligible, and
2. "umbrella" liability coverage is carried (see below).

SCOPE OF HOMEOWNERS INSURANCE

Coverage can be broken down into *people* coverage, *things* coverage, and *places* coverage:

1. A homeowners policy will cover each family member who is part of the household, e.g., the father, mother, children, in-laws, and other relatives living with the owner. If a son is in college but is planning to move back in, he is covered wherever he is.
2. The garage burns down with the client's car in it. Chances are that a comprehensive auto insurance policy covers the car, but the homeowners policy covers the garage. All personal posses-

sions on the premises can be covered, except for pets, but a "floater" may be needed for jewelry and other valuables.

3. Personal belongings may be covered regardless of where they are. Examples include property in transit while moving or traveling, goods in storage, and items in the car. However, for car thefts, the client may have to prove that it was locked and show that there was forcible entry.

If a home or apartment becomes unfit to live in after a fire or other damage, the client may have to live elsewhere. These *consequential damages* may be insured through an additional living expense endorsement. It is not automatic. If the client is turned down for theft insurance, a federal crime insurance policy may be obtained through the Federal Crime Insurance Agency (1-800-638-8780) of the Federal Insurance Administration (department of HUD). This policy must be obtained through an insurance agent.

¶ 821 SUGGESTED COVERAGE

When insuring a home, the homeowner should include major additions or improvements, such as a garage, a family room, trees, plants, personal property, other people's property while on premises, personal liability, and living expenses. If necessary, appraisals should be obtained. The insured should keep an inventory of the contents of the home with photographs. These should be kept in a safe-deposit box. Here is a suggested percentage breakdown of the kind of insurance the client should carry:

100%	The house itself
5%	Trees and plants
10%	Garages
50%	Personal property ("standard contents coverage")
20%	Extra living expenses
150%	Personal liability (absolute minimum)

Note that personal liability coverage should exceed the coverage on the house, while personal property normally accounts for one-half of the value of the home. These numbers are merely guidelines; each situation is different.

¶ 822 KNOW THE POTENTIAL LIABILITY

Unless the client is legally responsible for the loss of property, no insurance is necessary.

Consider how the client would feel in the following case:

> The client signed a real estate contract to buy a house for $150,000. Assume that the owner carried no fire insurance. Three weeks before the closing the house burned down to the ground.

Who suffered the loss? The client did, if the contract is silent on the issue. In most states the risk of loss passes upon signing the executory contract of sale. If the buyer is liable, the buyer must buy insurance. Because the above seems to be against most people's reasoning, "The Uniform Vendor and Purchaser Risk Act" has been adopted by several states (including California, Hawaii, Illinois, Michigan, New York, North Carolina, Oklahoma, Oregon, South Dakota, and Wisconsin). Under this Act, risk passes on the earlier of closing or possession, which makes more sense to most people. The lesson is clear: People must know when they are liable for what, so they can protect themselves. If a burglar gets in without signs of forcible entry, the client may not be covered. The client's tea cups from the Ming Dynasty were broken, but the policy excludes glass breakage.

The insured should know the coverage before learning the hard way. The burden of proof is generally on the insured to:

1. Prove that a loss was suffered.
2. Prove that the loss is covered.
3. Prove the amount of the loss.

¶ 823 CO-INSURANCE CLAUSES

Casualty insurance contracts usually contain either a *deductible* amount or a *co-insurance* clause. A deductible means the insured pays the first x dollars of damage. A co-insurance clause makes the insured a coinsurer in the event the insured fails to carry insurance on x% of the value of the property. For a partial loss the insurance company will pay the following fraction of the loss:

$$\frac{\text{Amount insured}}{\text{Amount required insured}}$$

Example: The client owns a home which has a fair market value of $150,000. The fire insurance policy contains an 80% co-insurance clause, meaning that unless the insured carries insurance of at least $120,000, the homeowner will suffer a portion of a partial loss personally. If the house burns down to the ground, the insured will simply collect $120,000, the face amount of the policy. However, if there is a partial loss of $48,000 and the insurance limit is $100,000, the insurance will pay

$$\$48{,}000 \times \frac{\$100{,}000}{\$120{,}000} \text{ or } \$40{,}000; \$8{,}000 \text{ comes out of the insured's pocket.}$$

The recent history of residential home prices indicates that the insured should review and possibly increase the coverage annually. A residence may go up $20,000 or more in one year. A fire might cost plenty unless the homeowner is fully covered, although the loss may be partially deductible as a casualty loss for tax purposes.

It should be evident from the above that the co-insurance clause only will have application when both the amount of insurance carried *and* the actual loss fall below 80% of the replacement value. If the loss is total, the face amount is paid, regardless of the co-insurance percentage.

¶ 824 INSURANCE CLAUSES TO KNOW ABOUT

There are three types of insurance clauses:

1. *Other insurance clause.* As a public policy, the insured is not supposed to be better off after suffering a loss than before. If people could easily make a profit on their insurance policies, abuses would be likely. Therefore, if the homeowner obtains multiple coverage, each insurance policy will pay the following:

$$\text{Damage} \times \frac{\text{insurance coverage}}{\text{total coverage}}$$

As a result it is hard to make a profit. The insurance will, at the most, make the client whole. This is a main reason for not being over insured. The client simply wastes premiums with no increase in total coverage.

2. *Mortgage clause.* If the homeowner has a mortgage on the house and it burns down, or is otherwise damaged, any insurance proceeds will first be paid directly to the lender (mortgagee) by the insurance company to the extent of the balance due plus accrued interest. Ordinarily, the mortgagee will release the funds to pay for repairs. This is to prevent the mortgagor from taking the money and running after collecting. In addition, the mortgage clause will provide that if the homeowner stops paying premiums, the lender will pay and add them to the loan balance.

3. *Arbitration clause.* If a dispute arises over a claim, this clause saves the parties a lengthy court trial. The insured's representative will simply appear with the claims adjuster before an insurance arbitration board and a settlement will be negotiated.

¶ 825 IMPORTANCE OF THE CAUSE OF A LOSS

The traditional homeowner's policy covered only fire damage to the house. Today the "broad form" coverage includes damage from explosions, hail and windstorms, riots, theft, falling aircraft, damage caused by vehicles and smoke, snow and ice, vandalism, water damage, etc. But even an "all-risk" policy will typically not cover damage caused by flood, earthquakes, volcanoes, landslides, nuclear radiation, and war.

The client should buy coverage suitable for the particular home. By far the most common losses are due to fire and theft. If the insured limits the property coverage to these, money will be saved on premiums. In addition, the deductible should be at least $500, maybe $1,000.

California experiences about two-thirds of all earthquakes in the U.S. If the home is located there, the homeowner should buy earthquake insurance. The lender may even require it.

In terms of personal property, such as furniture and clothes, the average policy does not cover "mysterious disappearances," wear and tear, gradual deterioration, insects and rodents, nor "inherent vice" (glass will break, bulbs will burn out). In addition, animals are excluded regardless of the cause of loss.

¶ 826 IMPORTANCE OF REPLACEMENT VALUE

The cash value (or fair market value) of the house and other possessions may be substantially less than their replacement cost. This is particularly true if the client has to replace used property with new. It is true that if a house burns down to the ground, the insured *could* buy a similar house of the same vintage in the same area for its cash value. However, if the destruction is partial, the client does not have the choice of buying new or used. One cannot rebuild or reconstruct second hand.

To make the homeowner's policy inflation-proof, an "inflation guard endorsement" must be added. This can be done for a 5%-7% increase in the premium, but it is not enough. Inflation increases based on the Consumer Price Index (CPI), for example, do not necessarily protect the insured fully. In many areas home prices have, on occasion, increased far faster than the general price level. Therefore, the client should consider a "Homeowners Replacement Cost and Inflation Protection Endorsement." Insuring for replacement cost, rather than cash value, is likely to cost about 15% more in premiums, but for a conservative homeowner, it is highly recommended. In any event, the client should review the coverage at least every two to three years.

¶ 827 INSURING AGAINST PERSONAL LIABILITY

Most people think of fire and theft of property, and little else, when homeowners insurance is mentioned. The personal liability coverage should not be forgotten. Here are some obvious and some less obvious situations which can occur and which a homeowner's insurance may cover:

1. A guest, delivery man or other invitee may be injured on the premises.
2. The dog may bite someone.
3. A child may injure a playmate with a toy.
4. A fire in the home may spread to other homes.

The client may injure another while playing golf, hunting, or riding (yes, these injuries may be covered).

In the client's situation, it may be best advised to have an "umbrella" policy which covers all personal liability everywhere.

¶ 828 USE OF "UMBRELLA" POLICIES

An "umbrella" policy covers the client for many kinds of personal liability, but not professional malpractice. It may go under the name of executive excess, executive umbrella, executive protector, etc. In the early years only physicians, lawyers, dentists, CPAs, etc., qualified. Today everyone can.

An executive once had car insurance with personal liability coverage of $500,000/$1,000,000 and another $500,000 through the homeowner's policy. Then the executive discovered "umbrella" insurance, took out a $1 million policy for $90 a year and cut the homeowner's insurance to $50,000 and the car insurance to $100,000/$300,000. Result: An increase in liability coverage and saved premiums.

The virtual necessity of carrying such a policy is caused by the following:

1. Many people are quite vulnerable to lawsuits, being in a high-income bracket with a visibly high status. People just do not sue paupers (unless they happen to know they are insured). On the other hand, the client does not have to be a millionaire to be sued like one. Accidents can happen in the home, the office, in traffic, or people may be sued for libel or slander.
2. To insure for various potential liabilities separately is more expensive than a "blanket" policy.
3. The policy picks up where other policies leave off. As a result the insured is typically required to carry minimum car and home insurance, such as $100,000/$300,000 on a car and $50,000 on a homeowner's policy. These limits vary from state to state and from company to company.
4. Umbrella policies are issued for $1 million and up. Three-million-dollar policies are common. The insured can rarely

obtain this kind of coverage through a homeowner's policy. Besides, the careful client wants comprehensive coverage for *all* activities.

Someone who gets hurt or injured looks around for someone with money to sue. This is the "deep pocket" theory. Make sure that, if someone gets a judgment against a client, it is the insurance carrier that pays, not the family.

¶ 829 HOW TO INCREASE COVERAGE

Here are some tips on obtaining more home insurance coverage:

1. *Shop* around. The insured may be able to obtain more coverage for the same premium.
2. *Review* the value of the home at least annually in times of rapid price increases. This is to make sure the home is at least 80% insured, so that under the co-insurance clause the client is fully covered for partial losses. The client should, of course, be 100% insured to be fully covered for a total loss.
3. *Add a "floater policy"* to cover jewelry, art, and other valuables. Certain collectibles are irreplaceable, but all the client can do is to insure cash values, which are often subjective. Without a "floater" the coverage is typically limited to $1,000 for jewelry, $2,500 for silverware, $200 for cash, $1,000 for securities, etc.
4. *Increase personal liability coverage* to $1 million or more through an umbrella policy. Consider paying for it by increasing the deductible. It is more important to be covered for large judgments than to only be covered for $15,000. The client may not even want insurance for affordable losses.

¶ 830 HOW TO SAVE ON CASUALTY AND LIABILITY INSURANCE

Here is a summary of basic ways to keep premiums down without losing needed coverage:

1. *Don't overinsure.* If the client overinsures, premiums are wasted, since the coverage is still limited to the loss suffered. By contrast, if the client is underinsured, coverage is incomplete. This is a bad way to save premiums.
2. *Pay the premiums* one, two, or even three years *in advance.* This gives the insured a lower annual cost.
3. *Use deductibles.* The client does not need insurance to cover a loss of $200 or $400, maybe not even $10,000. What must be protected against is the major financial risks, e.g., a $150,000

house burns down, or the client is sued for $2 million after a car accident. Yet most people use small deductibles and low maximum limits. It is not unlikely that the insured may be able to increase maximum liability coverage 10 times for the same premium, simply by doubling or tripling the deductible. Property damage coverage cost normally is 10% cheaper with a $250 deductible, 20% with a $500 deductible.

4. The best premiums on fire insurance can be obtained if
   (a) the house is built with fire-resistant materials;
   (b) there are several fire extinguishers;
   (c) the house is located within 1,000 feet from a fire hydrant and/or within five miles from a fire department;
   (d) the house is more than 10 feet from the next one; or
   (e) less than three families live in the house.
5. *Buy package policies.* Multiple policies are expensive.

The client needs a homeowner's policy, a car policy, and an umbrella policy. Low limits should be kept on the first two if the third is carried.

6. Live in a low crime area.
7. Valuable paintings, jewelry, coins, stamps, and the like are expensive to insure. Original bills or appraisals are needed. Small valuables the client rarely needs should be kept in a bank vault. Premiums may be cut by as much as 80%.

¶ 831 WHEN TO REVIEW INSURANCE COVERAGE

In addition to the annual or biannual review, property and casualty insurance coverage should be examined when

1. buying a home or a car;
2. moving, or even changing jobs;
3. acquiring anything expensive, from a boat to a mink coat, summer home, pool, or painting; or
4. property values appreciate.

¶ 832 HOW TO COLLECT ON A CLAIM

Here are some basic rules to follow to ensure that the client gets paid on time and pursuant to the promises in the policy:

1. *Buying the right policy* in the right amount in the first place. Anticipating probate needs, reading and *knowing* the policy before suffering a loss.

2. *Keeping inventories,* photos, and records of insured property, including serial numbers on things like television sets, typewriters, and the like in the event of loss.
3. *Minimizing losses* once they occur. Keeping fire extinguishers, calling the fire department, filing a police report in case of theft, making temporary repairs, etc.
4. *Following the claim procedures* in the policy. These may involve immediate written notice, notarized and sworn claim statements, filing a policy record, etc.
5. *Keeping records of losses,* if nothing else, for tax purposes. Casualty losses and medical expenses are deductible above certain limits.
6. *Seeking professional assistance.* If the insured has a complex claim, a *public adjuster* should be considered. This will cost 10%-15% of the settlement, but without one there may not be a settlement. A lawyer should be employed if personal injuries are involved. Lawyers often work on a contingent fee basis, e.g., for one-third of the settlement (plus expenses in any case).

Car Insurance

¶ 835 BENEFITS OF NOT OWNING A CAR

In terms of controlling car expenses, the first question to ask oneself is if a car is needed at all. Surprisingly often, the answer either is no or easily could be, if certain adjustments are made.

Consider the advantages of *not* owning a car:

1. There will be no car loans to pay off and the nondeductible depreciation is saved.
2. There will be no parking tickets, parking fees, or car insurance.
3. No time is wasted looking for parking space.
4. By reading on public transportation, the commuter may add up to two or three books a month on a reading list.
5. The client no longer has to worry about being caught driving under the influence.
6. No longer does the client have to dig the car out of the snow, have it towed away, change the oil, fill the gas tank, pay for car washes, change tires, waste time and money on repairs, etc.
7. No longer is it necessary to drive people home or give them rides because the client happens to have a car.

8. The client will contribute to the conservation of energy.
9. Life expectancy increases. Some 40,000 people a year are killed in car accidents in the U.S.

However, even if it is assumed that the client either needs a car in the business or wants one for convenience, the client should consider the use of a compact economy car. If gasoline is $1 a gallon and the client drives 30,000 miles a year, switching to a car which yields 30 miles a gallon rather than 15 mpg will save $1,000 a year in after-tax cash. In addition, money is saved on the purchase price, insurance, maintenance, and interest. Many people could save $2,000 or more a year in tax-free cash by using a smaller car. Unless the client is a giant, the slight inconvenience soon becomes unnoticeable.

¶ 836 NEED FOR CAR INSURANCE

Car insurance can be hard to get, hard to keep, and expensive to pay for, even though local law prevents unfair cancellation and non-renewals.

There are three good reasons to carry car insurance:

1. It is often illegal not to carry minimum personal injury and property protection.
2. If the car is purchased on credit, the buyer is required to buy insurance and keep the car insured. Eighty percent of cars purchased are financed by banks and loan companies.
3. A financial loss can be disastrous if the driver has no coverage, particularly in the personal injury area. In fact, car accident judgments against uninsured drivers are a major contributor to the one million personal bankruptcies filed in the U.S. each year.

No-fault insurance is rapidly becoming the norm since Massachusetts introduced it in 1970, meaning that an injured individual collects insurance benefits regardless of fault.

The goals of no-fault insurance are to reduce phony claims and the high legal fees resulting from contingent fee contracts. In the absence of no-fault insurance, a client injured due to someone else's negligence must meet with the claims adjuster of the other driver's insurance company.

SIX TYPES OF CAR INSURANCE

Car insurance can be broken down into six types, but all of them are rarely needed simultaneously:

1. *Bodily injury liability.* This coverage pays, up to the limit, for physical injuries caused by one's car to other people. The

minimum coverage offered is typically 10/20, meaning up to \$10,000 for one injured person but limited to \$20,000 for all persons injured in the same accident. This is incredibly low. The first \$1 million award to one plaintiff was awarded as early as 1936. To be able to sleep nights, the client should buy at least 100/300 coverage. It only costs about 50% more to increase the coverage about 10 times. It should be done unless the client is judgment proof. (See also umbrella liability insurance above.)

2. *Property damage.* Property is less expensive than people. Smashing up a car or three will probably only cost a few thousand dollars, and rarely will it cost more than \$20,000. Thus, the coverage should not run more than \$10,000—\$20,000 in most cases.

3. *Medical payments.* Chances are the client already has comprehensive medical coverage. If so, duplication should be avoided.

4. *Comprehensive coverage* (excluding collision). This covers the insured's car if it should be damaged or destroyed by *any thing:* rocks, flying objects, animals, floods, earthquakes, vandalism, explosions, hurricanes, hail-storms, riots, fire, and theft. The premium may be cut by as much as two-thirds simply by limiting the coverage to fire and theft. After the insured has owned the car for four years or so, comprehensive coverage may be dropped altogether because of the limited value remaining.

5. *Collision insurance.* This feature covers the cost of repairing or replacing the car if the insured bangs into another car or turns over. As with the comprehensive coverage, the client should consider dropping it after the car reaches its fourth birthday.

6. *Uninsured motorist coverage.* This protects an insured who "runs into" an uninsured driver. Thus, if the driver is liable but has no coverage, the client can still collect, but only for the personal injuries of the driver and any passengers. Property damage is typically excluded. The insured should carry enough coverage to match the liability coverage. The problem is the higher the cost of insurance, the fewer the drivers there are who buy insurance, and the more uninsured motorists, the higher the cost of insurance.

Other specialized coverage is available. One common rider is *towing* insurance, but, due to the limited expense involved, the coverage is rarely worth it.

CANCELLATION CLAUSES

The typical car insurance policy can be cancelled *by the company for any reason* the first 60 days. Once this probation period is over, a 30-day notice requirement is needed unless the following happens:

1. The insured, or a member of the household, has a driver's license suspended,
2. The insured suffers a heart attack or an epileptic seizure,
3. The insured commits three traffic violations within 18 months,
4. The insured is convicted of a felony,
5. The insured is found guilty of criminal negligence involving a motor vehicle, or
6. The insured is convicted of drunken driving.

Some companies issue *preferred risk* policies and enforce the above strictly. Others merely raise the rates.

¶ 837 RATING PROCESS

When buying car insurance, it is only right that the insured should pay a premium which reflects the risk of a person with the same characteristics.

Here are some factors which tend to increase premiums in order of decreasing severity:

1. Criminal convictions, being over age 75, being unemployed, being employed as an entertainer or a professional athlete, being physically disabled, or driving over 25,000 miles annually.
2. Getting a speeding ticket, being an unmarried male under age 25, owning a sports car, being an unskilled laborer, or being a student under age 25.
3. Being 66 to 70 years old or in the armed forces.
4. Having had a driver's license for less than three years, driving a car more than three years old, or having committed a moving violation.

¶ 838 SAVINGS CHECKLIST

To cut the cost of car insurance, the following should be considered:

1. Buy only needed coverage. This entails dropping comprehensive and collision coverage once a car is at least three or four years old. The insured may even consider a $25,000 deductible on personal injury liability. However, the maximum should be high, even $500,000 or more.

2. Claim every possible discount. This includes multiple car insurance, "safe driving" (merit-rating) plans, group plans, young driver plans, nonsmoking plans, nondrinking plans, etc.
3. Shop around for the cheapest rates. This may be delegated to an independent agent who offers a wide variety of insurance choices.
4. Don't use a high-powered car or a sports car.
5. Don't submit small claims.
6. Pay the premiums annually.
7. Keep the car in good condition.
8. Keep a car which is easily serviced and for which parts are readily available.
9. Get special discounts for installing special safety features like audible theft alarm and damage-proof bumpers.
10. Suspend coverage if the car is out of service for months.
11. When renting a car, skip optional collision insurance.
12. Notify the insurer when teenagers leave home. A discount may result.
13. Stop driving to work. The insurance will be lower. Better yet, never use the car within city limits. The rate will be reduced immediately. On the other hand, if the insured starts using a car long-distance, the rate will go up at the next premium renewal, maybe 11 months hence.
14. Car pools are fine, but if passengers for hire are taken, the insurance does not provide coverage.
15. Buy the insurance by *mail* if possible, for it will be cheaper.
16. Take advantage of special rates if mileage is less than 6,500 miles a year.
17. Get a special discount if over age 65.
18. Middle-aged executives who are married, have children, and have a good driving record may qualify for the lowest possible rates.
19. Note that car insurance premiums can vary by as much as 90%. However, if the service is good the insured should hesitate to change companies. If the client has had a recent accident, it is generally a waste of time to try shopping around.

20. Get a "safe-driving" plan if possible, but remember that the premium may jump 40% immediately if any driver of an insured car is
    (a) convicted of a traffic violation resulting in a loss or suspension of license,
    (b) is involved in an accident involving bodily injury, or
    (c) is involved in an accident causing property damage in excess of $100.

Once the premium is increased, the new level is effective for at least three years. Therefore, a "merit plan" may prove more expensive in the long run.

21. Make sure the insurance stays in force after the insured moves to another state.
22. Make sure the policy automatically covers a replacement car after a sale. Some policies require notice to the insurer within 30 days of a replacement; others automatically lapse.

¶ 839 WHAT TO DO IF TURNED DOWN FOR CAR INSURANCE

It should be kept in mind that there is a course of action if turned down for car insurance. First, it is difficult to be turned down, but the rate may be several times the minimum. But if the client's driver's license was recently suspended, the client may be rejected. If so, here is what the client should do:

1. Try another company.
2. If several companies refuse insuring for standard rates, take advantage of the so-called "Assigned Risk Plans," also called "Automobile Insurance Plans," which are available in each state.

   Under these plans, the insured is treated as an assigned risk. Each company licensed in a state is obligated to accept a certain number of applicants with a bad arrest and/or accident record. The premium may be three times the normal premium.

SAMPLE AUTO INSURANCE BILL

Although the bill will vary by person, car, time, and place, the following shows the components of the typical (annual) car insurance bill:

Bodily Injury Liability ($100,000 per person, $300,000 per accident)	$250
Property Damage Liability ($25,000 per accident)	100
Personal Injury Protection (PIP) ($100,000, no deductible)	75

Uninsured Motorist ($100,000 per person, $300,000 per accident)	50
Comprehensive	100
Collision ($500 deductible)	125
Additional Expense ($30 per day, $750 maximum)	10
TOTAL	$710

¶ 840 ECONOMICS OF NOT FILING A CLAIM

Under state law, every accident, however small, even if only minor property damage is involved, must be reported to the police. Failure to report an accident is a *crime.* But this does not mean the insured must file a claim with the insurance company. On the other hand, every accident involving personal injury should be reported to the company. A plaintiff may have as much as six years to sue, or, if a minor, until reaching majority. If the insured did not file a report, personal liability may result. If only minimal damage resulted, such as a bump, the insured may actually save money by not filing a claim. Of course, if the "deductible" is higher than the repair bill, the client won't collect even if filing a report. But even if the bill exceeds the deductible, the insured may save premiums by not filing a small claim.

Business casualty losses are deductible in full for tax purposes to the extent not compensated for by insurance. However, personal casualty losses are also each reduced by $100 before the total annual net losses are reduced further by 10% of adjusted gross income.[1] It should also be emphasized that personal casualty losses are nondeductible if covered by insurance *even if an insurance claim is not filed.*[2] In such cases, therefore, the casualty loss deduction is limited to the "deductible" (the self-insured portion) less $ 100 and less 10% of AGI.

[1] Code Sec. 165.

[2] Code Sec. 165(h)(4)(E).

CHAPTER 9

EQUITY INVESTMENTS

Stocks

¶ 901 INTRODUCTION

In this chapter equity investments are defined as stocks, as well as hybrid securities and derivative assets, deriving part or all of their value from being exchangeable or convertible into stock. Thus, convertible bonds, convertible preferred stocks, warrants, and put and call options are described. Investors in stocks must face the fact that there is no infallible way to pick a stock. While general principles are known, such as: "When interest rates go down, stock prices go up," or "Buy stock with low price-earnings ratios, selling below book value with a high cash flow per share," and "use dollar cost averaging," this is about as far as it goes. Therefore, the primary emphasis in this chapter is on proven investment *strategies* combining two or more investment positions, such as the writing of covered calls and "naked" puts, the use of convertible or warrant hedges, as well as practical information about brokers, mutual funds, and the use of margin accounts.

¶ 902 INVESTING IN STOCKS

Preferred stocks can safely be dismissed summarily for individual investors for the following reasons:

1. The investor gives up the relative safety of a bond to receive the stipulated dividend, which, unlike interest, needs never be paid.
2. The investor gives up the appreciation potential of common stock, because the preferred does not share in the good for-

tunes of the company to the same extent as the common due to the fixed dividend.

There are also several reasons *not* to buy *common* stocks:

1. The average dividend yield on stocks is generally less than the interest rate on savings accounts.
2. Despite fluctuations, long-term appreciation has on the average been less than the rate of inflation.
3. Common stocks are riskier than other securities, except for options to buy or sell stock, which are the riskiest of all.
4. An investor who is a corporate insider may be in a position to profit economically. Unfortunately, any profit made within six months belongs to the corporation under Code Sec. 16(b) of the Securities Exchange Act of 1934.

There are, however, some situations in which the investor should consider stocks:

1. If the employer *gives* the client stocks in the employer corporation, either outright or in the form of options, participation units or an interest in an Employee Stock Ownership Plan (ESOP), there is no reason to refuse, unless there is a choice of benefits.
2. In order to write covered calls (discussed below), the investor must maintain a long position. In most cases the client will buy the stock, but not before checking whether a suitable convertible is available.
3. A client who believes that the market can be consistently outguessed should try it. Unfortunately, a crystal ball is required to do so.

Traditionally, investors have been advised to look for three benefits in an investment: (1) safety of principal, (2) a good income, and (3) capital appreciation.

Stocks have never been safe, and they rarely yield high dividends. Someone in a high tax bracket does not necessarily want dividends. However, everyone *does* want appreciation. Since 1993, the maximum capital gains rate is 28%, even as tax rates on ordinary income reached a high of 39.6%. Many stock portfolios have gone up in the last two decades, but in a very uneven fashion. Adjusted for inflation, the stock market is probably lower at any given time than at the peak in 1929, applying the Dow Jones Industrial Average Index.

¶ 903 DOLLAR COST AVERAGING

It sounds trivial, but, to come out ahead, the investor must buy low and sell high. In addition, an investor should beat the market. Both of these objectives can be accomplished methodically, through the use of dollar cost averaging. The trick is to:

1. invest the same *amount* each time,
2. buy the same *stock* each time, and
3. buy at regular intervals.

The investor may apply the program to more than one stock, or diversify through the purchase of mutual fund shares. In order to be successful, the program relies on fluctuations. The stock does *not* have to go up above the initial value.

> ***Example:*** The client invests $300 a month in a low priced stock. One month the price is $5, the next it is $3. The average price is clearly $4, but what is the average cost? The client invested $600 and purchased 160 shares.
>
> $$\left(\frac{\$300}{\$\ 5} + \frac{\$300}{\$\ 3}\right)$$
>
> Thus, the average price paid was $3¾, less than the average price. If the third month the price is $4 and the fourth month the price is back up to $5 and the stock is sold, there is a profit as follows:
>
> | | |
> |---|---|
> | Proceeds: $5 × 235 | $1,175 |
> | less cost | 900 |
> | Profit | $ 275 |
>
> Since the average price paid is about $3.83, even a sale at $4 will produce a profit. The magic is simply that, by investing a constant amount, the investor automatically purchases more shares when the market is low, and fewer when the price is higher. It is obvious that the more volatile the stock, the less it has to recover to produce a profit. Had the client simply used a buy and hold strategy at one point in time, the investor could not produce a profit unless the price went up. Thus, it should not be difficult to beat the market.

¶ 904 AVOID TRADING

Once a stock is purchased, it should not be sold without careful consideration. If round-trip commissions are 2% of value, paying one round-trip commission monthly on a stock portfolio will wipe out one-quarter of the client's capital in a year. This is not to say that one should never sell. The investor may want a tax loss, or an option that had been written may be exercised.

¶ 905 DIVERSIFICATION

Diversification can take place in many ways, all of which can be achieved simultaneously. The investor may:

1. Invest in different vehicles, e.g., real estate and securities, or stocks and bonds.
2. Diversify stocks by investing in different industries from fast food to electronics.
3. Diversity *over time* by buying the same security at various prices or employing the same strategy at various times, such as writing calls weekly and monthly.
4. Buy mutual fund shares, preferably no-load funds, on which there is no sales commission. A client who diversifies may never make a killing but can sleep nights.

¶ 906 KEY STATISTICS—ANALYSIS

To buy sound values and stocks that are likely not to lose much ground, the following factors should be watched:

1. Everything else being equal, the price-earnings ratio (P/E) should be as low as possible. Theoretically, the price of a stock is equal to the discounted present value of future earnings. Since the future is by nature unpredictable, the client may be protected by buying low P/E stock. At least such stock is less vulnerable to bad news than high P/E stock.
2. The dividend-price ratio (D/P) should be as high as possible if the investor likes current income. A stock with a solid history of dividends is also likely to stay above a reasonable minimum.
3. Recent price increases do not represent good news, unless the investor owned it at the time. The higher the recent growth, the less likely it is that the growth can be sustained, and the more likely it is that the stock is overpriced with a high P/E and a low D/P. The time to buy the stock is *before,* not after, a price increase.
4. If the stock is selling *below book value,* so much the better, particularly if the assets are worth more than the numbers in the financial statements. Market values are often higher because of inflation, because goodwill does not appear unless purchased, because some assets have been fully depreciated or written off, etc. Stocks backed by assets are less vulnerable than stocks backed solely by perceived future earnings.

The ideal stock has the following characteristics:

(a) A dividend yield in excess of 5%.

(b) A price-earnings ratio below 7.

(c) A current asset to current liabilities ratio over 2.

(d) A book value per share higher than the stock price.

(e) A return on equity in excess of 18%.

(f) Net current assets in excess of the stock price.

Even four out of six is a solid buy. The ratio approach compares favorably with less scientific methods often recommended, such as buying the stock if the investor likes the product, or buying stocks in companies with headquarters close to home. Investors who care about facts relating to the company, industry, and economy are referred to as *fundamentalists*. Their bible is "Security Analysis" by Benjamin Graham and David L. Dodd. Published in 1934, it is still in print. People who feel that everything is reflected in the price of the stock and simply track price movements are referred to as *technical analysts*.

BUY INVESTMENTS, NOT MARKET LETTERS

As a general rule, expensive subscriptions represent wasted money, except for the tax savings when deducted as itemized expenses. One exception is a good convertible, warrant, and option service, such as Value Line, if the client needs information on volatility, conversion value premiums, exercise terms, etc., not available in the financial pages. The Oxbridge Directory of Newsletters contains a complete list of market letters and the Hulbert Financial Digest picks the best performing newsletters each year.

THE MARKET HAS NO MEMORY

There is substantial evidence that the stock market behaves in an unpredictable, random fashion. This is because 1,001 types of news affect the stock market, from the assassination of a president to interest rates and war news. A stock does not go up tomorrow because it did so today. Nor does it know who owns it. The stock should be purchased when it represents good value and sold when it no longer does.

STOCK DIVIDENDS AND SPLITS HAVE NO VALUE IN THEMSELVES

A 2-for-1 split means that all shareholders double their number of shares at the same time. The shareholder owns the same piece of the action. Similarly, a 5% stock dividend means that everybody owns 5% more pieces of paper in the same entity. No one is enriched, except the printers. Wealth cannot be created by issuing more stocks to share in the same assets and earnings.

TAKE ADVANTAGE OF TAX BENEFITS

On the average, everyone picks the same stock. All stocks are owned by the market. Someone who owns several stocks owns the market. Mutual funds cannot beat the market; they *are* the market. There are no proven ways to consistently pick the winners. One thing an investor can do is to consistently use every tax benefit available to investors. The timing of sales alone can put the investor ahead of the game *after taxes* only if breaking even before taxes on the average.

¶ 907 SHORT SALES

Selling property an investor does not own, which, in the case of securities, is generally borrowed through a broker, is known as selling short. Securities should be sold short under only two conditions:

1. As part of a hedge, such as a convertible hedge or option strategy, as discussed below.

2. To lock in a paper gain and postpone the taxation of it through a short sale "against the box."

The reasons *not* to sell short are:

1. The short seller must borrow the securities sold short from some other account through a broker. As a result, the lender must be reimbursed for any distributions made on the securities. In other words, the investor *pays* dividends or interest, rather than *collecting* them.

2. A listed stock cannot be sold short unless the price increased the last time it moved (an "uptick").

3. An investor who is an officer, director, or 10% or more shareholder is a corporate insider. A short sale of the corporation's stock is illegal under Code Sec. 16(c) of the Securities Exchange Act of 1934.

4. The short seller is putting a ceiling on potential winnings, since the stock can only become worthless, but the upside risk is potentially unlimited.

5. Although a short position theoretically may remain open indefinitely (unless the security expires or matures), any gain or loss will be short term. The holding period cannot start until stock is purchased, e.g., when the short position is closed out.

6. If the security is not readily available, the short seller may have to pay a fee or premium to the lending broker.

ILLUSTRATION OF A SHORT SALE "AGAINST THE BOX"

In October, a shareholder owns stock which has gone up from $10,000 to $15,000. The investor wishes to lock in the gain, but defer the tax until next year. If the stock is sold short for $15,000, the $5,000 gain is frozen, regardless of what happens to the price. When the short sale is covered in January (i.e., when the long position is delivered to the lender of the short stock), the gain is recognized for tax purposes. If the price went down to $10,000 in the meanwhile, the loss on the "long" stock is offset by the gain on the short position. Similarly, an increase to $20,000 would be offset by the loss on the short sale. Note that the investor locked in the exact gain existing at the time of the short sale.

¶ 908 USE OF MARGIN

Investing on margin means borrowing to invest, i.e., the investor is employing financial leverage. The use of margin will magnify gains and losses as a percentage of the cash investment in proportion to the reciprocal of the margin requirements. This means that a 10% change in price will double the money invested or lose it all if the investor only put up 10%, but will yield a return of 20% or a loss of 20% on 50% margin. Only an investor using margin can lose more than the investment. This is because the investor is personally liable for any deficit in the account.

When securities are purchased on margin, they are kept by the broker as collateral for the loan, i.e., in "street name." This means, for example, that the broker receives one check for dividends or interest paid on a given security held by the firm. The broker must then distribute the payment among the different margin accounts. Most investors keep their securities with their broker, even if they are fully paid for. This is less risky than in the past, because the account is insured within limits through the Securities Investors Protection Corporation (SIPC).

The broker does not have the cash to lend and therefore borrows money wholesale, at the prime rate, lending it to investors at one-half to two percentage points above retail. To obtain the loan, the broker puts up the customers' securities as collateral. (This is called rehypothecation.) Margin accounts are debited daily for the margin interest, i.e., the rate paid is compounded daily.

As a practical matter, a margin account is required:

1. to trade commodities,
2. to engage in short sales, and
3. to write options.

On the other hand, the following cannot be purchased on margin:

1. Puts, calls and rights.
2. Stocks that are not listed and not on the Federal Reserve Board's list of approved over-the-counter securities.
3. Low priced stocks or warrants, typically $5 or under.

Even a client who maintains a margin account should also have a *cash account* because interest and dividends paid on securities bought on margin can be transferred to the cash account. This allows a more intensive use of capital.

The use of margin tends to amplify both bull and bear markets. Purchasing power is increased as prices go up, leading to additional buying. When prices fall, the account holder may be forced to sell securities to meet a margin call. This flies in the face of the ancient dictum: Buy low, sell high.

Margin requirements are imposed by three sources:

1. The Federal Reserve Board sets the *initial* margin requirements (Regulations T, U and G).
2. The New York Stock Exchange sets its own margin, particularly the *maintenance* margin.
3. Each brokerage house has its own house rules, which cannot be less than above, but they often are tougher.

The initial margin on stocks varies from time to time, but is typically 50%, while the maintenance margin is typically 30% for both long and short positions. If the equity in the account falls below the maintenance margin, a *margin call* results. Unless the investor puts up more money or securities, the broker is authorized to sell enough securities to bring the equity up to 30%. The customer gives the broker this authority and the right to borrow securities to facilitate the short sale of another when signing the *margin agreement*.

Many successful investors have never seen a stock certificate, perhaps not even a broker. An investor who wishes to open an account can simply *call* a broker. The broker will mail the necessary forms, and the new customer fills them out and mails them back with a check. A few days later, the account holder can buy and sell on the phone. A client who wishes to change brokers may simply fill out a transfer of account form.

¶ 909 MARGIN RULES IN OPERATION

The following are examples of the margin rules in operation:

Example 1: *Purchase of stocks.* An investor buys stock for $10,000 and must put up $5,000 plus commissions. Each day the account will be charged interest on the $5,000 loan, which remains constant. If the stock goes up to $15,000, the account holder may remove $2,500 in cash or purchase another $5,000 worth of stock on margin. If the price goes down, the *equity* in the account must be at least 30% of the market value of the account. Thus, if the stock falls to $7,000, equity is only $2,000 ($7,000 less $5,000). As a percentage of the market value, it is only 28.57%. A margin call will result.

Example 2: *Short sale of stock.* An investor who sells stock short with a value of $10,000 must also put up $5,000 plus commissions. However, since the short seller did not buy anything, the $5,000 is merely a deposit, and there will be no interest charges. Any paper loss on the short sale will increase the overall debt balance. The $10,000 received when the stock is sold, in effect, belongs to the lender of the stock and remains in a special *short sale account.* This account must always show 100% of the market value. If the stock goes down by $2,000, a like amount of paper profit results. The short seller may withdraw up to $3,000 in cash as follows:

	Reduction of required short sale account	$2,000
+	Reduction in initial margin, 50% of $2,000	1,000
	Excess cash withdrawable	$3,000

If the price moves up by $2,000, there is a paper loss and the short seller must put up more money, as follows:

	The minimum maintenance margin is 30% of $12,000 or	$3,600
−	What is left of the initial margin $5,000 less $2,000	3,000
	Additional margin required to avoid closing out	$ 600

If the short seller does not put up the extra capital, the short position will be closed out automatically and the remaining $3,000, less commissions, is left.

Convertible Bonds

¶ 915 INTRODUCTION

The convertible bond was introduced to the U.S. in the 1840s by the railroad industry, but did not become widespread until the 1960s. It is like a straight bond with something added: the bondholder has the right, called the *conversion privilege,* to exchange it for stock at any time. Thus, the investor may hold on to the bond and collect interest every six months and sell it or hold it to maturity. Alternatively, the investor may surrender the bond to the issuer, typically through a broker, in exchange for a fixed number of shares, the *conversion ratio,* which does not depend on market values. This conversion ratio, say 20 shares, is often expressed as a *conversion price*. Thus, if par is $1,000, a conversion price of $50 would correspond to a conversion ratio of 20 shares since 20 shares times $50 equals $1,000.

¶ 916 WHY BUY CONVERTIBLE BONDS?

The investor should always look for a convertible bond before buying the stock, since some or all of the following advantages may exist:

1. A bond pays interest regularly, while the underlying stock may pay little or no dividends, and only at the discretion of the board of directors.
2. If the convertible bond is purchased below par on the market, a gain will automatically result if it is held to maturity and redeemed by the issuer.
3. Brokerage commissions are invariably lower on bonds, including convertibles, than on stocks.
4. If the underlying stock declines in value, the bond is still going to be worth its debt or bond value (the present value of the future interest payments and principal payment). Thus, the convertible limits downside risk without putting a ceiling on the appreciation potential.
5. The convertible bond represents a debt instrument, although usually unsecured. As a result, the bondholder enjoys priority above the shareholders in liquidation if the issuer goes out of business.

   On the other hand, the investor invariably winds up paying something for the conversion privilege:

   (a) The typical convertible bond is a *subordinated debenture,* i.e., it is unsecured and subject to the claims of all senior creditors and other unsecured creditors.

   (b) The interest paid is lower than on comparable straight bonds.

It should also be noted that the conversion price is commonly substantially in excess of the stock price at the time of issue.

¶ 917 CONVERTING A CONVERTIBLE BOND

The general rule and an old Wall Street adage says: "Never convert a convertible bond." Here are the reasons:

1. The accrued interest is lost if the bond is converted prior to the interest payment date.

2. The *conversion premium,* e.g., any excess value of the bond over the value of the underlying stock, is lost.
3. The bondholder incurs postage and handling charges.
4. It is cheaper to sell the convertible bond than the underlying stock.
5. It is never necessary to convert the bond to realize any gains, since the value will always reflect the *conversion value,* e.g., the price of the stock on which it confers an option.
6. Historically, the margin requirements for the stock have never been lower than for the convertible bond, but they have often been higher.
7. Conversion itself may lead to a taxable gain if the bond is convertible into securities of another company.

On the other hand, conversion may have to be considered if:

1. The bond is called for redemption (all convertibles are callable by the issuer at the *call price,* which is a few percentage points above par) and the stock value exceeds the call price. This is called a "forced conversion" since the investor would rather have, for example, $1,300 worth of stock, than cash of $1,050.
2. The dividends on the common stock are increased to a level in excess of the interest on the bond and the bondholder still likes the company.
3. The bond is about to mature and the conversion value exceeds its maturity value.
4. The conversion privilege is about to expire, which it sometimes does prior to maturity, and the stock is worth more than the bond value floor.
5. The conversion ratio is due to be decreased and the stock value exceeds the bond value.

INVESTMENT STRATEGIES INVOLVING CONVERTIBLE BONDS

Here are some of the many investment possibilities:

1. The convertible may simply be purchased and held for its interest and capital appreciation potential, coupled with downside risk protection. Deep discount bonds may be purchased for their high yields to maturity, but hardly for common stock potential.
2. The convertible may be used in *option writing* programs. Typically, calls are sold on the underlying stock which results in income from the premiums collected with good risk protection in both bull and bear markets.

3. A *convertible hedge* may be established, typically by buying the convertible and selling the underlying stock short. The convertible is sufficient margin for the short position, so that no additional investment is required. If the stock price declines, the short position can be closed out at a gain, while the hedger holds on to the convertible with a view to doing it again! Should the price increase initially, losses on the short side are balanced by the gains on the convertible. If the price bounces back after a successful sale, the hedger may sell short again.

4. *Arbitrage* is sometimes possible (the simultaneous purchase and sale of equivalent assets at a risk-less profit). For example, the conversion value may exceed the market value due to market imperfections. If so, the stock is sold short when the bond is purchased. Then the bond is converted and the stock used to cover the short position at a riskless profit.

TYPICAL PRICE RELATIONSHIPS

Here are examples of what happens to a convertible bond when stock prices are very low, normal, and very high:

	Low	*Normal*	*High*
Debt value	$700	$ 700	$ 700
Conversion value	300	950	1,400
Market value	700	990	1,400
Conversion value premiums	400	40	0
Bond value premiums	0	290	700

The inverse relationship between the premiums can be seen. If the stock is very low, the convertible will be priced as a straight bond. But if the stock value far exceeds its bond value, the bond premium is higher per definition. At this point, no premium over conversion value will exist, since the bond can be called any time and the downside risk protection has diminished greatly. The market value of a convertible can be regarded as the higher of:

1. The bond value plus the value of the options to buy the underlying stock, or

2. The conversion value plus the value of the downside risk protection.

¶ 918 PUT AND CALL ASPECTS OF THE CONVERTIBLE BOND

A *call* is an option to buy stock at a given price for a given time period, while a put is an option to sell stock at a given price for a given time. In effect, a convertible bond contains both options! Take the above '"normal" example. The bond could be viewed as a straight bond, worth $700, plus an "in the money" call worth $290. Of the $290, $250 is the immediate exercise value of the options with the remaining $40 representing the time value of the calls.

Conversely, the "low" example illustrates the put options aspect of the bond. The bond holder indirectly owns stock worth $300, but because of the $700 bond value may at any time sell the underlying stock by exercising the put and thereby selling the bond. The "exercise price" (bond value) is not a constant, however, but will gradually approach par as maturity draws near and, in addition, will fluctuate with changes in interest rates. It will, however, be largely unaffected by changes in the stock price.

¶ 919 CONVERTIBLE PREFERRED STOCK

Like a convertible bond, the convertible preferred bond is convertible into the common stock of the issuer at the conversion ratio at the option of the holder and is callable by the issuer at the call price. Here are the main differences between convertible bonds and convertible preferred:

1. Unlike a convertible bond, which is a debt instrument, the convertible preferred makes the owner an equity holder both before and after conversion.
2. The bond has a par value which is a debt due at maturity. The preferred may have any par, including no par, like common stock, and the par value, if any, is not payable at a future date.
3. The bond has a maturity date while the preferred does not. It remains outstanding until called, converted, cancelled, or redeemed in liquidation.
4. Failure to pay interest on bonds constitutes default, while preferred dividends are paid only at the discretion of the board of directors. Even though the dividend is fixed, either as a dollar amount or as a percentage of par, this ordinarily just puts a maximum yield on the instrument. Most preferred are *cumulative,* which merely means that dividends in arrears must be paid before any dividends are paid to the common shareholders. It does *not* mean that payments are certain.
5. Due to the lack of principal payments and interest, the preferred does not have a readily computable bond or debt value. This, in turn, prevents the instrument from providing the same downside risk protection as the convertible bond.

6. The bond holder as a creditor has a claim on assets in liquidation ahead of the equity holders which include the holders of convertible preferred.
7. On the other hand, preferred stock often carries voting rights. Bonds never do.
8. Preferred stock may be *participating,* i.e., its holders may share in dividends paid to common shareholders above certain limits.
9. Brokerage commissions payable on preferred parallel those payable on common and are therefore higher than on bonds.
10. The bond contract, the *indenture,* often provides for *sinking fund* payments to be made to a trustee to assure available funds for debt retirement. Few preferred stock agreements provide for the accumulation of retirement funds.

In conclusion, the individual investor is generally better off with a convertible bond than the preferred. The convertible preferred does not have the safety features of the bond because of the absence of interest and principal payments. At the same time, the appreciation potential is the same function of the underlying common stock in the case of both convertibles.

¶ 920 TAX ASPECTS OF CONVERTIBLES

If the convertible bond is converted into the underlying stock of the issuer, the investor is deemed to continue the original investment. As a result, no gain or loss is to be reported. Therefore, whatever is paid for the convertible becomes the cost basis in the common stock. The holding period, used to determine whether a short- or long-term gain or loss ultimately results, continues to run uninterrupted.[1]

Warrants

¶ 925 INTRODUCTION

Unlike convertible bonds which have an intrinsic value in themselves apart from the underlying common stock, the warrant does not. A warrant is merely an option, issued by a corporation, often as a bonus with bonds, preferred stock or common stock, or as a dividend. The typical warrant is an option on one share of common stock of the issuer, has a life of several years and has an exercise price in excess of the price of common at the time of issue. The warrant may be exercised any time by surrendering it, plus the exercise price to the issuer by the expiration date. The warrant pays no dividends, has no voting rights, nor any

[1] Code Sec. 1223.

claim on assets. As a matter of fact, they do not even show up on the financial statements of the issuer, except in footnotes.

¶ 926 WARRANTS AND CONVERTIBLES COMPARED

Convertible bonds have several advantages over common stock, notably the higher intrinsic value, the current yield, and lower transaction costs. The convertible preferred almost always displays the first advantage only, but the warrant not even that. But the warrant is more volatile, i.e., the leverage is higher. Like other options, the warrant is primarily a side bet on the performance of the underlying common.

¶ 927 WHAT TO LOOK FOR WHEN BUYING WARRANTS

Since the financial pages in a newspaper only give simple price and trading volume data, a good warrant service should be consulted to verify the following:

1. How many shares (including fractional shares) is the warrant exercisable into?
2. When does it expire?
3. Are the exercise terms due to change, or are they changeable? Some warrants have reducible exercise prices and/or postponable expiration dates.
4. Is the warrant protected fully against dilution from stock splits, stock dividends, mergers, spin-offs, and the like?
5. Some warrants are callable, some never expire, and some have unique terms, such as being exercisable through the tender of bonds, e.g., the exercise price is payable either in cash or usable securities, at the investor's option.

A good candidate for a purchase should have the following characteristics:

1. It should be listed, which makes it more probable that the market has depth, i.e., liquidity, and that it can be purchased on margin.
2. It should have a remaining life of at least three years.
3. The smaller the price of the warrant in relation to the common, the higher the leverage and the lower the downside risk.
4. The common stock should have a good appreciation potential.
5. Dividends should be low, since paying the shareholders does not do the warrantholder any good, but also limits price appreciation, given earnings per share.

¶ 928 MAIN WARRANT INVESTMENT STRATEGIES

Like convertibles, the warrant may be employed in several investment programs or strategies, such as:

1. The straight purchase of warrants for their leverage. But note that the stock must increase in value before expiration merely to compensate for the loss of time value.
2. The investor may buy warrants and treasury bills (or other safe bonds) to achieve the upside appreciation potential of the common at less risk.
3. The speculator may sell warrants short if they are expected to expire worthless. The best candidates are warrants which are due to expire within a year and have an exercise price well above the common price.
4. Warrants may be used for hedging purposes.

Like the convertible, the warrant purchase can margin a short sale of the associated common. In addition, a short sale of warrants may be coupled with a purchase of the common to provide upside protection.

¶ 929 TAX ASPECTS OF WARRANTS

If a warrant is sold, the result is a gain or loss. A loss will result if the warrant is allowed to lapse.

The cost of a warrant is what is paid for it, but if it came in a package, e.g., with a bond or stock, the cost of the package must be allocated between the warrants and the other securities in proportion to the respective market values.

If a warrant is exercised, the cost of the warrant plus the exercise price paid for the stock constitute the cost of the stock.

¶ 930 HEDGING WITH CONVERTIBLES AND WARRANTS

The upside and/or downside volatility are typically different for the convertible or warrant than for the underlying stock. This makes it possible to enter into potentially profitable hedges with full protection on the downside, upside or both.

ILLUSTRATION OF HOW HEDGES ARE CONSTRUCTED

Leverage projections are easily obtainable from good convertible and option services. Assume that a convertible bond, convertible preferred or warrant is projected to change its price in the following fashion:

If the common moves	+ 50% + 25% − 25% − 50%
the convertible would move	+ 40% + 20% − 10% − 20%

BULLISH HEDGE

If the hedger wishes to make the maximum profit from a price increase in the convertible, but with full downside risk protection, the hedger must sell some of the common stock short. Since the projected downside move for the convertible is only 40% of the potential decline in the common, the hedger would short common with a value of 40% of the value of the convertible. If the price goes up by 50%, the 40% profit on the convertible is reduced by a loss on the short position of 20% (50% times the 40% shorted). In other words, the hedger gives up half the profit, if any, for full protection.

BEARISH HEDGE

Since the projected increase in the convertible is 80% of the common, a short sale of the common in an amount of 80% of the value of the convertible will provide full protection on the upside. If the price declines, say 50%, the profit on the short sale of the common will be 40% of the value of the convertible (50% times 80%) reduced by the decline of 20% in the value of the convertible, or 20% overall. Note that no additional investment is required for the short position, except transaction costs.

NEUTRAL HEDGE

If the hedger desires a profit regardless of the direction of a price move in the common, the ratio to be shorted equals the sum of the projected upside and downside move in the convertible at the 50% level. Thus, the investor would have to short 60% of the value of the convertible (40% plus 20%). If the price of common went up 50%, the net profit would be 10% (40% on the long convertible less 50% times 60% on the short sale of common). Similarly, on a downside move of 50%, the net profit would be 10% (a gain of 50% times 60% on the short sales less a 20% loss on the convertible). Thus, a gain can be virtually guaranteed, but only if most of it is hedged away.

Understanding these hedging principles opens the door for participation in the increasingly popular option market to be discussed next.

Puts and Calls (Options)

¶ 935 GROWTH OF THE OPTIONS MARKET

Options, known as puts and calls, have been used by knowledgeable investors in the U.S. for many decades. Until 1973, the options were only traded in the Over-the-Counter (OTC) market, which still exists. Each OTC option is unique and there is a direct contractual link between the buyer and seller. On April 26, 1973, the Chicago Board Options Exchange (the CBOE) became the first exclusive options exchange in the world. Several other exchanges have followed suit. The reasons for the spectacular success of listed options are:

1. Puts and calls can be used in a variety of investment strategies, ranging from the highly complex to the simple, and from the most conservative to the highly risky. Options are within reach of anyone, regardless of income level.
2. Expiration dates and striking (exercise) prices have been standardized with two results:
   (a) The option markets have become more liquid; and
   (b) With standard terms, there is no longer any necessity for any direct link between each buyer and seller. Consequently, the investor may terminate a position anytime by simply calling the broker and ordering an offsetting trade.

¶ 936 WHAT ARE PUTS AND CALLS?

Anyone who is capable of trading securities may also buy or sell options. Puts and calls may be regarded as side bets on the performance of the underlying stock and are independent of the corporate issuer of the stock. Anyone who cares to may originate (write or sell) or purchase an option through a regular margin account. Here is the basic vocabulary of options:

A *call* is an option to buy 100 shares of stock for the striking (exercise) price any time prior to expiration. Listed options expire quarterly with a maximum life of three quarters. OTC options are issued for up to two years, but convertibles and warrants are the only instruments which offer truly long-term options. Different exchanges use different expiration months, and some options are listed on more than one exchange.

A *put* is the opposite of a call, i.e., an option to sell 100 shares of stock at a fixed price for a given period of time. Theoretically, no one must ever buy or sell the stock merely because options are bought or sold.

An *"in the money" option* is one with a current exercise value, e.g., a call with a striking price below, or a put with a striking price above, the price of the underlying common. An "out of the money" option is the opposite, e.g., the price of common must move for the option to have more than mere speculative value.

The *premium* is the price paid for the option. Unless the option is "in the money," the whole premium is paid for the speculative time value of the option. A long-term option commands a higher premium than a short-term option, everything else being equal.

An *option writer* is the grantor-seller-originator of an option, and may be an individual, partnership, corporation, or other legal person. Option writers are not necessarily more conservative than option buyers, but they usually employ less risky strategies. Sellers and buyers also overlap, since writers often buy one option and sell another as a hedge.

A *covered writer* sells options against a commensurate position, such as writing calls while holding the stock or a security convertible into it, or writing puts while being short the stock.

A *"naked" writer* has no position complementing the option sale, and puts up the applicable margin in cash, letters of credit, or other securities.

A *spread* consists of simultaneous option writing and buying. The options are in the same stock, but with different expiration dates and/or striking prices. Being, in effect, long and short at the same time reduces potential gains and losses. Because of the reduced risk, the margin requirements are substantially less than for the independent positions.

¶ 937 OPTIONS MARKET AS A ZERO-SUM GAME

If the writer sells a call and the stock goes up, the appreciation is given up to the option holder. The "loss" is reduced by the premium received and the buyer's gain is reduced by the premium paid. This is similar to a zero-sum game, particularly if the seller wrote "naked" calls and actually sustains the loss. But, unlike in the commodity markets, where no wealth is created in the aggregate, everyone can come out ahead in the options markets. If calls are written against stocks, for example, and the price increases, the writer at least collects dividends and the premiums. The broker makes commissions and the call buyer enjoys gain.

¶ 938 ADVANTAGES OF OTC OPTIONS

The old, established OTC market in puts and calls still exists and should not be disregarded for the following reasons:

1. While a few hundred options are listed, several thousand securities are under OTC options.
2. The investor may tailor the option to specific needs, since there is great flexibility in expiration dates and striking prices.
3. Options exist, not only on common stock, but on convertibles and warrants. Buying a call on a warrant is buying an option

on an option, which is truly superleverage *and* with limited risk.

4. Listed options expire within nine months, but OTC options may last up to two years.

5. The investor may wish to engage in arbitrage transactions, such as buying a long-term OTC call, and writing listed calls on the same stock.

¶ 939 OPTION WRITING

Sophisticated investors are more likely to write options than to buy them (except as part of the writing strategy and in closing transactions). The fundamental reason is simply: It is better to receive the premium than to pay it. Because of the premium received, a careful writer may achieve both a higher return *and* a lower risk than the traditional "buy and hold" strategy. Note the following:

1. When an option is sold, the writer receives the cash the next day. But there are no tax consequences until something happens to the option, often the following year.

2. Because of the call premiums received, the writer will preserve capital in down markets and receive a limited, but respectable profit in sideways or up markets. It is good to know that a profit can result without an increase in the stock price. If "naked" puts are written, one of two things will happen. Either the writer receives stock at a discount from what was an excellent buy in the first place, or annualized returns on the cash investment as high as 50%.

3. The writer may select a strategy suited to any temperament and risk-profile, from the most aggressive to the most conservative. Covered calls and naked puts are among the conservative strategies, while writing "naked" calls is a high-risk strategy.

4. An option writer is running a business. Premiums are collected, almost like an insurance company, from buyers who pay to limit their risks. This is done without the need for an office, personnel, or license. What is needed is capital, know-how, and a broker, preferably one who is an expert on options.

5. A the client who believes that options writing merely is a form of legalized gambling may be relieved to know that they are written by mutual funds, college endowment funds, pension funds, as well as by trustees and other fiduciaries.

¶ 940 OPTION WRITING STRATEGIES

The number of option writing strategies is only limited by the investor's imagination. The main ones are discussed below. As a practical matter, any combination of strategies may be employed simultaneously, so that the investor can diversify three ways:

1. Over time, by not writing all options with the same expiration date.
2. Over securities and industries, by buying stocks in several different businesses.
3. Over strategies, by writing covered calls *and* "naked" puts, using convertibles, etc.

The most popular strategies are discussed at ¶ 941-946.

¶ 941 WRITING "NAKED" CALLS

The writer who has no upside protection is hoping that the price of the common stock will stay the same or go down, in which case the writer pockets the premium. The transaction offers the same risk exposure as a short sale of the stock. The potential loss is unlimited, but reduced by the premium, while the gain is limited to the premium. If the stock starts moving up, the writer could cover by either purchasing a call or the stock itself. Should the call be exercised and the writer still be "naked," the writer must either buy the stock to deliver to the holder or sell the stock short, i.e., borrow the stock and sell it to the exerciser. The investor's option agreement with the broker authorizes the latter to sell short on the writer's behalf if necessary, without asking permission first. Writing "naked" calls is a high-risk strategy, unsuited to investors who like to sleep nights.

¶ 942 WRITING COVERED CALLS

Writing covered calls means that the writer maintains a long position in the optioned stock, directly or indirectly, so as to be protected from price increases. Thus the writer may have purchased the stock itself or a convertible or other option, such as a convertible bond or preferred, or a warrant or other call. Convertible bonds can often best offer downside protection as well as upside protection. Most options are not exercised, since both sellers and buyers normally close out their positions on the exchange. OTC options must be exercised. If the writer owns the common stock and the call is exercised, the writer may simply deliver the stock or keep it and buy another lot. With indirect ownership, such as a convertible bond, no such choice exists. Since the writer does not have the stock, it must either be purchased at a loss (offset by the gain on the convertible), or be obtained through a short sale. The latter results in a convertible hedge, described above. But why not convert? There are two reasons:

1. The writer would lose the conversion value premium and accrued interest since the last payment date.

2. There is no time. It takes more time to convert because of round-trip mailing, etc., than the few days between the exercise notice and the settlement date.

Example: "Writer" purchases 100 shares of XYZ stock for $5,000, simultaneously writing a six-month call for $500. Disregarding transaction costs, "Writer" puts up cash of $2,000 (50% margin less the call premium paid in advance). If the price goes up or stays the same, the return for the six months is 25% ($500 on $2,000) or an annualized return of 50%. Whether the call is exercised or not, the gain is short-term. Dividends paid on the stock will add to the return, while interest on the margin account and transaction costs will reduce the return. If the price falls more than 10%, the paper loss will exceed the option premium, but the writer can sell another call.

¶ 943 WRITING "NAKED" PUTS

The strategy of "naked" puts is as conservative as the writing of covered calls and economically similar. The writer earns the premium if the stock moves up or stays the same, while on the downside the loss is reduced by the premium. "Naked" puts have the following advantages over covered calls:

1. If the stock does not move to favor the option buyer, transaction costs are saved, since the writer never needed to buy the stock in the first place.

2. Even though put premiums are generally lower than call premiums due to the demand for calls, the return may be higher. This is because no capital is tied up in the stock initially. The only time the writer winds up buying the stock is if the price goes down, the writer does not enter into a closing transaction, *and* the put is exercised. Even then, the writer may immediately sell the stock or keep it to write covered calls.

3. If covered calls are written and the calls become "out of the money," no purchasing power is generated in the account due to paper losses on the stock. But if "naked" puts become "out of the money," cash is released, since less margin is needed.

If the stock price begins to fall, the writer can either do nothing, hoping for a turnaround, engage in a closing transaction, sell short the stock to cover, or write additional puts to average down.

A stock should never be purchased without considering writing a put first. If the client was wrong in believing that the stock was attractive, at least it is acquired at a discount. And if, right, the writer receives an excellent return on investment without acquiring the stock.

> ***Example:*** Writer sells a six-month put on XYZ against cash for $500 at a strike of 50. The margin requirement is $1,000 (30% of $5,000 less the $500 put premiums). If the price stays the same or goes up, Writer stands to make $500 in 6 months or a 100% annualized return. The figure may be less due to transaction costs or it may be more because Writer may remove cash if the price goes up. Unlike in the covered call situation, Writer has no interest cost, because there is no debt. This is due to the fact that Writer did not purchase any security. If Writer has substantial wealth, letters of credit may be obtained from a bank at a low cost, which many brokers will accept in lieu of a cash margin. If the stock drops by more than 10%, there is a loss. Should the put be exercised, Writer's cost basis equals the exercise price of $5,000 less the $500 received for the put, or $4,500, plus transaction cost. The basis is the same, regardless of how low the price is. At this point, Writer may wish to write covered calls. Should the put expire, Writer enjoys a gain. If Writer engages in a closing transaction, a gain or loss will result at that point.

One should never buy a stock without considering writing "naked" puts first.

¶ 944 WRITING PUTS AND CALLS SIMULTANEOUSLY

If an investor writes a put and a call on the same stock at the same time, only one side can be covered. Thus, the investor can write a "naked" put and a covered call or a covered put (against a short position) and a "naked" call. Since upside protection is more important than downside protection, the most popular strategy is a covered call and a "naked" put. If the price goes up, the writer pockets both premiums and if it goes down, a loss results on both the stock held and the put sold with the premiums as a cushion. Note that it is meaningless to talk about writing both a covered call and a covered put on the same stock, since the trader would have to be long and short in the stock simultaneously. These positions cancel each other out, leaving the writer with both options being "naked," with nothing but wasted transaction costs to show for it.

¶ 945 SPREADS

A spread means the purchase of one option and the simultaneous sale of another on the same stock, but with different striking prices and/or expiration dates. If the options have different expiration dates, the writer is doing a "calendar" spread. Typically, the writer purchases a long-term option at a price slightly higher than the short-term options sold, hoping to pick up the difference in time value or winding up with a free call at the end. A "money" spread involves options with various strike prices. Since the risk (and the profit potential) is reduced, the spread margin is less than on the individual positions. This practice was taken from the commodity markets.

¶ 946 MISCELLANEOUS STRATEGIES

All option strategies cannot be enumerated, since some of them have, no doubt, not even been invented yet. If the investor sells the stock while writing a call, for example, the upside risk exposure is doubled, while a short sale profit plus the premium is made on the downside.

If someone writes both a put and a call while being short the stock, the writer has again doubled the upside risk exposure, while the gains on the downside are limited to the premiums. An example of a *multiple hedge* would be the purchase of warrants, while simultaneously writing calls and buying the puts. If the writer purchases a call while writing a put, the writer effectively simulates the ownership of the stock, since the call becomes valuable on the upside, while the put loses on the downside. Finally, the investor may engage in arbitrage operations, such as buying options in one market and selling them in another. The markets may be different exchanges, or OTC and an exchange, or even be in different countries.

¶ 947 OPTION BUYING

Options are purchased for many reasons:

1. To close out a previously written option.
2. To engage in a spread transaction, e.g., as part of an option writing strategy.
3. As pure speculation, as a side bet on the performance of the underlying common stock with high leverage.
4. As insurance, to protect a long or short position in a stock or stock portfolio. Index options (available since 1983) are ideally suited for the latter. Several exchanges have them, they normally run for three months, and the trading unit is $100 multiplied by the index points.

5. As an alternative to the purchase of stock, particularly when the call is "in the money" with a low time value.

¶ 948 MAIN BUYING STRATEGIES

BUY CALL

Here, the normal loss is the maximum loss. If the stock does not move above its striking price, the call will expire worthless. However, if the stock climbs significantly, the call will go up faster in relative terms. The reasons for buying calls is the high leverage, coupled with no possibility of margin calls. Buying a call is equivalent to buying a warrant, except that the warrant has a longer life.

BUY CALL, SHORT STOCK

If done simultaneously, this is similar to a convertible hedge, discussed at ¶ 930. The short sale is protected by the call and, with luck, several successful short sales may be executed during the life of the call. If more than one call is purchased per 100 shares sold short, a neutral hedge will result so that a net profit can result if the price moves significantly either way. Should the investor short the stock and have a paper gain, it can be locked in by buying a call later.

BUY PUT

This basic strategy is equivalent to buying a call and shorting the stock. If the price goes down, the buyer stands to gain while having upside protection. There are numerous advantages over an unprotected short sale:

1. No margin account is needed to purchase options, but short sales require a margin account.
2. No short sale can be executed unless the last change in the stock price was an "uptick."
3. The put buyer does not borrow any stock and consequently need not reimburse the lender for cash dividends.
4. A short sale results in a short-term gain, if successful, because no purchase takes place until the position is closed out. The holding period of the put begins upon purchase and a long-term gain is possible.
5. The loss is limited to the put cost. A short seller's loss is theoretically without limit.
6. Since the leverage is higher, success will result in a higher percentage gain than a short sale.

7. No stock is borrowed by the put buyer. This results in no margin calls, nor any fees or premiums to the lender of stock in short supply.
8. Commissions are lower on options than stock. Only if the put is exercised, rather than sold on the exchange, will stock commissions be incurred.

On the minus side, there is the limited duration of the put, as well as its cost.

BUY PUT AND STOCK

This is an example of insurance, the converse of selling short and buying a call. If the put is bought with the stock, the investor enjoys full protection against a price decline at the cost of the put. The upside gain is unlimited. However, this strategy is equivalent to merely buying a call. The latter is easier, ties up less capital and at less transaction costs. However, if someone already has a gain on the stock and wishes to lock it in, until the following year, for example, buying a put will do the trick. An alternative is a short sale "against the box."

"SYNTHETIC" CONVERTIBLES

A client with some losses on paper might consider selling some securities to generate losses deductible from other income. The proceeds can be invested in a combination of Treasury bills or other short-term money market instruments and a few calls. Such a combination, consisting of, say, 90%-95% T-bills and 5%-10% calls may offer the same upside potential as a stock portfolio, but at much less risk.

ADDITIONAL STRATEGIES

As with writing strategies, buying strategies are virtually unlimited. Some investors have purchased convertible bonds while protecting themselves on the downside by puts. Due to the downside protection already inherent in the bonds, fewer puts must be purchased than if stock were to be protected. Warrants may also be protected by puts. Expiring warrants may be sold short, while calls are purchased as a hedge. Multiple hedges are also possible.

ILLUSTRATIONS OF OPTION PURCHASES

Investors may purchase calls "at the market" or "in the money."

Purchase of "at the market" call

"Buyer" purchases a six-month call for $500 on XYZ stock with a strike of 50, which is also the price of the stock. The premium of $500 is a true premium, since it is paid only for the time value and not for any intrinsic value. If the stock moves down or stays the same, the investment will gradually evaporate, and unless sold for a fraction of its value prior to expiration, it becomes a total loss. The loss will, however, offset other income. The stock must move up at least 5 points or 10% by expiration to reimburse Buyer for the premium paid. If it happens sooner, Buyer may still have a profit because of the remaining time value. But assume the stock goes up 10 points or 20% in three months. The option then has intrinsic value of $1,000. In addition, it sells at a premium of, say, $200. The premium is lower, not only because the option has less time to run, but because a buyer obtains less leverage when buying an "in the money" call, due to the higher investment necessary. Nevertheless, if $500 became $1,200 in three months, the annualized return is 560% as opposed to 80% if the stock had been purchased. On the other hand, the dollar return is $700 on the option and $1,000 on the stock. If the stock fluctuated only slightly, the option is a total loss while the stock investment would still be intact.

Purchase of "in the money" call

As an alternative to stock purchase, a deep "in the money" call is sometimes preferable. Assume that a call on XYZ stock can be purchased for $2,100 at a strike of $40 when the stock is at $60. $100 is paid for the time value, but consider the advantages:

1. The buyer ties up only $2,100 rather than $6,000.
2. The option has the same upside potential as the common stock, except for the $100.
3. The downside risk is reduced.
4. Commissions are lower.

As has been shown, convertibles and options can generate profits year after year, even if the stock market itself is rather sluggish. And with the number of strategies available, the client can gear investments to a special personality and risk profile. For anyone who likes to invest in the securities markets, it certainly makes sense to become less dependent on an upside move, given the frequent downswings over the years. Besides, it can generate a lot of excitement and satisfaction to become a sophisticated investor. By writing covered calls, for example, stocks are turned into money machines which generate premiums continuously without any increase in the stock prices.

The Securities Broker

¶ 950 WHAT IS A BROKER?

A broker works for a securities firm (brokerage house) which is a member of one or more stock exchanges. The firm does business with the public and maintains offices with a ticker tape. Brokers, also called account executives or registered representatives, buy and sell securities for their customers, in return for which they receive a percentage of the commissions generated.

¶ 951 BROKERAGE COMMISSION

Since May 1, 1975, minimum commissions have been abolished. Brokerage houses are now free to set any rates they want, but the following commission schedule, paid both on purchase and sale, is typical:

\$ 100 to \$ 800	2.5% of price plus \$7.50
\$ 800 to \$ 2,500	1.5% of price plus \$15
\$2,500 to \$ 5,000	1.1% of price plus \$25
\$5,000 to \$20,000	1.1% of price plus \$30

On large orders, commissions are negotiable. It can be observed that round-trip commissions on the typical round lot (100 shares) tend to be about 2.5%. On "over-the-counter" securities, the customer pays the spread between the bid and the asked price, often above 10%.

If the client simply wants someone to take an order, numerous "discount brokers" are available, rendering minimal service, but saving the customer up to 50% or more in commissions. (See below.)

¶ 952 EMPLOYING A BROKER

A broker is *not* an investment counselor, financial planner, or tax adviser, although many purport to be. The ideal broker should be knowledgeable, experienced, and ethical. It would be nice if the investor could manage investments personally, since no one will care more or charge less, but the typical investor may neither have the time nor the training for it. A broker is first of all a *salesperson*. The investor should go to a broker to buy, not to be sold. A broker may employ financial analysts and portfolio managers, but a broker is not necessarily either. The broker has three main objectives and in the order of their importance they are:

1. To earn a living, which can only be done by trading. The more the customer trades, the happier the broker, but the less capital the customer is left with. Excessive trading is called "churning."
2. To protect the firm against liability. If the investor loses more than initially invested, through the excessive use of margin or the sale of naked calls, for example (see below), the investor is personally liable. Should the investor be judgment proof or file personal bankruptcy, however, the brokerage firm must bear the loss.
3. To make the *customer* money, which, in the long run, is the only way to keep the account.

The broker is a "customer's man," spending a lot of time on the phone to generate commission business from old and new customers. There is a fair amount of paperwork and tape watching involved as well. One piece of advice: Stock should never be bought on the basis of a phone call. However, a broker is still needed for the following reasons:

1. To use financial leverage, the investor needs a margin account.
2. The prime function of a broker is to execute trades.
3. A broker can look up facts, such as price quotations, dividend and interest payment dates, and unique features of securities, such as convertibles and warrants.
4. The broker will send monthly statements, annual reports, etc.
5. The broker will explain financial expressions, being familiar with the unique vocabulary of the "street."
6. The investor can keep stock certificates with the broker for safekeeping on an insured basis (with limits) through the Securities Investors Protection Corporation.
7. A broker will exercise warrants or convert convertibles for a nominal fee as well as keep track of bonds called for redemptions.

DISCOUNT BROKERS

All of the above services are also available in the "third market" through discount brokers. The third market consists of off-the-exchange trading in listed stock by nonmember firms. The advantages of using discount brokers are:

1. Savings of up to 75% on commissions.
2. They do not try to sell anything, which reduces unnecessary trading.

The typical professional cannot beat the market. Studies have shown that once someone owns more than a handful of stock, the portfolio will conform very closely to the market average. A market average is particularly hard to beat if the investor must pay commissions and advisory fees. The client should therefore minimize overhead by not letting round-trip commissions become one of the biggest expenses in life. One way to do this is to "buy-and-hold." Commissions are not even deductible. Purchase commissions are added to the purchase price, while selling commissions reduce proceeds.[2] The net effect is that commissions reduce gains or increase losses.

---

[2] Code Secs. 263 and 1001.

¶ 953 SHOPPING FOR A BROKER

A customer has to shop for a broker as for any other product or service. Here are some factors to consider:

1. Since the abolition of minimum commissions, different brokers charge different commissions on like trades. In the area of bonds, for example, one may find one broker charging $5 per $1,000 per value bond without a minimum, another charging $5 per bond, but with a $25 minimum, a third using a sliding scale, etc.
2. Some brokers impose a net worth or high minimum investment requirement to open a margin account.
3. The extent to which an account is insured may vary from $100,000 to $500,000 or more.
4. The interest charged on the margin account will vary from broker to broker, but will always exceed the prime interest rate.
5. The house rules on margin requirements, particularly maintenance margin, will vary.
6. Brokers vary drastically in the area of option writing. Some will not permit the writing of "naked" calls, others have higher margin requirements, while some impose minimum equity requirements, etc.
7. Some brokers will let the customer use letters of credit to satisfy margin requirements for option writing, others will not. Other brokers will not release the advance cash payments generated by option writing, and so it goes.
8. Large firms have in-house research departments which supply the account executives with up-to-date information about the economy, the stock market, and specific securities.

The bottom line is this: Before selecting a broker, the client should make sure that the firm has the most favorable house rules with respect to the transactions and services that will be needed. Investors who engage in a variety of transactions or own substantial portfolios might consider more than one broker.

¶ 954 INVESTMENT COUNSELORS

As mentioned at ¶ 952 above, the advantage of being one's own investment counselor is that no one will care as much or charge less. But the disadvantages are the investor's lack of expertise and the time to be devoted to investment management. If someone else is to handle investment management, there are two ways to go: mutual funds, discussed below, for any portfolio size, and investment counselors for sizable sums. Generally, an investment counseling firm will not accept accounts of less than $50,000 because their annual fee, typically one-half to one percent of market value, must be at least a few hundred dollars a year for it to be worth their while. The investment counselor is regulated by the Securities and Exchange Commission and must register with it. The investment adviser will render services, such as furnishing information, planning future investments, and making buy and sell decisions. As a fiduciary, the adviser is subject to sanctions for any breach of fiduciary duty. The only way the firm will survive is to generate reasonable satisfaction for their clients.

¶ 955 MUTUAL FUNDS

Open-ended mutual funds act as a pipeline between the investor and the market. If they meet certain requirements, no tax is imposed at the fund level. There are several advantages of investing in mutual funds:

DIVERSIFICATION

Diversification is primarily an advantage for small investors. Once the investor has more than $50,000, for example, diversification can be achieved without incurring a significantly higher cost. An investor who owns shares in a fund owns a fraction of a securities portfolio. Further diversification may be achieved by investing in more than one fund.

DOLLAR COST AVERAGING

If a shareholder invests systematically, such as monthly or quarterly, he benefits from dollar cost averaging, discussed above. In other words, the investor automatically buys more shares when the market is low, fewer when the market is high.

PROFESSIONAL MANAGEMENT

Often cited as an advantage, mutual funds cannot beat the market on the average, because they *are* the average. The more money a fund manages, the harder it is to out-perform the market, and the more likely it is that the portfolio resembles a market index. Thus, the management may well be professional only in the sense that the shareholder must pay an annual fee.[3]

CONTINUOUS SUPERVISION

By giving up the fun of making personal decisions, the investor delegates the buy and sell timing decisions and the daily surveillance to

---

[3] Code Sec. 67.

the fund, for a fee. It does save time and somebody else can be blamed if the performance is poor.

INVESTING SMALL AMOUNTS

Again, what is an often-cited advantage of mutual funds must be taken with a grain of salt because:

1. The investor can always buy odd lots (less than 100 shares) by incurring additional commissions;
2. Many brokerage firms have monthly investment plans whereby as little as $40 a quarter can be invested in individual stocks; and
3. A growing list of companies have dividend reinvestment plans through which dividends automatically buy additional shares, often at a discount.

RETIREMENT PLANS

An investor who establishes an Individual Retirement Account or Keogh Plan with a mutual fund achieves the above advantages plus having any interest, dividends, or capital gains accumulate tax free. In addition, the investor may switch from group to group within the same mutual fund, or even from fund to fund.

SAFETY OF PRINCIPAL

A regulated investment company cannot go broke. It can write covered options, but not "naked" options, it cannot borrow or speculate or go short. The investor simply owns a share of its portfolio through thick and thin. The net asset value will fluctuate, but it will not go away. It presents a system of enforced self-control.

The main disadvantage of investing in mutual funds is the cost. There are two cost components:

1. The initial "loading charge" or sales commission at the time of purchase, typically about 5%. This is a one-time fee, but it is prohibitive, unless the investor plans a long-term investment program. There are no fees on redemption or for switching within the same group. The commission is not deductible, but is part of cost basis. ("No-load" funds are discussed below).
2. Management fees. The annual management fee is typically one-half of one percent of the asset value of the fund, but may be less for large funds. As a practical matter, the fee is deducted quarterly from dividends distributed. A one-half percentage fee amounts to 10% of the typical dividend yield of five percent, which is not insignificant.

The above fees are direct and in addition to the indirect charges, such as commissions paid by the fund itself on its own trading, and certain other expenses incurred.

The investor can beat the "load" by buying no-load funds, a growing number of open-end investment companies which sell their shares directly to the public without such middlemen as brokers and direct salesmen. These shares are bought, not sold. The investor has to initiate the transaction, but many investment companies advertise in the financial pages of newspapers. The shareholder must still pay management fees and commissions on their trades.

CATERING TO TASTE AND RISK PROFILE

Mutual funds specialize, and stock funds may be broken down in the following categories:

1. *Growth* funds, investing in stocks paying little or no dividends.
2. *Income* funds, investing on dividend-paying stocks.
3. *Market sector* funds, investing in broad industries, e.g., consumer products, transportation, etc.
4. *Specialized* funds, investing in specific industries, such as banking or auto.
5. *Socially responsible* funds, avoiding investments in arms, tobacco, liquor, pollution-prone companies, etc.
6. *Foreign stock* funds.
7. *Funds of* funds, investing in other mutual funds.
8. *Index* funds, simulating an index, such as the Dow Jones Industrial Average, by buying stock in proportion to size included in the index.

Thus, considerable choices exist. In addition, the investor may own more than one fund, or switch over time. Several excellent mutual fund newsletters are available.

Institutions account for 50% of ownership of New York Stock Exchange listed securities and for 75% of the trading volume. In fact, a stock owned by less than 50 institutions is known as "neglected" and a school of thought maintains that neglected stocks outperform the market.

CHAPTER 10

DEBT INVESTMENTS

Introduction to Bonds

¶ 1001 BOND MARKETS

Many investors have found more excitement in the bond market than the stock market in recent years. This is mainly due to the wide fluctuations in interest rates since the late '60s. As is generally known, bond prices vary inversely with the market rate of interest. They fall when interest rates increase, to stay competitive, and rise when rates fall. In addition, there have been notable opportunities in municipal bonds paying unusually high interest, and in the so-called "junk bond" market consisting of bonds selling at big discounts from par and therefore automatically paying proportionately higher interest (because interest is paid as a fixed percentage of par). Bonds provide a steadier income than stocks, and the issuer is obligated to pay off the principal amount at the stipulated maturity date.

¶ 1002 TERM STRUCTURE OF INTEREST RATES

The relationships between the bond price and the market rate of interest are as follows:

1. When interest rates fall, prices go up, and vice versa. This is because the price adjusts so as to provide a competitive yield to maturity at all times.
2. The further away the maturity date the more volatile ("risky") the bond price. This is because the price is primarily equal to the present value of interest payments for remote maturity bonds. The present value of $1,000 of par 30 years from now at 10% is only $57.
3. Because of 2, and as a reward for making a long-term investment, the yield on otherwise comparable bonds increases with the term to maturity. Thus, under normal conditions a 20-year bond offers a higher return than a 10-year bond, but less than a 30-year bond. However, under extreme market conditions the term structure may be reversed. Thus, if the interest rate is currently unusually high, a long-term investment may result in a slightly lower rate.

It has been generally believed that the so-called "junk bonds" yield more than traditional bonds as a reward for risk taking. However, statistics indicate that, *on the average,* the yield on junk bonds, if anything, is *less* than on other corporate bonds.

In a very general sense the same tax rules apply to bonds as to equity securities. Thus basis is computed by adding commissions to the purchase price, the holding period necessary to create a long-term capital transaction is the same, and the short sale rules apply. However, a number of unique rules, some of which are extremely complex, apply only to bonds and are surveyed below.

¶ 1003 TERMINOLOGY OF BONDS

Before investigating the many and varied aspects of bond investment, it is helpful to gain familiarity with bond features and bond terms:

BONDS

Briefly, a bond is a long-term promissory note, redeemable at some future time and yielding interest until then.

SECURED BONDS

Specific property is pledged as security for meeting the terms of the bond contract (the "indenture").

DEBENTURES

Unsecured bonds are issued on the general credit of the issuer.

SERIAL BONDS

A choice of several staggered maturity dates is offered.

REGISTERED BONDS

The issuer maintains a record of the owners and the holder receives interest checks by mail, typically semiannually.

BEARER BONDS

Also called coupon bonds. These are redeemable by whoever is in physical possession of them. Consequently, interest is not mailed. Instead, one dated coupon per interest payment is attached to the bond until maturity. When interest is due, the holder detaches ("clips") a coupon and deposits it with the bank for collection.

PRINCIPAL

Also called face value, par value, and redemption price, it is the amount of the loan repayable on the maturity date together with the final interest payment. The par value plus the last interest payment is called maturity value. The principal value of one bond is commonly $1,000 or $5,000.

INTEREST

Payment for the use or forebearance of money or credit.

COUPON RATE

The annual interest as a percentage of par. This rate is fixed and does not vary with the market price of the bond.

CURRENT YIELD

The annual interest as a percentage of the price paid for the bond.

YIELD TO MATURITY

The current yield adjusted for the discount or premium from par. This yield will exceed the current yield if the price paid was less than par, but will be smaller if a premium over par was paid.

ORIGINAL ISSUE DISCOUNT

This is the stated par value of the bond less the issue price at the time of the original sale.

MARKET DISCOUNT

This is the stated par value less unamortized original issue discount, and less the price paid in the market subsequent to issuance.

PREMIUM

Price paid less par value.

CALL FEATURE

A callable bond can be retired prior to maturity by the issuer if the issuer pays a *call premium* above par. The issuer thus pays for this added flexibility in long-range financial planning. If the issue is not callable for the first few years, a *call deferment* exists. The call price is adjusted downwards periodically until it becomes equal to the par value when maturity approaches.

¶ 1004 CAPITAL GAIN OR LOSS TREATMENT OF BONDS

A bond is a capital asset in the hands of an investor. Thus, if the holder sells or exchanges the bond, a capital gain or loss results. In 1939, the Supreme Court held that a sale or exchange did not include a redemption (retirement) by the issuer on maturity or earlier call date and denied capital gain treatment.[1] Since 1954, however, a redemption is treated as a sale or exchange.[2] Therefore, except for bond discounts, discussed below, a redemption or sale generally results in a capital gain or loss.

Bonds issued after July 1, 1984, to the public, by anyone other than an individual, are required to be in registered form.[3] If bonds required to be registered are not, the holder's gain on disposition is generally ordinary income.[4]

Under the general rules governing securities, the trade date is used to compute the holding period, as well as to determine when gain or loss is recognized. The latter date is also used to compute the amount of accrued interest to be paid to the seller who earned it.

¶ 1005 INTEREST ON BONDS

The (typically semiannual) interest received is includible in gross income. If interest received in any taxable year exceeds $400, the amounts and sources must be listed on Schedule B with form 1040. The "short form" may not be used. Interest is not defined in the Code, but case law defines it as compensation for the use or forebearance of money. It may be paid in cash or by the sale of an obligation at a discount, or a combination thereof. As has been shown, bearer bonds come equipped with dated coupons to be cashed in by the bearer, while interest on registered bonds comes as checks from the issuer to the holder of record. Interest is income when received from the issuer, and

---

[1] *Fairbanks v. U.S.,* 306 U.S. 436 (1939).

[2] Code Secs. 1232(a)(1) (now repealed), and 1271(a)(1).

[3] Code Sec. 163(f).

[4] Code Sec. 1287.

to the seller when the purchaser pays the accrued interest from the last payment date to the settlement date. If bonds are given away, the donor is taxed on the accrued interest up to the gift date in the year the *donee* is paid.[5] If the interest coupons are presented late, the holder is nevertheless taxed as of the due date, since the interest has been constructively received.[5a]

¶ 1006 PURCHASING BONDS

When a bond is purchased, the holder's cost basis equals the market value of the bonds and the brokerage commission.[6] The holder also pays the interest accrued from the last interest date (unless the bonds are traded flat) because on the next interest payment date, the holder will receive six months' interest, including the amount allocable to the time the seller held the bonds and earned the interest. Even a cash-basis investor cannot deduct this interest when paid but is required to wait (perhaps to the next taxable year) until the first interest payment is received. At that point, interest income is reduced by the previous payment to the seller. If the bond is sold before the first interest date, the amount paid originally to the seller would be deducted from the accrued interest paid by the next buyer. A seller is always taxed on the interest paid by the buyer when received.

¶ 1007 INCOME BONDS

Income bonds only pay interest if earned as explained in the indenture (the bond contract between the issuer and the bondholders). The interest may be cumulative (continuing to accrue in case earnings will later materialize) or noncumulative (gone forever for the year not earned). Since there is uncertainty as to whether the interest will be paid on the next interest date, such bonds are traded "flat" (meaning that the buyer does not pay accrued interest). Bonds in default are also often traded flat.

If interest is paid retroactively, the part representing interest associated with the period the bond has been held is taxed as ordinary income. The remaining amount reduces the basis in the bonds. If bonds are sold and any part of the sales proceeds is attributable to accrued interest, such amount would be ordinary income as well (to the extent accrued while the seller held the bonds).

---

[5] *Austin v. Comm.*, 47-1 USTC ¶ 9247, 161 F2d 266 (CA-6, 1947).

[5a] Reg. § 1.451-2(a).

[6] Code Sec. 1012.

Bond Discounts

¶ 1010 INTRODUCTION

The individual bond investor, holding a portfolio of bonds consisting of instruments issued at different times from the '50s to the '80s, is faced with a myriad of tax rules relating to the treatment of bond discounts. The 1984 Tax Reform Act added several wrinkles to an already complicated set of rules. Thus, for the *same* taxable year, a number of different rules may apply simultaneously to different bonds of the same bond investor, such as:

1. There are different rules for certain bonds issued before 1955, after 1954, but before May 28, 1969, after May 27, 1969, but before July 2, 1982, after July 1, 1982, after July 18, 1984, etc., etc.
2. There are special rules for taxable versus nontaxable bonds, original issue versus market discounts, short-term debt instruments, convertible and corporate bonds, and types of taxpayers.

Below are examined the many tax aspects of bond discounts to the investor in publicly traded bonds.

Original Issue Discounts

¶ 1015 WHAT IS "ORIGINAL ISSUE DISCOUNT"?

Original issue discount represents the stated redemption price at maturity (par or face value) less the issue price.[7] The issue price is the price at which a substantial portion of the bond issue was sold to the public. The original issue discount is treated as prepaid interest and may result in ordinary income. Whether it will or not, and the timing of the recognition of it, will, however, depend on when the bond was issued.

¶ 1016 DE MINIMIS RULE

An original issue discount not in excess of one-fourth of one percent of the redemption price at maturity times the number of complete years to maturity is considered to be zero.[8]

> ***Example:*** The stated redemption price of a 30-year corporate bond is $1,000. Up to $75 of original issue discount is disregarded (.025 × 30 × $1,000). Thus, if the issue price is $930, there is no original issue discount, but if it is $920, the discount is $80.

---

[7] Code Sec. 1273(a)(1).

[8] Code Sec. 1273(a)(3).

¶ 1017 BONDS ISSUED BEFORE 1955

Bonds issued prior to 1955 are treated the same as bonds issued after 1954 and before May 28, 1969 (discussed below), except that a redemption (retirement) results in ordinary income or loss, unless the bond was issued with interest coupons or in registered form (or was in such form on March 1, 1954).

¶ 1018 BONDS ISSUED BEFORE MAY 28, 1969 AND AFTER 1954

Corporate bonds issued before May 28, 1969 and after 1954 (and government bonds issued before July 2, 1982 and after 1954) are subject to special, lenient rules:

1. No amortization of original issue discount is required.
2. If, at issue, there was no intention to call the bond, a gain is ordinary income to the extent of the original issue discount attributable to the holding period.[9]

Example: Taxpayer purchases a $1,000 par value bond at issue for $760, due in 20 years (240 months). If the bond is sold on the market five years later for $920, the gain is $160. Of this amount, $240 × 60/240 or $60 is ordinary income, representing the portion of the "prepaid" interest earned up to that point.

¶ 1019 CORPORATE BONDS ISSUED BEFORE JULY 2, 1982 AND AFTER MAY 27, 1969

Corporate bonds which represent capital assets to the holder are treated in the following manner:

1. The ratable share of an original issue discount for each taxable year is includible in gross income as interest.[10]
2. The adjusted basis of the bond is increased by amounts included in gross income.[11]
3. If there was no intention to call the bond at issue, any gain or loss on disposition is capital in nature.
4. If there was an intention to call the bond at issue, any gain on disposition would be ordinary to the extent of the unamortized original issue discount.

Example: The investor acquired a $1,000 par value bond from the issuer for $760 on July 1, 1982, due July 1, 2002. The original issue discount is $240 or $1 a month. For 1982, the taxpayer must include interest paid plus $6 of amortization. Bond basis is in-

---

[9] Code Sec. 1271(c)(2).
[10] Code Sec. 1272(b)(1).
[11] Code Sec. 1272(d)(2).

creased to $766. For 1983 and later years, the required amortization equals $12. Should the investor keep the bond until maturity, its basis at that time would be $1,000, resulting in no gain or loss on redemption.

SUBSEQUENT HOLDERS

A subsequent buyer of the bond must continue to amortize the unamortized portion of the original issue discount, less excess amounts paid.[12]

Example: If, in the previous example, the original holder sold the bond on February 1, 1985, the situation would be as follows:

1. The seller's basis was $760 plus $1 × 31, or $791.
2. If the buyer pays $791 or less, the new owner must continue to amortize $1 a month of discount.
3. If $1,000 or more was paid, no amortization is required.
4. If more than $791, but less than $1,000 is paid, the remaining original issue discount is reduced accordingly.

Note that a seller who received less than $791 for the bond incurs a capital loss even to the extent the bondholder had "paid for" basis in part by recognizing ordinary income.

A third buyer is subject to the above rules, even if the second buyer was not required to amortize any discount because of paying at least par for the bond. Thus, a subsequent buyer receives no credit for a loss sustained by a previous holder.

Bonds Issued After July 1, 1982

¶ 1025 SCOPE OF PROVISION

Bonds issued after July 1, 1982, containing an original issue discount cannot be amortized on a straight-line basis. Rather, both the holder and the issuer must use the "constant interest rate" method.[13] This results in initially low, but annually increasing, amortization amounts. This procedure obviously favors the holder, but defers interest deductions to the issuer.

This rule is applicable to an expanded list of bonds, i.e., all "debt instruments" issued by anyone, including a natural person (after March 1, 1984), except tax-exempt, short-term obligations and U.S. savings bonds.[14]

---

[12] Code Sec. 1272(b)(4).

[13] Code Sec. 1272(a)(3).

[14] Code Sec. 1272(a)(2).

¶ 1026 COMPUTATIONAL PROCEDURE

The amortization of the original issue discount is to take place on a semiannual "yield to maturity" basis. The yield to maturity is the "internal rate of return" on the bondholder's investment. Thus, it is equal to the discount rate which would reduce the future interest payments and the redemption price to a present value equal to the investment. This number can be found mathematically or by referring to a bond table.[15] The yield to maturity is a constant. Once found, it is applied to the "adjusted issue price," defined as the issue price of the bond, plus previously amortized original issue discount for each "accrual period".[16] An accrual period is equal to each six-month period after the issue date.[17] Since an accrual period may span two taxable years, an allocation is made on a ratable daily basis. While the investor's gross income will include the allocated amortization amount for the year (or interest paid, if higher), the increase in basis will be limited to the amortization amount, less interest actually paid.

Example: The investor purchases a corporate bond at issue on August 1, 1993, for $800. The coupon rate is a semiannual 4% of the $1,000 par value and the semiannual yield to maturity is 7%. Here is the procedure:

1. The first accrual period runs from 8/1/93 to 2/1/94, or 184 days.
2. The amortization amount equals 7% of $800, or $56.
3. The adjustment to basis equals $56 less interest paid of $40, for a net basis increase of $16.
4. Gross income for 1993 equals $56 × 152/184 = *$46* (there are 152 days from 8/1/93 to 12/31/93).
5. For 1994, gross income from the bond includes the sum of three numbers:

Remaining portion from first accrual period	$12
Second accrual period: $816 × .07	57
Third accrual period: ($816 + $57 − $40) × .07 × $\frac{152}{184}$	48
	$117

[15] Mathematically, the yield to maturity can be found by solving for r in the equation

$$P = \$i \left(\frac{1 - (1+r)^{-2n}}{r} \right) + RP\,(1+r)^{-2n}$$

where

P = issue price

$i = interest paid during each 6-month period

r = yield to maturity (semiannual)

n = number of years from issue to maturity

RP = redemption price at maturity.

[16] Code Sec. 1272(a)(4).

[17] Code Sec. 1272(a)(5).

Thus, the yield to maturity is applied to the increasing basis until the adjusted basis equals par at maturity, if the bond is held that long.

The treatment of subsequent holders is equivalent to that applying to pre-July 1982 bonds. Thus, a subsequent purchaser continues to amortize the remaining discount unless paying more for the bond than the adjusted issue price at the time of purchase.[18]

¶ 1027 CONVERTIBLE BONDS

Despite the obvious value of the conversion feature, no reduction in the issue price of a convertible bond is to be made.[19] This is true, even if it can be established that the value of the bond without the conversion feature is far less than par upon issuance.

> ***Example:*** A convertible bond is issued at $1,050 with a par value of $1,000. It is convertible into 20 shares of stock, currently selling at $45 (conversion value $900). Similar bonds without the conversion feature trade at $800. There is no original issue discount. If the bond was issued for $930, the original issue discount is $70 and is treated under the general rules.

¶ 1028 BONDS WITH DETACHABLE WARRANTS

Bond/warrant packages are economically similar to convertible bonds. This is particularly true if the bonds are useable at par upon exercise of the warrants. Nevertheless, an allocation is to be made of the issue price between the bonds and the warrants, thereby frequently creating or increasing an original issue discount.[20] The allocation is to be made on the basis of actual market prices if both instruments are traded; otherwise, the allocation is to be made on the basis of prices of comparable traded securities. The creation of original issue discount is favorable to the issuer who receives an interest deduction over the life of the bond and unfavorable to the investor who must amortize the discount.

¶ 1029 SHORT-TERM GOVERNMENT OBLIGATIONS

Special rules apply to Treasury bills and other federal and local obligations issued at a discount, payable without interest and due within a year.[21]

For positions established and obligations issued after June 23, 1981, the following rules apply:

1. The obligation is a capital asset.

---

[18] Code Sec. 1272(a)(6).

[19] Reg. § 1.1232-3(b)(2)(i).

[20] Reg. § 1.1232-3(b)(2).

[21] Code Sec. 1271(a)(3).

2. On a sale or exchange, any gain is ordinary income up to the ratable share of the acquisition discount, determined on a daily basis.
3. Any excess gain is a capital gain.
4. A loss is a capital loss and is only incurred if the instrument is sold for less than the unadjusted issue price.

Sales of Interest Coupons and Stripped Bonds

¶ 1035 BONDS PURCHASED BEFORE JULY 2, 1982

The rules may be summarized as follows:

1. If the holder of coupon bonds sells the unmatured coupons, ordinary income results and is accelerated. No basis is allocated to the coupons.[22]
2. If the holder retains the coupons and sells the stripped bond, any gain is ordinary income to the extent of the difference between the fair market value of the bond with and without the coupons at the time of original purchase.[23]
3. The purchaser of the coupons will report interest income as the coupons mature. Any resale of the coupons will result in capital gain or loss.[24]

¶ 1036 BONDS PURCHASED AFTER JULY 1, 1982

The tax rules regarding stripped bonds purchased after July 1, 1982, are:

1. When a holder disposes of either the unmatured coupons or the stripped bond, but not both, the adjusted basis in the bond (as increased under rule 3) must be allocated between the coupons and the bond according to their respective fair market values at the time of sale.[25] Any excess of the redemption price of the retained portion over this allocated basis is subject to the original discount rules (as discussed above).
2. The purchaser of the coupons or the stripped bond is also deemed to have purchased an original issue discount bond if the redemption price exceeds the cost basis allocable to the coupons or bond.[26]
3. The seller includes in gross income any accrued interest on interest coupons disposed of, up to the date of disposition, and increases the basis in the stripped bond and the coupon by the accrued amount for purposes of rule 1, above.[27]

---

[22] Code Sec. 1286(c).
[23] Code Sec. 1286(c)(2).
[24] Rev. Rul. 54-251, 1954-1 CB 172.
[25] Code Sec. 1286(b).
[26] Code Sec. 1286(a).
[27] Code Sec. 1286(b)(1) and (2).

These earnings stripping rules have been extended to preferred stocks with fixed redemption prices acquired after April 30, 1993.

¶ 1037 MARKET DISCOUNTS

As noted in ¶ 1015, the original issue discount is the excess of par over the issue price. Whether or not there is original issue discount, the bond may be subsequently purchased for less than the issue price plus accrued original issue discount, if any. This decline in value may be caused by interest rate increases, a deteriorating credit rating, a default, a declining demand for bond investments, or a combination of these. An investor who acquires a bond at a given discount and a given yield to maturity has the same built-in economic gain whether the discount is one type, the other, or both. Historically, however, the market discount represents a built-in capital gain while the original issue discount, as has been shown, may result in ordinary income, currently or on disposition.

The Tax Reform Act of 1984 for the first time narrowed the gap between original issue discount (OID) and market discount (MD) on publicly traded bonds. Thus, for bonds *issued* after July 18, 1984 (the date of enactment), gain on disposition is ordinary income to the extent of accrued MD, a rule similar to the OID rules for bonds issued prior to May 28, 1969. In addition, for MD bonds *acquired* after the date of enactment, direct interest expenses must be deferred to the extent of accrued MD, an entirely new concept. To complicate the matter further, three elections with respect to MD bonds are provided that are analyzed below.

¶ 1038 EXCLUDED BONDS

The market discount (MD) rules do not apply to obligations maturing within a year, municipal bonds, installment obligations and U.S. savings bonds.[28] Any market discount less than 1/4 of 1% of the "stated redemption price" times the number of whole years to maturity is considered to be zero.[29] The Revenue Reconciliation Act of 1993 extends the market discount rules to municipal bonds and bonds insured before July 19, 1984, if acquired after April 30, 1993.

THE ORDINARY INCOME ON DISPOSITION RULE

When an investor disposes of an MD bond, the realized gain is generally recognized as ordinary income to the extent of accrued MD up to the date of disposition.[30] This rule also applies to short-term obligations.[31]

---

[28] Code Sec. 1278(a)(1)(B).
[29] Code Sec. 1278(a)(2)(C).
[30] Code Sec. 1276(a)(1).
[31] Code Sec. 1282(a).

Example: F purchases a par value of $1,000 MD bond for $800 and gifts it to S when the accrued MD is $50 and the fair market value is $835. F recognizes $35 of ordinary income, S's basis is $835 and his MD is $165.[32] Thus S is treated as having purchased the bond for $835, representing F's basis, plus gain recognized.

It should be noted that although gifts are subject to ordinary income recognition of accrued MD, as they have been for accrued interest generally, transfers on death and other nonrecognition transactions do not trigger income.[33] However, the ordinary income taint stays with the bond or the exchanged property traded for the bond if basis carries over in whole or in part.

OID AND MD COORDINATION

The MD rules work independently of the OID rules. Thus, whether a bond is an MD bond or not, OID on bonds issued prior to July 2, 1982, must generally be accrued and included in gross income on a straight-line basis, while OID on bonds issued after July 1, 1984, must be reported under the yield-to-maturity method.[34]

An OID bond issued prior to July 2, 1982, if acquired after July 18, 1984, is also subject to the MD accrual rules, but only for purposes of the interest deferral rule. Bonds issued after July 18, 1984, or acquired after April 30, 1993, may be subject to both the OID and MD accrual rules for gain and interest deferral rule purposes.

Example: A bond is issued with a face value of $1,000 and an issue price of $900. The OID is $100 and must be amortized on a yield-to-maturity basis. If the original holder sells the bond for $800 after having accrued $30 of OID, the new owner must amortize $70 of OID ($1,000 − $930) and will have MD of $130 ($930 − $800).

The OID and MD accrual rules may be summarized as follows:

Issue Date	*Acquisition Date*	*OID*	*MD*
5/28/69 - 7/1/82	Before 7/19/84	Yes, SL	No
5/28/69 - 7/1/82	After 7/18/84	Yes, SL	Yes (iD)
7/2/82 - 7/18/84	Before 7/19/84	Yes, YtM	No (Yes, if acquired after 4/30/93)
7/2/82 - 7/18/84	After 7/18/84	Yes, YtM	Yes (iD)
After 7/18/84	After 7/18/84	Yes, YtM	Yes(iD, OI)

SL = Straight-line accrual
iD = For purposes of interest deferral
YtM = Yield-to-maturity accrual
OI = For purposes of ordinary income on disposition

---

[32] Code Sec. 1276(c)(1).
[33] Code Sec. 1276(c).
[34] Code Sec. 1272(a) and (b).

MD ELECTIONS

The following elections relating to MD bonds are provided:

1. The amortization of MD may take place on the straight-line method on a daily basis or on the yield-to-maturity method on a semiannual basis with respect to each bond.[35] The latter should be done to minimize accrued MD.

2. If interest is deferred, the taxpayer may make an election for any taxable year to deduct currently any carried over amount to the extent interest income with respect to a bond (including OID) exceeds the annual net interest expense with respect to that bond.[36] This election should be made.

3. Taxpayer may elect to amortize MD (on either the straight-line or yield-to-maturity method) and include the amortization amounts in gross income each year. The election covers all MD bonds acquired in the year of election *and* in future years.[37] Bonds covered by the election are exempt from both the ordinary income on disposition rules *and* the interest deferral rules. This election should not be made as income is accelerated.

Example: An investor purchased an MD bond with a face value of $1,000 and no OID for $850. Accrued MD at the time of sale for $920 was $60 on a straight-line basis and $40 under the yield-to-maturity method. The possibilities are as follows:

1. If straight-line accrual was used, $60 of ordinary income and $10 of capital gain result.

2. If yield to maturity accrual was used, $40 of ordinary income and $30 of capital gain result.

3. If straight-line accrual was used for gross income purposes, $60 of ordinary income would have resulted prior to the sale, and basis would have been increased to $910 with a capital gain of $10 on sale.

4. If yield-to-maturity accrual was used for gross income purposes, $40 of ordinary income would have resulted currently and a capital gain of $30 on sale. The lesson is clear: Deferred accruals on the yield-to-maturity method should be employed.

---

[35] Code Sec. 1276(b)(2)(A).

[36] Code Sec. 1277(b)(1)(A).

[37] Code Sec. 1278(b)(1).

¶ 1039 BOND PREMIUMS

When the cost basis in a purchased bond exceeds the redemption price, a bond premium exists. Such a premium may be amortized.[38] The definition of bonds for this purpose is substantially the same as the definition of bonds above. Unlike the case of bond discounts, there is no attempt to distinguish between market premiums and original issue premiums. Normally, a price in excess of the principal amount is paid when the bond's stated rate of interest is higher than the prevailing market rate at the time of purchase. The premium thus effects a compensating downward adjustment of the bond yield. Because the bond premium is in the nature of a negative interest adjustment, the holder is permitted to amortize the premium over the life of the bond remaining at the time of purchase. Such a reduction in the interest income, however, is treated as an investment interest offset for tax purposes. With taxable bonds, the amortization must be elected. If the election is not made, all interest is taxed with no offsets, and upon maturity a long-term capital loss results, which may not result in maximum tax benefits. When the election is made, it applies to all taxable bonds bought at a premium and is binding for future years, unless the Commissioner grants a change. This election provides the bondholder with an interesting strategy explained below.

ILLUSTRATION OF CAPITAL GAINS NOW—ORDINARY DEDUCTIONS LATER

An investor who holds a bond that has increased in value substantially above par may sell it at a long-term capital gain. The investor may then immediately buy back the identical bond, make an election to amortize the premium and; thus, reduce ordinary income. The investor has created capital gains currently and must wait for the deductions, but long-term capital gains have been converted into ordinary deductions. The taxpayer does not have to worry about the "wash sale rule" since it does not apply to replacement of securities sold at a gain. Because of the timing difference, this should only be done after considering the marginal tax brackets and the present value of the tax savings. The strategy is of renewed interest in years since capital gains rates are again lower than ordinary income rates.

¶ 1040 BONDS WITH CALL FEATURES

The amortizable bond premium is the cost basis less the amount payable upon maturity, or if callable, *on the earlier call date.*

> ***Example:*** A callable $1,000 par bond is purchased for $1,250. The issuer has the option of calling the bond for redemption for five years at a call price of $1,150, and for the next five years at

[38] Code Sec. 171.

$1,100. The investor would be permitted to amortize a total of $100 the first five years.

If the issue was not called, an additional $50 could be amortized the following five years, and if still not called, the remaining $100 may be amortized over the remaining years to the maturity date. If the bond had been acquired for $1,100 or less, but more than par, no amortization deductions could be taken the first ten years, but the premium paid could be amortized over the remaining life of the bond after the expiration of the call feature at the end of ten years.

¶ 1041 INCOME SPLITTING WITH BONDS

If interest coupons are given away (to a child for instance) but the bonds retained, the interest is nevertheless taxed to the donor as an "anticipatory assignment of income." [39] The same result would follow if the *bonds* were given away, but the donor held on to the interest coupons. To get the tax benefit from income splitting, both the "fruits and the tree" must be parted with irrevocably.

¶ 1042 DEFAULTED BONDS AND WORTHLESS BONDS

If a bond in default is paid off, the investor is allowed to first recover basis. Any excess is a capital gain to the extent designated as principal or interest accrued prior to purchase.

If the bond becomes worthless, a capital loss results. The holding period runs until the last day of the year in which the worthlessness occurs. To claim a deduction, the bond must be completely worthless. For partial worthlessness, a sale or exchange must take place to establish and recognize the loss.

¶ 1043 PAYING ESTATE TAXES WITH "FLOWER" BONDS

Certain U.S. government bonds issued before March 4, 1971, may be used at par plus accrued interest to pay federal estate taxes. Since the typical coupon rate is 3% to 4% and the last bond matures in 1998, they sell at a discount, typically about 5% to 10% if maturity is at least five years away. This represents an attractive estate planning tool, but only for the dying. The reason is that the savings is eaten up by the interest foregone if the holder lives more than a couple of years. Also, the estate tax value equals par since they are redeemable at par (to the extent of estate tax payable). As is the case with other bonds, the accrued interest up to the date of death is "income in respect of a decedent" and includible in the gross estate as well as in the gross

[39] *Helvering v. Horst,* 40-2 USTC ¶ 9787, 311 U.S. 112 (1940).

income of the successor in interest.[40] A deduction is allowed for the estate tax, if any, caused by the estate inclusion.[41]

¶ 1044 U.S. SAVINGS BONDS

Like other government bonds, savings bonds are exempt from state and local taxes, but not from federal income, estate and gift taxes. Noncorporate cash-basis taxpayers may choose to report increases in the redemption value of Series EE bonds as annual income. A minimum yield of 4% is guaranteed. Alternatively, they may wait and report the redemption price less their cost in a lump sum upon redemption, maturity, or disposition.[42] Some parents register such bonds in the names of their children and elect to include the income on an annual basis, since their children may be in a zero tax bracket anyway. Series HH bonds are sold at face value, but pay interest to the registered holder semiannually. They cannot be sold, given away or used as collateral. EE bonds may be held past their original maturity, if extended, but interest still accrues, and is not taxed until cashed in. Some taxpayers hold on to their EE bonds until they retire, then exchange them for HH bonds in the same amount. Even on the exchange there, is still no tax on the interest on the EE bonds.[43] The retiree must pay tax on the interest from the HH bonds. The EE bond interest is not taxed until the HH bonds are cashed in or mature. Maturity dates are often extended, however.

E bonds issued from May 1, 1941, through April 1, 1952, reached final maturity 40 years after issue, i.e., on April 1, 1992, or earlier.

¶ 1045 TREASURY BILLS

Treasury bills (T-bills) cannot be beat for safety and liquidity. They are issued by the same entity which prints the money, i.e., the U.S. Government. The Treasury auctions 91-day (13-week) and 182-day (26-week) bills each Monday for issue the following Thursday. The 364-day (52-week) instruments are sold every four weeks on a Thursday for issue the next Thursday.

Prices are determined by bids, largely from institutional buyers. T-bills sell at a discount from par ($10,000 minimum initial investment, in multiples of $5,000) and are redeemed at par. Thus, a $10,000 T-bill for 364 days issued at $9.400 yields:

$$\frac{\$600 \times 100}{9{,}400} \quad \text{or} \quad 6.4\%$$

The investor sends the Treasury or a Federal Reserve bank a check (certified) for the par value and gets back the T-bill and a check for the

[40] Code Sec. 691.

[41] Code Sec. 691(c).

[42] Code Sec. 454.

[43] Code Sec. 1037(a).

discount. No commissions are incurred unless a bank or broker is employed. To order application forms and an informational brochure, "Information About Treasury Bills Sold at Original Prices," the investor writes to:

Bureau of the Public Debt

Department F

Washington, DC 20239-0001

The yield on T-bills has varied from 3%-12% since the '70s. To compute the annual yield, the following formula may be used:

$$Y = \frac{I \times D}{P \times M}$$

Y = effective rate of return, D = Number of days in the year.
I = $100 − P, P = Price per $100, and M = number of days to maturity.

Thus, if a 91-day T-bill is purchased for $9,826 in a non-leap year, the yield is:

$$\frac{(100 - 98.26)\ 365}{98.26 \times .91} \quad \text{or} \quad 7.103\%$$

¶ 1046 MORTGAGE-BACKED BONDS

There are several ways to invest in a pool of mortgages guaranteed by the United States or guaranteed or insured by a federal agency. Ownership in such a pool is evidenced by a "pass-through" certificate.

"GINNIE MAES"

"Ginnie Maes" are FHA/VA mortgage-backed bonds guaranteed by the U.S. Treasury. They are issued by Government National Mortgage Association, a U.S. government corporation within the Department of Housing and Urban Development.

The bonds are secured by government-insured mortgages, yield a high rate of return (mortgage rates tend to exceed the prime rate and corporate bond rates), and are quite liquid. Monthly payments of interest and principal are made (the latter a nontaxable return of capital). The average life of a mortgage is 8½ years, due to sales, refinancing, and default. As with other bonds, prices vary inversely with interest rates in the market.

"FANNIE MAES"

The Federal National Mortgage Association is a HUD-regulated, government-sponsored corporation owned by private shareholders. The "pass-through" certificates are backed up by conventional mortgages. Liquidity is limited and they are a little less safe than "Ginnie Maes."

"FREDDIE MACS"

The Federal Home Loan Mortgage Corporation was created by Congress and is owned by the 12 Federal Home Loan Banks. "Freddie Macs" are similar to "Fannie Maes."

A number of brokers represent mortgage-backed bond funds, such as "Ginnie Mae" funds. These are typically no-load, but with an "early withdrawal charge" the first four years. Automatic reinvestment of interest and/or principal is available. A $25,000 minimum investment is required if a direct purchase of bonds is desired. For funds, the minimum may be as low as $1,000.

¶ 1047 ZERO-COUPON BONDS

Zero-coupon bonds are Treasury securities paying no interest. However, they are redeemed at par, say $10,000 at maturity, and can be purchased for, say $2,000 or $4,000, depending on the term. They should only be bought to lock in a high interest rate and generally should not be purchased by a taxable investor. This is because the discount has to be taken into income yearly although not "paid" for many years. Different brokers have different markups. Customers beware.

Zeros are ideal for IRA and Keogh plans, since the tax is deferred until withdrawal. Zeros are quite volatile. Thus, prices of CATS—Certificates of Accrual on Treasury Securities—have been known to fluctuate from $20 to $100 for a $1,000 bond within two years.

Municipal Bonds

¶ 1050 QUALITY

Bonds issued by states or their subdivisions are referred to as municipal bonds and, except as provided in the Code, pay federally tax-exempt interest. There are two categories of such bonds:

1. *Revenue bonds,* secured by revenues from a specific project, such as a toll bridge or a hospital, and
2. *General obligation bonds* (GOs), backed by taxes.

GOs may be safer on the average, but it is more important how a particular bond is rated. Two services, Moody's and Standard & Poor's, rate municipal bonds from triple A to D. A single A rating or better is considered investment grade by both services.

Ultraconservative investors may obtain insurance against default of interest and principal through bond insurers. The two largest are Municipal Bond Insurance Association (MBIA) and American Municipal Bond Assurance Corporation (AMBAC).

¶ 1051 MUNICIPAL BOND INNOVATIONS

The percentage of municipal bonds owned by individuals has gone from 25% to 75% since 1979. This is due to a general congressional crackdown on tax shelters as well as the following innovations in the tax-exempt bond instrument itself.

¶ 1052 FLOATING RATE BONDS

Some bonds have floating rates which:

1. change the coupon rate weekly and
2. tie the rate to a combination of short- *and* long-term rates (typically discounted by 25%-35%).

The result is preservation of capital to the investor, since the market value will generally not stray far from par.

¶ 1053 PUT BONDS

The option tender bond gives the holder the right to tender his bond at par, typically once a year and not the first three years after issue. Unlike floaters, the put bond may fluctuate but cannot sell below par. The holder pays for the put by accepting a slightly lower coupon rate.

¶ 1054 ZERO-COUPON BONDS

The most popular innovation yet is the zero-coupon bond or "zeros", which offers the investor up to 25 times the original investment tax free, depending on the maturity date. This volatility also gives the holder an excellent capital gain potential if interest rates fall and the instrument is sold prior to maturity.

¶ 1055 TAXATION

For federal income tax purposes, "gross income does not include interest on the obligations of a State, a Territory or a possession of the United States, or any political subdivision of any of the foregoing, or of the District of Columbia;[44] . . . ." Nevertheless, there are numerous tax consequences associated with tax-exempt bonds, including federal income, estate and gift taxes, and state and local taxes. Since there are some 1,750,000 different issues of such bonds outstanding, from about 38,000 state and local governments and public authorities, a survey of the main tax aspects of these instruments is undertaken below.

---

[44] Code Sec. 103(a).

¶ 1056 COMPUTING THE EQUIVALENT TAXABLE INTEREST

To convert tax-free interest into the equivalent in taxable income, the bond holder simply divides the tax-free rate by one minus his marginal tax rate:

$$i = \frac{r}{1-T}$$

where

i = taxable interest equivalent,

r = tax-free rate, and

T = marginal tax rate.

Thus, if the marginal tax rate is 30% and the tax-free rate is 5%, the before-tax equivalent is 5/(1 − .3) = 7.14%.

¶ 1057 DISALLOWANCE OF EXPENSES AND INTEREST

The fact that no deduction is allowed for expenses allocable to interest exempt from income, nor for interest on indebtedness incurred or continued to purchase or carry tax-exempt bonds, could be viewed as an indirect federal income tax on tax-exempt income.[45] The loan and the investment on tax-free bonds need not take place at the same time. Thus, an elderly married couple was denied an interest deduction on a mortgage on their home, incurred to purchase taxable U.S. government bonds, since they could have sold their municipal bonds instead of borrowing.[46] On the other hand, if a business purpose exists for the loan, the interest deduction may be allowed, even if the taxpayer continues to "carry" tax-exempt bonds.[47]

¶ 1058 TAXATION OF SOCIAL SECURITY BENEFITS

Up to 85% of social security benefits received after 1993 may be includible in gross income.[48] The maximum includible amount equals the lesser of:

1. 85% of benefits received, or 85% of
2. The sum of one-half of the benefit plus provisional income, but less a base amount.[49] The base amount is zero for a married individual filing separately, $34,000 for a single individual and $44,000 for those filing a joint return.[50]

---

[45] Code Sec. 265(a)(1) and (2).

[46] *Levitt v. U.S.*, 74-1 USTC ¶ 9201, 368 FSupp 644 (S.D. Iowa).

[47] *Wisconsin Cheeseman, Inc. v. U.S.*, 68-1 USTC ¶ 9145, 388 F.2d 420 (CA-7); *Handy Button Machine Co.*, CCH Dec. 32,514, 61 TC 846 (1974).

[48] Code Sec. 86.

[49] Code Sec. 86(b).

[50] Code Sec. 86(c).

The most controversial portion of provisional income is the addition of "the amount of interest received or accrued by the taxpayer during the taxable year which is exempt from tax.[51] This adjustment will result in an indirect federal income tax on tax-exempt interest for some recipients of social security or railroad retirement benefits.

¶ 1059 BOND PREMIUMS

The following rules apply with respect to bond premiums on tax-exempt municipal bonds:

1. The premium must be amortized, whether it is a market or an original issue premium.[52]
2. The amount of the premium equals the bondholder's cost basis at the time of acquisition less the amount payable on maturity or earlier call date.[53]
3. No deduction is allowed for the amortization amounts since they have the effect of merely reducing tax-free interest.[54]
4. The bondholder's basis on the bond is reduced by the amount amortized.[55]
5. The amortization period extends from the date of acquisition to the date of maturity or earlier call date.[56]
6. The amortization method (e.g., straight-line, the "yield-to-maturity method," etc.) is elected by the investor and must be regularly employed. Most investors will elect straight-line amortization, since the basis is reduced at a slower pace, thereby making a capital loss on disposition more likely.

As a result of these rules, if the bondholder keeps the bonds until maturity, the basis will equal face value. No built-in capital losses are allowed. Nevertheless, a capital gain or loss may, of course, result from a disposition prior to maturity.

¶ 1060 ORIGINAL ISSUE DISCOUNT

If a tax-free municipal bond is issued at a price less than the stated redemption price at maturity, technically an "original issue discount" exists. Since this economically represents a "pre-payment" of tax-free interest, traditionally no income must be accrued or added to the basis. When the bond is subsequently sold, the gain attributable to the portion of the original issue discount "earned" up to the date of disposition is excluded from gross income.[57] If the bond is redeemed by

---

[51] Code Sec. 86(b)(2)(B).
[52] Code Sec. 171.
[53] Code Sec. 171(b)(2).
[54] Code Sec. 171(a)(1).
[55] Code Sec. 1016(a)(5).
[56] Code Sec. 171(b)(1).
[57] Code Sec. 1232(a)(2)(C) repealed, and Rev. Rul. 73-112, 1973-1 CB 47.

the issuer, the treatment of the original issue discount depends on when the bond was issued:

1. If the bond was issued prior to June 9, 1980, the full original issue discount, whether "earned" or "unearned" is excluded from gross income.[58]
2. If the bond was issued on or after June 9, 1980, only the "earned" portion of the original issue discount is excluded from gross income.[59]

A gain attributable to a market discount is includible in gross income, without diminution, as a short- or long-term capital gain.

> ***Example:*** A municipal bond was issued for $5,000, its redemption price. An investor who acquired the bond for $4,500 subsequently has received a $500 market discount. The basis in the bond remains at $4,500. Upon sale, a short- or long-term capital gain or loss results.

An investor acquired a $5,000 face value municipal bond, issued prior to June 9, 1980, from the issuer for $4,500. The original issue discount is $500. The bond basis remains at $4,500. Upon a sale, the gain is recognized only to the extent it exceeds the "earned" discount. Thus, if the maturity date is 200 months after issue and the bond is sold 120 months after issue, the first $300 of gain is excluded ($500 × 120/200). If the bond is redeemed, the first $500 of gain is excluded. A sale or redemption at a price below $4,500 would result in a capital loss.

Same as above, except the bond was issued on or after June 9, 1980. Whether a sale or a redemption occurs, the first $300 of gain is excluded from gross income.

SPECIAL RULE FOR MUNICIPALS

Municipal bonds issued after September 3, 1982, and acquired after March 1, 1984, are subject to the new original issue discount rules. Thus, an addition to basis is to be made on a yield to maturity basis, semiannually, for each accrual period.[60] The result is that a smaller amount of a gain on disposition will be considered attributable to tax-free prepaid interest.

¶ 1061 INDIVIDUAL RETIREMENT ACCOUNTS

Any amount paid or distributed from an individual retirement account funded with deductible contributions is includible in gross income and the basis of any person in such account is zero.[61] If the account invests in tax-exempt bonds, this rule effectively converts tax-

[58] Rev. Rul. 72-587, 1972-2 CB 74.
[59] Rev. Rul. 80-143, 1980-1 CB 19.
[60] Code Sec. 1288.
[61] Code Sec. 408(d)(1).

free income into ordinary income on distribution. As a result, an individual should never purchase municipal bonds through an IRA.

¶ 1062 ESTATE AND GIFT TAXES

Tax-exempt bonds and accrued interest thereon are fully includible in the decedent's gross estate. Similarly, such property, if transferred irrevocably during the owner's lifetime, is fully subject to the gift tax.

¶ 1063 STATE AND LOCAL TAXES

The interest received on tax-exempt obligations is not necessarily tax free locally, but may be subject to state, city and local income taxes.

TRIPLE EXEMPTS

The only bonds never taxed locally regardless of where the investor lives were issued by Hawaii or Alaska prior to statehood, or are issued by the District of Columbia, Puerta Rico, Guam, the Virgin Islands, or any American Indian Nation.

¶ 1064 TAX-EXEMPT BOND TRUSTS AND BOND FUNDS

Unit investment trusts in the municipal bonds area originated in 1961. This provided the only way to maintain a tax exemption for individual investors who pooled their funds. Trusts normally do not sell their holdings or purchase new bonds.

As a result, once the initial unit is purchased, the investor does not receive any proceeds until the first bonds reach maturity and are redeemed by the issuer. Therefore, trusts are long-term investments, usually 10 to 20 years, but sometimes as long as 30 years. Typically, the investor either saves for retirement or for the children's college education.

Since the trusts do not trade, no management fees are charged, but the sales charges normally range from 3.5% to 4.5%. The minimum investment is from $1,000 to $5,000 in most instances. A sale prior to maturity in the secondary market will cost the investor a "spread" of up to 3% of the proceeds. In addition, a capital gain or loss will result.

With the passage of the Tax Reform Act of 1976, a green light was given to mutual funds to enter the arena. Shareholders in municipal bond funds are no longer taxed on dividends paid out of tax-exempt interest earned by the fund, assuming at least 50% of the assets are invested in municipals.[62] To avoid local taxes, some funds currently specialize in the bonds of a single state. The funds offer full liquidity, unlike the bond trusts, and most are no-load funds with no charge for

[62] Code Sec. 852(a)(1).

sales, redemptions, or reinvestments. However, management fees, quality standards and minimum investments vary considerably. The investor may collect or reinvest the interest earned in most funds.

¶ 1065 YEAR-END TAX SWAPS

Tax swapping is a legitimate way to offset capital gains on bonds, stocks, options, real estate, or other capital assets for a specific tax year, and apply excess losses, up to $3,000, against ordinary income. In addition to mere tax reasons, the investor may simultaneously improve the quality of his holdings, or shorten maturity dates, and/or increase current yields. Because of the "wash sale rule," the replacement bonds cannot be "substantially identical" to those sold. However, the issuer and the coupon rate may be identical if the maturities differ by at least three years.

> ***Example:*** The investor purchased $50,000 of 5% Campfield Causeways municipal bonds at par years ago, maturing in 2007. Due to higher interest rates, the market value declined to $40,000. At the point of sale, the investor sustained a $10,000 loss and invested the proceeds in $50,000 par value of Williamstown Turnpike bonds, paying 7% interest. These bonds, maturing in 2010, had also declined 20%. As a result, the investor recognizes a $10,000 long-term capital loss. If this loss would offset $10,000 of short-term gain, substantial tax savings would be enjoyed. At a minimum, a $3,000 deduction from ordinary income would be taken in the current year, with a $7,000 capital loss carryover to the succeeding year.

COMMISSIONS

Here are the main ways to save on bond transaction costs:

1. *Shop around.* Some brokers may charge $5 a bond, no minimum, others a $25 minimum, or even $50 per transaction.
2. *New issues.* If the broker is a member of an underwriting syndicate, customers may buy new issues of corporate and municipal bonds commission free.
3. *New issues, T-bills, notes, and bonds* may be purchased with no transaction costs from any Federal Reserve Bank.
4. *Bond funds,* if purchased, should be no-load funds.

¶ 1066 COLLECTIBLES AND PRECIOUS METALS

Investing in collectors' items is very difficult without the benefit of hindsight. We all wish we had purchased a few copies of Action Comics for June 1938, containing the first story of Superman. Each 5¢ investment would today be worth up to $20,000, depending on the condition. The problems with buying art, stamps, jewelry, coins, etc. are:

1. The investor is likely to buy retail and sell wholesale. It may be true that the same diamond engagement ring that cost $1,000 a few years back today costs $2,000; but a purchaser who tries to sell it the following day may be lucky to get back one-third of what was paid for it.
2. To obtain bargains, the investor must become an expert and in addition spend a lot of time looking for bargains, going to auctions, or having people come to the investor's specialty shop. The average person cannot compete with experts.
3. Money doubles in nine years at 8% and in six years at 12%. A painting or a coin does not pay interest or dividends. Silver and gold may cost storage, and any valuables in the home should be insured. As a result, the collector pays out cash every year, instead of earning money. The charges may even be considered nondeductible personal expenses, unless the items are clearly held for investment purposes.

Collecting stamps, coins, books, or art may provide great personal pleasure, but unless the collector specializes so heavily as to qualify as an expert, it is a hobby, not an investment.

CHAPTER 11

TAX-SHELTERED INVESTMENTS

¶1101 INTRODUCTION

The Tax Reform Act of 1986 reduced (but did not eliminate) the demand for tax shelters. This was due to the lowering of maximum tax rates to 28% for most investors after 1987 (31% for some taxpayers), the repeal of the capital gain deduction and the investment tax credit, the retention and fortification of the alternative minimum tax, as well as the deferral of passive activity losses.

With the Revenue Reconciliation Act of 1993, maximum tax brackets were increased to 36% for the upper middle class and 39.6% for the wealthy starting in 1993 while the maximum capital gains rate stayed at 28%. As a result, tax shelters are back in vogue!

Tax Shelter Characteristics

¶1102 POSSIBLE TAX ADVANTAGES

A tax shelter represents an investment in a specific activity involving risk capital for which Congress has seen fit to grant specific tax incentives. Thus, a tax shelter normally does not consist of "loop-holes" discovered by a smart tax lawyer, but is an investment qualifying for tax breaks enacted by Congress to attract that investment. This is typically done by permitting a deliberate mismatching of revenues and expenses.

A tax shelter can be organized as an individual investment, a trust, a corporation, or, most commonly, a partnership. The tax benefits have historically involved:

1. Accelerated depreciation or rapid amortization.
2. The investment credit (not available after 1985).
3. A deferral of tax payments.
4. Ordinary current deductions may increase later capital gains.
5. Special deductions, such as a depletion allowance.
6. Lower tax rates.

¶1103 TAX SHELTER ANALYSIS

Tax incentives alone, however, cannot turn a bad investment into a good one. Ideally, a shelter will turn deductions into future assets. Deductions alone will only reduce after-tax economic loss.

The main points to consider before investing in a tax shelter are:

1. What is the reward/risk ratio? The riskier the investment, the greater the potential rewards should be.
2. What is the client's overall financial situation? Can the client afford the investment, i.e., can the client comfortably tie up the money and, if necessary, take a total loss?
3. Is the investment consistent with the client's personal goals, in terms of the type of investment, its relative size as part of the portfolio, investment horizon, and retirement goals, etc.? The typical tax shelter is not for the worrier.

Tax shelters have been badly abused and often misunderstood. High-bracket individuals have been so anxious to reduce their tax liabilities that they have shown no concern about losing money on the investment itself. A common belief has been that if the short-term tax savings exceeded their cash investment, they could not lose. This is clearly erroneous because even if the investment becomes worthless, nonrecourse liabilities turn to income. If investors are *personally* liable, they have to pay off the notes. Even the best shelters rarely effect more than a postponement of taxes, which, of course, is a benefit. To postpone the tax liability indefinitely, one shelter leads to another. Here are the main reasons why an investment must make economic sense in its own right *before* taxes:

1. Even if the liabilities are nonrecourse and do not have to be paid off, the investor has income when default or sale occurs.
2. If personally liable on the notes, the investor must pay them off even if the properties are worthless, unless judgment-proof. The client may also be jointly and severally liable and have to pay *all* the partnership's liability, left with only the right to sue the other partners for their share.
3. In addition to a possible liability far beyond the value of the investment, the deductions may be disallowed in the absence of a possibility to make a profit. Thus, the "hobby-loss" rule requires a showing of a profit at least three out of five years in order to overcome the presumption that a transaction was not entered into for profit. As a partner, the investor must qualify; it is *not* sufficient that the *partnership* has profit motive. Here is a list of what the IRS looks for to determine whether a profit motive exists:
   (a) How is the business conducted?
   (b) What specialized knowledge does management possess?
   (c) How much time and effort are devoted to the project?
   (d) Is the investment expected to appreciate in value?

(e) What is the profit and loss history of the enterprise?

(f) What is the dollar amount of profits versus losses?

(g) What is the financial status of the taxpayer?

(h) Are there any elements of pleasure or recreation involved?

(i) How are a tax-sheltered investment and its profit potential judged?

Ideally, the investor hires an independent expert to physically inspect and appraise the proposed activity. In any event, here are some possible danger signals:

1. Are the properties located far away so that the client may not even geographically verify that they exist?
2. Has the investor been asked for a last-minute investment? In addition to being suspicious, remember that "December partners" are not allowed retroactive losses.
3. Does the investment lack a sound business purpose? One indication of this is failure to supply information other than tax benefits, which may or may not materialize.
4. Is the projected income consistent with industry projections and possible when considering the general market for the product or service?
5. Is there a commingling of operations of several enterprises which makes it difficult to figure out the return on one share?
6. Are the claims made about the business and the tax situation too general to be useful?
7. Has anyone ever heard of the promoter? If not, be careful. If the investment is marketed by a reputable broker, there is some assurance that the *brokerage firm* may believe in the prospects.
8. If the shelter is marketed by mail, asking for immediate cash, it is better to stay away. This would be a long shot. Mail solicitations are often encountered during the last two months of the year, when taxpayers become agitated over how much tax they are going to owe.

In conclusion, it must be remembered that unless the investment is economically sound, if the investor merely cuts the after-tax loss, the investor still loses money. There are worse things in life than paying taxes, and a tax shelter going sour is one of them.

¶ 1104 TYPES OF SHELTERS

Tax shelters come in all types and sizes, limited only by the imagination of the promoters. The general principles outlined in this chapter apply to them all. Any examples presented are by way of illustration only, and are not to recommend specific shelters. As the saying goes, some investors may have been beefing about being slaughtered in the cattle market, but this does not mean that no one should invest in cattle.

Most tax shelters can be divided into five broad groups:

Real estate, ranging from shopping centers and hotels to low-income housing and historic structures (discussed in the next chapter).

Energy, from coal to oil and gas.

Leasing activities, from airplanes and computers to boxcars.

Entertainment, from plays and movies to books and records.

Agriculture, from timber and cattle to beaver-breeding and shrimp-raising.

A sixth type, *securities* (silver straddles, leveraged Treasury bond investing, etc.), was wiped out by changes in the tax law, e.g., straddle deferral rules in Code Sec. 1092, the "mark to market" rule in Code Sec. 1256 and the amortization of bond discount rules in Code Secs. 1272 and 1277.

Regardless of the activity, the investor must be concerned with the rate of return and the timing of future cash flows, as well as present and future tax consequences.

¶ 1105 WHAT CAN GO WRONG WITH A SHELTER?

Of the many things that can go wrong with a shelter, the following are among the most significant:

1. The investor's tax situation changes, rendering the shelter less attractive, even though it delivered what it promised. Examples include:
   (a) The investor's tax bracket increased due to increased income or changes in the tax law.
   (b) Investment interest deductions had to be partially carried over due to the limitation on the deductibility of investment interest above and beyond net investment income.
2. There may be adverse changes in the tax law. An extreme example was the Tax Reform Act of 1986, which lengthened real estate depreciation time, deferred passive activity losses and investment interest, taxed capital gains at ordinary in-

come rates, etc. The Revenue Reconciliation Act of 1993 further lengthened the cost recovery period for commercial buildings to 39 years!

3. Upon audit, the IRS may fight the deductions, resulting in a lengthy court battle that the taxpayer may not win. Even if successful, the legal fees may be staggering.

   Typical IRS arguments are that the activity was not entered into for profit or that the "partnership" is really an incorporated association and is therefore taxable as a corporation.

4. The shelter itself may prove to be fraudulent, or at least without chance of economic viability. Examples of both are regrettably common.

5. It may be difficult or expensive to terminate the investment. Minimally, there is often a lack of liquidity for many years.

ILLUSTRATION OF A FRAUDULENT OFFERING

As the news attests, there have been fraudulent tax shelter offerings, where the promoters pocket the money and run. Here is a real example:

> Two lawyers marketed a fraudulent $112 million tax shelter consisting of a nonexistent Wyoming coal mine. They received $20 million in *cash* and $92 million in uncollected nonrecourse notes. Investors included famous sports and entertainment figures and other high-bracket individuals. Within three months, most of the cash had vanished. It was converted to the personal use of the promoters or their associates, put into other investments or foreign accounts, etc. When the time came to make a mere $300,000 payment on the Wyoming real estate, to which they did not even own the advertised rights, even *that* money was unavailable.

¶ 1106 OIL AND GAS

The investor probably needs no reminder of what has been happening to energy costs, notably oil and gasoline prices, the last few years. They have successfully tackled inflation by a wide margin. It therefore makes sense to be an owner of, as well as a consumer of, oil and gas. Investments in oil and gas drilling programs have never been more attractive from an investment viewpoint vis-à-vis other tax shelters. Although the "at-risk" provision (explained below) and the minimum tax on intangible drilling cost deductions apply, working interests in which the investor has unlimited liability are exempt from the passive activity deferral rules so that tax losses may shelter income from all sources.

In 1971, gas was 35¢ per thousand cubic feet (at the wellhead) and a barrel of oil was \$2.35. Since the 1980s, these prices have fluctuated between \$1.50 and \$15.

There are many publicly offered oil and gas exploration programs and they are able to find new reserves both in the United States and Canada on a consistent basis. The oil and gas depletion allowance is still available for wildcatters. In general, a successful program will yield high current deductions and partly sheltered cash flows in a year or two, with most distributions made within 8-10 years.

With as little as \$5,000 the taxpayer may buy an interest in such an inflation-hedging investment and claim intangible drilling cost deductions up front and depletion allowances when cash is collected. Some 80-90% of the initial investment is deductible. As prices increase, so does the reward/risk ratio. Despite attempts to develop alternative sources of energy (nuclear power, solar energy, etc.) from nuclear power to solar energy, there is little doubt that oil and gas will remain the main energy resource until the next century.

ILLUSTRATION OF AN OIL OR GAS INVESTMENT—A REALISTIC VIEW

A taxpayer invested \$100,000, all of which was deductible (\$40,000 in dry-hole costs and \$60,000 in intangible drilling costs (IDC)) and expects to collect income of \$200,000 over 10 years. Sounds good? If it does, there are drawbacks. Even assuming a 36% bracket, the taxpayer is still investing \$64,000 after taxes.

What about the return? The \$200,000, less a depletion allowance of, say, \$40,000, could leave the investor with only \$102,400 as follows:

Income	\$200,000	
Depletion	40,000	
Income tax	(57,600)	(36% of \$160,000)
	\$102,400	

Thus, the taxpayer really invested \$64,000 to get \$102,400 in 10 years. Even an investment of \$64,000 in 7% (8%) municipals with the interest reinvested would have grown to about \$131,800 (\$144,646) in 10 years with a lot less work, inconvenience, expense, and more peace of mind. IDC and percentage depletion may also be subject to the alternative minimum tax.

¶ 1107 MASTER LIMITED PARTNERSHIPS (MLPs)

After the passive activity loss deferral rules came in with the Tax Reform Act of 1986, the Master Limited Partnership (MLP) was heralded as one way out. This was because many MLPs generated passive income that would be capable of being offset by losses from other passive investments, and because they are readily available on stock exchanges and over-the-counter, making them easy to purchase and sell.

The Revenue Act of 1987 all but obliterated the tax advantages of MLPs in two ways:

1. Under Code Sec. 7704, MLPs are taxed as corporations after 1987, thus locking income and losses in the entity. Pre-existing MLPs, defined as MLPs actively traded by December 17, 1987, *and* with at least 90% of gross income generated from "portfolio" type income such as interest, dividends, and gains from securities, etc., are not taxed as corporations until after 1997 (unless they add a substantial new line of business).

2. MLPs not taxed as corporations under the ten-year moratorium rule are subject to special limitations. Thus, passive losses are locked in each MLP for each owner, until the earlier of the generation of passive income by that particular MLP, the taxable sale of the interest, or the death of the owner. Furthermore, income from whatever source in the MLP is treated as nonpassive. However, business income is treated as passive, but only for the purpose of absorbing carryovers of business losses from previous years from that particular MLP.[1]

¶ 1108 PARTNERSHIP TAXATION—GENERAL

Most tax shelters are organized as partnerships for the following reasons: a partnership is not a taxable entity.[2] All items of income, gain, loss or credit flow through as such to the individual partners who pick them up on their own individual returns.[2a] The partnership, as a true conduit, simply files an information return, Form 1065, showing the results of operations and each partner's distributive share.

Unlike a Subchapter S corporation, for example, there is no limit on the number of investors who can own an interest.

The Uniform Limited Partnership Act is in effect in most states and permits all investor-partners to be limited partners with limited liability, as long as there is at least one general partner with personal liability. In fact, a corporation can be the only general partner in a limited partnership.

---

[1] Code Sec. 469(k).
[2] Code Sec. 701.
[2a] Code Sec. 702(b).

¶ 1109 COMPUTING THE BASIS IN A PARTNERSHIP INTEREST

The formation of a partnership is not a taxable event.[3] The investor's investment at any given point in time is arrived at by adding the following:

1. Cash and cost basis of assets invested.[4]
2. Share of taxable and nontaxable income.[5]
3. Share of partnership liabilities.[6]

From this is subtracted:

1. Share of liabilities repaid.[7]
2. Share of losses and nondeductible expenses.[8]
3. Distributions made in cash or property.[9]

The basis is needed to compute any gain or loss on a disposition of the partnership interest and it also limits loss deductions since these may reduce basis, but not below zero.[10] If the "at-risk" rules apply (explained below), the losses may be suspended, if in excess of the lower "at-risk" basis.[11] These rules are complex enough that the investor probably needs a tax advisor. The trick is to get competent advice *before* getting into a shelter. It is so much easier to buy than to sell a tax shelter interest.

> ***Example:*** Robert purchases an interest in a new tax shelter partnership requiring an investment of $100,000. He puts up $10,000 in cash and borrows the rest on a nonrecourse note on commercially reasonable terms. Of the downpayment, $800 goes for commissions, $500 for legal fees and $300 for organization costs, leaving a $8,400 investment in cash and a note for $91,600 ($100,000 less $8,400). (Incidentally, only the $300 qualifies for a five-year write-off as organization expenses.) The basis for gain or loss is $101,600 ($10,000 plus $91,600). This is also the limitation on deductions if it is a real estate venture. If not, the "at-risk" basis is only $10,000, not $101,600.

The "At-Risk" Provisions

¶ 1115 HOW "AT RISK" WORKS

An investor may have different "bases," e.g., one basis for determining gain or loss on sale and another basis for limiting loss deduc-

[3] Code Sec. 721.
[4] Code Sec. 722.
[5] Code Sec. 705.
[6] Code Sec. 752(a).
[7] Code Sec. 752(b).
[8] Code Sec. 705.
[9] Code Sec. 733.
[10] Code Sec. 704(d).
[11] Code Sec. 465.

tions. The "at-risk" rules simply limit the basis for deducting losses by excluding nonrecourse liabilities for that limited purpose, keeping the gain or loss basis on disposition unchanged.[12] Here is an example of an abuse the rules are designed to prevent:

Taxpayer purchases a feature film for $10 million which costs the producer $1 million to produce. It is really only worth $2 million, so the buyer puts up $2 million as a downpayment, signing a nonrecourse note for $8 million. The seller is happy, having received his 100% profit. The investor is happy because depreciation can be claimed on $10 million with no personal liability for the note. If this were done in partnership form, the investor would also pay stiff fees to the promoter plus management fees. Under current law, only $2 million in losses can be deducted unless the investor is personally liable on the note.

WHO ARE AFFECTED

The "at-risk" rules apply to individuals, whether in partnership or not, and certain closely held corporations.

ACTIVITIES AFFECTED

Although initially only farming, oil and gas, equipment leasing and movies, records and books were affected, currently *all* activities, except real estate (unless the loan is commercially unreasonable or the seller is the lender) are subject to the "at-risk" rules. Being "at risk" is therefore necessary for a tax shelter to really work, but it is often unattractive financially. To make personal liability tolerable, the investor should either be judgment proof or the project should be economically viable.

¶ 1116 WHEN THE INVESTOR IS NOT "AT RISK"

The taxpayer is not "at risk" if:

1. borrowing on a nonrecourse basis;
2. covered by a guarantee, insurance, "stop-loss" clause, reimbursement agreement, or similar arrangement;
3. borrowing from a "related party," e.g., close relatives, controlled businesses, etc.; or
4. the amount was borrowed from a person with an economic interest in the activity, e.g., the partnership borrowed from the general partner.

---

[12] Code Sec. 465.

¶ 1117 "AT RISK" IN OPERATION

All deductions, such as interest and depreciation, are computed as usual, and reduce the gain or loss basis without regard to the "at-risk" rules. The taxpayer then deducts losses until the "at-risk" basis is reduced to zero. Any excess losses are suspended and can only be deducted if and when the taxpayer acquires more "at-risk" basis. There are three ways to acquire basis without disposing of the interest:

1. Adding a share of profits.
2. Making additional investments.
3. Assuming personal liability (and becoming a general partner).

¶ 1118 SUSPENDED LOSSES UPON DISPOSITIONS

Any gain recognized from the transfer of an "at-risk" activity or any interest in such an activity is income. Accordingly, it is added to a taxpayer's "at-risk" basis and, to that extent, absorbs any suspended losses.[13]

> ***Example:*** Taxpayer's "at-risk" basis was zero, the adjusted basis was $10,000 (share of nonrecourse liabilities) and suspended losses were $8,000 when Taxpayer sold the partnership interest for $3,000 in cash. Seller's gain is $3,000 ($3,000+$10,000−$10,000) and is offset by $3,000 of suspended losses. The remaining $5,000 of losses evaporates. Buyer's basis is $13,000, but the "at-risk" basis is $3,000.

GIFTS

When a gift is made, suspended losses are added to donor's basis which carries over to the donee, but no losses are allowed. The donee's "at-risk" basis equals that of the donor's (computed as of the end of the year of the gift) plus gift taxes paid, if any.[14]

> ***Example:*** Same as above, except Taxpayer gifted the property. Donee's "at-risk" basis remains zero, but the gain or loss basis is increased by $8,000 to $18,000.

TRANSFERS AT DEATH

Upon death, the successor's gain or loss basis equals the estate tax value, e.g., the fair market value of the interest.[15] The "at-risk" basis, however, equals that of the decedent, plus any step up, or less any step down, in basis, resulting from Code Sec. 1014.[16]

> ***Example:*** Same as above, except Taxpayer died when the interest was worth $3,000. Successor's basis for gain or loss is $13,000, the

---

[13] Prop. Reg. § 1.465-66.
[14] Prop. Reg. § 1.465-68.
[15] Code Sec. 1014(a).
[16] Prop. Reg. § 1.465-69.

estate tax value ($3,000, plus share of liabilities). Since this represents a step up in basis of $3,000 ($13,000 – $10,000), Successor's "at-risk" basis is increased from zero to $3,000.

¶ 1119 LOSS RECAPTURE RULES

Being personally liable for a limited time does not work either. Thus, any losses deducted above the "at-risk" basis resulting from:

1. a switch to nonrecourse financing,
2. a guarantee, or
3. a distribution.

It will be taxed and added to the above-mentioned expense account in search of basis. Thus, if a taxpayer is only comfortable with nonrecourse financing, real estate is the only game in town.

ILLUSTRATIONS OF THE SCOPE OF THE "AT-RISK" RULES

Dry holes

Here is an example of a real-life tax shelter which sounded almost too good to be true:

Investor puts $100,000 in an oil-drilling venture, all of which would be currently deductible if the hole was dry. Furthermore, if the hole was dry, an oil company was contractually obligated to buy the worthless hole for $60,000. Why would they pay for a dry hole? Because it is cheaper than doing it themselves. In other words, they would rather expend $60,000 for a dry hole than spend $100,000 to get the same result. The two alternatives were advertised to be:

1. Investor winds up with an oil well, or
2. investor gets back close to the after-tax cost.

In addition, Investor is not subject to the minimum tax on tax preferences if a dry hole results. Here is the drawback: because Investor is guaranteed a $60,000 minimum, even if the hole is dry, Investor is really only "at risk" for $40,000. The deduction will therefore only reduce the investment by $20,000. The transaction is likely to be construed as a loan or as an option.

What is real estate?

Pat and Mike bought a building for $10,000 in cash each and an $80,000 nonrecourse mortgage to operate a movie theater on the premises. Even though the only asset in the partnership is real property, Pat and Mike are subject to the "at-risk" rules, being in the movie, not the real estate, business. Thus, losses in excess of $20,000 are suspended. After several years of losses and small profits, Pat and Mike lease the building to someone who is going to operate a business on the premises. Even if the lessee is running a movie theater, Pat and Mike are now in the real estate business, the "at-risk" basis are increased by $40,000 each and suspended losses become deductible to that extent.

Passive Activity Losses

¶ 1125 INTRODUCTION AND SUMMARY

One of the biggest changes in the Tax Reform Act of 1986 was the passive activity loss deferral rules.[17] In a nutshell the rule provides that losses from activities in which the investor does not *materially participate,* including any limited partnership and real estate, can only be used currently to the extent of income from such activities. Excess losses are suspended one year at a time to offset passive activity income. However, suspended losses are allowed in full in the year the activity is disposed of in a taxable transaction (capital losses are limited to capital gain plus $3,000 a year under Code Sec. 1211). Exceptions are provided for "working interests" in oil or gas property where the investor's liability is not limited and for 10% or more owned real property in which the investor "actively participates" (for the latter, see next chapter). The rules apply to individuals, estates, trusts, and personal service corporations. Even though losses are suspended, a basis reduction results in the interest. Thus, even if the partner has sufficient basis to absorb the loss under Code Sec. 704(d) and even if the partner has "at-risk" basis, the loss is still deferred if the activity is "passive" and the partner has no other income from passive activities. Income from compensation and investments (portfolio income) is irrelevant.

¶ 1126 PORTFOLIO INCOME AND "PAYCHECK" INCOME

Portfolio income includes such items as interest, dividends, royalties and capital gains. Such income, *even if generated in an entity engaged in the "passive activity"* cannot be offset by passive activity losses. Compensation is treated the same way.

1. Partner's share of limited partnership loss is $50,000. Partner has $60,000 of investment income and $75,000 of salary. The full $50,000 is deferred.

2. Same as 1, except the partnership had interest and dividends of $20,000 allocable to Partner. The investment income is passed through to Partner, increasing investment income to

[17] Code Sec. 469.

$80,000 and the loss to $70,000 which is disallowed and carried forward.

3. Same as 1, but Partner has income from another partnership of $35,000. Only $15,000 of losses are required to be deferred, even if the passive activities are quite different, e.g., cattle and Broadway shows.

¶ 1127 YEAR OF DISPOSITION

Suspended losses under the passive activity deferral rules (*not* losses suspended because of Code Sec. 704(d) or Code Sec. 465) are deductible without limit in the year of a taxable disposition of the entire interest.[18] This rule also applies when the investor dies, but only to the extent the suspended loss exceeds the step-up in basis, if any.[19] In a gift situation, the donee's basis is increased by the suspended losses.[20]

1. *Sale at gain.* Partner has suspended losses of $10,000 and sells the interest at a gain of $3,000. Partner also has income from another passive activity of $2,000. The suspended loss offsets (1) gain of $3,000, (2) income of $2,000, and (3) any other income, including portfolio or paycheck income, in that order.
2. *Sale at loss.* Same as 1, except the interest is sold at a capital loss of $5,000. The suspended loss is allowed, first to offset passive activity income, then against other income. In the absence of capital gains in the current year, only $3,000 of the $5,000 capital loss is allowed, with $2,000 carried over to the subsequent year.
3. *Gift.* Partner gives the interest to a daughter at the time basis is $11,000 and suspended losses are $8,000. The suspended losses evaporate, but the daughter's basis equals $19,000.
4. *Death.* Same as 3, except the gift was testamentary and the estate tax value was $16,000. $5,000 of the suspended losses evaporate ($16,000 – $11,000), $3,000 are allowed on the decedent's final income tax return and the daughter's basis is $16,000.

¶ 1128 MATERIAL PARTICIPATION

A passive activity is a trade or business in which the taxpayer does not materially participate. The following are generally passive interests:

1. Limited partnerships.

---

[18] Code Sec. 469(g).
[19] Code Sec. 469(g)(2).
[20] Code Sec. 469(j)(6).

2. Real estate rentals.
3. Activities in which taxpayer is a mere investor.

The following are *not* passive interests:

1. "Working interests" in oil and gas ventures, as long as the investor's liability is not limited.
2. Dealerships, including real estate dealers.
3. Trades or businesses where the taxpayer "materially participates" (for definition, see below).
4. The following rental activities are not passive activities, assuming the owner materially participates:
   (a) The rental period is seven days or less, on the average (hotel rooms, tuxedos, cars).
   (b) The rental period is 30 days or less, and significant services are rendered.
   (c) The rental period is of any length if extraordinary services are rendered (boarding schools, nursing homes, hospitals).
   (d) The rental is incidental to nonrental activity (the property is held for sale or investment, or used in a trade or business).
   (e) The property is available to customers during regular business hours for their nonexclusive use of (i.e., a golf course).

The taxpayer "materially participates" if any one or more of the following seven tests are met:

1. The taxpayer works more than 500 hours a year in the activity.
2. The taxpayer's participation constitutes substantially all participation in the activity of all individuals (including nonowners) in the year.
3. The taxpayer works more than 100 hours in the activity in the year, and no one else works longer hours.
4. The taxpayer significantly participates more than 100 hours in more than one activity and they total more than 500 hours in one year.
5. The taxpayer materially participates in the activity for at least any five years out of 10.
6. The taxpayer materially participated in a personal service activity for any three years prior to the tax year at hand.

7. The taxpayer materially participated on a regular, continuous, and substantial basis during the year, based on facts and circumstances.

It should be noted that the seven tests are designed to see if *losses* are deductible currently and not subject to passive loss deferral rules. If *income* is generated the IRS takes the position that 100 hours of participation is sufficiently material to render the income nonpassive, and thus not shelterable by passive losses.[21]

¶ 1129 HOW TO DEDUCT PASSIVE ACTIVITY LOSSES

Since passive activity losses are only currently deductible to the extent of passive activity income, three possible approaches to avoid loss deferral include:

1. *Converting assets yielding portfolio income into passive activities.* Examples include selling securities and investing the proceeds in partnerships (limited) which generate taxable income, or in income partnerships, such as unleveraged real estate partnerships and parking lots.
2. *Converting an active profitable trade or business into a passive activity.* Under the rules, even a shop could become a passive activity if the owner hires a manager and no longer materially participates in the business.
3. *Converting a passive activity, with tax losses, into an active trade or business.* This could involve converting an apartment house into a hotel, or firing a store manager and taking over the latter's duties, for example.

¶ 1130 CREDITS

Credits are treated similarly to deductions. Thus,

1. Credits from passive activities are allowed only against the tax liability generated by net passive income.
2. Excess credits are suspended in search of taxes from net passive income and cannot be carried back.
3. In the year the entire interest is disposed of in a taxable transaction suspended credits are allowed, but are limited to their *deduction equivalent*, which is a deduction reducing regular tax liability by the amount of the credit.
4. General credit limitations also apply. Thus, most credits may reduce the annual tax liability by $25,000 plus 75% of the excess.

---

[21] Temp. Reg. § 1.469-1T.

¶ 1131 SUMMARY OF THREE LOSS SUSPENSION RULES

Partnership losses, as we have seen, are subject to three loss limitations:

1. Losses are limited to the partner's overall gain or loss basis. Any excess is carried forward one year at a time, is personal to the taxpayer, and evaporates on a transfer by sale, exchange, gift, or death.

2. Losses allowable under rule 1. may nevertheless be suspended to the extent they exceed the taxpayer's "at-risk" basis.[22] However, on a sale, suspended losses are allowed to the extent of gain; on a transfer by gift, they are added to donee's basis; and on a transfer by death, they evaporate, but the transferee receives "at-risk" basis to the extent of a step-up in basis to estate tax value.

3. Losses from passive activities allowable under rules 1. and 2. are deferred to the extent they exceed passive activity income.[22a] Upon a taxable disposition, however, suspended losses are allowed; upon a gift, they are added to basis; and upon death, they are allowed to the extent they exceed any basis step up.

¶ 1132 SECURITIES LAW ASPECTS OF TAX SHELTERS

The Security Act of 1933 applies to securities very broadly defined. Thus, any investment contract, whereby an investor buys an interest in an enterprise, and looks for the efforts of a third party to bring a profit, is a "security." The term "security" can encompass such diverse investments as a partnership interest, a whisky future, an option, a coin portfolio, a condominium unit (sold as an investment), etc. An interest in a tax shelter is a security, meaning it must either be registered or exempt from registration. The most common exemption sought is the "private placement exemption." In brief, this entails offering the investment to only a few people (35) who are both "smart and rich," e.g., informed, capable of understanding the risks, and able to bear it. There is also an intrastate exemption from filing with the SEC and a "short-form" (Regulation A) filing procedure for issues up to $1.5 million. Not uncommonly, a tax-shelter offering may have violated either federal or state securities laws. And here is the point:

1. If a shelter flops economically, the investor has no recourse apart from deducting the loss.

---

[22] Code Sec. 465.

[22a] Code Sec. 469.

2. If the tax benefits do not materialize, the taxpayer may have to pay back the taxes plus interest and penalties.
3. If a securities violation is found, the investor is entitled to a refund of the investment from the organizers/promoters.

As a result, the promoters are more worried about the securities laws than the tax laws. Tax problems are the investors' worry, but securities law problems involve the promoters directly. Having a just lawsuit does not, however, mean that the investors can collect. But if a shelter fails, investors invariably look for a securities law violation.

¶ 1133 DISPOSING OF A TAX SHELTER

A common mistake of the individual reluctant to pay tax when evaluating a tax shelter is to consider only the up-front, immediate tax benefits, i.e., the ratio of deductions to invested cash. The tax consequences which will inevitably result a few years later are often conveniently forgotten, one reason being the promoter's failure to mention them. The later the investor reaches the cross-over point when moving from a tax loss to a taxable income situation, the better. But when it happens, it is difficult to get out without sustaining considerable inconvenience and/or costs. Here is a summary of the main ways to terminate tax-sheltered investments:

SELL THE INTEREST AND PAY THE TAX

This is probably the course of action the investor wishes to avoid because it may lead to a tremendous tax liability all in one year and with little or no cash generated. The problem arises because the face amount of the indebtedness discharged is counted as sales proceeds. These proceeds less the often low or zero cost basis (due to previous deductions) will all turn into income, even though nothing may actually change hands. The tax consequences are the same whether there is a foreclosure, a partnership sells its assets, or the inventor sells the interest in the partnership. The released liabilities are included in the proceeds.[23] Certain items, such as depreciation recapture, will be ordinary income, and any investment credit recapture will result in a tax liability, not merely taxable income. However, losses suspended under the "at risk" rules are deductible to the extent of gain, and losses suspended under the "passive activity" rules are deductible in full in the year of sale.

Most people adjust their spending to their after-tax income. As a consequence, if the sale results in no cash proceeds, only a tax liability, many investors find themselves without the means to pay the tax even

[23] Code Secs. 1001, 752(b) and 7701(g).

if they wanted to. In the future, however, this may become the most popular strategy. This is because of the extent losses have been suspended after 1986.[24] Most taxable dispositions will make these losses deductible against *any* taxable income in the year of sale. (See next chapter.) The following sales methods exist:

1. The sponsor or the broker sometimes buys back shelters or helps find buyers.
2. Investors with publicly registered shelters may have them listed through their broker on the National Partnership Exchange (1-800-356-2739). Potential buyers can bid for a week, but the owner may reject any offers made.
3. There is an institutional secondary market in tax shelters. However, not only are they selective, but they also pay less than the net asset value. Three of the largest are Oppenheimer and Bigelow (212/599-0697), Partnership Securities Exchange (415/763-5555) and Equity Resources Group, Inc. (617/876-4800).

PERSONAL BANKRUPTCY

This alternative may be unattractive for several reasons:

1. If the investor owns considerable assets and is not insolvent, a discharge will be denied by the bankrupty court.
2. By planning ahead, the petitioner can transfer all assets to a spouse, for example. This must be done more than one year prior to filing, otherwise it is a *fraudulent conveyance* and the property can be reached by the trustee in bankruptcy. If done, it must be done irrevocably. This means lost control of assets with the attendant risk. Making oneself "judgment-proof" may result in gift tax liability unless the transfer is to the spouse.
3. The fact of a bankruptcy stays on the petitioner's credit record for 10 years and may prove embarrassing professionally.
4. Historically, all kinds of tax shelters were financed with nonrecourse loans. A taxpayer who is not personally liable for the debt cannot be discharged from it. Therefore, the taxpayer will still have income upon sale or foreclosure of the property.

Despite the above disadvantages, bankruptcy does work if the investor owns few assets *and* is personally liable for the debts of the shelter. This is because the discharge of the indebtedness is *not* income.

[24] Code Sec. 469.

Although cancellation of indebtedness generally is taxable, an exception is provided for bankruptcies to assist the petitioner in obtaining a fresh start.[25]

THE DEFECTIVE TRUST GAMBIT

In the middle '70s, this strategy was heralded as a specially attractive tax-shelter device. A high-bracket individual would have a trust, owning the interest with the children as beneficiaries. This would be a *grantor trust* for income tax purposes because the grantor would retain certain powers, typically the power to revoke.[26] As a result, the trust would be disregarded for tax purposes and the grantor could therefore deduct all tax losses. Also, no gift tax liability would be incurred because the transfer to the trust would not be complete. A few years hence, when the cross-over point was reached, the grantor would release the power to revoke, and the children would receive the taxable income, but little cash. Because of the limited value of the interest at that time, the gift tax liability would be minimal.

Unfortunately, the IRS treats the release of power under these circumstances as a transfer, a sale, or an exchange, thus resulting in the same tax liability as if the interest were sold outright. The face amount of the debts again becomes proceeds from a sale.

DEATH

Dying can save a lot of income taxes, but is typically of limited utility as a planning device. If the tax shelter investor is old, it would be advisable to consider the life expectancy and the investment horizon, i.e., time to the cross-over point in tandem. Taxable income could be postponed until death by a continuous tax shelter program. Death is not a taxable event. An heir who does not want the interest due to the high potential tax liability can disclaim the bequest. Or the interest could be left to the state, which cannot disclaim. If the interest has zero or negative value, no charitable contribution deduction is available.

DIVORCE

A taxpayer would purchase the tax shelter interest in the spouse's name, take all the deductions on a joint return, and then obtain a divorce after the cross-over point is reached. This strategy, however, is hardly consistent with domestic harmony, and most people do not plan a divorce several years in advance. And, even if done, assuming the spouse has little income, the loss of the availability of joint returns will be expensive. The latter could be resolved, of course, through an early remarriage.

---

[25] Reg. § 1.61-12(b).

[26] Code Sec. 676.

INVESTMENT IN NEW SHELTER

If the investor's experience with tax shelters has been a good one, a continuous program makes sense. Thus, when one tax shelter interest is disposed of, another one is purchased. The disadvantage is that the sale may produce little or no cash, while the purchase requires an investment. Consider the following:

1. The investor could save on taxes by investing in liquid assets, such as tax-exempt municipal bonds.
2. The investor could get out of a shelter early in the year and invest later in the year to allow time to save up. If done, the investor's deductions for the year are limited, due to the unavailability of retroactive allocations to "December partners."[27]

CHARITABLE CONTRIBUTIONS

Contributing a tax shelter interest to charity presents several problems:

1. After the "cross-over" point, most charities will refuse the "gift." This is due to the fact that the interest may be cumbersome, have no value, and generate "unrelated business income" on which an otherwise tax-exempt institution will still be taxed.
2. If the interest passes by will, but the named charity refuses to accept, it will pass as a residuary distribution. Alternative charities should be named. The investor might consider forming a private foundation and contribute the interest to it (but see 3).
3. When the interest is contributed to charity, the investor is deemed to have received a share of the face amount of liabilities in the shelter. If this exceeds both the basis and the fair market value of the interest, no contribution deduction is possible and the "donor" still winds up with the gain.
4. If the interest is a partnership interest, the investor has an additional problem. In general, there are restrictions on the admission of new partners, even in the absence of a specific prohibition in the partnership agreement. The doctrine of *delectus personarum* means that a partner may not be able to force the other partners to accept a third party, including a charity, as a partner.

---

[27] Code Sec. 706(c)(2)(B).

As a conclusion, it is hard to recommend this alternative as an effective way to terminate a shelter.

TRANSFER OF REMAINDER TO A TRUST

Here, the interest is transferred to a trust irrevocably with the investor retaining an income interest until the estimated "cross-over" point, whereupon the remainder goes to minor children or grandchildren in low brackets, or, for that matter, a charity or a corporation. Retaining the income interest for a term of years assures the taxpayer his deduction, because a tax loss is nothing but "negative income." The IRS may, however, treat this type of arrangement as equivalent to a "defective trust."

GIFT TO FAMILY MEMBER

Giving away a tax shelter interest to a low-bracket family member may present several problems:

1. It is a part sale, part gift, so that the donor's share of liabilities less basis are translated into a taxable gain.
2. If the liabilities involved exceed the fair market value of the assets transferred, the transferee may be deemed to have made a gift of the difference with possible gift tax consequences. This, however, may be much more attractive than the income tax consequences of a deemed sale. Each donor can make a tax-free gift of up to $610,000, corresponding to the amount of the unified estate and gift tax credit plus the annual exclusion of $10,000, without any gift tax being due. This is worth considering.

A TAX-FREE EXCHANGE

The tax law permits an exchange of "like-kind" property without the recognition of a gain or loss.[28] Thus, by trading in an investment for another, the gain is postponed. A sizeable additional investment in cash may be required, but the gain is rolled over in addition to accomplishing the goals under "invest in new shelter." Although partnership interests are not eligible for tax-free exchanges, the same result may be reached by receiving a tax-free property distribution from *one* partnership, then contributing such property to another partnership in exchange for a partnership interest.

INCORPORATION

If a partnership interest is incorporated, liabilities in excess of basis result in an immediate gain.[29]

---

[28] Code Sec. 1031(a)(2)(D).

[29] Code Sec. 357(c).

INSTALLMENT SALES

Through a sale on the installment plan, a gain is postponed until the proceeds are collected. Unfortunately, liabilities in excess of basis count as proceeds and may indeed be the only proceeds.

ABANDONMENT

Walking away from a tax shelter has probably received the most attention in the literature. The investor simply notifies the other partners in writing of the withdrawal. This is permissible under the Uniform Partnership Act, but may be contrary to the partnership agreement. Because the remaining partners presumably pick up the ex-partner's share pro rata, they may be so upset if the share actually has negative value that they may sue for damages. In any event, the investor's share of liabilities still counts as proceeds.

¶ 1134 PENALTIES AND INTEREST

There are penalties for promoting abusive tax shelters, failing to register a tax shelter with the IRS, and penalties aimed at advisers and return preparers. In addition, there are a number of penalty provisions aimed at the "aggressive" taxpayer, such as:

1. The interest on tax underpayments is equal to the short-term Treasury Bill rate plus 3%, while the IRS will pay only the T-bill rate plus 2% on overpayments.[30]
2. The interest rate is further increased by 20% if the underpayment is due to fraudulent tax-motivated transaction.
3. Underpayments of estimated taxes are subject to a penalty of 1% a month.[31]
4. Substantial understatements of tax liability (the greater of 20% of tax required or $10,000) caused by items for which no "substantial authority" exists or undisclosed items are subject to a 25% penalty.[32]
5. Underpayments caused by negligence are subject to a 5% penalty.[33]
6. A 75% fraud penalty is applicable to underpayments of tax caused by fraud.[34]
7. 1% a month up to 25% is assessed for taxes shown as due on the return, but paid late. A ½% rate is used until the taxpayer receives a notice of intent to levy on taxpayer's assets or a notice and demand for immediate payment.[35]

---

[30] Code Sec. 6621.
[31] Code Sec. 6654.
[32] Code Sec. 6661.
[33] Code Sec. 6724.
[34] Code Sec. 6653.
[35] Code Sec. 6651.

8. An overvaluation penalty of 10%-30% of an overvaluation of property in excess of 150% of basis.[36]
9. A $250 penalty is assessed for each failure by the taxpayer to include a tax shelter ID number on his return.[37]

To add insult to injury, penalties are nondeductible. Even interest on underpayments is fully nondeductible since, for personal taxpayers, the interest is personal interest.

¶ 1135 ALTERNATIVE MINIMUM TAX—THE LAST STRAW

An alternative minimum tax is computed on alternative minimum taxable income (AMTI) and is payable to the extent, if any, it exceeds regular tax.[38] AMTI equals taxable income, plus tax preferences, and less a $45,000 exemption for joint filers ($33,750 for single filers). The exemption is reduced by 25 cents for each dollar that AMTI before exemption exceeds $150,000 for joint filers ($112,500 for singles). The tax rate is 26% on the first $175,000 of AMTI (reduced by the exemption) and 28% on any excess.

The most important "add-backs" to taxable income include:

1. Miscellaneous itemized expenses;
2. IDC in excess of 65% of net income;
3. Regular cost recovery on personal property less accelerated cost recovery over a longer period;
4. Straight-line real estate cost recovery less straight-line cost recovery over 40 years;
5. Passive activity losses allowed as a phase-in;
6. Bargain element of incentive stock options upon exercise; and
7. Tax-exempt interest on nonessential private activity bonds.

¶ 1136 TAX BENEFITS OTHER THAN TAX SHELTERS

Before running out to buy interests in long-distance, esoteric tax-shelter investments, the investor should recall some of the other tax relief provisions that are available with or without an investment:

1. The *maximum capital gains tax* rate of 28% and the maximum rate on ordinary income of 39.6% are available, regardless of how high the individual's taxable income is.
2. *Exemptions* ($2,450 in 1994) are available for the taxpayer, a spouse and dependents.[39]

---

[36] Code Sec. 6659.
[37] Code Sec. 6707.
[38] Code Secs. 55-59.
[39] Code Secs. 151-152.

3. The *standard deduction* provides a minimum of tax-free income for everyone ($3,800 for singles, $6,350 on a joint return in 1994).
4. When property is sold on the *installment method,* the seller defers the tax liability until collection.[40]
5. A greater portion of compensation may be taken in the form of nontaxable fringe benefits and deferred compensation.
6. If self-employed, a professional corporation can provide numerous tax savings opportunities.
7. The taxpayer can always invest in tax-exempt *municipal bonds,* directly or through a fund.[41]
8. The estate and gift tax *marital deduction,* thanks to which unlimited assets may be transferred between spouses free of transfer taxes.[42] Usually, there is no income tax either.[43]
9. The *unified credit* exempts the first $600,000 transferred to anyone by death or gift from estate and gift taxes.[44]
10. After age 55, a homeowner may exclude up to $125,000 of a gain on the principal residence from taxation.[45]
11. A wage earner may deduct up to $2,000 a year of contributions to an individual retirement account.[46]
12. Taxpayer may invest in deferred, variable annuity programs or universal life policies.

CONCLUSION

The reduction of tax rates, the expanded alternative minimum tax, lengthened cost recovery periods, repeal of the investment tax credit, and the passive activity loss deferral rules, all reduce the demand for traditional tax shelters. However, tax shelters are not dead because, among other reasons:

1. Starting in 1993, ordinary tax rates reach a maximum of 39.6% while capital gains rates remain at the pre-1993 level of up to only 28%.
2. Real estate losses up to $25,000 per year are allowed from "active participation interests."
3. Losses from shelters are allowed in full against income from other shelters and upon taxable dispositions.

---

[40] Code Sec. 453.

[41] Code Sec. 103.

[42] Code Secs. 2056 and 2523.

[43] Code Sec. 1041.

[44] Code Sec. 2010.

[45] Code Sec. 121.

[46] The deduction is phased out at AGIs of $40,000 to $50,000 on a joint return ($25,000-$35,000 if single) if the taxpayer or the spouse is a participant in a qualified plan.

4. Trades or businesses generating income may be converted to passive activities.
5. Passive activities generating losses may be converted to a trade or business in which taxpayer materially participates.

Although hit hard by the Tax Reform Act of 1986 and the Revenue Reconciliation Act of 1993, real estate remains the most viable of tax shelters and is deserving of a separate chapter, which follows.

CHAPTER 12

REAL ESTATE INVESTMENTS

INTRODUCTION

PASSIVE LOSS RESTRICTIONS

Introduction

¶ 1201 REAL ESTATE INVESTMENTS IN GENERAL

There are numerous advantages and disadvantages to real estate investments. (Investing in a residence was analyzed in an earlier chapter.)

Advantages

Compared to other investments, such as securities, real property offers the following benefits:

1. Real estate has a better record as an inflation hedge. Over the last few decades, values have more than compensated for the diminishing purchasing power of the dollar. Residential property in particular has skyrocketed in some parts of the country.
2. Someone who buys rental property may immediately start expensing the purchase price through depreciation deductions. This is true even though the *value* may be going up.
3. Should a poor investment be made in rental property, any loss is generally a deductible ordinary loss, *not* a less useful capital loss.
4. A buyer may be able to purchase real estate with only 20% or less down, creating more leverage, with more solid backing than securities.

Disadvantages

On the other hand, real estate has some drawbacks:

1. Each piece of real estate is unique. It is therefore much easier to buy than to sell. Real estate broker commissions comprise a high percentage of the selling price, often 6%-8%.
2. There is considerable work involved. Buying an apartment building, for example, may turn the owner into a part-time janitor. Managers may be needed to oversee the property, lawyers to evict tenants, and brokers to sell it, etc.

¶ 1202 COMMERCIAL REAL ESTATE INVESTMENT

The client does not have to be wealthy to invest in commercial properties as an alternative to residential structures. Individual commercial property owners are on the increase and the investments range from stores and office buildings to warehouses and parking lots. And the increases in value are comparable to those of residential properties. The tax advantages are similar as well, with the addition of a few extras, discussed below.

Advantages of commercial properties over rental structures are as follows:

1. It is *easier to raise the rent,* for several reasons:
   (a) Rent control only applies to residential units.
   (b) If the rent is a percentage of gross receipts, which is common when the tenant is a store, the landlord automatically receives increases as the price level goes up. If sales go up in real terms, an additional bonus is paid.
   (c) It is more cumbersome to move a business than to change a residential address. As a result, the commercial tenant is more likely to accept a rent increase, unless it is outrageous.
2. *Favorable financing* is often available. It is not unusual in tight mortgage markets for the seller to finance the purchase, often with only 10% down. A mortgage given by the seller is called a purchase money mortgage. An older seller, near retirement, who received the advantage of, say, a 10% return on a mortgage secured by the property could at the same time report the gain on the installment method, spreading any tax liability over many low-income years. If the buyer needs an institutional loan, however, the downpayment is typically considerably higher than the 20% commonly used for residences.
3. *Longer leases* are common. It is not unusual for commercial leases to run for up to 20 years. This cuts the costs of negotiations, advertising for new tenants, vacancies, repairs and maintenance, etc. However, the owner must make sure it is possible to raise the rent during the life of the lease.
4. There are *fewer maintenance problems.* Commercial occupants rarely spend 24 hours a day on the premises. There will be few midnight calls, no noisy parties, etc. Ideally, the premises may only be in use during normal business hours, say, from 8 a.m. to 6 p.m., Monday through Friday.

5. Commercial tenants are *less difficult to evict.* Locally, numerous ordinances protect even nonpaying residential tenants from being evicted except after substantial periods of time. Commercial tenants are not protected to this extent. The other side of the coin is that a business may close in a recession, but a family must live somewhere in any event. Note also that the owner of a service business, with few assets on the premises, can more easily walk away than a store owner, for example.

¶ 1203 WHAT TO LOOK FOR BEFORE BUYING

Here are some basic factors to consider before buying property:

1. If possible, the investor should stay within a familiar neighborhood. Ideally, the investor should live close by in order to keep an eye on the property. It is not necessarily an advantage to lease to family members or close friends. Such people may expect favors and may not take their obligations as seriously as when dealing at arm's length.
2. An investor may find what is wanted through newspaper ads, but not without checking the reason for the sale. Surprisingly often, an owner may be amenable to an offer, even if the property is not listed for sale. Consequently, if an investor finds an attractive piece of real estate, it would be worthwhile to find out who owns it and if the owner might sell.
3. When looking for a long-term investment, the investor must be concerned with location, physical appearance, and most of all, the long-term income potential of the property. However, if a quick profit is desired, the primary concern is the price. The potential income outlook becomes secondary.
4. Since real estate is much easier to buy than to sell, the buyer should be prepared to own it for at least several years. The property should therefore be in good physical condition, well located and occupied by financially stable tenants.
5. A suburban site with good parking and preferably near a major highway is a good location for a store. However, the investor should not necessarily shy away from stores in downtown business centers, either. Office buildings, on the other hand, need not be located directly on a major street if there is easy access to one. Warehouses should, in most cases, be located near major highways for trucking convenience.
6. The investor should not hesitate to look for uncommon situations. A hotel could be converted into an apartment building, a warehouse into a discotheque, etc.

¶ 1204 LEASE CONSIDERATIONS

Here are some points to keep in mind about *leases:*

1. As a rule of thumb, the gross purchase price should not exceed 100 times the *gross* monthly rent collected currently. This ratio should not deteriorate with time. Thus, the future gross monthly rents should be at least one percent of the fair market value of the property. As another rule of thumb, the annual cash *net* income should be at least 10% of the cash downpayment. Due to noncash expenses, such as depreciation, the investor may collect cash while sustaining a tax loss. (See below for tax aspects of real estate.)
2. If one can be negotiated, a *net* lease should be obtained. In a net lease situation, the *tenant* assumes the responsibility for property taxes, insurance, utilities, and maintenance of the premises. The owner's responsibility is limited to the structure itself. Naturally, the rent charged will be less under these conditions, but income is stabilized.
3. The investor should not agree to a long-term lease unless the lease contains an *escalation* clause. Here are the main possibilities:
   (a) Tying the rent to a price index, such as the Consumer Price Index or the implicit price deflator in the Gross Domestic Product.
   (b) Having the lease provide for increases necessary to cover rising costs in property taxes, utilities, and upkeep.
   (c) When renting to retail stores, charging rent which equals the larger of a flat amount or a percentage of gross sales. Gross sales tend to go up with inflation. The owner will collect extra rent if the store is successful, while the floor serves as a guaranteed minimum.

¶ 1205 RESIDENTIAL REAL ESTATE INVESTMENTS

One typical example of a real estate investment plan is to buy a six-flat, live in one unit, and rent out the rest. On paper, at least, it looks good. Theoretically, the owner has "free" rent plus a tax shelter (current deductions and future appreciation). Here is the picture the *seller* may present:

Cash-Flow Analysis for Six-Flat

Gross rental income $440 per month per apartment		$26,400
Operating Expenses:		
Taxes	$6,000	
Insurance	800	
Utilities	1,800	

Supplies	200		
Other services	400		9,200
Net operating income			$17,200
Loan payments			
10% interest on $150,000 mortgage		$15,000	
Principal		1,600	$16,600
Net before tax cash flow			$ 600

According to the seller, therefore, the investor lives free and collects $600 a year while generating a tax loss due to depreciation deductions. In addition, future appreciation is a capital gain.

The problems with these calculations are as follows:

1. The owner receives no direct compensation for being the janitor, plumber, painter, manager, rental agent, maintenance man, and bookkeeper.
2. The owner puts up a sizeable down payment, on which no interest is paid (and money doubles every six years at 12%, for example).
3. The property may be hard to sell.
4. The cash-flow statement make no provisions for vacancies, eviction costs, advertising, replacement of carpeting, appliances, major repairs, etc.
5. There are risks, such as a changing neighborhood, economic slumps, and difficulties in selling at a profit.

A more realistic cash-flow picture may be the following:

Gross rental income		$ 26,400
Less vacancies and uncollectibles		2,000
Operating expenses:		
Taxes	$6,000	
Insurance	800	
Utilities	1,800	
Advertising	150	
Legal fees	400	
Supplies	400	
Replacements	1,000	
Decorating	500	11,050
Net operating income		$ 13,350
Loan payments		16,600
Negative before tax cash flow		($3,250)

The investor might still receive a current benefit from the tax loss, but the bottom line may be quite sensitive to small changes in the basic assumptions. The extreme case, of course, is a one-flat, where the occupancy rate is either 100% or 0%.

¶ 1206 BUILDING "SWEAT EQUITY"

Everyone hears stories about people who buy property which may be in less than perfect condition and a little mismanaged. They work on the property, put it in shape, raise the rent, then finally sell at a big profit. Before doing this, the following example should be considered.

Example: Two identical two-flats are in need of extensive rehabilitation and sell for $50,000. One buyer does all the work on weekends and evenings, spending $7,000 on materials; the other pays a contractor $25,000. They both receive $600 a month in rent and pay property taxes of $1,000 a year and interest on a $40,000 mortgage of approximately $4,000 a year. The first buyer maintains the property himself, spending $50 a month on materials, while the other pays a management company $175 a month. Two years later, they both sell for $90,000, being in the 30% bracket. Here are the after-tax results for the "janitor" and the "investor."

	"Janitor"	*"Investor"*
Gross rental income	$7,200	$ 7,200
Interest	4,000	4,000
Property tax	1,000	1,000
Maintenance cost	600	2,100
Depreciation	1,710	2,364
Taxable income or loss	($110)	($2,264)
After tax income or loss	(77)	(1,585)

The depreciation differential is due to the fact that the "janitor" can only depreciate the $7,000 of materials purchased, while the "investor" can depreciate the full $25,000 paid the contractor. The calculation assumes that $10,000 of the purchase price is allocated to the land and that the building is depreciated straight-line over 27½ years. It is apparent that the hard-working "janitor" clears only some $124 a month more after taxes than the "investor."

Here is what happens upon sale:

	"Janitor"	*"Investor"*
Selling price	$90,000	$90,000
Cost basis	53,580	79,272
Capital gain	$36,420	$19,728
Tax at 28%	10,198	5,524
After-tax gain	$26,222	$14,204

The "janitor" incurs a capital gain tax of some $4,600 more than the "investor" but made $12,000 more after taxes. However, it took two years' labor to do it (and closing and selling costs are disregarded). It was not an investment profit; it did not come easy. Unless an individual has a limited earning power in alternative pursuits, this is possibly the hardest way to turn personal services into capital gains.

¶ 1207 INVESTING IN RAW LAND

The trouble with buying raw land is threefold:

1. It is nondepreciable,
2. it yields no current income, and
3. due to property taxes, principal and interest (if mortgaged), the cash flow is negative. The sole advantage is the appreciation potential.

For the nonprofessional investor the following is sound advice:

1. Invest only locally where the investor knows the community, the politics, and the property.
2. Predict the path of progress and expansion of the city.
3. Take into account zoning and environmental protection.
4. Reduce the negative cash flow by parking fees, billboard rental, timber removal, tenant farming, or other applicable revenue sources.
5. The investor may use the land personally, e.g., buying a home with an oversized lot or using it as a summer or winter home, a retirement home, etc.

¶ 1208 BENEFIT OF REAL ESTATE PARTNERSHIPS

The reasons that real estate has been such a popular investment vehicle for a partnerships boil down to the following factors:

1. *Safety of capital.* Real estate is a substantial, tangible asset, which generally retains its value in the long term.
2. *Future appreciation.* Real estate tends to increase in real value, since "they don't make more of it."
3. *Inflation hedge.* Even if it does not appreciate in real terms the nominal value should, in the long run, reflect price level changes.
4. *Cash flow.* To the extent gross rent collected exceeds cash expenses and mortgage repayments, there may be a (tax sheltered) positive cash flow.
5. *Tax advantages.* Due to the deductibility of depreciation, interest and taxes, rental income is generally received tax free. Some tax losses, however, must be deferred until sale, or offset

against other "passive activity income." Rehabilitation or low-income housing tax credits may also be available.

6. *Leverage.* Gain and loss are magnified through third-party borrowing.

By purchasing real estate through a partnership the investor is hoping for all the advantages of real estate plus the benefits of professional management, diversification, economics of size, and limited liability. The investor pays dearly for these advantages in the form of fees, such as:

1. Acquisition fees, such as real estate commission (a 6% commission equals 24% of equity when 75% leveraged).
2. Property management fees of 3-6% of gross rents.
3. Partnership management fees of 1-2% of gross income.
4. Share of profits, losses, and cash distributions during ownership to general partner.
5. Share of gain on sale to general partner.

The sum of all these fees can turn a quality project into a loser for the investor.

As a result, large, public real estate partnerships investing in many properties in many locations are the safest for the average investor. These are registered and available through brokers and dealers.

¶ 1209 GENERAL OR LIMITED PARTNERSHIPS

A limited partner's liability is limited to the amounts the investor is obligated to invest under the partnership agreement. However, the partner only "gets basis" (limit on loss deductions) in the partnership interest for a share (using the profit-sharing percentage) of nonrecourse liabilities.[1] Nonrecourse liabilities carry a higher interest rate, however, since the lender has no recourse against any person upon default, but is limited to the value of property subject to the mortgage. A small group of investors are probably better off as a general partnership, due to the simplicity and greater ease of financing. To avoid sales charges, commissions, and fees to promoters and others, they should form their own partnership. They might, however, hire a professional property manager (for 5% of gross rents) to avoid having to perform the daily chores.

¶ 1210 RISKS IN REAL ESTATE

It is important to recognize that things *can* go wrong in real estate investments, regardless how rosy the picture may have been the last

[1] Reg. § 1.752-1(e).

few years. If something does go wrong, it is likely to be because of one or more of the situations discussed below.

INFLATION MIGHT TAPER OFF, OR STAY LOW

Although most people hope inflation will be curbed, real estate investors do not. Anyone who uses high leverage builds equity automatically if inflation continues. The reason is that the mortgage stays the same but the value of the property goes up in nominal dollars. If the property is owned outright, no equity is built in real terms, unless the property goes up at a rate higher than inflation. But once the property has a mortgage on it, the difference between the value of the property and the fixed mortgage keeps growing. Conversely, if property values fall, the equity will also fall, magnified by the fixed mortgage. Lower inflation will also make stocks and bonds more attractive vis-à-vis real estate. A shift into securities on the part of the average investor will contribute further to falling real estate values.

ENERGY COSTS ARE GOING UP

The astronomical increases in energy costs affect housing mainly in two ways:

1. Suburban houses get less and less attractive due to the higher transportation costs (including the Revenue Reconciliation Act of 1993 4.3-cent-per-gallon federal fuel tax).
2. Individual family homes, in particular, become costlier to heat and air-condition.

CHANGES IN THE TAX LAW

Until the 1986 Tax Reform Act, real estate had been left relatively untouched by changes in tax policies intended to curb tax shelters. The 1986 tax law changes include the following:

1. All buildings acquired after 1986 must be depreciated straight-line, residential buildings over 27½ years, commercial buildings over 31½ (39 years since 1993).
2. Tax losses from rental properties are deductible only from taxable income from other "passive investments" (other than portfolio incomes). Excess losses are carried forward and deducted in the year the investment is sold.
3. If the investor owns at least 10% of a real estate business *and* "actively participates," up to $25,000 of tax losses are deductible from other income. However, the limitation is phased out pro rata as adjusted gross income goes from $100,000 to $150,000.

4. Capital gains are taxed at the same rates as ordinary income after 1987 for most taxpayers, except for a cap of 28%.

LOCAL POLICIES MAY CHANGE

Perhaps the most important aspect of real estate investments is to consider local conditions. Some of the factors which affect real estate values are school busing, zoning regulations, and rent controls. Environmental and zoning restrictions are particularly important if land is purchased with a view to either developing it or selling to a builder.

THERE MAY BE A RECESSION

A national recession will, at least temporarily, affect real estate values. When interest rates are high, a phenomenon called *financial disintermediation* occurs, e.g., savers may take money out of savings accounts where it earned 2.5% in interest and invest it in Treasury notes. This leads to a drying up of mortgage loans. Even more disastrous may be a local recession. Property values in cities with very few employers are particularly vulnerable. The failure of just one large employer may lead to numerous foreclosures and prices are slashed to the bone. Commercial tenants become scarce as well, even if the area does not become a ghost town.

THE SOUTH SEA BUBBLE SYNDROME

Something is worth only what somebody else is willing to pay for it. In a speculative frenzy, investors sometimes buy, not because they think the property has a high intrinsic value, but because they think they can turn around and make a big profit. In the early 1980s, mortgage rates of 15%-20% did not bother them, because the loan was "free" in the sense that the after-tax interest expense was less than inflation. Eventually any bubble bursts. At a minimum, real estate prices cannot go up indefinitely at a rate in excess of inflation. After all, buildings get older and this intrinsic value goes down, not up.

¶ 1211 NO-DOWN-PAYMENT STRATEGIES

Since the '80s, books, seminars and TV programs have proclaimed the magic of 100% financing, or how to buy real estate with little or no money down.

Here is a brief summary of some of the financing methods. All examples assume a $100,000 selling price.

SELLER FINANCING

Three basic rules for seller financing are as follows:

1. Seller takes back a mortgage for $100,000, or two or more mortgages totalling $100,000.

2. Buyer assumes an existing first mortgage, seller finances the balance with a second.
3. Buyer obtains a first mortgage from a lending institution, for, say, $70,000. Buyer then hands the cash over to Seller who takes back a second mortgage for $30,000.

BORROWING THE DOWN PAYMENT

The down payment is borrowed from finance companies by taking cash advances on credit cards or from friends or relatives. The balance is then borrowed by assuming the existing mortgage and/or from the lending institution and/or from the seller.

MORTGAGING OTHER PROPERTY

Here, the buyer offers the seller a second mortgage on a home or other property owned as a down payment. Alternatively, the buyer obtains a second mortgage from someone else, then uses the proceeds from the loan as a down payment or perhaps several.

THE SECONDARY MORTGAGE MARKET

Due to cash flow problems, many sellers who took back a mortgage originally are willing to sell the paper in the secondary market at a discount from face value:

> Buyer takes out a second mortgage on a home, pocketing $20,000. With the proceeds, Buyer acquires a second mortgage with a face value of $25,000. The newly purchased paper is used as a down payment (at face) and the rest is borrowed from a lender and/or Seller.

CONTRACT ASSIGNMENTS

In some cases, the buyer will have a new purchaser for the property prior to closing. In this case, the contract may be assigned to the ultimate buyer at a profit *without* the need for a closing and without the need for a down payment. The earnest money, if any, may be a note. The intelligent buyer should always make sure that the real estate contract is assignable.

¶ 1212 OPTIONS

An option is a promise to keep an offer open. For a price, the option premium, often as little as 1%-5% of the property value, the buyer obtains the unilateral right to buy the property for a given price for a given length of time.

> ***Example:*** Buyer pays Seller $5,000 for the right to purchase a $100,000 building for $100,000 at any time during the next nine months. If Buyer finds another purchaser at more than $105,000,

Buyer will exercise the option or assign it. If not, Buyer may let the option lapse or purchase the building personally.

¶ 1213 WRAPAROUND

Here, the seller finances the buyer but does *not* pay off the existing mortgage, which the seller continues to amortize.

Example: Seller has an existing first mortgage of $60,000 on a $100,000 building. Seller grants Buyer an $80,000 mortgage and Buyer pays $20,000 down (borrowed from other sources). Seller collects on his $80,000 mortgage, say at 11%, and continues being liable for, and making payments on, the $60,000 mortgage, say at 9%.

¶ 1214 USE OF PARTNERS

A buyer with no funds may consider going into partnership with another. For example:

1. The buyer locates, purchases, and manages the property. The partner puts up the down payment for a 30% interest.
2. The buyer uses partner's credit to obtain financing. The partner receives a 20% interest.

LEASE AND SUBLEASE

Here, the "buyer" does not buy, but obtains a favorable long-term lease. The buyer then turns around and sublets for short or long periods at a profit.

PROPERTY EXCHANGES

1. The buyer puts down a piece of land as a down payment on an apartment building.
2. The buyer exchanges unwanted property for property the buyer *does* want. This is a "tax-free exchange." [2]

SELLER REFINANCING

The seller refinances the property, the buyer takes over the mortgage and the seller takes back a second for the balance.

Example: Seller has an old $30,000 mortgage. Seller obtains a new $75,000 mortgage, pays off the old one and pockets $45,000. Seller then grants Buyer a second $25,000 mortgage.

MOVING MORTGAGES

Here, the seller grants a second or third mortgage with security in other property owned by the buyer.

---

[2] Code Sec. 1031.

Example: Buyer assumes an existing $30,000 mortgage, Seller takes back a second for $50,000 and also lends Buyer the $20,000 down payment on a "second second" secured by Buyer's home.

MISCELLANEOUS TECHNIQUES

Some buyers may be able to offer "free" performance of future services or rent-free occupancy of premises or, with the consent of creditors, take a seller's place as a debtor.

1. *Trading services.* If the buyer has useful, marketable skills, e.g., accountant, dentist, plumber, the buyer may be able to offer future services as a down payment ("10 years of dental services free").
2. *Prepaid rent.* If the seller lives in the building, part of the down payment may be a free 10-year lease.
3. *Assuming liabilities.* The buyer may be able to negotiate with the seller's creditors so as to become the substitute debtor (a "novation") as part of the down payment.

¶ 1215 TAX ASPECTS OF REAL ESTATE

Tax aspects of home ownership, such as the age-55 exclusion, replacement provisions, the office-at-home deduction, etc., are covered in ¶ 440-482.

¶ 1216 CAPITAL GAINS

Capital gains are taxed at ordinary income rates with a cap of 28%. Thus, even a taxpayer in the 39.6% tax bracket is in the 28% capital gains bracket.

¶ 1217 RENTAL INCOME

A landlord is taxed on rental income when received, whether the rent is prepaid or is paid late. Thus, any security deposit should not be labeled last month's rent. If it is, it is taxable when received, regardless of the life of the lease.

¶ 1218 CASH DEDUCTIONS

A current deduction is available for payments for interest, taxes, insurance (unless prepaid), repairs and maintenance, utilities, management fees, advertising, legal fees, etc. *Improvements,* on the other hand, must be capitalized and depreciated.[3] There is often a fine line between improvements and maintenance. The test is whether the expenditures materially increase the useful life or value of the property. Thus, the following are typical improvements: the installation of a

---

[3] Code Sec. 263.

central air-conditioner, replacing a roof, landscaping, new plumbing, and the purchase of permanent storm windows.

¶ 1219 "AT-RISK" LIMITATIONS

After the Revenue Act of 1978, *all* activities, *except* real estate, are subject to the "at-risk" limitations. Briefly, this means that in other activities, the investor may only deduct tax losses (caused by depreciation, for example) to the extent of the investment that may be personally lost. Thus, nonrecourse debt, secured only by property for which no one is personally liable, does not count.[4] For post-1986 acquisitions, this rule applies to real estate in the cases where a loan on a nonrecourse basis is granted by the seller or does not have arm's-length terms. Thus, the "at-risk" limitations are not applicable to institutional loans or to loans from related parties, as long as the terms are "commercially reasonable".

¶ 1220 DEPRECIATION

One of the greatest advantages in owning buildings is that the cost can be depreciated ("cost recovered") over their estimated useful lives. Such noncash deductions are valuable for tax purposes because they reduce ordinary income dollar for dollar even if the building is appreciating in value. Depreciation is a system of *cost allocation,* not of valuation, so that the deductions do not depend on price fluctuations. Here are the main rules to keep in mind:

1. The owner is allowed to depreciate the part of the cost reasonably allocable to the building (land is not depreciable). The following expenses are part of the cost and cannot be immediately expensed: Purchase commissions, finder's fees, legal fees associated with the acquisition, title search, title policy, survey costs, appraisal fees, recording fees plus improvements, but the cost is reduced by depreciation and casualty losses. If a structure is purchased to be demolished, the costs must be added to the basis in the *land.*

2. The holder of a present interest, such as a life tenant, is entitled to the whole deduction. The remainderman cannot claim any deductions.[5]

3. If an owner converts real estate from personal use to rental property, the depreciable basis, as well as the basis for determining loss, is limited to the value at the time of conversion.[6]

---

[4] Code Sec. 465.

[5] Code Sec. 167(d).

[6] Regs. § § 1.165-9(b) and 1.167(g)-1.

¶ 1221 COST RECOVERY

Residential buildings, defined as properties where at least 80% of gross rent is from dwellings, are to be depreciated straight-line over $27\frac{1}{2}$ years, commercial buildings over 39 years.[7]

Example: An apartment building was purchased for $500,000 on April 2, 1993. If $100,000 is allocable to the land, the cost recovery deduction for 1993 is

$$\$400{,}000 \times \frac{8.5}{27.5 \times 12} = \$10{,}303$$

Note that the "half-month convention" applies, e.g., one-half of a month's write-off is allowed for the month placed in service.

If the property is an office building, the 1993 deduction is

$$\$400{,}000 \times \frac{8.5}{39 \times 12} = \$7{,}265$$

Buildings acquired prior to 1987 continue to be written off over 15, 18, or 19 years, or over their "useful life" (if acquired prior to 1981).

Passive Loss Restrictions

¶ 1225 INTRODUCTION

Individuals, estates, trusts, certain closely held corporations, and personal service corporations are subject to severe restrictions on the current deductibility of losses from "passive activities."[8]

RULE IN A NUTSHELL

Any tax loss from a "passive activity," including rental real estate, is deductible currently only to the extent of income from other "passive activities" (not including portfolio income, such as interest and dividends). The remaining loss is deferred until the activity interest is disposed of. Exceptions for "real estate professionals" were introduced in the Revenue Reconciliation Act of 1993.

PASSIVE VERSUS PORTFOLIO INCOME AND LOSSES

Passive activity losses (PALs) cannot generally reduce taxable income from nonpassive sources, such as wages, interest, and dividends.

Example: Taxpayer earns $100,000 one year from taxable interest on certificates of deposit and has a share of a tax loss from a limited real estate partnership interest of $100,000, including allocable interest expense of $80,000. No portion of the loss is currently deductible, but $100,000 in interest income is taxed as earned.

---

[7] Code Sec. 168(e).

[8] Code Sec. 469.

¶ 1226 ACTIVE PARTICIPATION LOSSES

If an individual "actively participates" in a real estate venture, up to $25,000 of losses may be deducted annually from income from whatever source, such as salaries and portfolio income. The deduction is phased out as adjusted gross income (before IRA deductions, taxable social security, and passive activity losses) goes from $100,000 to $150,000 (for married persons filing separately, the limitation is $12,500, phased out from $50,000 to $62,500 of adjusted gross income).

> ***Example:*** Helen and Blake have adjusted gross income of $50,000 and $100,000, respectively, and in excess of $25,000 of real estate losses each from projects in which they actively participate. If they file as single (they are not married), each person may deduct $25,000. On a joint return, *no* real estate losses are allowed. If they are married filing separately, Helen gets to deduct $12,500, while Blake must carry forward the whole loss.

In order to constitute an active participation loss, the taxpayer must own (or together with the spouse) at least 10% of the value of all interests in the activity. In addition, taxpayer and/or spouse must participate in management decisions other than through an agent.[9]

¶ 1227 ILLUSTRATION OF INTEREST DEDUCTIONS

The restrictions on deductions of real estate-related loans are illustrated by the following examples:

1. A taxpayer invests in a limited real estate partnership that generates a $30,000 tax loss, including $12,000 of mortgage interest. In the absence of income from passive activities, the full $30,000 is deferred. This is so, even if interest income is earned from savings or by the partnership on its investments.
2. Same as 1 above, but the taxpayer also borrowed money against stocks in order to purchase the real estate investment. Any interest on the loan is deferred also as a passive activity loss.
3. Same as 2 above, but the investor borrowed against a home. To the extent that the equity loan does not exceed $100,000, the interest is fully deductible, even if the proceeds are used for tax shelter investments.
4. A homeowner borrows $145,000 on the home and uses $115,000 to invest in an apartment building; later $10,000 is used to buy stocks, and $20,000 is spent for a vacation.

---

[9] Code Sec. 469(i).

Interest on the first $100,000 is qualified residence interest and, deductible without limit, interest on $15,000 is deferred as a *passive activity loss,* interest on $10,000 is *investment interest* (deductible to the extent of net investment income with the excess deferred), and interest on $20,000 is simply disallowed as *personal interest*.

5. Taxpayer operates a hotel and the mortgage interest was $17,000 one year. The interest is deductible in full (as are depreciation and other expenses) since it constitutes trade or business interest.

¶ 1228 DISPOSITIONS OF ENTIRE INTEREST

Suspended losses are allowed in full when the passive activity is disposed of in a taxable transaction. The following special rules should be noted:

Capital losses. A net capital loss is only deductible to the extent of capital gains plus $3,000.[10]

Sales to related parties. These do not count. Thus, if the sale is to a spouse, sibling, ancestor, descendant, or controlled entity, the suspended loss is not deductible by the transferor until a disposition by the transferee to an unrelated party.[11]

ABANDONMENTS

An abandonment qualifies as a taxable disposition; testamentary and inter vivos gifts do not.

INSTALLMENT SALES

If installment reporting is used, a proportion of the suspended loss is available which equals the proportion of the total profit reported. Since the installment method is unavailable for loss sales, suspended losses are immediately allowed in cases where there is an installment sale of the entire interest at a loss.

¶ 1229 TRANSFERS BY GIFT

When an interest in a passive activity is gifted, the basis, increased by suspended losses, carries over to the donee.[12]

Example: If, in the example below, Joe Brown, Sr., did not die, but gifted his partnership interest to Joe Brown, Jr., the donee succeeds to donor's basis of $20,000, increased by the $40,000 of suspended losses. Thus, Joe Brown, Jr., may *never* deduct the suspended losses, but his cost basis is $60,000.

---

[10] Code Sec. 1211.

[11] Code Sec. 469(g)(1)(B).

[12] Code Sec. 469(j)(6).

¶ 1230 TRANSFERS AT DEATH

When an investor in a passive activity with suspended losses dies, the suspended loss is deductible on his final return. However, the loss is reduced by any step-up in basis resulting from the estate tax value.[13]

> ***Example:*** Joe Brown, Sr., died with a limited real estate partnership interest. His basis immediately prior to his death was $20,000, the fair market value was $50,000, and his suspended losses were $40,000. Joe Brown, Jr., who inherited the interest, has a tax basis of $50,000.[14] The suspended loss of $10,000 ($40,000 less the step-up in basis of $30,000) is deductible on Joe Brown, Sr.'s final tax return.

¶ 1231 REAL ESTATE EXEMPT FROM LOSS DEFERRAL RULES

Real estate rental activities are not subject to the passive loss deferral rules, if

1. The average rental period is seven days or less (e.g., hotels, motels).
2. The average rental period is 30 days or less and *significant* services are rendered.
3. The average rental period is of any duration and *extraordinary* services are rendered (e.g., hospitals, nursing homes, boarding schools).
4. The rental activity is merely incidental to the main activity (e.g., the property is held for sale, investment, or used in a trade or business).
5. The property is available to customers on a nonexclusive-use basis during regular business hours (e.g., golf courses).

In addition, real estate professionals can shelter their income from real estate activities.

¶ 1232 REHABILITATION TAX CREDIT

A 10% credit is allowed (and reduces the basis of the building) for rehabilitation expenditures relating to a pre-1936 nonresidential building. At least 75% of both external walls and the "internal structural framework" must be retained.[15] For certified historic structures, the credit is doubled to 20% and it applies to both residential and commercial structures.

---

[13] Code Sec. 469(g)(2).
[14] Code Sec. 1014(a).
[15] Code Sec. 46(b)(4).

¶ 1233 LOW-INCOME HOUSING CREDITS

In 1987, three new low-income housing tax credits became available for acquisitions, construction, or rehabilitation of low-income housing.[16] The credits for 1987 expenditures were:

1. A 9% credit each year for ten years for a total of 90% of new construction cost or rehabilitation expenditures.
2. A 4% credit each year for ten years for expenditures financed with municipal bonds or federal subsidies.
3. A 4% credit each year for ten years for acquisition costs without rehabilitation or construction work.

   Because of the time value of money, the 9% a year for ten years is far less than a 90% credit in present value terms. For example, since the present value of an annuity of $1 for ten years is $6.145, the present value equivalent of the 90% credit at 10% is 6.145 × 9%, or 55.3%.

The following features of the low-income housing credit should be noted:

1. The 9% and 4% numbers are linked to the federal interest rates after 1987 and change annually.
2. The units for which the credit is claimed must be residential and must be occupied by nontransients with low income, paying low rent (specific tests are provided).
3. The qualification rules must be met for 15 years; otherwise, part of the credit may be recaptured with interest.
4. No basis reduction is required for the credit claimed, but the general business credit limitation applies (e.g., the low-income housing credit plus a number of other credits may offset the first $25,000 of tax liability, plus 75% of the excess).
5. State or local agency authority is needed as well as the filing of a certification with the IRS.

¶ 1234 CREDIT PHASEOUTS

The rehabilitation and low-income housing credits are phased out (i.e., must be carried forward) as adjusted gross income goes from $200,000 to $250,000. The credits are allowed without regard to active participation, except for post-1989 low-income housing.

The low-income housing credit was made permanent by the Revenue Reconciliation Act of 1993.

---

[16] Code Sec. 42.

¶ 1235 DISPOSING OF A REAL ESTATE INVESTMENT

For tax consequences of disposing of a tax shelter by divorce, bankruptcy, sale, exchange, gift, death, incorporation, etc., see ¶ 1133 in the chapter on "Tax-Sheltered Investments."

In general, real estate is illiquid and is much easier to buy than to sell. The closing costs may be as high as 12%-13% of the purchase price. Thus, real estate should be purchased with a view to holding it for at least five years. Due to selling commissions, legal fees, mortgage registration, title insurance, appraisal, and survey fees, etc., expenses and appreciation typically just offset each other the first three years.

¶ 1236 CONCLUDING REMARKS

Real estate investing is *not* dead after 1992. The 27½-year and 39-year depreciation periods allowed are shorter than the 40 to 45 years typically used prior to 1981. Rental income can still be sheltered completely by deductions for interest, taxes, and depreciation, providing tax-free cash flow. *No* losses are disallowed; they are only deferred. Income from any passive activity (real estate or other tax shelter) which has passed the "crossover point" may be offset by passive activity losses. In any event, rents and prices invariably adjust so as to provide a market competing for resources with at least a minimum acceptable after-tax return on invested capital.

CHAPTER 13

FAMILY TAX PLANNING

¶ 1301 INTRODUCTION

The Internal Revenue Code of 1986 changed many of the rules for family tax planning, but many opportunities still exist and many established principles still remain.

JOINT OR SINGLE TAX RETURNS

Significant marriage penalties still exist where both spouses have income. Due to the bias inherent in the tax tables themselves, as well as the general tendency on the part of Congress not to double tax benefits from single to joint returns, substantial tax savings may be available for persons choosing to remain or become single.

JOINT OR SEPARATE TAX RETURNS

Due to floors on various deductions and the reduced progressivity in rates, many cases will exist where married couples may save taxes by filing separately. See ¶ 1310.

INCOME SPLITTING WITH CHILDREN

Severe limitations now exist on investment income splitting with children under 14 years of age, and it has become less attractive to split income with anyone due to the lowering of maximum tax rates. However, opportunities still exist to reduce overall family taxes. See ¶ 1320.

DIVORCE TAX PLANNING

With half of all marriages in the U.S. breaking up, and with complex new rules related to exemptions, alimony, and property transfers, tax planning in the event of divorce is important and valuable. See ¶ 1330.

The tax aspects of surviving one's spouse and matters concerning a decedent's final returns are covered at ¶ 1350 and 1352, respectively.

Joint or Single Tax Returns

¶ 1302 INTRODUCTION

The "marriage penalty" is a phrase referring to the phenomenon that some joint return filers would pay less income tax in the aggregate if they were eligible to file as single. This phenomenon has been caused in part by the progressivity of tax rates and in part by a number of tax benefits which are not doubled on a joint return as compared to a single return. An increasing number of married couples have been affected adversely by this bias against two-earner couples. The Tax Reform Act of 1986 reduced the progressivity of tax rates, and the Revenue Reconciliation Act of 1993 increased it. However, the "marriage penalty" is still very much with us.

¶ 1303 COMPARING JOINT AND SINGLE RETURNS—GENERAL OBSERVATIONS

By inspecting the tax tables (see Appendix), the following conclusions may be drawn with regard to how marital status affects aggregate tax liability:

1. If only one party has income, a couple is always better off filing a *joint* return. Even if taxable income is not in excess of the 15% bracket, joint filing still makes a difference because of the higher standard deduction allowed and the extra exemption.
2. If both spouses have similar income they are *always* better off filing single returns.
3. If both parties have income but their incomes are dissimilar, they may or may not be better off filing as single.

¶ 1304 MARRIAGE PENALTY PROVISIONS IN THE CODE

The following tax provisions discriminate against joint return filers:

1. *Taxing Social Security benefits.* The threshold level of adjusted gross income for purposes of taxing up to 85% of Social Security benefits is $32,000 for singles and $44,000 on a joint return.[1]
2. *IRA reduction.* The threshold level of adjusted gross income for purposes of phasing out deductible IRA contributions for participants in qualified plans is $25,000 for singles and $40,000 on a joint return.[2] Furthermore, a married person can be denied an IRA deduction because the spouse is a participant in a qualified plan.
3. *Residence gain exclusion.* Each single individual is eligible for one gain exclusion of up to $125,000 on the sale of a principal residence.[3] A married individual, however, is *not* eligible for the exclusion if the spouse or the spouse's previous spouse has ever claimed the exclusion.
4. *Loss disallowance.* Losses and certain expenses between related taxpayers, including spouses, are disallowed.[4]
5. *Moving expenses.* Indirect moving expenses carry the same limit per individual as they do per married couple.[5]
6. *Capital losses.* Capital losses in excess of capital gains can only be deducted against ordinary income to the tune of $3,000 a year whether on a single or a joint return.[6]
7. *Real estate losses.* The maximum deductible loss from real estate rentals in which a taxpayer actively participates is $25,000 for singles and $25,000 on a joint return.[7]
8. *Deductions subject to a floor—*
   (a) Medical expenses are deductible only to the extent they exceed 7.5% of adjusted gross income (AGI).[8]
   (b) Casualty losses are subject to a 10% of AGI floor.[9]
   (c) Miscellaneous itemized deductions are reduced by 2% of AGI.[10]

   Clearly, such expenses are less likely to exceed the floor on a joint return than a single return if they are incurred disproportionately to income generated.
9. *Credits.* The child care credit under Code Sec. 21, the credit for the elderly and disabled under Code Sec. 22, and the earned income credit under Code Sec. 32 are all phased out

[1] Code Sec. 86(c).
[2] Code Sec. 219(g).
[3] Code Sec. 121.
[4] Code Sec. 267.
[5] Code Sec. 218(b)(3).
[6] Code Sec. 1211(b)(2).
[7] Code Sec. 469(i).
[8] Code Sec. 213(a).
[9] Code Sec. 165(h)(2)(A).
[10] Code Sec. 67(a).

faster on a joint return than on two single returns if both parties have income.

If one or more of the above items apply, the "marriage penalty" inherent in the tax table is aggravated.

¶ 1305 FILING STATUS AND THE LIFE CYCLE

If minimizing taxes and maximizing tax benefits are paramount in a couple's mind, the following scenario can readily be envisioned:

1. As long as they are both working they will file as single.
2. If they have one or more children but both keep working, one or both will file as head of household.
3. If one stays home for any reason and has little or no income, they will marry and file a joint return.
4. If the nonworking spouse goes back to work, they will divorce and file as single or head of household.
5. If the first party to die will have a taxable estate in excess of $600,000, they will marry (on the deathbed, ideally) so as to qualify for the estate tax marital deduction.[11]

The simplest way to reduce the marriage penalty is to give married couples the option to file as singles and repeal all provisions relating to "married filing separately." This is, in fact, the case in a number of countries today.

Joint or Separate Tax Returns

¶ 1310 INTRODUCTION

Two individuals who are married on the last day of the taxable year may no longer file single tax returns. If both have gross income, they may file either

1. one joint return with joint and several liability for the tax due,[12] or
2. two separate returns with each party being liable only for that individual's tax liability.

The alternative that minimizes the spouses' combined income tax liability, including state and local taxes, should be chosen each year.

¶ 1311 EXEMPTIONS

A joint return is the return of two taxpayers. Each spouse has a separate exemption. Both parties' exemptions, including dependency exemptions, are allowed in full on a joint return, even if only one party has gross income.

---

[11] Code Sec. 2056.

[12] Code Sec. 6013.

On separate returns, each taxpayer is allowed only personal exemptions. However, if one spouse has no gross income so that only one separate return is filed, the spouse who files a return is entitled to the nonfiling spouse's personal exemptions under Code Sec. 151(b) unless the nonfiler is the dependent of another.

¶ 1312 STANDARD DEDUCTION CONFORMITY REQUIREMENT

To avoid a situation where one spouse pays all itemized deductions then itemizes, while the other claims the standard deduction, the rules are as follows under Code Sec. 63(e):

1. If both parties itemize or both take the standard deduction, no adjustments are necessary.
2. If only one party itemizes, the nonitemizer must add to AGI the excess of the standard deduction over expenses qualifying as itemized deductions.

¶ 1313 REASONS TO FILE SEPARATELY

The following reasons exist for filing separately:

1. To avoid liability for one's spouse's taxes if a taxpayer suspects that the spouse is less than honest or the marriage is in trouble. However, under Code Sec. 6013(e), a spouse is not held liable for the other spouse's tax if it would be "inequitable" to do so and the taxpayer was ignorant of a "substantial understatement of tax" attributable to "grossly erroneous items" of the other spouse.
2. To reduce the impact of progressive state and local taxes, e.g., those of New York.
3. To reduce adjusted gross income (AGI) so as to maximize deductions attributable to one spouse which depend on the level of AGI, e.g., medical, casualty, and miscellaneous itemized expenses.

The optimal situation is where one spouse has the combination of earning a low AGI while paying for such items attributable to personal expenses. This may happen, for example, in the year of death of a spouse when the taxable year is shorter and medical expenses may be high. However, it should be noted that although a deduction may be increased when separate returns are filed, it is likely to be deducted in the 15% bracket rather than in the 28% bracket.

The following traditional reasons to file separately no longer exist:

1. To avoid offsetting one spouse's long-term capital gain against the other spouse's short-term capital losses, since "net capital

gains" no longer are reduced by 60%, but are taxed like ordinary income (with a cap of 28%).

2. To qualify one spouse for income averaging, since the averaging provision has been repealed.

¶ 1314 DEDUCTIONS DEPENDENT ON ADJUSTED GROSS INCOME

The main reason for filing separately is to increase deductions which are reduced by a percentage of adjusted gross income (AGI). These deductions are:

1. Medical expenses, which are reduced by 7.5% of AGI under Code Sec. 213(a).
2. Casualty losses, which are reduced by 10% of AGI under Code Sec. 165(h)(2)(A).
3. Miscellaneous itemized deductions, which are reduced by 2% of AGI.[13]

Incurring any one of these or a combination thereof may make it beneficial to file separately in any given year.

¶ 1315 FILING STATUS RESTRICTIONS

To file a joint return, two people must be legally married under local law (including common law) by the end of the taxable year.[14] Thus, they cannot be legally separated or divorced by year-end.[15] They must also have the same taxable year.[16]

Marital status is determined as of the end of the taxable year or at the time of death of the spouse.[17] Thus, a single return may not be filed by a married individual, even if the spouses are living apart or in the year a spouse dies.

CHANGING FILING STATUS RETROACTIVELY

If a couple files separate returns, they have the full statute of limitations (generally three years from the later of the due date or when the return was filed) to change their mind and file jointly.[18] However, once a joint return has been filed and the parties have assumed joint and several liability for their combined taxes, they can only switch to separate returns up to the original due date of the return.

---

[13] Code Sec. 67(a).

[14] Code Sec. 6013(d)(1)(A).

[15] Code Sec. 6013(d)(2).

[16] Code Sec. 6013(a)(2).

[17] Code Sec. 143(a).

[18] Code Sec. 6013(b)(1).

¶ 1316 JOINT RETURN ADVANTAGES

Even though the income-splitting advantages of a joint return have been reduced with the lowering of top rates and the number of tax brackets, some advantages of filing joint returns remain:

1. There is less paperwork with only one mailing and one set of schedules.
2. There is no need for tracing. Thus, it does not matter who paid which expenses, made charitable deductions, whose names are on the bank and brokerage accounts or on the securities, who made the deposits, etc.
3. Certain tax benefits are only available to married couples if joint returns are filed.

¶ 1317 SITUATIONS REQUIRING JOINT FILING

To claim the following tax benefits, joint filing is required:

1. The earned income credit under Code Sec. 32(d);
2. The child care credit under Code Sec. 21(e)(2);
3. The retirement credit under Code Sec. 22(e)(1);
4. The additional $250 IRA deduction for a nonworking spouse under Code Sec. 219(c)(1); and
5. The $32,000 base amount for taxability of social security benefits under Code Sec. 86(c)(2).

If any of the first three benefits is available, a joint return should invariably be filed.

Income Splitting with Children

¶ 1320 UNFAVORABLE CHANGES

Time-honored techniques of transferring income to children to escape higher income tax rates have been narrowed by legislation.

The following provisions in the Tax Reform Act of 1986 made income splitting less attractive:

1. No personal exemption is allowed an individual eligible to be claimed as a dependent by someone else.[19]
2. *Clifford* trusts, also known as 10-year trusts, short-term trusts, reversionary trusts, and Code Sec. 673 trusts, are no longer available for income-splitting purposes if the transfer was made after March 1, 1986.

---

[19] Code Sec. 151(f)(2).

3. Spousal remainder trusts, e.g., trusts where income goes to a child and remainder to grantor's spouse after one or more years, can no longer be used to split income for transfers after March 1, 1986.[20]
4. Unearned income, e.g., investment income, of a child under age 14 is generally taxed at the parent's tax rate without regard to the source of funds, except for the greater of a $600 standard deduction or itemized expenses allocable to unearned income, and $600 taxed at the child's tax rate.[21]
5. After 1992, estates and trusts are taxed at high rates and reach the 39.6% bracket at only $7,500 of taxable income.[22]
6. Trusts must be on the calendar year except for tax-exempt and charitable trusts.[23]
7. Average tax brackets for most people have been reduced to a maximum of 28%.[24]
8. The $100 dividend exclusion in Code Sec. 116 was repealed.
9. Dependents with unearned income in excess of $600 will have to file a return, even if there is no tax liability.[25] However, after the Miscellaneous Revenue Act of 1988, the parent may elect to include a child's unearned income over $600, but less than $5,000, on the parent's return if the income consists of interest and dividends only.
10. Dependents under age 14 who are required to file a return must be provided with the parent's social security number to do so.[26] Also, *parents* who claim exemptions for children age 2 or over must report such children's social security numbers on *their* return.[27]
11. A $5 penalty per omission applies.[28]

¶ 1321 PROVISIONS FAVORABLE OR UNCHANGED

The following rules benefit children with income or parents of children with income:

1. A standard deduction of $600 (in 1993) is available to offset unearned income on a dependent's return.[29]
2. Nondependent donees of income-producing properties have available a $3,800 standard deduction (in 1994) and a personal exemption of $2,450 (in 1994).

---

[20] Code Sec. 672.
[21] Code Secs. 1(i)(2) and 63(c)(5)(A).
[22] Code Sec. 1(e) and (g).
[23] Code Sec. 645.
[24] Code Sec. 1.
[25] Code Sec. 6012(a)(1)(C).
[26] Code Sec. 1(i)(6).
[27] Code Sec. 6109(c).
[28] Code Sec. 6676(e).
[29] Code Sec. 63(c)(5).

3. *Earned* income is still taxed to the person who renders the services, including children under age 14.
4. Individual retirement accounts (IRAs) are still available for children regardless of age.
5. A grantor-parent may retain a reversion in a trust which takes effect only upon the death of the only child-beneficiary prior to age 21.[30]
6. After 1989, all or part of deferred interest on U.S. savings bonds issued after 1989 is tax free (subject to a high-income phase-out) under Code Sec. 135, if the bonds are used to pay for higher education for the taxpayer, the spouse, or the dependent.

¶ 1322 CHILDREN UNDER AGE 14

The tax provisions related to children under age 14 may be summarized as follows:

1. All income, earned or unearned, is taxed *to the child.* No exemption is allowed.
2. Earned income is taxed at the child's tax bracket. The standard deduction of $3,800 (in 1994) is available (for earned income) or deductions may be itemized.
3. *Net unearned income,* e.g., investment income from whatever source (such as income on savings from the child's own earned income), is taxed to the child at the parent's marginal tax bracket. However, to arrive at net unearned income, unearned income is reduced by $600, and itemized deductions allocable to unearned income are taken or a standard deduction of $600 is taken, whichever is higher.[31] The following special rules apply:
   (a) A child under age 14 is a person who has not reached age 14 by the end of the taxable year and who has at least one living parent at the end of such year.
   (b) If both parents are alive, the custodial parent's marginal tax bracket is used. In joint custody cases, or where the parents file as "married filing separately," the taxable income of the parent in the highest bracket is used to compute the tax.[32]

These rules apply to income from custodial accounts and trusts, including *Clifford* and spousal remainder trusts, even if set up prior to March 2, 1986.

---

[30] Code Sec. 673(b).
[31] Code Sec. 1(i)(4).
[32] Code Sec. 1(i)(5).

ILLUSTRATIONS (1993 RATES, STANDARD DEDUCTION, AND EXEMPTIONS)

As illustrated below, the treatment of a child's income depends on the age of the child, whether income is earned or unearned, and the amount of deductions.

1. *Child under 14, unearned income only, no deductions.* The child has $3,000 of unearned income. Net unearned income is $1,800 ($3,000 less $600 and less the greater of a standard deduction of $600 or allocable itemized deductions). $1,800 is taxed at the parent's tax rate, and $600 is taxed at the child's rate.
2. *Child under 14, unearned income only, deductions over $600.* Same as 1, above, except that itemized deductions (reduced by the 2% floor for miscellaneous itemized deductions) related to the unearned income equal $700. Net unearned income equals $1,700 ($3,000 less $600 and less the greater of $600 or itemized deductions of $700). Thus, $1,700 is taxed at the parent's rate, and $600 is taxed at the child's rate.
3. *Child under 14, both earned and unearned income, no deductions.* Same as 1, above, except the child also has earned income of $900. The standard deduction is $900, of which $600 is allocated to unearned income. Net unearned income is still $1,800, and earned income is $900 less $300 ($900 – $600). Thus, $1,800 is taxed at the parent's tax rate, and $600 of unearned income as well as $600 of earned income are taxed at the child's rate.
4. *Child under 14, both earned and unearned income, itemized deductions exceeded by standard deduction.* The child has $3,000 of unearned income, $2,000 of earned income, and itemized deductions of $1,200 of which $700 is directly related to the unearned income. The standard deduction is $2,000. Net earned income equals $3,000 less $600 of the standard deduction and less $600, or $1,800, which is taxed at the parent's tax rate. Itemized deductions, including those allocable to unearned income, are irrelevant since they are exceeded by the standard deduction. The remaining standard deduction of $1,400 is allocated to earned income. Thus, $600 of earned income and $600 of unearned income are taxed at the child's rate, and $1,800 of unearned income is taxed at the parent's rate, for a total of $3,000 of taxable income ($5,000 – $2,000).
5. *Child under 14, both earned and unearned income, expenses itemized.* Same as 4, above, except earned income is $1,100.

Net unearned income equals $1,700 ($3,000 – $600 – $700). Net earned income equals $600 ($1,100 – $500 ($1,200 – $700)). Thus, taxable income is $2,900 ($3,000 + $1,100 – $1,200) of which $1,800 is taxed at the parent's rate.

6. *Child under 14, both earned and unearned income, no taxable income.* The child has $1,300 of unearned income, $500 of earned income, and $1,800 of deductions of which $400 is allocable to unearned income. Unearned income equals $100 ($1,300 – $600 and less the greater of $600 or $400). However, unearned income cannot exceed taxable income, which is zero ($1,800 – $1,800).[33]
7. *Child over 14, both earned and unearned income.* A child over age 14 has unearned income of $11,000 and $5,000 of earned income. This gross income of $16,000 is reduced by the greater of $3,700 (the standard deduction) or itemized expenses. The net is taxed at 15%, the child's bracket.

¶ 1323 INCOME-SPLITTING STRATEGIES WITH CHILDREN UNDER AGE 14

The following strategies and vehicles are useful when transferring property to children under age 14:

1. The first $600 of investment income is completely tax free to the child, sheltered by the standard deduction. Thus, at least $600 may be from taxable sources, such as interest and dividends.
2. The next $600 is taxed at the child's rate, or 15%. As a result, the first $1,200 of income per year per child may be from taxable sources.
3. The child's 15% bracket is up to $22,100 (in 1993). Thus, earned income of $22,100 plus the IRA deduction, if any, plus the standard deduction of $3,700, but less up to $600 in unearned income, is taxed at this low bracket.
4. Once the $1,200 threshold is reached, the following investment vehicles should be considered:
   (a) *Series EE U.S. Savings Bonds* on which taxes on interest may be deferred until redemption or maturity under Code Sec. 464. Bonds issued currently carry a guaranteed yield of only 4% if held for at least 5 years.
   (b) *Growth stock or mutual funds* paying little or no dividends with a high appreciation potential.

[33] Code Sec. 1(i)(4)(B).

(c) *Tax exempt municipal bonds* or bond funds, including zero coupon bonds. At most, the interest, including bond discount, is subject to state and local income taxes.

(d) *Precious metals* and other collectibles with good appreciation potential.

(e) *Insurance products,* such as single payment deferred annuities, single payment whole life policies, or universal life policies. Cash values still accumulate tax free, and funds may be borrowed tax free against cash values.

During the taxable year, if the child turns 14, tax-deferred investments may be liquidated and reinvested to the extent desired in securities with a higher taxable yield since at this point income distributed to the child is taxed at the child's low tax rates.

(f) *Regular C corporations* may be used to defer income. After 1987, corporations are taxed at 15% on the first $50,000 of taxable income, 25% on the next $25,000, and 34% on the excess of $75,000.

Example: Parents transfer $20,000 of cash to a corporation which buys a building using the cash as a down payment and borrows the rest. The stock is given to the five-year-old child. Since the equity in the corporation is $20,000, no gift tax consequences result. Until the child is age 14, the corporation pays no dividends. In the meantime, the building appreciates, tax-sheltered rental income is accumulated, and the personal holding company tax is avoided due to deductions for depreciation, property taxes, mortgage interest, and repairs and maintenance. Once the shareholder is age 14, dividends may be paid and taxed at 15%. (This strategy does *not* work with securities, due to the personal holding company tax.)

¶ 1324 TAX INCENTIVES TO EMPLOY ONE'S CHILDREN

Employing one's children, when bona fide and feasible in the light of the child labor provision in the Fair Labor Standards Act of 1939, can be quite beneficial for tax purposes. This is due to the following:

1. Income splitting is achieved since each child is a separate taxpayer with a separate standard deduction.
2. Earned income is taxed to the child, regardless of age, even if under age 14.
3. Each child, regardless how young, may have a separate IRA.
4. If the spouse is not employed, the child(ren) should be covered under a medical reimbursement and/or medical insurance plan as employees. However, if the spouse is employed, the

children may be included as dependents without being employees.

5. Wages of children under the age of 18 paid by a parent-sole proprietor are exempt from social security and employment taxes.[34]

Example: Joe Mendez, the sole proprietor of a grocery store, employs his 16-year-old son, Richard, as a part-time bagger and delivery boy. His salary is $5,700 a year. Richard's tax return for 1993 (required to be filed) may be summarized as follows:

Gross Income	$5,700
IRA Contribution	2,000
Adjusted Gross Income	$3,700
Standard Deduction	3,700
Taxable Income	0

The $5,700 paid is deductible to the proprietorship. Thus, Joe's self-employment tax may be reduced in full or in part by the payment made. In any event, Joe's gross income is reduced by $5,700, which stays in the family. Assuming Joe still pays over one-half of Richard's support, the dependency exemption is still available as well. If more than $5,700 is earned by Richard, the excess, up to $22,100 (in 1993), is taxed at 15%.

INCOME-SPLITTING STRATEGIES BY AGE OF CHILD

The following is a breakdown by age of income-splitting possibilities:

Children Under Age 8

- Appreciation Vehicles, such as Growth Stocks
- Tax-Exempt Vehicles, such as Municipal Bonds
  - Single Premium Life Insurance and Deferred Annuities
- U.S. Savings Bonds

Children Over Age 8, but Under Age 14

- Continue the above
- Hire child in business (at relatively low wages)

Children Over Age 14

- Switch to taxable current yield securities and investments
- Hire in business (at higher wages)

¶ 1325 DEPENDENCY EXEMPTION

Claiming an exemption for a child or other dependents is the ultimate income-splitting device since no income results to the dependent. To claim a *dependency exemption,* five tests must be met:

[34] Code Sec. 3121(b)(3)(A).

1. *Taxpayer must provide more than half of the support.*[35] Total support includes support from all sources and can be rendered in cash, property or services, such as free rent. The test is who *paid* the support. Thus, if a mother banks her social security, her child can still support her. The fact that she *could have* supported herself is irrelevant. Support items include food, shelter, clothing, education, medical and dental expenses, recreation, transportation, and reasonable spending money, but *not* income and social security taxes paid by the dependent, funeral expenses, life insurance premiums, and scholarships. If free lodging is provided, the fair market value counts; however, it works both ways. The dependent may live in a separate own home or pay rent, in which case this counts toward total support.

The support test may be met one year and not the next. Each taxable year stands on its own and cannot be averaged.

2. *The dependent must have less than the exemption in gross income,* even if he is a close relative (except a child) depending on taxpayer for almost all support.[36] Thus, gross income must be less than $2,450 in 1994. Fortunately, gross income does not include such items as social security, welfare, insurance proceeds, municipal bond interest, and gifts and inheritances. But if these items are spent on support, they enter into the 50% text.

There is one significant exception to the gross income test—a child. Children, including adopted and foster children, can have any amount of gross income, if they are either under age 19 or full-time students for five months during the year. The Technical and Miscellaneous Revenue Act of 1988 provides that the full-time student exception only applies to children under age 24. The support test must still be met.

3. *The dependent must either be a member of the household or meet specific relationship tests.* Unless the dependent is a qualifying relative, the dependent must live with taxpayer the whole year and the relationship cannot violate local law. Qualifying relatives include: children, grandchildren, stepchildren, foster children, brothers, sisters, parents, grandparents, uncles and aunts by blood, parents-in-law, sons-in-law, daughters-in-law, brothers-in-law, and sisters-in-law). Once an in-law relationship is established, it survives divorce and death.[37]

---

[35] Code Sec. 152(a).

[36] Code Sec. 12(e)(1).

[37] Code Sec. 152(a).

4. *A dependent cannot file a joint return* unless done solely to obtain a tax refund. Thus, typically, the exemption is lost when a child gets married.[38]
5. *The dependent must be living in the U.S., Canada, or Mexico for at least part of the year* for which the exemption is claimed.[39]

If two or more people share the support of another, chances are neither one would qualify for the exemption under the above rules. The solution is to file a *multiple support declaration* (Form 2120). Through this device one person can claim the exemption each year.[40] The requirements are simply that two or more persons could have claimed the exemption, except for the support test, that such persons together provide more than 50% of the support and that only one person claims the exemption and provides more than 10% of total support. This is most often done when two or more children support one or both parents.

¶ 1326 TRANSFERRING ASSETS TO HIGHER BRACKET TAXPAYERS

In the following situations, tax savings may result when low tax bracket individuals transfer property to higher tax bracket relatives:

1. A retired parent gifts or sells the home to an adult child, then leases it back. If sold, the parent's gain may be excluded up to $125,000 under Code Sec. 121 and the child may shelter rental income with depreciation deductions (straight-line over 27½ years for post-1986 purchases) on the stepped-up basis.
2. A parent is subject to tax on up to 85% of social security benefits caused fully or partly by municipal bond interest. The parent may gift the bonds to a child. Subsequently, the child may make nontaxable gifts to the parent out of the tax-free income.
3. An individual without earned income, e.g., a retiree, may transfer up to $2,000 a year to a working, but broke, child so as to enable the child to make deductible IRA contributions.
4. A retired parent sustains large medical expenses. The child may claim these medical expenses if the child pays them, even if the funds were received as a gift from the parent.
5. A parent may transfer funds to a child so as to later qualify for VA or other benefits.

---

[38] Code Sec. 151(e)(2).
[39] Code Sec. 152(b)(3).
[40] Code Sec. 152(c).

¶ 1327 HOW PROPERTIES ARE TRANSFERRED TO MINORS

Traditionally, transfers to minors have been made in trust, or by a parent to the other parent as custodian for a minor. Typically, a custodial account is opened at a savings institution or a brokerage firm. The Uniform Gifts to Minors Act (UGMA), originally adopted by most, if not all, states, is being rapidly replaced by the Uniform Transfers to Minor Act (UTMA). Under UGMA, assets transferred to minors were generally limited to cash, securities and insurance policies. UTMA also allows transfers of tangible assets, e.g., precious metals, collectibles and real estate.

The Tax Reform Act of 1986 significantly limited income-splitting opportunities with trusts and children under age 14. The lower maximum marginal tax rates also reduced the incentive to split income with anyone. However, income splitting is not dead, not even with minors under age 14. With the Revenue Reconciliation Act of 1993, maximum brackets for many increased to 36% (39.6% for taxable income over $250,000). Thus, several tax strategies and tax-deferral vehicles still exist that are suitable for minimizing taxation of the family as a whole.

Divorce Tax Planning

¶ 1330 INCOME SPLITTING

As the divorce rate has climbed over the years, a growing number of parents pay or collect alimony and/or child support. The Tax Reform Act of 1986 made numerous changes affecting divorced parents. Thus, tax rates have been lowered for many and the standard deduction has been increased. Exemptions have grown but are phased out at high income levels; income splitting with children under age 14 is affected, and there are new recapture rules of front-loaded alimony. Thus, more than ever, a close look at the pertinent tax provisions should be taken whenever a marriage is dissolved.

Restructured income tax rates make it desirable to avoid wasting the benefits of the 15% income tax bracket (as opposed to the 28% and higher brackets). Furthermore, it may not be assumed that allocating exemptions to the parent with the most taxable income will save the aggregate tax.

THE 15% BRACKET

The prime candidates for income splitting are individuals in the 15% bracket. In 1993, the 15% brackets were as follows:

Singles	Up to $22,100
Heads of household	Up to $29,600
Joint return	Up to $36,900

THE INCREASED EXEMPTION

Personal and dependency exemptions were increased to $1,900 in 1987, $1,950 in 1988, and $2,000 in 1989. After 1989, an inflation adjustment has been made annually.[41] For the typical taxpayer in the 28% bracket, therefore, the exemption is worth $658 in 1993 ($2,350 × .28).

EXEMPTION PHASEOUT

At high taxable income levels, exemptions are phased out. Thus, exemptions are phased out in 1993 as taxable income increases beyond $108,450 for singles, $135,600 for heads of households and $162,700 on joint returns. Therefore, the exemption strategy for high income individuals is the reverse of the traditional one. The exemption for a dependent child should be allocated to the parent who can use it, even if that parent is in the 15% bracket.

> ***Example:*** Jasper and Marcia are divorced. In 1993 Jasper files as single, and Marcia files as head of household, having custody of Lolita, age 12. Marcia is in the 15% bracket. If Jasper's taxable income is in excess of $108,450, Lolita's exemption is being reduced, and, at a taxable income of $230,950, it is completely wasted. In a situation like this the exemption should be claimed by the custodial parent regardless of her tax bracket.

¶ 1331 WHICH PARENT CLAIMS DEPENDENT?

The custodial parent is entitled to the dependency exemption without regard to who pays child support if:

1. Such parent had custody for a greater part of the year than the other parent;
2. The parents are divorced or legally separated, or have lived apart the last six months of the calendar year;
3. They together provided most of the child's support; or
4. Both parents had custody more than half of the year.[42]

However, if the custodial parent agrees in writing, for any year the noncustodial parent can claim the exemption.[43] Ideally, the parent in the highest tax bracket in the year should claim the exemption. This is particularly true since neither head-of-household status nor the child care credit requires that a dependency exemption be claimed (see below).

---

[41] Code Sec. 151(d).

[42] Code Sec. 152(e)(1).

[43] Code Sec. 152(e)(2).

¶ 1332 MARRIAGE PENALTY

The marriage penalty refers to the extent to which a couple pays more federal income taxes on a joint return than they would if they got divorced or stayed single, filing two single returns. For example:

1. Deductions reduced by a percentage of adjusted gross income may virtually disappear on a joint return but be available to a greater extent on single returns, e.g., casualty losses, medical expenses, and miscellaneous itemized deductions.
2. Many tax benefits available on a single return are less than doubled on a joint return. Examples include capital losses, losses from active real estate participation, IRA deductions, the standard deduction, the earned income credit, etc.

¶ 1333 INCOME SPLITTING WITH CHILDREN UNDER AGE 14

Investment income of a child under age 14 by the end of a taxable year after 1986 is taxed to the child but at the parents' tax bracket.[44] Thus, *net unearned income,* defined as unearned income less the sum of $600 plus the greater of a standard deduction of $600 or itemized expenses allocable to such income, is taxed at the parents' rate. Since a child would rarely itemize, in most cases, therefore, $600 is tax free, $600 is taxed at the child's rate (typically 15%) and the excess at the parents' rate (typically 28%). If the parents' bracket is 31%, the maximum tax savings would be 31% of $600, plus 16% of $600, for a total of $282 a year. In the 28% bracket, the savings could be $264.

¶ 1334 MARGINAL TAX WHEN PARENTS ARE DIVORCED

The tax rate at which a child under age 14 pays tax on unearned income is that of the custodial parent if the parents are divorced or legally separated.[45] If the custodial parent is remarried, the tax rate may be determined from a joint return with the new spouse. In any event, the tax rate used may be higher or lower than that of the noncustodial parent.

In the case of divorced parents with joint custody, the highest tax rate applicable to either parent is used.

> ***Example:*** Jasper and Marcia are divorced. Jasper is in the 15% tax bracket. Marcia has custody of Lolita, age 12, and is remarried to Jason. Marcia has no income and files a joint return with Jason, who is in the 31% bracket. Any net unearned income of Lolita is taxed at the 31% rate. Thus, no income splitting with Lolita should take place until the year during which she attains the age of 14.

---

[44] Code Sec. 1(i).

[45] Code Secs. 1(i)(5)(A) and 7703.

¶ 1335 TAX ASPECTS OF ALIMONY AND CHILD SUPPORT

Cash alimony constitutes gross income to the recipient under Code Sec. 71 but is deductible by the payor from gross income.[46] However, the divorce or separation instrument may specify that alimony payments are to be nontaxable and nondeductible.[47]

In contrast, child support payments are always nontaxable and nondeductible.[48] If the amount of child support is unspecified, all payments made are considered alimony. If the payor pays less than the amount agreed and such amount is combined alimony and child support, the latter is deemed paid first.[49]

¶ 1336 MAKING FIXED AFTER-TAX PAYMENTS TO AN EX-SPOUSE

If the payee is to receive a fixed after-tax sum, such as $10,000 a year, this is all that need be paid if it is designated as child support or nondeductible alimony. However, if any part of it is taxable alimony, such position must be grossed up by the payee's marginal tax rate.

> ***Example:*** Marcia is in the 15% tax bracket and is to receive $10,000 a year in after-tax cash, $6,000 of which is child support, the rest taxable alimony. Her alimony payment must equal $4,000/(1 − .15) or $4,706. This is because 85% of $4,706 is $4,000. Thus, to gross up an after-tax amount, it is necessary to divide by one less the tax rate.

¶ 1337 CHILD SUPPORT OR ALIMONY: NONTAX CONSIDERATIONS

Alimony is more flexible than child support for tax purposes in the sense that it may be designated as taxable and deductible or nontaxable and nondeductible. Also, alimony may be paid without regard to the existence of minor children. On the other hand, a divorced individual with children is likely to prefer child support since it, unlike alimony, does not cease upon remarriage. The opposite may be true, if the custodial spouse has no plans to remarry before the last child reaches majority.

¶ 1338 DECISION RULES

Based on the analysis above, the following decision rules may be articulated:

1. If the payor's tax bracket is higher than the payee's in a given year, all payments should be designated as alimony until their

---

[46] Code Sec. 215(a).
[47] Code Sec. 71(b)(1)(B).
[48] Code Sec. 71(c).
[49] Code Sec. 71(c)(3).

tax brackets are equalized. The excess payments, if any, should be designated nondeductible alimony or child support.

2. If both parties have the same filing status, such as single or head of household, and the payor's income is higher, deductible alimony should be paid until their taxable incomes are equal.
3. If the payor's marginal tax bracket is less than the payee's, any payments made should constitute nondeductible alimony or child support.
4. The dependency exemption should be claimed by the parent in the higher tax bracket, unless such parent would have the exemption phased out.

¶ 1339 RECAPTURE OF EXCESS FRONT-LOADING OF ALIMONY PAYMENTS

The more-than-six-year-alimony-payment-period requirement has been repealed. The cumbersome six-year recapture period mechanism of excess up-front alimony has been replaced by a slightly less complicated three-year recapture period procedure.[50] The rules work as follows:

1. Only three consecutive years are considered, starting with the first year any deductible alimony is paid.
2. If the annual payment drops by more than $15,000 from year one to year two or three and/or from year two to year three, "excess alimony" is gross income to the payor in the third year and deductible to the payee.
3. The rules' purpose is to reduce the incentive to deduct as alimony what is really a property settlement.
4. The rules do not apply under the following circumstances:
   (a) Payments are treated as nondeductible alimony, child support, or as a property settlement.
   (b) Payments stopped or were reduced because of the death of the payor or payee or the payee's remarriage.
   (c) Payments fluctuate due to forces not under the payor's control, such as being a percentage of gross revenues of a business.
   (d) Payments are reduced or discontinued after the third year of payments ("the third post-separation year").
   (e) Payments are reduced by $15,000 or less.
   (f) Payments increase by any amount from year to year.

---

[50] Code Sec. 71(f).

¶ 1340 COMPUTING EXCESS ALIMONY

The excess payment in year two (E_2) is simply equal to deductible alimony paid in year two (A_2) less deductible alimony paid in year three (A_3) and less $15,000. This may be written as:

$$E_2 = A_2 - A_3 - \$15{,}000$$

The excess alimony payments, which are taxable and deductible in the third post-separation year, equal the excess payments in year two, plus the excess payments in year one. The latter equals the alimony paid in year one (A_1) less the average of alimony paid in year two (reduced by excess payments in year two and alimony paid in year three, and less $15,000. This excess may be written as:

$$E_1 = A_1 - \frac{(A_2 - E_2) + A_3}{2} - \$15{,}000$$

Thus, the excess alimony recaptured in year three may be written as:

$$E = E_2 + E_1 = E_2 + A_1 - \frac{(A_2 - E_2) + A_3}{2} - \$15{,}000$$

where $E_2 = A_2 - A_3 - \$15{,}000$.

Examples: The following are examples of how recapture provisions may affect the payment of alimony:

(a) Jasper pays Marcia $60,000 of alimony in 1991, none in 1992 or 1993. $45,000 will be recaptured in 1993 whether or not Jasper pays more alimony after 1993.

(b) Jasper pays Marcia $3,000 a month alimony March through December 1991, $1,500 a month in 1992 and $500 a month in 1993. There is $3,000 of recapture computed as follows:

The payments were $30,000 in 1991 (10 × $3,000), $18,000 in 1992 and $6,000 in 1993. $30,000 exceeds average alimony in years two and three by $18,000.

$$\frac{(\$18{,}000 + \$6{,}000)}{2} = \$12{,}000$$

Since $18,000 exceeds $15,000 by $3,000, this amount is excess alimony. It should be noted that, if Jasper had started payments in April 1991, *no* recapture would have taken place.

(c) Jasper pays Marcia $70,000 in 1991, $35,000 in 1992, and nothing in 1993.

$$E_2 = A_2 - A_3 - \$15{,}000$$
$$= \$35{,}000 - \$15{,}000 = \$20{,}000$$
$$E_1 = A_1 - \frac{(A_2 - E_2) + A_3}{2} - \$15{,}000$$
$$= \$70{,}000 - \frac{(\$35{,}000 - \$20{,}000) + \$0}{2} - \$15{,}000$$
$$= \$70{,}000 - \$7{,}500 - \$15{,}000$$
$$= \$47{,}500.$$

Thus, $67,500 ($47,500 + $20,000) is includible in Jasper's income in 1993 and deductible by Marcia. Of course, Marcia may have little or no income in 1993 to deduct the excess alimony from, particularly since she received no alimony in 1993.

(d) Jasper and Marcia divorced in December 1991, and he paid her $1,000 in alimony. In late December 1992, he paid her $49,500, and, in early January 1993, he paid her another $49,500. Technically, there is no recapture.

These rules are effective for divorce and separation instruments executed or amended after 1986. However, in the case of unamended pre-1987 agreements, the old six-year recapture rules will be applied only to the first three post-separation years.

¶ 1341 PROPERTY SETTLEMENTS—APPRECIATED ASSETS

Under Code Sec. 1041, the transferor recognizes no gain or loss when property is transferred to a spouse or ex-spouse as a property settlement (unless the transferee is a nonresident alien.) As a result the transferee's adjusted basis is that of the transferor. Upon sale the transferee spouse will have to recognize gain, including the built-in gain at the time of the transfer. Prior to 1987, if such gain was a capital gain, only 40% was taxed, while, currently, such gain is fully taxed at a rate of up to 28%.

Example: When Jasper and Marcia were divorced, Marcia received securities with a basis of $15,000 which she later sold for $25,000. Prior to 1987 Marcia's tax bracket was 34% and her tax on the $10,000 gain therefore would be 34% of $4,000, or $1,360. If the sale took place after 1986, when her bracket had been *reduced* to 28% her tax on the gain is *increased* to $2,800 (28% on the full $10,000).

¶ 1342 TRANSFERS IN TRUST FOR BENEFIT OF SPOUSE

Code Sec. 1041 provides generally that gain or loss is not recognized on a transfer to, or for the benefit of, a spouse or former spouse (if incident to divorce). Two exceptions have been added if the transfer is to a trust:

1. *Gain* must be recognized to the extent that the amount of the liabilities assumed, plus the amount of the liabilities to which the property is subject, exceeds the adjusted basis of the property.[51]
2. *Gain or loss* must be recognized on a transfer of installment obligations.

Example: When Jasper and Marcia got divorced, Jasper funded an alimony trust with a number of assets. Two of these were an office building with a basis of $20,000, a mortgage of $35,000 and a value of $70,000 and an installment obligation with a face value of $50,000, a gross profit percentage of 40% and a fair market value of $45,000. Jasper will recognize a $15,000 gain on the transfer of the building, some or all of which may be ordinary income due to depreciation recapture. The trust's basis is increased by the amount of gain to $35,000. Jasper will also recognize a $15,000 gain on the installment obligation ($45,000 less 60% of $50,000) and the trust's basis becomes $45,000. If Jasper had simply transferred the assets outright to Marcia, neither gain would have been recognized.

¶ 1343 DEFERRED COMPENSATION AND QUALIFIED DOMESTIC RELATIONS ORDERS

The Retirement Equity Act of 1984 introduced requirements that plan administrators make payments to "alternate payees" pursuant to Qualified Domestic Relations Orders (QDROs). Typically, this means that, when an employee is divorced, a court may order payments out of a pension or profit-sharing plan to the former spouse and/or children. The Tax Reform Act of 1986 made it clear that distributions to someone other than the spouse are taxed to the employee, while payments to the former spouse are taxed to such spouse. If a lump sum is paid, five-year forward averaging may be available, while an annuity is taxed under the annuity rules.[52] If the spouse receives an annuity and the employee has an investment in the contract (e.g., if it is a contributory plan), a proportional share of such investment is allocated to the payee who can then apply the resulting exclusion ratio.

Examples:

(a) Jasper is a participant in a noncontributory pension plan. At the age of 50, when his life expectancy is 30 years for income tax purposes, he is divorced and, pursuant to a

[51] Code Sec. 1041(e).

[52] Code Secs. 402(a)(9) and 72(m)(10).

QDRD, $8,000 a year is paid to his daughter, Simone. Jasper has gross income of $8,000 a year.

(b) Same as in (a) above except the annuity is paid to Jasper's ex-wife, Marcia. Marcia has gross income of $8,000 a year.

¶ 1344 HEAD-OF-HOUSEHOLD STATUS

An individual is a "head of household", qualifying for tax rates lower than on a single but higher than on a joint return, if the taxpayer:

1. maintains a household for a dependent for more than half the taxable year;
2. is entitled to a depending exemption for such dependent, except an unmarried child;
3. furnishes more than half the cost of maintaining the household; and
4. is divorced, legally separated, or married but living apart with a dependent child.[53]

If the divorced parents are single and retain custody of at least one child each, they may both qualify as heads of household.

¶ 1345 CHILD CARE CREDIT

Under rules similar to the head-of-household tests, the custodial parent of a child under 15 (or a handicapped child) is entitled to the child care credit without regard to who claims the dependency exemption.[54] If both parents qualify, they may both claim the child care credit for one or more children in their care.

¶ 1346 IRA DEDUCTIONS

Alimony, if taxable, is "earned income" for purposes of the IRA deduction.[55] Furthermore, the IRA deduction of up to $2,000 is allowed without diminution even if the former spouse/payor is an active participant in a qualified pension or profit-sharing plan, and even if neither spouse qualified for an IRA deduction prior to the divorce.

Example: Jasper and Marcia are married, file a joint return, have adjusted gross income of $50,000 or more and Jasper participates in a qualified pension plan. Neither spouse may claim an IRA deduction.[56] If the couple is divorced, Marcia receives alimony, and is not covered by a qualified plan, she may deduct IRA contributions, while Jasper may not (unless his adjusted gross income is under $35,000).

---

[53] Code Secs. 2(b)(1)(A) and 143.

[54] Code Sec. 21(e).

[55] Code Sec. 219(f)(1).

[56] Code Sec. 219(g).

¶ 1347 ALIMONY TRUSTS

Alimony trusts can play a valuable role in estate, tax, and financial planning. In fact, the use of such a trust can have distinct advantages over an outright settlement or direct support payments to a former spouse and minor children.

The alimony trust has the following advantages to the former spouse who is the beneficiary:

1. Without a funded trust, support payments often stop upon the payor's death. Unfortunately, the need for support payments does not go away. The trust can continue automatically until the payee's death or remarriage and until the last minor child reaches majority.
2. Because the trust is funded initially, subsequent setbacks, such as disability or unemployment, will not affect the support payments.
3. The beneficiaries are no longer faced with chasing the breadwinner across the country if the latter should decide not to pay in the future.
4. The former spouse is relieved of the responsibility to manage a lump-sum settlement. In addition, a one-shot settlement may prove inadequate because of subsequent price level increases.

A typical alimony trust works like this:

1. The payor creates an irrevocable trust with a corporate trustee to continue even after death, if necessary.
2. The trust agreement will be referred to in the divorce decree.
3. The payor transfers cash and/or property needed to fund the trust.
4. The trustee will normally have the discretionary authority to invest and reinvest the trust funds.
5. All income generated will be paid quarterly to the former spouse for support with a guaranteed minimum. Any deficit will reduce the principal (corpus).
6. A percentage of the guaranteed minimum can be designated as child support.
7. The trustee's commissions are payable out of principal.
8. The trust continues until the former spouse dies or remarries and for the duration of the children's minority. If the former happens before the latter, a portion of the trust (based on point 5, above) terminates.

9. In all events, the trust corpus reverts to the payor or the payor's estate.

TAX CONSEQUENCES TO PAYOR

1. Appreciation on property transferred is not taxed to the payor unless, and only to the extent that, liabilities in excess of basis are transferred.[57]
2. The payor is taxed on amounts paid as child support.
3. Upon the payor's death prior to termination of the trust, the trust principal, less the actuarial value of the outstanding income interest, is includible in the payor's gross estate.

TAX CONSEQUENCES TO SPOUSE

1. The payee is taxed on all alimony received, including principal payments, but not on payments made out of tax-exempt income.
2. The payee is not taxed on child support payments.[58]

CONCLUSION

Percent changes in the law may have simplified some areas of taxation, but the tax aspects of divorce and separation are not among them. New rules relating to IRA deductions, property settlements, recapture of excess alimony, and income splitting may all have to be considered when a marriage is dissolved, as well as major changes in tax rates and exemptions that affect everyone.

Death of the Spouse

¶ 1350 "SURVIVING SPOUSE"

The advantages of a joint return are available to a surviving spouse for the year of the decedent's death and, in some cases, two more years. However, subject to the gross income test, a year-of-death return must be filed for the decedent spouse.

"Surviving spouse" is a separate filing status and is independent of age. A taxpayer can file a joint return if married at the end of the year and for the year in which the spouse died even if the taxpayer did not remarry. The tax advantages of the joint return are also available to the taxpayer as a "surviving spouse" for an additional two years. Even though the return is not a joint one, the taxpayer is entitled to use the joint return rates and the joint return standard deduction. The taxpayer is no longer entitled to an exemption for the deceased spouse. To

[57] Code Sec. 1041.

[58] Code Sec. 682.

be eligible, the surviving spouse must meet the following requirements.[59]

1. The taxpayer remains unmarried. (A taxpayer who remarries may, of course, file a regular joint return with the new spouse.)
2. The taxpayer maintains a household that is the home of at least one dependent child for the whole year.
3. The taxpayer was eligible to file jointly with the deceased spouse for the year of death.

After the two years are up, the taxpayer may be able to qualify as a "head of household" and be taxed at rates that are higher than the joint return rates but lower than the single rates.

¶ 1351 LIABILITY FOR THE DECEASED SPOUSE'S TAXES

As this actual fact situation illustrates, the filing of separate returns may benefit a deceased spouse:

> A man operated his own business in Chicago and made a reasonable profit. For the last several years of his life, he filed no returns and paid no taxes. His wife had no income of her own, except interest on joint savings accounts, which was below the taxable limit. Upon his death, she became the sole owner of the savings and the residence owned in joint tenancy, and received life insurance. She sold the house and ended with approximately $200,000 in savings altogether. Because of her husband's failure to pay tax, she was worried that the IRS would inquire into the situation, but she need not have worried, because of the following circumstances:
>
> 1. No part of her husband's income could be attributed to her as community property, because Illinois is not a community property state.
> 2. She was not a partner in the business; therefore, no business income could be allocated to her.
> 3. Because no joint returns were filed, she never became liable for his taxes under the "joint and several liabilities" rule.
> 4. The IRS could sue his estate, but there was no estate to sue. His assets were held in joint tenancy with rights of survivorship, and she was the beneficiary of the life insurance. Therefore, except for some personal belongings with negligible value, all property held passed to her automatically by operation of law.

---

[59] Code Sec. 2(a).

5. She had no transferee liability because her husband had not been rendered insolvent through the creation of the joint tenancies.

6. A taxpayer's liability is *personal* to the taxpayer. If she had paid his tax, it would have constituted tax deductible donations to the United States government.

¶ 1352 DECEDENT'S FINAL RETURN

Death does not excuse the failure to file, or the nonpayment of tax. On the date of death, a new taxpayer, the estate, comes into being, and the decedent's taxable year ends. The return for this year, which could consist of a week, a month, or a year, is due on April 15 of the following year regardless of the date of death. The decedent's personal representative, i.e., the executor, if named in the will, or the administrator, if there was no will or if the executor was unwilling or unable to serve, may have to file a minimum of three federal tax returns:

1. The decedent's final return.
2. The estate tax return.
3. The estate's income tax returns.

These are in addition to state and local returns. Form 1040 is used to file the final return. It may be a joint return, signed by the surviving spouse and by the personal representative, if one has been appointed. If a refund of tax paid by the decedent is claimed, the return must include Form 1310, Statement of Claimant to Refund on Behalf of Deceased Taxpayer.

The income on a final return includes income earned by the decedent up to the date of death, and if joint, income for the whole year attributable to the surviving spouse.

Also, all allowable expenses paid by the decedent can be deducted on the final return, and if it is a joint return, all deductible expenses of the spouse for the whole year are included. Any medical expenses paid on behalf of the decedent by the surviving spouse can be deducted on the final return, whether paid before or after death, whether separate or joint returns are filed, and independent of whether the survivor remarried or not by year-end. In addition, medical expenses paid by the estate may be deducted on the final return if paid within 12 months of death, unless deducted on the estate tax return.[60]

Net operating loss and capital loss carryovers not absorbed on the final return expire because they are personal to the taxpayer.

---

[60] Code Sec. 213(c).

¶ 1353 DEATH OF A SPOUSE PRIOR TO DUE DATE

The earlier in the year a person dies, the less likely it is that a return has been filed for the preceding year. When a return is filed by the survivor, this return is *not* a final return. It may, however, also be a joint return, signed by the surviving spouse alone, explaining the circumstances. An appointed personal representative must also sign. As a result, there may be a maximum of four returns filed at joint return rates *after* the death of a spouse:

1. One return for the preceding year.
2. One return for the year of death (the final return).
3. Two returns as a surviving spouse.

¶ 1354 INCOME IN RESPECT OF A DECEDENT

The decedent has almost always been on the cash basis. Assuming this to be the case, only income actually or constructively received and expenses actually paid will be included in the final return. Income and expenses received and paid after death will wind up in the returns of the estate and/or the heirs. In general, estates are taxed like trusts, meaning that the income is taxed to the estate, unless and to the extent distributed to the beneficiaries. In other words, an either/or approach is used. Here are some examples:

1. If the widow receives the right to her husband's future renewal commissions, *she* will have gross income when she collects them.
2. If the decedent rendered services, but the checks are received after death, the estate is taxed on them.
3. Dividends and interest on securities owned by the decedent, but paid after death, will be taxed to the recipient estate or heir.[61]
4. If the decedent was a partner the income will be taxed to the recipient when the partnership year ends, unless a buy/sell agreement is effective immediately. The rule is that the partnership year ends *as to the selling partner* on the date of sale. Thus, if the partnership agreement provides for a sale of the partnership interest as of the date of death, the income up to that time will be includible in the decedent's final return.

The estate exists as a separate taxpayer from the death of the individual, regardless of when the personal representative is appointed, and lasts as long as necessary for the administration of the estate.

[61] Code Sec. 691.

CHAPTER 14

TAX ASPECTS OF CASUALTY GAINS AND LOSSES

¶ 1401 INTRODUCTION

A series of recent natural disasters, including Hurricane Andrew, which hit Miami and the surrounding area on August 24, 1992, as well as the flooding in the Midwest in the summer of 1993, has made it necessary for an unprecedented number of taxpayers and their advisors to become familiar with the tax consequences of casualty gains and losses (as well as building codes, insurance and mortgage provisions). The main tax considerations relating to involuntary conversions are discussed below, with special emphasis on examples of personal casualties relating to homes and personal use property.

¶ 1402 LIMITATIONS ON PERSONAL CASUALTY LOSS DEDUCTIONS

Casualty losses are deductible under Code Sec. 165(a). However, the deduction for losses of money or property *not* connected with a trade or business or a transaction entered into for profit ("personal casualty losses") are subject to *four* special limitations:

1. The deduction is only allowable to taxpayers who itemize expenses as opposed to taxpayers who claim the standard deductions. The standard deduction on a joint return was $6,200 in 1993 and is $6,350 in 1994.
2. In the case of a total loss of property, the amount of the loss is limited to the *lesser* of the fair market value of the property immediately prior to the loss or its adjusted basis under Reg. § 1.165-7(b)(1)(i). The loss is, of course, reduced by insurance proceeds received.
3. Each casualty loss (total losses from the same casualty, as opposed to each item damaged or lost) must be reduced by $100 under Code Sec. 165(h)(1).
4. Casualty losses after the application of the above limitations are deductible only to the extent they exceed 10 percent of taxpayer's adjusted gross income under Code Sec. 165(h)(2)(A).

Example: Taxpayer's house was completely destroyed by a tornado. Immediately prior to the casualty, the house had an adjusted basis of $100,000 and a fair market value of $80,000. Insurance proceeds of $60,000 were received. If the house was Taxpayer's residence and the homeowner's adjusted gross income (AGI) was $40,000, the casualty loss deduction is computed as follows:

1. The lesser of adjusted basis or fair market value is $80,000.
2. $80,000 less insurance proceeds equals $20,000.

3. $20,000 is reduced by $100 to $19,900.
4. $19,900 is reduced by $4,000 (10 percent of AGI) to $15,900, which is deductible on Schedule A as an itemized expense.

If the house was being rented or used for business purposes, the deduction would simply equal adjusted basis of $100,000 less insurance proceeds of $60,000, or $40,000. The deduction would be claimed on the appropriate form, e.g., Schedule E for rental property or Schedule C for self-employed individuals who used the building in their business.

It should be noted that in the case of a personal casualty, no deduction is possible if insurance proceeds equal the fair market value of the property as reduced by $100 and 10 percent of AGI.

¶ 1403 PERSONAL USE PROPERTY

Because of the severe limitations on the amount deductible as personal casualty losses, it is important to be aware of which items constitute personal property. Examples include:

Personal residences, such as the principal residence, vacation homes, hunting lodges;

Private automobiles, boats and aircrafts;

Home furnishings, carpeting and appliances; and

Jewelry, antiques, art works, books, stamps and other collectibles held for personal purposes.

In addition, the damaged or destroyed property must actually belong to the taxpayer, the taxpayer's spouse (if a joint return is filed), or the taxpayer's dependents.

The casualty loss is increased by debris removal and cleanup expenses.

¶ 1404 THE REDUCTION IN VALUE APPROACH TO CASUALTY LOSSES

Although not technically required, appraisals, photographs and physical evidence will make it more likely that a casualty loss deduction will withstand possible IRS challenges. Thus, conducting appraisals before and after the casualty, i.e., establishing the decline in the fair market value of the property due to the casualty, is one way to compute the amount of the casualty loss (before limitations). Obtaining an appraisal of a damaged house is obviously easier than an after-the-fact appraisal of the home as it was prior to the disaster. However, an estimate may be made by real estate professionals based on sales prices of comparable properties just prior to the loss. For autos, "Blue Book" values may be used to establish pre-loss values, while a detailed inventory showing original cost and estimates of fair market values and replacement costs can be used for household furniture and other personal property.

The costs of professional appraisals, photographs, videotaping, etc., are *not* deductible as casualty losses. However, such expenses constitute "miscellaneous itemized deductions," the sum of which is deductible to the extent it exceeds two percent of AGI.

¶ 1405 THE REPAIR COST APPROACH TO CASUALTY LOSSES

As an alternative to proving the decline in fair market value of property partially destroyed, a taxpayer may elect to use the cost of restoration to original condition. The IRS requires the following information under Reg. § 1.165-7(a)(2)(ii):

1. the repairs are necessary to restore the property to its pre-casualty condition;
2. the amount expended is not excessive;
3. repairs performed are limited to the damage sustained; and
4. the property's value after the repairs have been made does not exceed the property's pre-casualty value.

¶ 1406 THE "REPAIRS VS. DECLINE IN VALUE" ELECTION

Since a taxpayer has a choice between deducting actual repair costs required to restore the property or the decline in value caused by the casualty prior to repairs, the greater amount should clearly be claimed. However, it should be kept in mind that it is easier to prove repair costs (with receipts and canceled checks) than a decline in value, since the latter is more subjective.

> ***Example:*** Homeowner's house was partially destroyed by lightning. Competent appraisals show a decline in fair market value from $100,000 to $60,000. If repair costs only amount to $15,000 (for example, because Taxpayer does much of the work himself or has friends and/or relatives in the construction business), the $40,000 decline in value (less limitations) should be deducted. The value decline cannot exceed the adjusted basis in the house, however, as previously stated.

It should be noted that regardless of how the casualty loss is computed, the loss deduction available for tax purposes reduces the adjusted basis in the property with respect to which it is claimed under Code Sec. 1016.

¶ 1407 GENERAL MARKET DECLINES

When a casualty results in a decline in values of both damaged and undamaged properties, Reg. § 1.165-7(a)(2)(i) requires that before and after appraisals take this phenomenon into account.

> ***Example:*** Taxpayer's home was damaged by a hurricane and was worth $300,000 before the storm and $200,000 after. However, had the home been worth only $240,000 after the hurricane, *even if undamaged,* the casualty deduction is limited to $40,000. This frequently happens because of a flight from hurricane-prone areas, depressed market prices, destruction of businesses and public attractions in the area, etc.

Since the computations are made immediately after a disaster, it is irrelevant that the market value may eventually recover to the former level. This limitation may make the election to use the cost of repairs and restoration more attractive.

¶ 1408 REQUIRED INSURANCE CLAIMS

Personal casualty losses covered by insurance are not deductible unless an insurance claim has been filed under Code Sec. 165(h)(4)(E). However, if the loss exceeds insurance proceeds, a deduction is allowed subject to the limitations discussed above.

INSURANCE SETTLEMENT EXPENSES

Expenses incurred in reaching a settlement with the insurer may include lawyer's fees, accountant fees, fees of umpires, arbitrators, or mediators, etc. Such fees are not deductible as casualty losses. Rather, they reduce the insurance proceeds recovered.

PENDING INSURANCE SETTLEMENTS

Insurance proceeds which have a reasonable likelihood of being collected reduce the amount of casualty losses which can be claimed. It follows that:

1. No casualty loss deduction is allowed if it is expected that a full insurance recovery will be made.
2. A casualty loss can be claimed in the year sustained (or the previous year in a disaster area) even though insurance proceeds are pending as long as the casualty loss exceeds the expected coverage. Coverage is expected if a lawsuit is filed.
3. An additional casualty loss may result in a subsequent year if insurance proceeds actually collected (if any) fall short of the expected amount assumed in the loss year.

SUBSEQUENT INSURANCE RECOVERIES

A taxpayer may deduct a casualty loss unreduced by insurance, in good faith, even after filing an insurance claim, believing that a recovery is highly unlikely. If an insurance payment is unexpectedly made in a subsequent taxable year, such amount constitutes gross income in the year received under the tax benefit rule in Code Sec. 111. An amended return is not required. The amount received is gross income only to the extent of the casualty deduction actually claimed unless the amount is so substantial as to also generate a casualty gain. It is also possible that a casualty gain was originally reported but has been increased by a higher than expected insurance payment. An amended return should then be filed. Finally, it is possible that a casualty gain was reported but that the insurance payment turned out to be smaller than assumed. Again, an amended return should be filed to reduce the casualty gain retroactively or even to claim a casualty loss.

¶ 1409 CASUALTY LOSSES AS NET OPERATING LOSSES

Even personal casualty loss deductions in excess of taxable income result in net operating losses under Code Sec. 172(d)(4)(C). As a result, such excess losses may be carried back three years and forward up to 15 years under Code Sec. 172(b)(1)(A).

> ***Example:*** Taxpayer sustained a deductible $30,000 casualty loss from hurricane damage in 1992. If Taxpayer's taxable income was $18,000, the excess $12,000 may be carried back to 1989, 1990 and 1991, then to 1993, etc. If taxpayer lived in an area declared a disaster area, the deduction may be claimed for 1991 by election with any excess carried back to 1988, 1989 and 1990, then to 1992, etc.

A taxpayer who expects to be in a higher tax bracket the year(s) after the year of loss may wish to elect to forego the carryback under Code Sec. 172(b)(3).

¶ 1410 CASH GIFTS RECEIVED BY DISASTER VICTIMS

Many disaster victims receive cash gifts from friends, relatives and neighbors or from emergency disaster funds set up gratuitously by their employers. The IRS takes the following positions:

1. Amounts received are excluded from gross income as gifts under Code Sec. 102.
2. The casualty loss deduction, if any, does *not* have to be reduced by the amounts received *unless* "the money received must be used by the recipient to rehabilitate or replace the

property which is the subject of the claimed casualty deduction."[1]

Example: An employee suffers a casualty loss of $40,000 to her home, $28,000 of which is deductible for tax purposes. If the employee receives $15,000 tax free from her employer's emergency fund without limitations or directives relating to how the money is to be used, she still can claim a casualty loss of $28,000. If the money is required to be used to repair and restore the house, the casualty loss deduction is reduced to $13,000.

¶ 1411 THE UNITARY APPROACH TO PERSONAL RESIDENCES

A personal residence includes the building and the land, *including* trees, plants and shrubs. As a result, a homeowner does not have to allocate adjusted basis and fair market values to the various items of realty comprising a home.

Example: Homeowner created an impressive garden from scratch which over the years developed into an attractive collection of ornamental and fruit- and nut-bearing trees at a nominal out-of-pocket cost. Although the house suffered minimal damage, the garden was totally destroyed by a hurricane, resulting in a reduction in value of the overall property of $20,000 plus $5,000 in debris removal cost. The casualty loss deduction is $25,000 before limitations.

It should be noted that gain or loss must be computed separately for *personal* property in the residence, such as furniture, appliances and glassware.

Casualty Gains with Respect to a Principal Residence

¶ 1415 INTRODUCTION

A homeowner's adjusted basis in the home itself is often lower than expected due to two factors:

1. Because of the two-year rollover of gain rules in Code Sec. 1034, an older homeowner's adjusted basis in a residence may be little more than the cost of the first home ever purchased, five homes ago, since deferred gains reduce the adjusted basis in the replacement home.

Example: Homeowner purchased a first home for $10,000. Many years later, it was sold for $100,000, whereupon a new home was purchased for $105,000. The adjusted basis in the new home is $15,000 ($105,000 less $90,000 of realized gain deferred).

---

[1] Rev. Ruls. 131, 1953-2 CB 112 and 64-329, 1964-2 CB 58.

2. From the purchase price of the property must be subtracted the cost of the land, furnishings, appliances, curtains, rugs and other personalty, to arrive at the adjusted basis of the house itself.

¶ 1416 TOTAL DESTRUCTIONS

If a homeowner suffers a complete loss of a principal residence and collects insurance proceeds in excess of the adjusted basis in the house, such excess is gross income. However, under Code Sec. 165(h)(2)(B), a net personal casualty gain for a given year is a capital gain. If the home was held over one year, the gain is a long-term capital gain. Furthermore, if taxpayer's long-term capital gains for the year exceed short-term losses, the excess is a "net capital gain" subject to a maximum tax rate of 28 percent under Code Sec. 1(h).

The homeowner may, however, defer the gain by investing the insurance proceeds in another home or rebuilding. It should be noted that the mandatory two-year rollover of a home provision in Code Sec. 1034 does *not* apply to involuntary conversions (casualties) under Reg. § 1.1033(a)-3. Rather, a taxpayer who wishes to defer the casualty gain must *elect* to do so under Code Sec. 1033. On the other hand, in lieu of the rigid two-year rule in Code Sec. 1034, taxpayer has the rest of the taxable year of the casualty, plus two more years, plus possible extensions to replace the home without recognizing gain. If less than all insurance proceeds are reinvested, a capital gain results to the extent of the extra funds retained.

> ***Example:*** Taxpayer purchased a home for \$100,000, \$20,000 of which was reasonably allocable to the land. Several years later, the home was completely destroyed in a hurricane on January 2, 1993, when the home was worth \$300,000, of which \$50,000 represented the value of the land. The insurer paid \$250,000 for the value of the house and Taxpayer promptly sold the land for \$50,000. Taxpayer realized gain of \$170,000 on the house (\$250,000 less \$80,000) and \$30,000 on the land, for a total of \$200,000. Since the casualty necessitated the sale of the land, the full gain of \$200,000 is realized from an involuntary conversion and is a casualty gain. Taxpayer has until the end of 1995 (plus possible extensions) to acquire another home. If the new home costs \$300,000 or more, no gain is recognized and the adjusted basis in it equals its cost less \$200,000 of deferred gain. If the new home costs less than \$300,000, e.g., \$230,000, \$70,000 of capital gain is recognized and the new home's basis equals \$100,000 (\$230,000 less \$130,000 of deferred gain).

If the home was seized, requisitioned, or condemned, and the homeowner received a condemnation award in excess of basis, the homeowner may elect to fall under the two-year rollover of a residence provision rather than the involuntary conversion provision pursuant to Code Sec. 1034(i). Possible advantages of making the election include:

1. If Taxpayer happened to have purchased another home within two years prior to the casualty, it may be treated as the replacement residence even though there was no contemplation of an involuntary conversion. An example is the case where Taxpayer moved into a "new" home and had not yet sold the "old" one but rented it out with an option to buy.
2. Under Code Sec. 1034(b), the "adjusted sales price," which must be reinvested to defer all gain, is reduced by "fixing-up expenses" not otherwise deductible or added to basis.
3. Members of the armed forces may extend the two-year replacement period by up to two more years under Code Sec. 1034(h).

¶ 1417 THE $125,000 EXCLUSION

Under Code Sec. 121, a homeowner over age 55 has a once-in-a-lifetime election to exclude up to $125,000 of gain from the sale or exchange of a principal residence. Under Code Sec. 121(d)(4), the election may be made with respect to a gain from an involuntary conversion as well. Thus, a homeowner over age 55 who has not made the election previously and who does not plan to buy another home should make the Code Sec. 121 election. It is made on Form 2119, "Sale of Your Home," the same form used for the two-year rollover provision. The homeowner must have owned the home for at least three of the last five years and have used it as a principal residence at least three of the last five years prior to the conversion, but not necessarily concurrently. If the insurance proceeds result in a realized gain in excess of $125,000, the remaining gain may be deferred by reinvesting the insurance proceeds (less $125,000) in related property, e.g., improvements within the "two-year-plus" replacement period under Reg. § 1.121-5(g).

¶ 1418 MORTGAGE INSURANCE AND THE TOTAL DESTRUCTION OF A RESIDENCE

Due to a depressed real estate market, many homeowners who put up a small down payment have a "negative equity" in their homes (the mortgage loan balance exceeds the value of the home). If such a home is destroyed as a result of natural disaster, the lender (mortgagee) collects the mortgage balance from its insurer and the ex-homeowner deeds the land to the insurance company.

Example: Homeowner purchased a home for $100,000, $20,000 of which allocable to the land. At a time when the property was worth $80,000 and the mortgage balance was $90,000, the home was totally destroyed by a tornado. The insurer paid off the $90,000 mortgage, and the ex-homeowner deeded the land to the insurer. No casualty deduction is allowed since Taxpayer was relieved of a mortgage in excess of fair market value. Taxpayer has sustained a loss of $10,000 ($100,000 less $90,000). However, this is a *personal loss,* nondeductible under Code Sec. 262, *not* a casualty loss. If the value of the home was in excess of the mortgage, a casualty loss would be possible.

PARTIAL DAMAGE

In most cases, even Hurricane Andrew caused only partial damage to a residence. Even in situations where the insured received a flat sum from the insurer which proved more than sufficient to repair or replace a roof, walls, or ceilings, casualty gains only result if the insurance proceeds exceed the total basis in the home. Any amount left over merely reduces the homeowner's adjusted basis in the home. In other words, in the absence of a realized gain there can be no recognized gain, even if the homeowner is enriched!

Example: Homeowners have an adjusted basis of $100,000 in their home, which suffers substantial damage during a hurricane. They receive $75,000 from their insurer for the damage to the real property. They spend $40,000 on capital improvements, e.g., replacing the roof and rebuilding a wall, $10,000 on repairs, e.g., indoor and outdoor painting, new wallpaper, etc., and invest the remaining $25,000 in the stockmarket.

Homeowners do *not* realize a gain since the insurance proceeds of $75,000 did not exceed their $100,000 basis. However, the amount not spent on capital improvements, $35,000, reduces their adjusted basis in the home to $65,000. No reporting requirements exist (see below).

Casualty Gain on a Home Followed by Resale

In some cases, a taxpayer who sustains substantial damage to a home may collect insurance proceeds in excess of the home's adjusted basis then decide to sell the home either "as is" or after making minimal repairs to make it more salable. If the home is reparable, this approach results in two separate transactions for tax purposes. However, if the home must be razed, the sale is a direct and mandatory result of the involuntary conversion so that only one transaction has occurred.

> ***Example 1:*** Homeowner's house with an adjusted basis of $90,000 was so badly damaged by a hurricane as to unreparable. The insurance company paid $150,000 for the damage whereupon Homeowner sold the property for $50,000. For tax purposes, Homeowner has received the full $200,000 on account of an involuntary conversion and has realized a $110,000 gain from an involuntary conversion. Homeowner has the usual "two-years-plus" to reinvest in another home to defer the gain. However, if Homeowner is over age 55, an election may be made under Code Sec. 121 to simply exclude the gain since it does not exceed $125,000.

> ***Example 2:*** Same as Example 1 except the home is reparable. In this case, Homeowner first realizes a gain of $60,000 from the involuntary conversion. At the time of sale, another $50,000 of gain is realized in a separate transaction (sale of a home). The full $50,000 is gain because Homeowner recovered the basis in the home plus $60,000 from the insurer and thus had a zero basis at the time of sale. To fully defer the two gains, the total $200,000 received must be reinvested. Technically, $150,000 must be reinvested within the "two-years-plus" period mandated by Code Sec. 1033 (the involuntary conversion section) and $50,000 within the "two-years-after-closing" period mandated by Code Sec. 1034 (the replacement of a principal residence section). As a practical matter, a new house must be purchased by the earlier of the two replacement periods. This scenario poses a problem for taxpayers over age 55 since the Code Sec. 121 election to exclude gain may only be applied to one disposition of a home. Thus, Homeowner in this example may elect to include the $60,000 gain or the $50,000 gain, but not both. This makes a replacement, even a temporary one, more attractive for tax purposes.

¶ 1420 CASUALTY GAINS ON PERSONAL PROPERTY

Since personal property is nondepreciable, the adjusted bases in furniture and household goods equal their original cost. However, if the insurance policy provides for replacement value, gains on numerous items may result, particularly with respect to jewelry, art works and collectibles. Technically, gain or loss must be computed on each item, or at least on classes of items (e.g., the stamp collection, the wardrobe). To defer gain, the Code Sec. 1033 election must be made for each identifiable item or category of items. Any cash left over is taxable as a capital gain to the extent of realized gain.

Example: Taxpayer's piano, purchased for $7,000, was destroyed and the insurance company paid $15,000. A new piano was purchased for $13,000. Taxpayer's realized gain equaled $8,000 ($15,000 less $7,000). The taxable gain (recognized gain) equals $2,000, the cash left over. The cost basis in the new piano equals $7,000, the carryover basis of $7,000, less "boot" of $2,000 and plus $2,000 of gain recognized.

If Taxpayer has both casualty gains and losses from the same casualty, the gains and losses (not reduced by $100) are netted. A casualty gain, taxed as a capital gain only results to the extent gains exceed losses. If losses exceed gains, a net casualty loss results, deductible subject to the $100 and ten percent of AGI limitations, described above.

¶ 1421 TEMPORARY LIVING EXPENSES

When a home becomes uninhabitable because of a casualty, due to extensive damage, lack of utilities, etc., a homeowner with a family may incur temporary living expenses such as hotel bills or short-term rent. Such living expenses, like all personal expenses, are nondeductible under Code Sec. 262. However, insurance coverage for temporary living expenses is usually partly tax-free under Code Sec. 123. The exclusion is limited to expenses actually incurred in excess of normal living expenses saved (expenses which would have been incurred during the relevant time period, but were not).

Example: After a disaster, Taxpayer and family moved into a hotel for 30 days at a cost of $4,000 plus $1,000 for meals. If the insurance company paid $4,200 and normal living expenses would have been $1,500, the exclusion is $3,500 ($5,000 less $1,500). Thus, Taxpayer must report $700 of gross income ($4,200 less $3,500).

It should be noted that fixed costs, such as mortgage payments, property taxes and minimum phone charges, are payable even if the homeowner is absent and are not part of normal living expenses. As a result, the exclusion tends to be a large portion of insurance proceeds.

¶ 1422 DISASTER AREAS

If the President of the United States declares a disaster area under the Disaster Relief and Emergency Act, a taxpayer may elect to claim a casualty loss resulting from the disaster in the previous taxable year under Code Sec. 165(i). If a return has already been filed for the previous year, an amended return is necessary, e.g., Form 1040X. Possible advantages of making this election include:

1. A refund check is available within weeks.

2. Interest is paid on the refund.
3. If the taxpayer's AGI was lower the previous year, the deduction is higher due to the 10 percent floor.

Disadvantages of the election may include:

1. An amended return may have to be filed.
2. The taxpayer may not have the information required to compute the loss, e.g., the insurance company has not yet processed the claim.
3. AGI for the previous year may be higher than for the current year.

Example: Taxpayer's home was destroyed by Hurricane Andrew on August 24, 1992. The estimated loss is $15,000 after insurance proceeds and the $100 deductible. AGI on the 1991 tax return, filed in April, was $50,000 and is estimated to be $40,000 for 1992. Taxpayer thus has a choice between filing an amended return for 1991, claiming a deduction of $10,000 ($15,000 less 10 percent of $50,000) and getting a quick refund or waiting until 1993 and claiming a deduction of $11,000 ($15,000 less 10 percent of $40,000).

In cases where immediate cash flow is not a concern, a taxpayer may be advised to wait until 1993 when AGI for both 1991 and 1992 are known before making the election. However, the election to claim the loss in the prior year must be made by the due date of the loss year without extensions, e.g., by April 15, 1993.

¶ 1423 CASUALTY GAIN RELIEF FOR DISASTER AREAS UNDER THE 1993 REVENUE ACT

The Revenue Reconciliation Act of 1993 provides three items of tax relief in Code Sec. 1033(h) for occupants and owners of principal residences who suffered property damage in a Presidentially declared disaster on or after September 1, 1991:

1. No realized gains resulting from insurance proceeds received for unscheduled personal property ("contents"), such as clothing and furniture, are to be recognized, whether or not the property is replaced.
2. Insurance proceeds received for damage to the residence and scheduled property, such as jewelry, furs, art works and antiques, are to be treated as one common fund. As a result, no realized gain is recognized as long as the total proceeds are reinvested in the involuntarily converted residence and/or scheduled property within the replacement property.

3. The replacement period is extended from two to four years after the year the gains from the involuntary conversion were realized.

Example 1: Taxpayer received $10,000 for a piano (unscheduled property) purchased for $4,000 which was constructively destroyed by water damage during Hurricane Andrew. Taxpayer spent the insurance proceeds on college tuition for the children. None of the $6,000 realized gain is recognized.

Example 2: Taxpayer's home was damaged by Hurricane Andrew. Insurance proceeds of $100,000 were received for the home with an adjusted basis of $40,000 and $30,000 for scheduled jewelry with an adjusted basis of $10,000. As long as Taxpayer expends the full $140,000 on jewelry and/or replacing the damaged residence within four years after the end of the tax year when the insurance proceeds were received, no gain will be recognized.

THE TWO PERCENT FLOOR ON "MISCELLANEOUS ITEMIZED DEDUCTIONS"

Casualty losses are excluded from the definition of "miscellaneous itemized deductions" under Code Sec. 67(b)(3), presumably because of the number of other limitations placed on personal casualty losses.

THE PHASEOUT OF ITEMIZED EXPENSES

Casualty losses are excluded from the definition of "itemized deductions" subject to an up to 80 percent phaseout for high income taxpayers under Code Sec. 68(c)(3), again because of the other limitations applicable.

THE ALTERNATIVE MINIMUM TAX

Casualty losses are deductible in computing alternative minimum taxable income under Code Sec. 56(b) to the same extent they are deductible for regular income tax purposes.

EMERGENCY LOAN INTEREST

After a disaster, a number of low-income, uninsured, or underinsured homeowners receive federal loans on favorable terms from (among others) the Small Business Administration or the Federal Emergency Management Agency (FEMA). Receiving such a loan to repair, rebuild, or reconstruct a residence has no impact on the casualty loss deduction. Furthermore, the interest on the loan is deductible as long as the loan qualifies under Code Sec. 163(h)(3)(C) as "home equity indebtedness," i.e., it cannot exceed $100,000 and must be secured by a "qualified residence." However, such interest is *not* deductible for alternative minimum tax purposes, since Code Sec. 56(e)(1) requires that the loan be used to acquire, construct, or substantially improve a residence, not merely to repair it.

SPECIAL RULES FOR BUSINESS/INVESTMENT CASUALTIES

The main differences in the tax treatment of business casualty losses are as follows:

1. In the case of total destruction of business property, the adjusted basis is deductible even if the fair market value is less.
2. The casualty loss is not reduced by $100 or by 10 percent of AGI.
3. An insurance claim is *not* a prerequisite to claiming a deduction.
4. Each item of property damaged must be handled individually even if part of a whole, e.g., trees and buildings.

In cases where property is used partly for business and partly for personal purposes, e.g., taxpayer lives on the first floor and rents out the second, the property is treated as two separate assets, one of which is subject to personal casualty loss rules, the other to the business casualty loss rules.

¶ 1424 IRS REPORTING REQUIREMENTS

The following duties apply with respect to reporting to the IRS:

1. Insurance companies have *no* duties to report insurance proceeds paid to any taxpayers to the IRS, regardless of the amount.
2. Taxpayers who receive insurance proceeds, regardless of amount, have *no* duty to report the receipt of such funds *if no gain is realized.* Thus, where insurance proceeds received on account of a damaged home do not exceed its adjusted basis the IRS need not be notified. This is true even if a homeowner has substantial sums left over after completing repairs. However, the taxpayer should keep track of amounts not spent on capital improvements, so as to be able to compute the reduced basis in the home in case of a later sale or disposition.
3. If insurance proceeds with respect to property exceed its basis, a realized gain results. A taxpayer who does not intend to replace or restore the property will, of course, have to recognize the gain in the return for the year during which proceeds are received. If the taxpayer intends to reinvest the insurance proceeds in similar property within two years after year-end, thus deferring the gain, the election to do so is *deemed made*

even if the taxpayer *does nothing*, i.e., does *not* report a gain "even though the details in connection with the conversion are not reported . . ." under Reg. § 1.1033(a)-2(c)(2). The same regulation, however, states, somewhat inconsistently, that when a gain results from an involuntary conversion "[a]ll of the details . . . shall be reported . . ." in the return for the year the gain is realized.

4. A taxpayer who winds up with a previously unreported gain when the replacement period expires due to the failure to reinvest all insurance proceeds must report the gain in an amended return for the year the insurance proceeds were received.

5. When an election to defer a gain is made or deemed made all the details regarding any reinvestment must be provided with the returns for the years involved.

It should be noted that the three-year statute of limitations does not start with respect to a gain from an involuntary conversion until the IRS has received notice of replacement, intention to replace, or failure to replace under Reg. § 1.1033(a)-2(c)(5). Thus, if a taxpayer reports nothing, the statute never starts even if a return is filed with respect to the gain realized from the involuntary conversion.

¶ 1425 IRS FORMS AND PUBLICATIONS

IRS Publication 584, "Casualty Loss Workbook," explains how to identify damaged property and compute casualty losses.

IRS Form 4684, "Casualties and Thefts," is required to be filed if a casualty loss is claimed. The form with instructions illustrates how to compute casualty gains and losses from personal as well as business properties. Although no substantiation is required to be filed with the return, the taxpayer must be prepared to present proof of loss if audited.

¶ 1426 CONCLUDING REMARKS

A taxpayer who is a victim of a natural disaster may have a casualty gain or loss for tax purposes, depending on factors such as insurance coverage, the relationship between basis and value of affected properties and whether the loss is personal or a business loss. Casualty gains are easily deferred by election if the property is to be replaced. However, personal casualty losses are subject to severe limitations. The key to a successful deduction is adequate proof of loss, such as appraisals, repair costs, photographs and good records.

CHAPTER 15

CLOSELY HELD BUSINESS PLANNING

¶ 1501 INTRODUCTION

Small businesses are organized (in the order of importance) as sole proprietorships, partnerships, and corporations. They are discussed here and compared in that order. The unique S corporation is covered in a comparison with partnerships and comes out a loser. As in practice, tax considerations tend to dominate the choice of business organization.

Sole Proprietorships

¶ 1502 SOLE PROPRIETOR

A sole proprietor is self-employed, and income and deductions appear on Schedule C of Form 1040. The net income from the business is added to the owner's other income on Form 1040 and is subject to self-employment (social security or FICA) tax. Thus, the proprietorship is *not* a separate entity apart from its owner.

¶ 1503 TAX INCENTIVES TO EMPLOY ONE'S SPOUSE

At first blush, it may appear that few or no tax benefits are possible when a sole proprietor employs a spouse with whom a joint return is filed. However, significant tax savings are in fact possible.

¶ 1504 INDIVIDUAL RETIREMENT PLANS

Each employee or self-employed person may contribute and deduct the lesser of either $2,000 or earned income to an IRA each year.[1] A sole proprietor *not* employing the spouse is limited to $2,000 a year, plus an extra $250 if the choice is made to include a nonworking spouse. Thus, an extra $1,750 a year deduction from gross income is possible. The contribution may be made as late as the due date of the return, by April 15 the following year, even if the return is filed earlier. However, if the sole proprietorship is on the cash basis, the *wages* to the employee-spouse must be paid by year-end. The sole proprietor may also be covered by an H.R. 10 plan (Keogh plan) which may be a defined contribution or defined benefit plan. Deductible IRA contributions are

[1] Code Sec. 219(b)(1).

phased out, however, for participants with AGI above $25,000 ($40,000 for joint filers).

¶ 1505 MEDICAL REIMBURSEMENT PLANS

Medical reimbursement plans are attractive, since payments made are deductible while excluded from gross income, circumventing the 7.5% of adjusted gross income limitation on medical expense deductions. However, the sole proprietor is not considered an employee for this purpose and cannot be covered *as such* under the plan.[2] Once one spouse is covered as an employee, the other spouse and the children may be included. Thus, the sole proprietor will be covered as an employee's spouse.[3] This is so, even if the spouse is the only employee, since the Regulations provide that a plan may cover one or more employees.[4]

¶ 1506 MEDICAL INSURANCE

Unlike medical reimbursements, medical *insurance* may be provided on a discriminatory basis.[5] Thus, where there are other employees, medical insurance may nevertheless be offered to the employee-spouse only and cover the proprietor as the spouse of the employee. Premiums paid are not gross income but are fully deductible, both for income tax and self-employment tax purposes.[6] In comparison, if the spouse is not an employee, premiums paid on behalf of the family of the proprietor are only 25% deductible.[7]

¶ 1507 MISCELLANEOUS CONSIDERATIONS

1. The IRA and medical benefits are available to partnerships as well as proprietorships.
2. State and local tax savings are possible when employing a spouse due to the deduction for medical benefits and IRA contributions.
3. If the employee-spouse's participation in the business is quite extensive, the arrangement may be considered a *coproprietorship.* In this case the IRS's position is that both parties are subject to self-employment tax.[8]
4. It is *not* sufficient to put one's spouse on the payroll. Services commensurate with the salary must be rendered.

---

[2] Code Sec. 105(g).

[3] Rev. Rul. 71-588, 1971-2 CB 91.

[4] Reg. § 1.105(a).

[5] Reg. § 1.105-11(a) and (b).

[6] Reg. § § 1.162-10(a) and 1.402(a)-2(a).

[7] Code Sec. 162(m).

[8] Let. Rul. 8123044.

¶ 1508 TAX INCENTIVES TO EMPLOY ONE'S CHILDREN

Employing one's children, when feasible in the light of the child labor provisions under the Fair Labor Standards Act of 1939, is even more beneficial than employing one's spouse. This is due to the following:

1. Income splitting is achieved since each child is a separate taxpayer.
2. Each child, regardless of age, may have a separate IRA.
3. If the spouse is not employed, the child(ren) may be covered under a medical reimbursement and/or medical insurance plan. However, if the spouse is employed, the children may be included as dependents.
4. Wages of children under the age of 18 paid by a parent/sole proprietor are exempt from social security and employment taxes, similar to those of an employee-spouse.[9]

Example: Joe Mendez, the sole proprietor of a grocery store, employs his 16-year-old son, Richard, as a part-time bag boy and delivery boy. His salary in 1993 was $8,050. Richard's tax return for 1993 (required filed) may be summarized as follows:

Gross income	$8,050
IRA contribution	2,000
Adjusted gross income	$6,050
Standard deduction	3,700
Taxable income, taxed at 15%	$2,350

The $8,050 paid is deductible to the proprietorship. Joe's self-employment tax base may be reduced in full or in part by the payment made. In any event, Joe's gross income is reduced by $8,050, which stays in the family. Assuming Joe still pays over one-half of Richard's support, the dependency exemption of $2,350 is available to Joe, but not to Richard. If Joe pays more than half his own support, his taxable income is zero since he can claim his own exemption.

Partnerships

¶ 1510 INTRODUCTION

A few large firms, notably CPA firms and law firms, are operated as partnerships, along with thousands of small enterprises, including tax shelters. In addition, numerous sole proprietorships are (or should be) operated as family partnerships, particularly for tax purposes. This section provides a survey of the law of partnerships, as well as financial

[9] Code Sec. 3121(b)(3)(A).

planning and tax aspects. Common problem areas and their solutions are outlined for partnerships in general, with special emphasis on family partnerships, and professional service partnerships. The information provided should assist anyone who is or who may become a partner, whether on a full or part-time basis.

¶ 1511 PARTNERSHIP CHARACTERISTICS

Here is a summary of the main legal aspects of partnerships:

1. Any legal person competent to contract may become a partner.
2. A limited partnership must have at least one general partner with unlimited liability.
3. A general partnership is governed by agency law. Mutual agency means that each partner may bind the partnership and the other partners within the apparent scope of the partnership business.
4. A partnership interest is *personal property,* even if the main assets of the partnership are real property (the doctrine of equitable conversion).
5. A partnership interest is a capital asset for tax purposes (with some refinements).
6. A partnership may be *express* (i.e., a written or oral agreement), or *implied* (from acts of the partners).
7. The firm name may be actual (e.g., Jones and Smith) or fictitious (ARC Associates).
8. Creditors must exhaust partnership assets before going after the partners' personal assets.
9. Partners share profits and losses equally and are not entitled to payment for services or interest on their capital, unless contractually agreed.
10. Partners are not employees but are self-employed.
11. Partners have the right to an accounting, to be informed of what is occurring, and to their capital interest upon dissolution.
12. Although the majority can make normal operating decisions, unanimous consent is required for major business decisions (absent an agreement to the contrary).
13. What constitutes partnership assets depends on the following:
    (a) Does the partnership have title?
    (b) Were the assets purchased with partnership funds?

   (c) Are the assets used in the business?
   (d) Are the assets recorded on the partnership's books?

14. Partnership assets must be available to the partnerships' creditors in order of priority before the excess is applied to a partner's debts.
15. Partners' assets must be available for the individual partner's debts before any excess is applied to partnership debts.
16. A partnership may file bankruptcy as an entity.
17. A creditor of a partner who attaches a partnership interest acquires no right in partnership property, does not become a partner, and cannot compel liquidation. The creditor can, however, collect future distributions of profit and capital.
18. A partnership may be dissolved at any time (absent a contrary agreement).
19. Each partner owes the other partners a fiduciary duty.
20. All general partners are jointly liable for partnership debts.
21. A partnership is dissolved if a partner dies, files bankruptcy, or is incapacitated.
22. If a partnership is liquidated, the order of priority is:
    (a) Creditors of the partnership.
    (b) Individual creditors of insolvent partners (but only if the partnership is insolvent).
    (c) Partner creditors for loans and advances.
    (d) Partners' capital accounts.

¶ 1512 TYPES OF PARTNERS

Partners may be classified as follows:

1. A *general* partner actively and publicly engages in the business of the partnership. The partner may or may not make an investment but is liable for partnership debts and shares in profits and losses.
2. A *nominal* partner shares in neither management nor profits but is held out publicly as a partner. Because of the latter, the partner is liable for partnership debts.
3. A *silent* partner does not share in management but is publicly known as a partner, makes investments, is liable, and shares in profits.
4. A *secret* partner is unknown to the public but participates in management and shares in profits.

5. A *dormant* partner neither participates in management nor is known to the public but makes an investment and shares profits.
6. A *limited* partner cannot participate in management but makes an investment. The partner's liability is limited to such investment, but the partner shares in profits.

To summarize, all the above are personally liable for partnership debts, except limited partners. All the above share in profits, except nominal partners.

¶ 1513 STATE LAW REQUIREMENTS

A partnership exists for tax purposes, whether or not state law is complied with. As long as two or more legal persons (individuals, corporations, trusts, or even partnerships) enter into a business for profit, a partnership exists as far as the IRS is concerned. Mere co-ownership of property does not constitute a partnership, but joint ventures, syndicates, pools, or other unincorporated businesses do.[10]

Under local law no formalities need be observed for a partnership to be recognized, but there may be penalties for not observing them. Four basic factors are looked at by the courts to determine whether a partnership exists:

1. Did the parties *intend* to be partners? If they held themselves out as partners, the intent is inferred.
2. Did they *share* profits and losses?
3. Do they *jointly own* and control property?
4. Do they *jointly control* and manage the business?

The Uniform Partnership Act (UPA) was approved in 1914 and has since been adopted by almost all states. The Uniform Limited Partnership Act (ULPA) has a more recent history. In the absence of a partnership agreement, and only then, the UPA and ULPA govern the relationships between the partners. This is also true if the agreement is ambiguous or silent as to issues. A minimum of activity can result in a partnership, even inadvertently.

¶ 1514 PARTNERSHIP AGREEMENT

The contract that spells out the rights and duties of the partners is known as the partnership agreement. It should try to anticipate the maximum number of questions which may need to be answered while providing a mechanism for periodic revisions. Some of the points covered in the typical agreement include:

---

[10] Code Sec. 761(a).

1. The name of the partnership.
2. The identity of each general and limited partner and each partner's interest in profit, loss, and capital.
3. Required investments to be made by each partner.
4. Procedures for expelling old, or admitting new, partners, as well as for sales and other transfers of partnerships interests.
5. The scope of the partnership should be spelled out, e.g., can it borrow, buy securities or real estate, be in more than one line of business, etc.?
6. Who owns the furniture, who is responsible for leases, who pays expenses, who collects and deposits fees, etc.?
7. Who has what rights to clients or retention of clients?
8. What happens on the dissolution of the partnership? Does the partnership have a limited duration? Can it merge with other partnerships?
9. Who makes the day-to-day decisions? What percentage vote is required for major business decisions?

From these few examples it is obvious that the partnership agreement can be, and probably should be, a lengthy document. The more that can be spelled out up front, the more clear-cut the relationship. A tentative partnership agreement is possible as a short-term solution, but there should be a termination date, otherwise the partners may never get around to changing it. A partnership agreement can be revised any time, but only if all partners agree (unless there is a different provision in the agreement).

MAKING DECISIONS

If the partnership consists of only two or three people, it may be practical to require unanimous consent for any decisions. This is the rule of the UPA, but it is impractical in large partnerships. The obvious solution is to have an agreement spelling out who makes what decisions. It could be broken down as follows:

1. One partner or any one partner can make decisions relating to day-to-day operations.
2. A majority or even all partners must agree on major decisions, such as admitting a new partner, obtaining financing, moving to new offices, or merging or selling the business.

¶ 1515 FORMATION OF THE PARTNERSHIP

The partnership agreement serves a function from the start. Although the formation is not a taxable event, subsequent payments of salaries and interest depend on what assets, if any, each partner transfers. In a service partnership the main asset is the earning power of the partners. But even in such a business, assets such as a lease, office equipment, and receivables are common.

If one or more partners receives a partnership interest merely in exchange for services, such as forming the partnership, the value of the partnership interest will be income to the recipient with a corresponding deduction to the partnership.[11]

PROFIT AND LOSS SHARING RATIOS

In the absence of an agreement, all partners share profits and losses equally, with no one getting paid for services rendered or receiving interest on investments made. Here are some alternatives:

1. The profit-sharing ratio can be different from the loss-sharing ratio.
2. The partners can have profit and loss-sharing ratios different from their fractional capital interest.
3. Some partners can receive compensation for services rendered and/or their capital accounts.
4. A profit-sharing interest can be coupled with a guaranteed minimum.
5. The profit and/or the loss-sharing ratios can vary through time or be subject to amendment, for example by majority vote.
6. In a service partnership it is not uncommon to give the partner who produced the client a percentage of the gross billings to that client, while all partners share in the rest, based on actual work done, for example.
7. In some partnerships, notably law firms, an executive committee votes on each partner's profit percentage for the preceding year based on performance during the year.

In conclusion, the arrangement that can be made can be flexible or inflexible, constant over time or subject to change. Any number of factors can be considered, i.e., skill, prestige, longevity, degree of practice development, overall contribution, investments, time commitment, etc.

¶ 1516 DEATH OF A PARTNER

Because death is inevitable what happens when a partner dies should be spelled out up front. The partnership can in fact be a

[11] Code Sec. 83.

valuable estate or retirement-planning tool once the possibilities are known. One frequent provision is that when the partner dies, the partnership or the surviving partners will purchase the interest and pay the estate or designated beneficiaries in installments over a number of years. This buy/sell agreement has several advantages:

1. It provides the estate or beneficiaries with liquidity, income to live and a guaranteed market for the partnership interest. In fact, the arrangement fulfills many of the functions of life insurance and is often financed through life insurance contracts.
2. To the extent these payments constitute income to the successor in interest, the surviving partners receive tax deductions.[12]
3. Liquidation of the interest can be funded by life insurance, i.e., the partnership may carry insurance on the lives of its partners with a proviso in the partnership agreement that the proceeds will in fact be used for this purpose.
4. A formula can be designed to meet any objectives the parties may have and can therefore be quite flexible. Thus a lump sum can be provided on death, plus periodic payments thereafter.
5. Payments provided will be in addition to the accumulated funds in the self-employment retirement plan (H.R. 10 plan).

For tax purposes the partnership does not end with the death of a partner.[13] Therefore, the taxable year of the partnership does not end with respect to the decedent, unless there is a buy/sell agreement providing for an automatic sale upon death. In the latter case, the income of the partner is taxed on the partner's final return, otherwise the successor in interest will pick up the income.

¶ 1517 DISABILITY OF A PARTNER

The smaller the partnership and the more recent its formation, the greater the impact on operations if a partner becomes disabled. Auto accidents are the most likely source. Statistics show that the probability is substantial that at least one partner in a multipartner partnership will suffer long-term disability prior to ordinary retirement. The average partnership does not have the resources to continue payments to a disabled partner for an extended period of time. As a result the following is recommended:

1. The partnership should decide on a period of time during which it would be willing and able to make disability payments, should one occur.

[12] Code Sec. 736(a).

[13] Code Sec. 706(c).

2. The partnership or the partners should buy disability insurance. If payments are to start six months after disability occurs, for example, premiums can be kept down.
3. If disability occurs, payments will be made to the disabled partner, say in the amount of 75% of normal payments, until the insurance takes over.

In larger partnerships self-insurance may be a viable alternative. In any event the disability problem is one which also should be handled up front.

¶ 1518 HOW TO ADMIT A NEW PARTNER

Assume that a partnership has two equal partners but wishes to admit a third equal partner. The following approaches could be used:

1. The new partner receives a one-third interest in capital. If purchased, even with appreciated property, there are no tax consequences at the time. But if nothing is paid, the partner will have income in the amount of the value of the interest, unless it is an intra-family gift.
2. The new partner receives a one-third interest merely in profits and losses. If nothing is paid for it, the partner may have compensation income in the amount of the value of the interest. However, if receiving and keeping the interest is contingent on future performance of substantial services, there will not be income currently.[14]
3. The new partner receives a one-third interest in the receivables as well as in profits and losses. The problem with receiving an interest in already existing receivables is that the partner may have taxable income in the year of collection. In most cases it is recommended that the incoming partner merely receive one-third of receivables generated after admission. This is also the fairest, since the receivables did not result from the new partner's services.
4. The new partner receives a profit and loss interest for services *and* buys a one-third capital interest from the old partners. This would lead to taxable income to the old partners who will be deemed to have sold a share of the unrealized receivables.[15] The new partner receives a cost basis in the partnership's interest as well as in the assets (if an optional basis adjustment is made under Code Sec. 754). The partnership agreement can provide for an allocation of the purchase price to exclude receivables, if desired. In most cases, this alternative is the

[14] Code Sec. 83.

[15] Code Sec. 751.

most desirable, assuming the incoming partner is not purchasing a part of already existing receivables.

¶ 1519 TAX ASPECTS OF PARTNERSHIPS

Here is a summary of the main tax aspects of partnerships:

1. A partnership is *never* taxed as such, but must file a Form 1065 which is strictly an information return, showing the partnership's income and deductions and each partner's distributive share. The form must be signed by one of the partners.

2. If the partnership has at least three of the following four corporate characteristics, i.e., continuity of life, centralized management, limited liability, and free transferability of shares, it runs the risk of being taxed as a corporation. This could only happen if the IRS is successful in labelling the entity as an unincorporated association.

3. The formation of the partnership and its incorporation, if desired, can generally be done tax free.[16]

4. Each partner picks up a share of partnership income or loss in the partner's taxable year with which, or within which, the partnership's year ends.[17] Only a limited deferral is available, however, because the tax year of the business generally has to be the same as that of the majority partners.

5. The partnership is a true conduit, i.e., long-term capital gains, tax-free income, qualifying dividends, etc., flow through as such to the individual partners.[18]

6. Partners are not employees but are self-employed. As a result, there is no withholding, and no employer's share of Social Security tax must be paid. On the other hand, no corporate type qualified pension and profit-sharing plans can be established. The partners and their employees have to make do with H.R. 10 plans for the self-employed.

7. A partner who sells property to the partnership is generally treated as an outsider, i.e., the partner is treated as having sold the property to a third party, not as having sold it to the other partners, retaining a proportional share.[19] Gain is recognized, but a loss is disallowed if the partner owns more than 50% of the capital and/or profits, directly or indirectly.[20]

---

[16] Code Secs. 721-723.
[17] Code Secs. 702 and 706(a).
[18] Code Sec. 702(b).
[19] Code Sec. 707(a).
[20] Code Sec. 707(b)(1).

8. Income, gains, losses and credits can be allocated disproportionately if
   (a) the partnership agreement specifies it,
   (b) the allocation changes the actual dollar amounts, not merely the character of gain or loss,[21] and
   (c) the capital accounts reflect all allocations made and will be followed on liquidation of the partnership.

   The partnership agreement can be changed after the end of the year, with retroactive effect, if done by the due date of the return. Thus profit and loss ratios, for example, can be changed after the fact.
9. All tax elections must be made at the partnership level.[22] Examples include accounting methods, such as cash reporting or accrual and installment reporting, inventory, and depreciation methods. It would be an administrative nightmare if each partner could adopt a different method, so this is an eminently practical rule. For this purpose the partnership is treated as an entity, while the general scheme is to view the partnership as a multiple proprietorship.
10. The partnership as such has no net operating losses, but the loss is deductible to the partners. Each partner can deduct a share of the partnership loss in accordance with the loss-sharing ratio from any other income. The deduction is limited to the basis in the partnership interest.[23] Once this has been reduced to zero, any excess loss is carried forward indefinitely in search of basis. Such basis is obtained by future profits, additional investments, or from increases in partnership liabilities. In addition, a loss may be suspended under the "at risk" or the "passive activity" rules.
11. If a partner sells a partnership interest, this is a transaction between the outgoing and incoming partner. The partnership is not affected, but the partnership's taxable year ends *as to the selling partner.* Thus, the former partner picks up the share of profits for the current taxable year of the partnership up to the date of sale when the new partner takes over.[24]
12. Upon the sale of a partnership interest a capital gain or loss results.[25] However, any gain is ordinary income to the extent of the selling partner's share of appreciation on ordinary

---

[21] Code Sec. 704(b).
[22] Code Sec. 703(b).
[23] Code Sec. 704(d).
[24] Code Sec. 706(b)
[25] Code Sec. 741.

income assets, e.g., depreciation recapture, inventories, and unrealized receivables.[26]

13. Distributions generally merely reduce a partner's basis in the partnership interest and are not taxed currently.[27] Property distributions receive the same basis in the hands of the partner as they had in the partnership.[28]

14. A partnership only ends for tax purposes if it either ceases operations or if at least 50% of the capital and profit interests change hands during one 12-month period.[29]

¶ 1520 SYNDICATES, POOLS AND JOINT VENTURES

At least for tax purposes, a partnership is broadly defined and includes the following types of businesses:

1. *Syndicates.* A syndicate refers to an enterprise with one particular purpose requiring a large capital. The most typical example is a securities underwriting syndicate, formed by several investment firms to launch a particular stock or bond issue. Once the securities are sold, the syndicate ceases to exist.

2. *Pools.* The typical example is an investment club, whereby individuals pool their funds and make common investments for firm and profit. An election may be made for the members to file individually, without a partnership return.[30]

3. *Joint ventures.* Individuals, partnerships, or corporations join in a venture for their common benefit. Although most common in the construction field, the term is used in show business (the production of a play), operation of a business, development of mineral properties, etc.

There is a fine line between the three, but a syndicate has more members than a joint venture. The latter may have only two. A pool is limited to investment activities. All these are taxed as partnerships, unless they have too many corporate characteristics. If they do, they may wind up as unincorporated associations and be taxable as corporations.

For a discussion of tax shelter partnerships, see the chapter on tax shelters.

---

[26] Code Sec. 751.
[27] Code Secs. 731 and 733.
[28] Code Sec. 732(a).
[29] Code Sec. 708(b)(2).
[30] Code Sec. 761(a).

Tax Planning with Family Partnerships

¶ 1525 INTRODUCTION

A partnership can be an important vehicle to redistribute family income and capital, but it is underutilized. It may be created either by gifting or selling an interest in the business to a child or other relative, thereby making the relative a partner.[31] The relative may be admitted into an existing partnership or a sole proprietorship may be transformed into a partnership. Below, we will look at the mechanics of family partnerships and the tax aspects of each.

¶ 1526 FAMILY MEMBERS AS PARTNERS

The basic reason for admitting a relative as a partner is to split taxable income with people in low brackets. Estate and gift tax savings can also result. There are significant nontax considerations as well:

1. Does the client really want a relative as a partner? A partner does have more powers than a shareholder, due to the fact that a partnership is governed by mutual agency rules. Maybe a corporation is a better solution?
2. Does the sole proprietor want to give up ownership and control over part of the capital?
3. Is a partner with experience needed?

¶ 1527 HOW TO EFFECT INCOME SPLITTING

In the typical situation the taxpayer wishes to have a close family member as partner for tax purposes, so as to have the relative's distributive share of income taxed in lower brackets. Normally the relative is a child. The younger the child, the less likely it is that the child will render services. If nothing else, there are laws against child labor. In a licensed profession, e.g., lawyer, CPA, M.D., or D.D.S., an additional requirement is that each partner be licensed.

¶ 1528 FAMILY PARTNERSHIPS AND INCOME TAXES

Here are the rules governing the recognition of family partnerships for tax purposes:

1. The motive for selling or giving a relative a partnership interest is generally irrelevant.
2. In a service partnership each member must render services, otherwise there is an assignment of income problem.[32] The general rule is that income is taxed to whoever earns it.

---

[31] Code Sec. 704(e).

[32] Code Sec. 704(e)(2).

3. A family is defined rather narrowly. The other members must either be
   (a) the transferor's spouse, lineal descendants (child, grandchild) or ancestors (parent, grandparent), or
   (b) a trust with such relatives as beneficiaries. But if the trust is a "grantor" trust, e.g., the grantor retained the power to revoke, borrow, alter, amend, etc., the trust is not taxed, but the grantor still is.
4. The transferor must transfer a *capital* interest in the partnership, i.e., an interest in the assets of the partnership. This interest must be distributable to the owner upon withdrawal or liquidation. Thus, the grantor cannot simply transfer an interest in profits and still shift the income.
5. A child will be recognized as a partner whether the capital interest is purchased or received by gift. But unless services are rendered, capital must be a material income-producing factor. This means that the business employs capital to a great extent, such as substantial inventories or plant, machinery, or equipment. Outstanding receivables will not suffice. Businesses primarily collecting fees, commissions, or other compensation for services rendered do not qualify.
6. The transfer to the relative must be complete so that the transferee is the true owner of the interest. The IRS obviously scrutinizes family transactions. If the transaction lacks economic substance, at a minimum the tax benefits will be denied, at a maximum the grantor may be charged with tax evasion.
7. When the new partner is recognized as such depends on the substance of the transaction, i.e., the conduct of the partner is more important than paper work.
8. In any event, unearned income in excess of $1,200 of a child under age 14 is taxed at the parents' tax rate.[33]

RETAINED CONTROLS

There are four main controls, the retention of which (one or more) may indicate that the transferor is, in reality, still the owner of the interest purportedly transferred:

1. *Control over distributions.* Restrictions on the relative's right to withdraw profits is a negative factor, but retaining income for the reasonable needs of the business is fine.

---

[33] Code Sec. 1(i).

2. *Transfer restrictions.* The donee should have the power to sell or liquidate. Buy-sell agreements are so common and serve a business purpose, so that a *reasonable* agreement should be okay.
3. *Control of partnership assets.* If the donor retains complete control over the assets—for example, through outright ownership with the partnership as lessee—this tends to indicate that the transfer lacks substance.
4. *Management controls.* Being a managing partner is one thing, but powers inconsistent with normal partner relationships are another. The retention of voting control is acceptable, assuming that the control is common and that the donee is free to liquidate his interest. If the partner is a child, it is generally necessary to set up a trust to own the interest. It is important that the donee's share of income is distributed (to the extent not needed in the business) and that the share is received for the donee's benefit. A client who retains control of the funds may be taxed on them, too. The above controls may also constitute a retained life estate for estate tax purposes.[34]

¶ 1529 PARTNER'S ROLE IN THE BUSINESS

The following seven factors are important in considering whether the donee is *in fact* a partner:

1. Is the donee publicly held out as a partner?
2. Is the donee treated as a partner under state law?
3. Is the donee authorized to use business bank accounts?
4. Does the donee have rights to receive distributions?
5. Is the donee recognized as a partner in contracts, insurance policies, or other such documents?
6. Is the donee treated as a partner on the books and records of the business?
7. Is the donee listed as a partner on Form 1065, the partnership's tax information return?

¶ 1530 WHO SHOULD THE PARTNER BE?

Particularly if the donee is a child, the client has to consider whether a trustee or a custodian should be the *legal* owner. In addition, the client may wish to make the trust or custodian a *limited* partner. If the trustee is independent and unrelated to the grantor, the trust is most likely to be recognized as a separate partner. If the client is the

[34] Code Sec. 2036.

trustee, the trust instrument has to give the client much less discretion than can be granted an independent trustee.

A guardian is an alternative to a trustee if acting as a fiduciary for the sole benefit of the minor. But note that if the child's share is spent on support, the parents (who have the support obligation) will be taxed on the amounts so expended.[35] The Treasury Regulations require that the fiduciary is subject to judicial supervision, including the filing of accountings and reports. A trust is probably the cleanest alternative in most cases.

The donee will be recognized as a partner, whether a general or limited partner. A donee who takes no active part in management is eligible to be a limited partner and does not have to *render any* services to shift the income, assuming capital is a substantial income-producing factor. Recall that certain formalities are necessary to have a limited partnership under local law. If the child is only a partner for income tax reasons, it makes sense to protect the child from partnership creditors.

¶ 1531 HOW MUCH INCOME CAN BE ALLOCATED?

The basic limitation as to the amount of income that can be shifted to the donee partner is that a reasonable allowance has to be made for the grantor's own services. Thus, if the grantor works full time and the donee is a passive equal partner, the grantor must, as a practical matter, be allocated more than 50%. After the adjustment for services rendered, the allocation can be proportional to the capital interests owned.[36] This rule presumably also applies in a loss situation. Thus, if the reasonable compensation to the donor partner exceeds partnership income, the donee will be allocated a share of the resulting loss. The fact that the donee is a limited partner should not change the above approach.

¶ 1532 PURCHASED INTERESTS

A purchased interest, like a gift, results in a capital interest equal to its fair market value. In fact, a purchase is treated as a gift, not as a purchase, unless one of the following requirements is met:

1. The purchase by a family member meets the tests of an arm's-length transaction.

2. The purchase has a bona fide business purpose.

The main advantage of structuring the transaction as a purchase, rather than a gift, is the avoidance of the gift tax. To facilitate

---

[35] Code Sec. 677(b).

[36] Code Sec. 704(e)(2).

payment, a deferred payment sale for an installment note or a private annuity may be employed.

Corporations

¶ 1535 ADVANTAGES OF INCORPORATING

1. There may be some tax advantages of incorporating, such as tax-free fringe benefits and low corporate rates. It should be kept in mind that the IRS can disregard the corporation if it is formed for tax avoidance rather than to facilitate the transaction of business.
2. If a new, risky venture is started and the corporation goes "belly up," the shareholder's liability is limited, keeping the residence, investments, and salary from being attacked by creditors. However, a shareholder is still personally liable for malpractice after incorporation, relating to personal negligence. There simply is not any liability for debts owed by the corporation itself. Incorporation is not the only way to limit liability. Others include:
   (a) Reimbursement or guarantee contracts.
   (b) Becoming judgment proof.
   (c) Being insured against loss.
   (d) Utilizing a limited partnership.

   In fact, it may be difficult for a small corporation to get a loan, unless the shareholders cosign or pledge noncorporate assets.
3. Lenders are not subject to usury laws when dealing with a corporation, a useful aspect in inflationary times.
4. Corporations continue as legal entities after the owner dies, goes bankrupt or becomes incompetent, unlike a partnership or proprietorship.
5. Corporate shares can easily be transferred to family members.
6. Additional capital can be raised through the sale of new stock.

¶ 1536 DISADVANTAGES OF INCORPORATING

Before rushing out to incorporate a consulting practice and/or royalty income and/or a stock portfolio, consider the following drawbacks:

1. Even though the incorporation process is simple, a lawyer or CPA is needed for every aspect of corporate life.
2. Before incorporating, the potential shareholder should analyze assets, family situations, earning power, and the nature of the

business. Maybe all that is needed is a will or an insurance policy.

3. Large tax savings are possible only if the owner can afford to be without a large share of the earnings of the corporation by putting it into a retirement plan or letting it ride at low tax rates.
4. Double taxation can only be avoided by adopting an S corporation, a unique creature of the tax law entailing numerous complexities (compared with partnerships below).
5. Unless earnings are large, it may not be worth the legal and accounting fees resulting initially and continuously, due to filing of necessary documents monthly, quarterly, or annually.

¶ 1537 CHARACTERISTICS OF CLOSELY HELD CORPORATIONS

Four basic advantages of corporations are widely cited:

1. Limited liability,
2. Continuity of life,
3. Free transferability of shares,
4. Tax advantages.

In reality, *none* of these advantages may be present in a small business corporation. If not, a corporation simply means more paperwork and legal plus accounting fees. Consider the following:

1. Limited liability is a myth if the owner has to personally gaurantee the debts of the corporation. The smaller the business, the more likely this is. In addition, the owner and other employees are still liable for malpractice.
2. There can be no *actual* continuity of life in a small business. When the one-man owner dies or retires, so does the business regardless of legal form. A corporation merely lives on as a legal entity.
3. Free transferability of shares is the exception to the rule for small businesses. Not only are buy/sell agreements extremely common among the shareholders or between the corporation and each shareholder, but even in the absence of restrictions, there is a limited market for untraded shares.
4. Historically, the main tax advantages of a closely held corporation were two and probably accounted for most small incorporations.
   (a) Liberal deductions for pension, profit sharing, and fringe benefits, without current tax liability for the owners.

After 1982, self-employment plans are generally available to the same extent.

(b) Low corporate tax rates of 15-34% (15% on the first $50,000). The problem is that to take advantage of these benefits, the owners must be financially able to go without the funds for a long time. Currently, maximum individual rates are down to 28% for most people. In addition, there are many pitfalls. The major ones are briefly discussed below. These problems exist even if the corporation is recognized as such for tax purposes.

¶ 1538 CORPORATE FORMALITIES

To prevent the IRS from "piercing the corporate veil" by claiming the corporation has no substance, it is strongly recommended that the shareholders religiously perform the corporate rites, such as holding shareholders' and directors' meetings, keeping minutes and separate bank accounts, and dealing with the corporation on an arm's-length basis, etc.

To get rid of the corporation is simple legally. Although many just walk away from a corporation which failed, particularly if there are few assets, the following typical steps should be taken: file a Statement of Intent to Dissolve with the State, record it with the County Recorder, then file Articles of Dissolution with the State. Before liquidating a successful corporation, tax aspects of liquidations should be considered and are discussed briefly below.

¶ 1539 STEPS IN INCORPORATING

Legally, there is no corporation unless the following major steps are taken:

1. *Obtain a certificate of incorporation.* The incorporator goes to the office of the Secretary of State, Corporation Department, and fills out the certificate of incorporation. Most states require three incorporators, although a proprietor may typically become the sole shareholder subsequently. For a payment of about $100, a proprietor becomes the president and founder of the corporation, a separate legal entity and taxpayer, and, incidentally, an employer. Information required includes: a name for the corporation, business purpose, names and addresses of incorporators, location of business office (could be the residence), capitalization (number, type, amount of shares), initial capital, names of subscribers, directors, etc.
2. *Shareholder meeting.* A meeting of the shareholders (at least one) completes the incorporation process. They elect a board of

directors, which then elects corporate officers. Bylaws are adopted, covering such issues as date and place of meetings, how such meetings are to be conducted, voting procedures, salaries, terms of office, dividend declarations, and powers to amend the bylaws.

¶ 1540 RIGHTS OF SHAREHOLDERS

A shareholder in a corporation typically has the following rights and is entitled to:

1. a stock certificate,
2. transfer stock,
3. vote for directors (typically cumulative voting),
4. have and participate in shareholders' meetings,
5. dividends (when declared),
6. inspect books, records, and stock lists,
7. financial statements,
8. subscribe to new stock to maintain his ownership,
9. sue officers and directors.

¶ 1541 RIGHTS AND DUTIES OF DIRECTOR

The rights and duties of the Director are as follows: to

1. elect and supervise officers,
2. declare dividends,
3. have a fiduciary duty to the corporation,
4. be personally liable for acts outside the scope of the corporation's purpose,
5. act only with the other members of the board, not individually,
6. not be automatically entitled to director's fees,
7. retain the power to bind the corporation contractually beyond its term, and
8. seek shareholder approval on major policy decisions, e.g., a merger.

¶ 1542 HOW TO INCORPORATE TAX FREE

In order to incorporate tax free, two main requirements must be met:

1. The transferors of property to the corporation must be in at least 80% control immediately after the transaction.[37]
2. Only stocks must be received from the corporation.
3. A tax-free incorporation means that neither gain nor loss can be claimed. A *sale* to the corporation will be taxable, but a loss will be disallowed if the shareholder owns more than 50% of the value of the stock directly or indirectly.[38]
4. Gain is taxed to the extent the shareholder receives "boot," i.e., anything except stock, such as options, cash, bonds, short-term notes, etc. Losses are still *not* allowed.
5. The shareholder may dispose of stocks or securities after a reasonable time without worrying about violating the 80% test retroactively.

¶ 1543 DEBT-VS.-EQUITY PROBLEM

Various tax advantages flow from funding a closely held corporation more through shareholder loans than through payment for corporate shares.

Example: Hilda forms a corporation with a capital of $100,000 put up by her and her associate. Because of her expertise and time commitment, she receives a 60% interest and the associate 40%. If Hilda gets 60% of the stock, she has 60% control, whether the whole $100,000 is called stock or whether $1,000 is called stock and $99,000 is called debt.

The advantages of using debts are:

1. Interest is deductible to the corporation, while dividends are not.
2. Repayment of principal is not taxable to the creditors. The IRS will, in extreme cases as the above, contend that the debt is really equity and label all payments from the corporation dividends to the extent of earnings and profits. To avoid reclassification the following rules should be observed:
   (a) Avoid extremely high debt/equity ratios.
   (b) Make sure there are written promissory notes bearing a reasonable rate of interest with a maturity date.
   (c) Create a track-record of timely repayments not dependent on earnings.
   (d) The debt should not be subordinated to other liabilities or convertible into stock.

---

[37] Code Sec. 351.

[38] Code Sec. 267.

(e) Avoid proportional holdings of debt and equity.

¶ 1544 STOCK REDEMPTIONS

A stock redemption is a repurchase of its own stock by a corporation and is therefore one method to get money or property out of the corporation. However, unless care is taken, the full proceeds will be deemed a dividend rather than sales proceeds from stock, the latter resulting in a capital gain or loss.

The distinction may be illustrated as follows:

Example 1: Hilda owns 100% of a corporation, then sells half her stock to it for $20,000. The "proceeds" are a dividend, since she still controls the corporation.

Example 2: Same as *1* above except she owns only 50% of the corporation, while her spouse and children own the other half. Under attribution rules applicable to redemptions, she still is deemed to own 100% of the corporation, because a shareholder constructively owns what the spouse, parents, children and grandchildren own.[39]

There are two practical ways to avoid dividend treatment upon redemptions:

1. *Complete terminations.* If the shareholder retains *no* stock in the corporation and no interest or position other than as a creditor for ten years, family attribution rules are waived.[40]
2. *Disproportionate redemptions.* If the shareholder owns less than 50% of the corporation after the redemption, directly or indirectly, *and* the ownership interest was reduced by more than 20% through the redemption, dividend treatment is avoided.[41]

When a business is incorporated, it may be good tax planning to give the spouse and/or children some of the stock because:

1. There will be little or no gift tax on the initial low value.
2. Dividends paid to the children will be taxed in low brackets.
3. Under the "complete termination" rule, the stock of the spouse and/or children can be redeemed at capital gains rates later when the value is higher and there are funds in the corporation.

Note that the *corporation* is taxed if it redeems stock with appreciated property.[42]

Dividend treatment is avoided under the following circumstances:

---

[39] Code Sec. 318.

[40] Code Sec. 302(b)(3).

[41] Code Sec. 302(b)(2).

[42] Code Sec. 311(b).

Example 3: Hilda's spouse plays no role in the corporation other than as a 20% shareholder. If the corporation buys him out after ten years for $20,000, $20,000 less his cost basis in the stock is a capital gain to him. There is no dividend.

Example 4: Hilda owns 40% of a corporation and her brother owns the other 60%. If she sells more than 20% of her stock to the corporation, i.e., more than 8% of the total stock, none of the proceeds will be a dividend to her under the "disproportionate redemption" rule.

¶ 1545 DISALLOWED DEDUCTIONS

Deductions that are disallowed are as follows:

If the IRS finds a shareholder/employee's salary to be excessive, i.e., beyond reasonable payments for services actually rendered, a deduction for the excess is denied and is treated as a dividend. This is because the owners of a small business have an obvious incentive to use salaries as a tool to minimize double taxation. Compensation is broadly construed to include contributions to retirement plans, bonuses and fringe benefits. Year-end bonuses are particularly vulnerable to dividend treatment because they resemble distributions of earnings to owners. Here are some ways to minimize the problem:

1. Avoid year-end bonuses.
2. Have the employment contract spell out increases due to inflation, extra work, and increased billings.
3. Structure salaries in such a way that they are not proportional to stock ownership.
4. Be in line with salary levels in the industry.
5. Pay some corporate tax. The rate is only 15% on the first $50,000.
6. Pay some dividends from time to time.
7. Spell out all compensation decisions in writing, including corporate minutes.
8. Consider a Subchapter S election (discussed below).

BUSINESS EXPENSES

If the corporation pays for and deducts a shareholder's travel and entertainment expenses, some of these may be disallowed as excessive or personal in nature. As in the unreasonable compensation case, the corporation loses a deduction and dividend income results. A contract to repay any disallowed expenses to the corporation will avoid the dividend problem, but the mere existence of the agreement may precipitate an audit.

¶ 1546 SALE OF RESIDENCE TO CORPORATION

A shareholder's home is appreciated from $50,000 to $100,000 and the corporation has substantial undistributed earnings. The idea comes to mind to sell the home to the corporation and rent it right back, i.e., the shareholder deeds the home to the corporation, signs a lease and cashes in. The corporation is now in the rental business and can claim depreciation and other deductions. It works, but consider the following:

1. If the home is sold at a price above its fair market value, the premium is a dividend.
2. If sold above $50,000, the shareholder realizes a gain with the following possible wrinkles:
   (a) If the shareholder owns at least 50% of the value of the stock, directly or indirectly, the gain is ordinary income under a special tax rule because the property is depreciable to the corporation.[43]
   (b) A shareholder age 55 or over may use the once-in-a-lifetime election to exclude up to $125,000 of gain.[44]
   (c) By renting the home to a third party, the shareholder may postpone the gain by reinvesting the proceeds in a new home. But then the shareholder has to move out in addition to again tying up the funds.
3. If the home is sold for its cost the shareholder may be able to avoid gain, but the IRS may argue that it is a part sale, part contribution to capital.
4. If the home is sold at a loss, the loss is nondeductible as are all losses from personal-use property.

¶ 1547 ACCUMULATED EARNINGS PROBLEM

To enforce double taxation of corporations, Congress enacted penalty provisions for corporations which do not make dividend distributions. One such provision is the tax on the "improper accumulation of surplus."[45] Another is the personal holding company tax (PHC), discussed below. In the absence of a tax on accumulated earnings, corporations could simply keep all earnings in the corporation until liquidation, at which time the shareholders could cash in their chips at capital gain rates. The accumulated earnings tax is 39.6% of the tax base once it applies. There are two relief provisions:

---

[43] Code Sec. 1239.
[44] Code Sec. 121.
[45] Code Sec. 531.

1. There are no questions asked and there is no tax on the first $250,000 of "surplus," i.e., retained earnings.
2. The corporation is not taxed on earnings accumulated for the reasonable needs of the business, such as expansion and increased working capital.

The obvious means of limiting the needs for accumulations is for the corporation to take deductions for as much reasonable compensation and other "ordinary and necessary" business expenses as possible, including paying dividends.

¶ 1548 PERSONAL HOLDING COMPANY PROBLEM

It would be nice if dividends and interest could be sheltered by incorporating a securities portfolio. Unfortunately, Congress thought of that. The result is a 39.6% tax, equal to the maximum marginal tax rate on individuals, on undistributed PHC income *after* the regular corporate tax![46] A corporation is a PHC in any year it meets the following:

1. It is more than 50% owned by five or fewer individuals.
2. At least 60% of its income is from passive sources such as interest, dividends, rent, and royalties.

The PHC tax is an alternative to the accumulated earnings tax. Due to the 60% test, up to 40% of the income can be from passive sources without a problem. It may therefore be a good idea to transfer securities to a profitable corporation within the limit to obtain such special benefits as the dividend received deduction. A U.S. corporation only pays tax on 30% of dividends from other taxable U.S. corporations.[47] In addition, the corporation can let the investment income accumulate until it runs into either the personal holding company problem or the accumulated earnings problem.

Passive income includes income from personal services if:

1. the person furnishing the services owns at least 25% of the stock, and
2. someone other than the corporation can designate who is to render the services.

As a practical matter, this is a problem only if the client or patient has the right to designate. Furthermore, the mere fact that an individual solicits business and renders the services personally is not a problem. The test is whether the relationship is terminable at will and whether substitution is freely permissible.

---

[46] Code Sec. 541.

[47] Code Sec. 243.

Dividend Alternatives

¶ 1550 INTRODUCTION

Dividends are only one means of transferring wealth to a shareholder. The following are some of the means for a closely held prospering corporation to transfer wealth to shareholders wishing to receive funds and/or benefits at the lowest after-tax cost:

1. salaries,
2. loans,
3. dividends,
4. fringe benefits, and
5. redemptions.

The alternatives should be considered in the order which maximizes the after-tax benefit to the shareholder, considering both corporate and individual taxes.

To pay dividends is widely regarded as the least desirable way to transfer wealth to the owners of a corporation. It should be used only as a last resort, such as to avoid the accumulated surplus tax or the personal holding company tax.[48] Dividends are both nondeductible to the corporation and taxable as ordinary income to the shareholder.

¶ 1551 SALARIES

Salaries are an effective means of transferring wealth because:

1. Payments are deductible to the corporation.
2. The shareholder-employee is taxed on the salary, but at least the funds are received currently.

If the compensation is "unreasonable," any excess will be treated as a dividend. In this event, both employer (corporation) and employee (shareholder) must pay Social Security tax, and the latter is nondeductible.

¶ 1552 FRINGE BENEFITS

There are two kinds of fringe benefits, both of which are deductible to the corporation:

1. Pension and profit-sharing plans have the unique dual disadvantages of providing no current benefits to the employee/shareholders while also being taxable when ultimately received. In addition, considerable expenses are incurred in administering the plans.

---

[48] Code Secs. 531 and 541.

2. Other fringe benefits, like medical and legal plans, group-term life insurance, and educational assistance plans, provide current benefits while not ever being subject to tax.

¶ 1553 LOANS

At first glance it is tempting to borrow money from the corporation since borrowed funds can be received tax free, but consider the following:

1. The payments are nondeductible to the corporation;
2. The amounts have to be repaid; and
3. A dividend will result unless the formalities of an arm's-length transaction are observed.

It is particularly helpful that loans are disproportionate to stock ownership percentages.

¶ 1554 PROPERTY TRANSACTIONS

The sale of property to the corporation at fair market value (followed by a leaseback, if desired) bails money out of the corporation, but:

1. If the sale is at a gain, the gain is taxable; and if the property is depreciable and the shareholder is in at least 50% control, directly or indirectly, the gain is ordinary.[49]
2. If the sale is at a loss, the loss is nondeductible to the extent that the shareholder controls over 50% of the value of the stock.[50] If the property is sold for more or less than fair market value, any excess received is a dividend and any discount is a contribution to capital, or even a part sale/part contribution.

¶ 1555 REDEMPTIONS

If the corporation buys back some of its stock, the shareholder is taxed on the proceeds as a dividend (keeping the aggregate basis in the remaining stock) unless:

1. The shareholder owns less than 50% of the corporation's stock, directly or indirectly, after the redemption, and such ownership was reduced by more than 20%.[51]
2. The stock ownership is terminated and a 10-year agreement is filed not to reacquire stock or to be a director or officer.[52]

If the stock is depreciated, a "redemption" may thus lead to a dividend, to the extent of proceeds, or a deductible capital loss, depending upon whether the above tests are met. Also, a corporation that

[49] Code Sec. 1239.
[50] Code Sec. 267.
[51] Code Sec. 302(b)(2).
[52] Code Sec. 302(b)(3).

redeems its stock with appreciated property will be taxed on the appreciation.

¶ 1556 SUGGESTED PREFERENCE RANKING

Here is a suggested list of the main ways to get money out of a closely held corporation, ranging from the most to the least desirable:

1. Payments deductible to the corporation that are tax free to the shareholders and provide a current benefit, including
   (a) fringe benefits, such as medical and legal reimbursement plans, and group-term life insurance (up to $50,000),
   (b) pension and profit-sharing plans to the extent the participant-owner-shareholder can borrow from the qualified plan, and
   (c) travel and entertainment expenses.
2. Payments that are deductible to the corporation and taxed to the shareholder, but which provide a current benefit, including salaries, bonuses, and taxable fringe benefits.
3. Payments that are currently deductible to the corporation, but are taxable to the shareholder when received, which will not be received until later. The typical pension and profit-sharing plans fitting in here (assuming no amounts are borrowed from the plans), e.g., deferred compensation structured as qualified plans, as well as thrift plans.
4. Payments that are nondeductible to the corporation, that result in current benefits to the shareholders, that do not have to be repaid, and that result in either capital gains or losses. (This is the world of redemptions. The corporation buys back some of its stock resulting in capital gains or losses to the shareholders. Also included are sales of property to the corporation at a gain or loss.)
5. Payments that are nondeductible to the corporation and nontaxable to the shareholders, but that have to be repaid, including loans from the corporation to the shareholders.
6. Payments that are nondeductible to the corporation and fully taxable to the shareholder, but that provide a current benefit. This is the last and least desirable alternative, the dividend option, to be used if all others fail.

To summarize, transfers to shareholders should generally be made in the following order:

1. Fringe benefits,
2. Salaries,

3. Qualified deferred compensation plans,
4. Stock redemptions and property sales to the corporation,
5. Shareholder loans,
6. Dividends.

Nontax considerations should, of course, be noted as well.

Losses and Liquidations

¶ 1560 HOW TO GENERATE ORDINARY LOSSES WHEN SELLING STOCK

Capital losses are less useful than ordinary losses. Although they are deductible without limit from capital gains, an individual can only offset $3,000 of ordinary income each year.[53]

Code Sec. 1244 provides an incentive for small businesses. Briefly, any loss incurred on Code Sec. 1244 stock is an ordinary loss up to $50,000 in one taxable year, or $100,000 on a joint return. The requirements are as follows:

1. The corporation is domestic.
2. The stock is issued for money or property (other than stocks or securities).
3. More than 50% of gross receipts is from sources other than passive investment income.
4. The amount received by the corporation for issuing the stock is limited to a maximum of $1 million.
5. No built-in losses are allowed, i.e., if depreciated property is contributed for stock, the deduction is based on fair market value. The rest is a capital loss.
6. The losses are ordinary whether the stock becomes worthless or is sold or exchanged at a loss, including liquidations and partial liquidations.
7. The favorable treatment is personal. Thus, an estate acquiring the stock from a decedent, a donee, purchaser, or any transferee is denied ordinary losses.
8. If the loss exceeds income, the excess can be carried back or forward as a net operating loss.
9. The provision is applicable only to individuals, not to estates, trusts, or corporations.

---

[53] Code Sec. 1211.

10. An S corporation can issue Code Sec. 1244 stock. Thus, double taxation can be avoided if the business succeeds and can provide ordinary loss treatment if the business fails.

¶ 1561 LIQUIDATIONS

Corporations are liquidated not only when they fail, but also when shareholders wish to pull out and go on to other things. The following liquidation tax rules are quite unfavorable:

1. Property distributions are taxable, resulting in gain or loss to the corporation.[54]
2. The corporation recognizes gain or loss on liquidation sales as well.[55]
3. Whether the corporation sells the assets and distributes the proceeds or simply distributes the assets to the shareholders, the shareholders are taxed on the value of what they receive, less their cost basis in their stock.[56] Because the distributions are taxable, the assets receive a fair market value basis.[57] Gains will generally be long-term capital gains.

Overall, then, a liquidation is not a powerful method to bail out accumulated earnings and assets since the result typically is double taxation.

Valuation of Closely Held Stock

¶ 1565 WHEN VALUATIONS ARE NECESSARY

Because closely held stock, as defined, does not trade in established markets, a price may not be readily available. Valuations must, however, be made from time to time, notably in the following circumstances:

1. For a shareholder who wants to sell stock, borrow against it, or give it to charity.
2. If stock is given away, the gift tax liability is based on value.
3. When a shareholder dies, the estate tax is based on value.
4. The corporation may wish to establish an Employee Stock Ownership Plan, go public, or merge with another corporation.

In some of these situations, a high value is desirable and in others a low value is. For example, a shareholder who sells stock, borrows on it or gives it to charity wants a high value, but for gift and estate tax purposes, the shareholder wants a low value. (For a discussion of

---

[54] Code Sec. 336.
[55] Code Sec. 1001.
[56] Code Sec. 331.
[57] Code Sec. 334(a).

"Business Continuation Insurance," "Key Employee Coverage" and the like, see ¶ 1529—1532.)

¶ 1566 VALUATION PRINCIPLES

Established financial theory postulates that the price of a stock is simply equal to the present value of future dividends. Because two variables are needed, the discount rate and the future dividends, both of which are unknown, tax practitioners have focused on other variables. According to the IRS, the pertinent variables are:

1. Nature and history of the business from the start.
2. The economic outlook in general and for the industry in particular.
3. Book value and liquidity situation.
4. Earning capacity for the last five years.
5. Ability to pay dividends.
6. Intangible values, such as goodwill.
7. Recent sales and size of interest to be valued.
8. Prices of comparable traded stock in the same business.[58]

These are all reasonable factors, but they do not tell us *how* to *compute* the value. Therefore, value is the subject of frequent litigation, particularly in estate tax cases. There can be little doubt, however, that of the above the value of the assets and the earning power of the business are the most important factors.

Since valuation is not an exact science, all relevant factors must be considered. The IRS definition of fair market value is not very helpful. It states, "the fair market value is the price at which the property would change hands between a willing buyer and a willing seller, neither being under any compulsion to buy or to sell and both having reasonable knowledge of relevant facts."[59] If fair when entered into, the price under a buy/sell agreement (see below) will often be binding as "fair market value," but that does not solve the problem of how to determine the price in such contracts.

Buy/Sell Agreements

¶ 1570 INTRODUCTION

The corporation may continue indefinitely as a legal entity, but this does not ensure the continuity of the business itself. In the typical family business the first place to look for new management is among family members. Because of this and because of the typical owner's

[58] Rev. Rul. 59-60, 1959-1 CB 237.

[59] Reg. 20.2031-1(b).

desire to prevent a disposition of the business or even a minority interest to outsiders, restrictions on sale are common.

BUY/SELL AGREEMENT DEFINED

A buy/sell agreement is a contract between the shareholder or between the shareholders and the corporation, providing for the sale and purchase of stock upon the death, retirement, or disability of the shareholder. Obviously, the agreement should be in writing and specify the price, which could be a given number, i.e., $50 per share, or a formula, i.e., 125% of book value, seven times the last three years' average earnings, etc.

ADVANTAGES OF BUY/SELL AGREEMENTS

1. The value of the stock can be set for tax purposes.
2. Liquidity is provided the selling shareholder's estate. A ready buyer is provided so as to avoid a forced sale at bottom prices of nonmarketable stock.
3. The stock stays in the family so that control is not lost.
4. Employees of the corporation will be less concerned about losing their jobs.

¶ 1571 KINDS OF BUY/SELL AGREEMENTS

Sometimes the shareholder only gives the prospective buyer a right of first refusal, in effect, an option to buy. In other cases the corporation and/or other shareholders are committed to buy. There are only two fundamental types of agreements:

1. A redemption agreement, whereby the corporation itself will buy the stock, thereby receiving basis. This is the simplest method if there are several shareholders.
2. A cross-purchase agreement, whereby the remaining shareholders buy the stock. This works best if there are only two or three shareholders. A combination of the two is also possible. Capital gain treatment can be obtained through either method.

¶ 1572 FUNDING THE PURCHASE

Life insurance is commonly used to pay for the purchase of stocks from a deceased shareholder's estate. Upon disability or retirement, an installment sale may be effected. Under a redemption agreement, the corporation owns a policy on each shareholder. The premiums are nondeductible, but the proceeds are tax free. It is also unlikely that the accumulated cash values, if any (term insurance can be used), would be subject to the accumulated earnings tax, since this is done for business reasons. The other shareholders' cost basis in their stock remains the same after the redemption.

In a cross-purchase situation, each shareholder carries insurance on the lives of the other owners. They cannot deduct the premiums and the proceeds are nontaxable. The corporation has no tax consequences when stock is bought or sold. Whatever is paid becomes the basis in the stock purchased. The main tax disadvantage of the cross-purchase is that the buying shareholder pays for the stock with after-tax money. Another point is that younger shareholders may eventually buy the stock owned by older shareholders with the financing problem this entails. The last survivor may have a real problem.

Taxation of Corporations and Partnerships

¶ 1575 ADVANTAGES OF PARTNERSHIPS

There is no income tax on formation with few exceptions.[60]

Partnerships are not taxable entities.[61]

Income splitting is often available through family partnerships.[62]

Net operating losses flow directly through to the partners.

All items of income, gain, loss, deduction or credit flow through to the partner.

All items of income, gain, loss, deduction, or credit flow through to the partners as such without changing character, e.g., capital gains, dividends, foreign source income, etc.[63]

Different items of income and loss can be allocated disproportionately according to the partnership agreement.[64]

There are no special taxes on partnerships, e.g., accumulated earnings taxes, personal holding company taxes, etc.

It is easy to incorporate a partnership, but less convenient to go from a corporation to a partnership, due to the corporate liquidation provisions.[65]

¶ 1576 DISADVANTAGES OF PARTNERSHIPS

The partners are taxed on their share of earnings whether they are distributed or not.[66]

The partnership ends for tax purposes if 50% or more of the capital and profit interests are sold or exchanged within one year.[67] This

[60] Code Sec. 721.
[61] Code Sec. 701.
[62] Code Sec. 704(e).
[63] Code Sec. 702(b).
[64] Code Sec. 704(b).
[65] Code Secs. 331-338.
[66] Code Sec. 702.
[67] Code Sec. 708(b)(2).

terminates the taxable year and leads to a constructive partnership liquidation.

The partnership must have generally the same tax year as the majority partners.[68]

The IRS may argue that the partnership has too many corporate characteristics and should be taxed as a corporation.

¶ 1577 ADVANTAGES OF CORPORATIONS

Corporate tax rates are low initially, e.g., 15% on the first $50,000. The average tax rate of 34% is not reached unless $335,000 in taxable income is reported.[69]

The *shareholders are not taxed* unless a distribution is made.[70]

Affiliated corporations may elect to file *consolidated returns.*

Many *tax-free fringe benefits* are only available to corporations, i.e., deductible to them, without being taxed to the employees. Examples include group-term insurance and disability insurance.

Shareholders are generally not liable for corporate taxes.

Because a corporation's reason for being is presumed to be for business, *travel and entertainment expenses* have traditionally been allowed liberally.

Corporations facilitate estate planning due to the divisibility of the shares.

Corporations can engage in several different forms of tax-free mergers and reorganizations.[71]

¶ 1578 DISADVANTAGES OF CORPORATIONS

The IRS has been known to attack the reality of the corporate form if the shareholders treat it as a "dummy" or as their alter ego.

Since dividends are taxable and paid out of after-tax earnings, double taxation results.

A dollar in dividends paid out of earnings and profits is ordinary dividend income, regardless of the original source, be it tax-exempt interest, or capital gains. Because of this lack of tracing, a corporation is not a conduit.

Corporations are subject to a host of special taxes, ranging from capital stock taxes to accumulated earnings taxes. Often, state taxes are higher for corporations than for individuals because corporations do not vote. A corporation can never claim the Fifth Amendment privi-

---

[68] Code Sec. 706.
[69] Code Sec. 11.
[70] Code Sec. 301.
[71] Code Sec. 368.

lege. Corporations are frequent targets of special tax legislation. If an owner-shareholder is found to have received excess travel and entertainment expense reimbursement or an unreasonably high salary, a double penalty results: The corporation's deduction is reduced *and* the owner-shareholder winds up with a dividend.

Tax Advantages of Partnerships Over S Corporations

¶ 1580 INTRODUCTION

The Subchapter S Revision Act of 1982 narrowed the gap between S corporations and partnerships. Nevertheless, numerous advantages of operating in partnership form still exist. In addition, virtually any benefit that can be derived from an S corporation can also be enjoyed by a partnership. These include the absence of tax at the entity level, flow-through of losses and tax benefits, limited liability, income splitting potential, tax-free formation, etc.

¶ 1581 ELIGIBILITY REQUIREMENTS

For S corporations, the following eligibility requirements exist, none of which are applicable to partnerships:

1. The number of shareholder is limited to 35.
2. Shareholders have to be individuals, estates, or certain trusts.
3. No shareholder may be a nonresident alien.
4. Only one class of stock may be issued.[72]

A partnership may have both general and limited partners, corporate partners, foreign partners, more than 35 partners, etc.

In addition, an S corporation cannot be a member of an affiliated group, i.e., it cannot be a parent or a subsidiary.[73] A partnership may be a partner in other partnerships.

¶ 1582 TAX-FREE FORMATION

To incorporate assets tax free, the transferors must transfer property solely in exchange for stock or securities and be in 80% control immediately thereafter.[74] To form a partnership, no such restriction exists.[75] Thus, a person who transfers appreciated property to a partnership in exchange for less than an 80% interest is not taxed, regardless how small the interest received. A person who received stock would be taxed immediately (unless part of a transferor group who, in the aggregate, received at least 80% of the stock).

---

[72] Code Sec. 1361(b)(1).
[73] Code Sec. 1361(b)(2)(A).
[74] Code Sec. 351.
[75] Code Sec. 721.

Even if the 80% control requirement is met, the new shareholder would be taxed on liabilities transferred in excess of basis.[76] A partner would often avoid the tax since basis is received for a share of these liabilities.[77]

> ***Example:*** Mr. P transfers property with a value of \$60,000, a basis of \$30,000, but subject to a liability of \$40,000, to a partnership in return for a 25% interest. Since he, in effect, is relieved of only 3/4 of the liability, or \$30,000, which does not exceed his basis, no gain is recognized, his basis in his interest is zero and the partnership's basis in the property is \$30,000.[78]
>
> In a corporate setting, Mr. P would have to recognize his full gain of \$30,000. Even if he was part of an at least 80% transferor group, the \$10,000 of liabilities in excess of basis would result in a current gain. The latter would be true in the partnership case only if Mr. P is a limited partner and the liability is with recourse.

¶ 1583 THIRD-PARTY LIABILITIES

Both partners and S corporation shareholders may deduct their share of loss to the extent of their basis in their interest.[79]

However, while S corporation shareholders receive no basis for S corporation liabilities, a partner's basis is increased by a share of partnership liabilities.[80] All partners add their share of nonrecourse liabilities in accordance with their profit-sharing ratios, but recourse liabilities are shared only by general partners and in proportion to their loss-sharing ratios.[81]

Slightly offsetting this partnership advantage is the fact that S corporation shareholders receive basis for loss deduction purposes for the full amount of their loans to the corporation regardless of the ownership percentage.[82] In any event, both S corporation shareholders and partners may be subject to the "at risk" rules in Code Sec. 465 and the "passive activity" loss deferred rules in Code Sec. 469.

¶ 1584 OPTIONAL BASIS ADJUSTMENTS

By making a Code Sec. 754 election at the partnership level, a partner who purchases or inherits an interest will have the allocable share of basis in the partnership's assets stepped up (or down) to the basis in the partnership interest under Code Sec. 743(b). This will equalize "inside" and "outside" basis, but does not affect the basis in partnership assets with respect to the other partners. Since the election can be made retroactively (by the due date of the partnership return

[76] Code Secs. 337(c) and 351(b).
[77] Code Sec. 752(a).
[78] Code Sec. 723.
[79] Code Secs. 704(d) and 1366(d).
[80] Code Sec. 752(a).
[81] Reg. § 1.752-1(c).
[82] Code Sec. 1366(d)(1)(B).

for the tax year the interest was acquired), a step-down in basis is avoided, at least initially. However, since the election, once made, is irrevocable, future partners may have to accept a step-down. The election also covers basis adjustments on certain distributions. In any event, optional basis adjustments are not available to S corporations.

¶ 1585 DEBT-VS.-EQUITY PROBLEMS

An S corporation, like any corporation, is subject to a possible reclassification of debt as equity. This has the effect of transferring debt repayments and interest into dividends. The problem is especially acute for S corporations since a reclassified debt may be held to be a second class of stock, terminating the S election. A new set of stringent "straight debt safe harbor" rules for S corporations now exists.[83] In a partnership, the debt versus equity issue is rarely a problem.

¶ 1586 OWNERS AS EMPLOYEES AND SELF-EMPLOYED

A partner is not an employee but is considered self-employed. This means that no withholding from partners' salaries is required at the partnership level. Consequently, it is the individual partner's responsibility to file declarations of estimated tax, pay the tax quarterly, and pay the self-employment tax. Thus, the paperwork is reduced substantially. If the partnership is on a fiscal-year basis, up to 11 months deferral of a partner's "salary," e.g., the "guaranteed payments," is possible.[84]

> ***Example:*** A partnership's taxable year ends January 31. A calendar year partner with a monthly salary of $5,000 receives the full $5,000 each month with no withholding, and the February through December salary is not taxed until the following year. By contrast, an S shareholder's salary is subject to withholding and is taxable when paid.

¶ 1587 ALLOCATION OF TAXABLE ITEMS

An S shareholder is required to pick up a pro rata share of each item of gain, income, loss, deduction, or credit on a per share per day basis, on the last day of the S corporation's year.[85]

No flexibility exists in varying this by agreement. In a partnership, disproportionate allocations may be made and changed annually, even retroactively, since the allocation is made according to the partnership agreement.[86] It may be revised up to the due date of the return.[87]

---

[83] Code Sec. 1361(c)(5).

[84] Code Secs. 707(c) and 706(a).

[85] Code Secs. 1366(a) and 1377(a)(1).

[86] Code Sec. 704(a).

[87] Code Sec. 761(c).

A 10% S shareholder shares capital, profits, and losses 10%. A partner can have a different percentage of all three and these may be changed automatically or by agreement at any time. In fact, a partner is recognized as such even if the partner has only a profit interest and even if the partner does not share in losses.

While it is true that disproportionate allocations only are upheld if they have "substantial economic effect," this requirement generally is satisfied by making sure that the capital accounts reflect the allocations made, and that liquidating distributions are made in accordance with the respective account balances. Thus, it is possible for a partnership to allocate cost recovery deductions, tax-exempt interest, and capital gains to high-bracket partners, while allocating fees, dividends, and short-term gains to low-bracket partners.

¶ 1588 CAPITAL GAINS TAXES

S corporations are taxed on built-in gains existing on the effective date of the election under certain circumstances described in Code Sec. 1374, and at regular corporate rates. Partnerships are not so taxed.

¶ 1589 TAX ON PASSIVE INCOME

Unlike partnerships, S corporations are taxed on passive income in excess of 25% of gross receipts in any taxable year, and at a flat 35% rate.[88] The tax is applicable only if the corporation had subchapter C earnings and profits at the close of the taxable year in question. In fact, if the tax is applicable for three consecutive years, the S election is terminated.[89] Once terminated, a five-year waiting period is required before reelection may be made.[90]

¶ 1590 DISTRIBUTIONS OF APPRECIATED PROPERTY

When the S corporation distributes appreciated property to its shareholders, the gain must be recognized.[91] A partnership generally does not recognize gain on such distributions to its partners.[92] Note that neither entity can recognize a loss on property distributions. A shareholder will, however, receive a fair market value basis in the property, while a partner receives a carried-over basis.[93]

¶ 1591 REDEMPTIONS OF OWNERSHIP INTERESTS

An S corporation shareholder who sells stock to the corporation can, at the most, hope for a capital gain or loss with no corporate deduction.[93a] A partnership, however, may receive ordinary deductions for some payments made to the withdrawing partner, if payments exceed

[88] Code Sec. 1375.
[89] Code Sec. 1362(d)(3).
[90] Code Sec. 1362(g).
[91] Code Sec. 1363(d).
[92] Code Sec. 731(b).
[93] Code Sec. 732.
[93a] Code Sec. 302.

the payee's interest in the fair market value of the partnership's tangible assets. Although payments constitute ordinary income to the partner, in most cases ordinary income, coupled with an ordinary deduction, is better in the aggregate than a capital gain with no deduction, particularly when there is a limited rate differential.

¶ 1592 IN-KIND DISTRIBUTIONS IN LIQUIDATION OF THE ENTITY

S CORPORATIONS AND PARTNERSHIPS

A shareholder who receives property from a corporation in liquidation of stock must generally recognize a gain or loss equal to the fair market value of property received, less the basis in the stock.[94]

A partner who receives property upon liquidation of the partnership receives a basis in such property equal to the basis in the interest reduced by cash received.[95] The partnership recognizes neither gain nor loss on a distribution.[96] The partner recognizes no gain under Code Sec. 731(a)(1) but recognizes a loss if the partner receives no property other than cash, unrealized receivables, and inventory, and the basis in the interest exceeds the basis in such items.

> ***Example:*** An S shareholder with a basis of $5,000 in the ownership interest receives property with a basis of $3,000 and a value of $12,000 in liquidation of the interest. The shareholder recognizes a gain on $12,000 – $3,000, or $9,000, but receives a fair market value basis of $12,000 in the property.[97]
>
> A partner on equivalent facts will recognize no gain but will have a basis of $5,000 in the property received.

¶ 1593 DEATH OF AN OWNER

When an S shareholder dies, the final return must include a share of income, loss deduction or credit of the S corporation up to the date of death.[98] In effect, the S year ends with respect to the late shareholder. This may or may not lead to a bunching of income. In the most extreme case (e.g., the S year ends on January 31, and the decedent died at the end of December, and was on a calendar-year basis), 23 months of income will appear on the decedent's final return.

A partner has more flexibility. Even though the partnership's taxable year generally continues uninterrupted with respect to the deceased partner under Code Sec. 706(c)(1), this result may be changed through either pre-death or post-mortem planning. A buy/sell agreement which obligates the partner to sell at death will close the year

---

[94] Code Sec. 331.

[95] Code Sec. 732(b).

[96] Code Sec. 731(b).

[97] Code Sec. 334(a).

[98] Code Sec. 1375(a)(1).

with respect to the partner.[99] Even if the partnership's taxable year ends after the death of the partner, the distributive share will still wind up on the final return if:

1. It is a joint return with the surviving spouse;
2. Such surviving spouse inherits the partnership interest or it is distributed before the end of the joint return year and before the end of the partnership year; and
3. The partnership year ends no later than the last day of the joint return year.

In the case of the S shareholder, there will be no income in respect of a decedent. A deceased partner will have such income in the amount of the distributive share up to the date of death, unless it is reported on the final return for the above-mentioned reasons. It should also be noted that under local law, but not for tax purposes, the partnership terminates on the death, bankruptcy, or incapacity of a partner, as well as on the withdrawal or admission of a partner.

¶ 1594 FROM CORPORATION TO PARTNERSHIP AND VICE VERSA

Incorporating a partnership can generally be accomplished tax free unless liabilities exceed basis in property transferred.[100] However, to go from the corporate form to the partnership form necessitates a corporate liquidation. Not only is this taxable at the corporate level,[100a] but the shareholders would also be taxed on fair market value of assets received less their basis in their stock. [101]

CONCLUSION

Before incorporating a business in order to make an S election, the many tax advantages of the partnership should be considered. In most cases, the partnership appears to be far superior even after 1982 legislation narrowed the gap. However, if a corporation already exists the choice is less obvious since a liquidation is a taxable event and is necessary if a partnership is to result.

Should the small business owner simply wish tax deferral, a C corporation is still the answer since a 15% tax on the first $50,000 of taxable income and 25% on the next $25,000 may be a small price to pay for indefinite deferral of the owner's personal tax. What is clear, however, is that for maximum flexibility and absence of entity tax the partnership is still the leading vehicle for a business venture.

---

[99] Code Sec. 706(c)(2)(A).

[100] Code Sec. 351.

[100a] Code Sec. 336.

[101] Code Sec. 331.

Among the few tax advantages of the S corporation *not* available to a partnership are the ordinary loss provisions of Code Sec. 1244 on sale or worthlessness of stock.

CHAPTER 16

FRINGE BENEFITS, PENSIONS, AND SOCIAL SECURITY

¶ 1601 INTRODUCTION

Most employees live on their salary, or what's left of it after taxes. Many of them have no systematic savings program for retirement, unless their employer provides them with a pension or profit-sharing plan or similar arrangement. The purpose of this chapter is two-fold:

1. To provide a survey of pension and profit-sharing plans and other fringe benefits.
2. To provide some basis for making a choice of compensation packages in view of a client's financial and tax-planning needs.

This chapter covers such topics as qualified versus nonqualified plans, tax-free rollovers, pension versus profit-sharing plans, and tax aspects of lump-sum distributions, as well as self-employment plans and other fringe benefits, such as options, employee stock ownership plans and stock bonus plans.

Few people except the poor can maintain their standard of living after retirement. An employee who retires at age 65 can expect to live past 80. To do the job of financing retirement, a systematic program should be started at age 35, if possible. Social Security payments for a married couple waiting until age 65 to retire have passed a maximum of $10,000 a year tax free (assuming other income is limited), but a retired $100,000-a-year executive may find that spendable income upon retirement is cut by as much as one-half despite a good pension plan. To narrow the gap, the executive must rely on savings and investments.

The higher a client's income, the smaller the fraction needed to live on upon retirement. The client needs a smaller house after the children are gone and may no longer need the extra car, for example.

Government workers, police officers, or firefighters may often retire with half pay after 20 years of service, then go into a new job, such as teaching, and by age 65 have at least two retirement plans; these retirees are sometimes referred to as "double dippers." In any event, this chapter provides a survey of what an employee may expect from an employer, plus a few things which can be done if the client has outside self-employment income, such as director's fees.

¶ 1602 FUNDING REQUIREMENTS AT RETIREMENT

The table below shows the investment required to provide $100 a month in retirement benefit for 5-30 years assuming rates of return ranging from 5½ to 15%.

Years	*5½%*	*8%*	*10%*	*12%*	*15%*
5	$5,235	$4,932	$4,706	$4,496	$4,205
10	9,214	8,242	7,567	6,970	6,198
15	12,238	10,464	9,306	8,332	7,145
20	14,537	11,955	10,362	9,082	7,594
25	16,284	12,956	11,005	9,495	7,807
30	17,612	13,628	11,395	9,722	7,909

For example, if at retirement, $10,362 is available and is invested at 10%, the retiree may withdraw $100 a month for 20 years before funds run out. If the obtainable return is only 8% the funds would run out after 15 years ($10,464).

To look at it differently, if a pension of $1,000 a month is desired for 15 years and the obtainable return is 8%, $104,640 is the required capital ($10,464 × 10).

From the table it is also clear how a small increase in capital can make possible a large increase in the retirement period funded. Thus, at 12%, the capital requirement is $9,722, rather than $8,332 to fund 30 years rather than 15. In other words, a mere 12% increase in funds will suffice to double the payout period, while still paying the same fixed pension.

¶ 1603 FUNDING FUTURE RETIREMENT

The table below shows the future value of $1 a year invested at rates from 8-15% for 5-15 years.

Years	8%	10%	12%	15%
5	6.33	6.71	7.11	7.75
7	8.63	10.43	11.23	12.72
10	15.64	17.53	19.65	23.23
12	20.50	23.52	27.02	33.35
15	29.32	34.95	41.75	54.71

Thus, if $1,000 a year is invested at 10% for 15 years (tax-deferred), a nest egg of $34,950 (34.95 × $1,000) will result. However, again at 10%, this is only sufficient to fund a retirement annuity of $300 a month for 25 years ($34,950 ÷ $11,005 from the previous table). Another way of using the table is to ask: How much must be invested annually at 8% for 12 years to accumulate $100,000? The answer if $100,000/20.5, or $4,878.

The two tables taken together provide basic insight into how retirement annuities are funded as well as helping an individual save for retirement.

RETIREMENT PLANNING WORKSHEET

The following worksheet quickly provides a rough estimate of how the client's retirement situation is at any given time:

A.	Desired annual income upon retirement typically 60-80% of current income		$_____
Sources of retirement benefits:			
B.	Expected social security benefits	$_____	
C.	Expected pension benefits	_____	
D.	Remaining income required (A − B − C)		$_____
Other post-retirement income:			
E.	Income from services	$_____	
F.	Investment income	_____	
G.	Total retirement income (B + C + E + F)		$_____
H.	Remaining income required (A − G)		$_____
Investments:			
I.	Current savings		
J.	Projected retirement savings		
K.	All other assets		
L.	Expected assets at retirement (J + K)		$_____
M.	Retirement income from total investments (Liquidation or preservation of capital may be assumed)		$_____
	Amount still needed (A − G − M)		$_____

To reach the desired goal, the tables above may be used to compute the required funding level and to implement a savings plan.

¶ 1604 NONQUALIFIED DEFERRED COMPENSATION

Simply put, a nonqualified deferred compensation plan is an agreement providing that someone will be paid in the future for work performed currently. The plan is nonqualified because it does not meet the funding, vesting, and nondiscrimination rules applicable to qualified plans, described below. It is generally offered to highly paid executives who can afford to wait until retirement, death, or disability, and offers the dual advantages of saving for the future while deferring the income tax.

An employer may cover the bulk of its employees with a qualified pension plan, but still offer some key executives a nonqualified plan. At least for tax purposes, it may make more sense than a salary increase taxed currently. The agreement is included in the employment contract and stipulates that the payment will be made to the employee or his beneficiaries. The payments may be conditional upon a minimum period of employment and the contract may even stipulate a noncompete agreement and/or provide for part-time consulting services after retirement.

To obtain the tax deferment, the plan cannot be funded or secured by third-party financial agreements, such as life insurance. Neither does the employer get a deduction until the employee is taxed. Because the only security for the payments is a legally enforceable, but unfunded, promise, an employee should not enter into this arrangement without a profound belief in the employer's financial future.

In summary, deferring some compensation that the employee does not need until retirement, without paying tax currently, may be more attractive than receiving a third of it up front, despite the risks.

¶ 1605 TAX ADVANTAGES OF QUALIFIED PLANS

The attractiveness of a qualified deferred compensation plan, such as a thrift, pension, or profit-sharing plan, can be summarized as follows:

1. The payments made by the employer are currently deductible.
2. These payments are not currently taxed to the participant.
3. Upon retirement, the employee may be in a lower bracket.
4. If distributed as a lump sum, the amount may be eligible for special forward averaging and a capital gain portion.
5. All contributions are allowed to accumulate tax free in the plan until distributed.
6. Although the participants' own contributions, if any, are nondeductible, they too can accumulate tax free.

¶ 1606 QUALIFIED PLAN REQUIREMENTS

Below are listed the main requirements for a qualified pension, profit-sharing, or stock bonus plan.[1] The tax advantage of being qualified is that contributions are deductible to the employer without being taxed to the employee currently. There are also substantial nontax advantages, such as the vesting and funding standards which safeguard the participant's interests.

1. The plan must in essence provide for deferred compensation.
2. It cannot merely be a temporary agreement.
3. The plan must be for the exclusive benefit of employees and their beneficiaries.
4. The plan cannot discriminate in favor of highly compensated employees. Thus, it must be available to either a specified percentage of employees or a representative cross section of employees. To a limited extent, employees may be excluded because of being either too young or too old or new employees.
5. The plan must be written and available to employees to read.
6. The trust funds cannot be transferred or borrowed for the benefit of other than plan participants.
7. The plan can, in effect, provide employees with income below certain levels with smaller benefits, by "integrating" the plan with Social Security.
8. A profit-sharing plan and a defined benefit plan must contain a formula for allocating contributions and other benefits.
9. There are ceilings on contributions and/or benefits.
10. There are funding requirements. An IOU won't do it.

¶ 1607 VESTING REQUIREMENTS

Prior to the Pension Reform Act of 1974 vesting abuses were common. An employee might be terminated the day before the 65th birthday and receive no pension (except for employee contributions) if the pension contract specified that the employee had to be employed at age 65 to be eligible.

Vesting refers to the point at which the employee "owns" the *employer's* contributions, regardless of whether the job is kept or not, and regardless of the reason for termination or resignation. Under current law the meter starts ticking when the employee is enrolled in the plan. Each employee 18 years or older with at least one year of

[1] Code Sec. 401(a).

service must be enrolled if eligible. (If 100% vesting is provided, two years of service may be required.)

For plan years beginning after 1988, an employer has two choices as far as minimum vesting requirements are concerned:[2]

1. Full vesting after five years of service.
2. One hundred percent vesting after seven years of service phased in as follows:
   (a) 20% after three years of service
   (b) 20% for each year, years four through seven.

Note that vested benefits are *not* necessarily inheritable, nor do benefits have to be paid until normal retirement age.

¶ 1608 DEFINED BENEFIT VS. DEFINED CONTRIBUTION PLANS

There are two main ways to compute contributions made to a pension plan:

1. *Defined benefit plan.* Because the company tells the employee up front how much will be paid upon retirement, i.e., "80% of the average of the highest three years' salary prior to retirement, but not exceeding $67,000," several complex determinations are necessary, such as:
   (a) The composition of the labor force in terms of age, sex, and salaries.
   (b) The turnover of the employees.
   (c) Their life expectancies.
   (d) The estimated return on investments.
   (e) The funding requirements, adjusted for actuarial gains and losses and experience gains and losses.
   (f) Past service liabilities to employees present when the plan was instigated.

   An actuary is required.

   The maximum pension which can be paid and funded is adjusted annually and linked to the Consumer Price Index. For example, an employee could get as much as $115,641 a year from a plan in 1993.
2. *Defined contribution pension plan.* This is also called a "money-purchase" plan. An actuary is unnecessary and no specific benefits are promised. The employer simply says: "Look, we are contributing X percent of your salary to the

[2] Code Sec. 411(a).

plan every year. Whatever retirement benefit that we purchase is what you get." This is simple, yes, but the employee does not know how much will be ultimately received.

As a comparison, in 1993, the maximum deductible amount per employee was $30,000 a year or 25 percent of compensation if less. Not a niggardly sum to be invested in a nontaxable trust to be accumulated with interest and compound interest, tax deferred until distribution. Small firms tend to sacrifice certainty for simplicity.

¶ 1609 PENSION AND PROFIT-SHARING PLANS COMPARED

Below is a checklist comparing nine features of pension and profit-sharing plans to help an employee or employer decide which is the best if a choice exists.

	Pension		*Profit-Sharing*
1.	Contributions are based on covered wages and are made in fat as well as lean years.	1.	Contributions need only be made in profitable years.
2.	The contributions are not discretionary, but are either a percentage of covered wages (for a defined contribution plan) or based on actuarial computations and promised benefits (for a defined benefit plan).	2.	Contributions may be left to management's discretion.
3.	Few fringe benefits can be included.	3.	Many fringe benefits can be included.
4.	The employer may recover excess funds on plan termination. An excise tax may be imposed.	4.	The employer cannot recover anything ever.
5.	Retirement benefits must be provided.	5.	There is no need to provide retirement benefits.
6.	Retirement plans, almost per definition, tend to benefit older employees.	6.	The younger the employee, the more favored is a profit-sharing plan.
7.	Subject only to actuarial justification, there is no limit on contributions, but a given individual is limited to a maximum benefit per year ($115,641 in 1993).	7.	Deductible contributions cannot exceed 15% of covered payroll.
8.	Can be invested in life insurance contracts (up to 50%).	8.	Some limitations on amounts which may be invested in life insurance.
9.	Forfeitures will be applied in reducing future employer costs (defined benefit) or may be allocated to remaining participants (defined contribution).	9.	Forfeitures may be allocated to remaining plan participants.

Most noncontributory profit-sharing plans are rather inflexible. But some, in addition to many contributory plans, offer withdrawal and/or loan privileges. This is very useful in case of emergencies. In any event, distributions are permitted after two years. Withdrawals in excess of the employee's own contributions are taxable, loan proceeds are not. There may be restrictions on withdrawals except to the extent of voluntary contributions.

Cash or Deferred Arrangements (CODAs)

Subject to additional requirements, an appropriate type of plan will not fail to be a qualified plan just because it provides a choice between the receipt of cash and payment into the plan.

¶ 1615 REQUIREMENTS FOR 401(K) PLANS

After 1978, the deferred cash arrangement (the Code Sec. 401(k) plan) became more attractive. The employer contribution, if any, is deductible even though the employee may elect to receive cash currently or in the future. The plan is typically used to shelter part of the employee's regular pay, i.e., as a "salary reduction plan." As a qualified plan, it must meet all general requirements under Code Sec. 401(a), discussed above. In addition, the plan must:

1. Provide for immediate vesting;
2. Not allow distributions until retirement, death, disability, separation from service, attainment of age 59½, or financial hardship defined as "heavy and immediate" financial need;
3. Not allow distributions with the mere passage of time or upon completion of a time period in the plan; and
4. Meet a special set of nondiscrimination and participation standards.[3]

Even though the employee contributions are not subject to income taxation currently, they are subject to Social Security taxes.

Example: Brickell Corp. adopted a 401(k) plan which provides that its employees defer up to 15% of their salaries, up to $6,000. Brickell will match the first 6% of employee contributions. Doris Hall elected to defer 10% of her $25,000 salary this year. The results are as follows:

1. The full $25,000 is subject to Social Security tax.
2. Doris's gross income from compensation this year is $22,500.
3. Doris's total 401(k) contribution is $4,000 (16% of $25,000).
4. Brickell Corp. has a compensation deduction of $26,500, plus Social Security taxes.

ADVANTAGES

Subject to the income limitations discussed below, IRA accounts may be established in addition to 401(k) plans, but, if the employee cannot afford both, it should be noted that the 401(k) plan has several advantages over the IRA:

[3] Code Sec. 401(k)(3).

1. A lump-sum distribution may be eligible for special forward averaging. The IRA is not eligible for any tax benefits upon distribution.
2. Contributions by highly paid employees may exceed the $2,000 limitation on individual IRAs, since the limitation is higher ($8,994 in 1993). However, such employees would not also be eligible to deduct IRA contributions.
3. Withdrawals may be made any time upon "financial hardship" (without penalties after age 59½), defined as "immediate and heavy financial need," but only to the extent of the need.[4]
4. If the deferral is 10%, the W-2 Form would actually show $36,000 in gross income, rather than $40,000, for example. The result is the same as if a $4,000 deduction were allowed from gross income.

¶ 1616 SELF-EMPLOYMENT PLANS (H.R. 10 OR KEOGH PLANS)

Here are some special features of an H.R. 10 plan:

1. The percentage of compensation which is deductible as a contribution is 20% of gross earnings for a money purchase pension plan, up to $30,000 a year.[4a]
2. A nonworking spouse cannot be included.
3. A lump-sum distribution is eligible for special forward averaging.
4. Only self-employed (unincorporated) individuals are eligible, but the client may shelter self-employment income from outside activities, even if an employee covered by other qualified plans.

   Eligible income includes:

   (a) Director's fees.

   (b) Consulting income.

   (c) Income from lecturing.

   (d) Royalties from books.
5. A client with employees is subject to the general coverage and minimum participation requirements of other qualified plans.

---

[4] Prop. Reg. § 1.401(k)-1(d)(2).

[4a] 20% of the gross equals 25% of the net.

6. The client may use a profit-sharing H.R. 10 plan to avoid contributions in less profitable years, but the annual contribution limit is then reduced from 20% to 13.05%.[4b]

H.R. 10 plan contributions are deductible from gross income, accumulate tax free until withdrawal, can be made until the due date of the return (including extensions), are subject to excise taxes on missing contributions, and are subject to the 59½- and 70½-year-old withdrawal rules.

7. Owners (sole proprietors or more than 10% partners) may not borrow from the plan. Others may borrow up to $50,000 and repay it over no more than five years.
8. If a money purchase pension plan is used to qualify for the 20% contribution limit, the contribution must be made even if the business reports a loss. The IRS assesses a penalty of 5% on any underfunding. If not made up within 90 days of notification, a 100% penalty on the missing contribution must be paid.
9. If self-employment income is significant, say $30,000 a year or more, it may be worth establishing a defined benefit plan. If the client is over age 40, as much as 50% or more of the self-employment income may be contributed and deducted. However, due to the high cost of employing an actuary (required), it is not worth it for small plans.

Individual Retirement Accounts (IRAs)

¶ 1620 ELIGIBLE INDIVIDUALS

Individuals with earned income from any source (even taxable alimony) are generally eligible to make tax-deferred contributions to an IRA. However, individuals who participate in a Keogh plan or a qualified corporate deferred compensation plan have their permissible *deductible* contributions reduced if their income exceeds certain levels. Thus, single individuals' deductions are phased out evenly as adjusted gross income goes from $25,000 to $35,000, married individuals' deductions as AGI goes from $40,000 to $50,000, and the deductions for married individuals filing separately are phased out as AGI goes from zero to $10,000.

The following are examples:

1. John Grow is single and makes $80,000 in AGI from his bookstore, a sole proprietorship. He may contribute $2,000 to an IRA.

[4b] 13.05% of the gross equals 15% of the net.

2. Same as 1, but John has established a Keogh plan. No deductible IRA contribution is allowed.

3. Same as 2, but John's AGI is $30,000. A $1,000 IRA deduction may be taken.

4. Same as 1, but John is married and Mrs. Grow is covered by a qualified pension plan. Neither spouse may take an IRA deduction.

5. Same as 4, but taxpayers have $44,000 of AGI on a joint return. A maximum of $2,400 may be deducted ($2,000 for each, less 40% of $4,000, since $44,000 – $40,000 is 40% of $50,000 – $40,000).

Anyone may make *nondeductible* IRA contributions up to $2,000 a year (or earned income, whatever is less). However, total contributions may not exceed $2,000 a year for both deductible and nondeductible transfers. The income on nondeductible contributions is also permitted to accumulate on a tax-deferred basis.

¶ 1621 TAX CONSEQUENCES

Contributions (up to $2,000 of earned income, plus up to $250 for a nonworking spouse) are deductible from gross income even if the standard deduction is used. The IRA may be set up and the contribution made by the due date of the return (without extensions) with full effect for the preceding year. Thus, a contribution for a given year may be made during such year and/or before April 15 of the following year. In fact, the deduction may be claimed on an early return and the resulting tax refund then used to make the contribution, so long as the contribution is made by April 15.[4c] The accumulated income of the IRA is not taxed until distributed, allowing for maximum growth. Upon distribution, the full account balance is subject to taxation, i.e., the basis in the IRA is zero (assuming only deductible contributions).[5] Thus, capital gains, tax-exempt interest, etc., are all converted to ordinary income on distribution. Annual trustee and management fees are currently deductible subject to the 2% floor on miscellaneous deductions under Code Sec. 212 and do not count as part of the $2,000 or $2,250 limitation. Commissions are not deductible, however, but neither do they "count." [5a]

Unlike other "qualified plans" no special tax benefits are available, even on lump-sum distributions.

[4c] Rev. Rul. 84-18, 1984-1 CB 8.

[5] Code Sec. 408.

[5a] Rev. Rul. 84-185, 1984-1 CB 222.

¶ 1622 PERMISSIBLE INVESTMENTS

The IRA contributions may be invested in almost anything, e.g., securities, money market funds, mutual funds, savings accounts and certificates, life insurance (with limitations), real estate, partnerships, etc. Most financial institutions, such as commercial banks, savings and loan associations, credit unions, brokerage firms, insurance companies, and investment companies, offer IRAs. If desired, the participant may manage an IRA personally or have more than one IRA. Due to convenience, low risk (insurance up to $100,000), and fixed interest levels, most people contribute to savings accounts. Municipal bonds are in the unique position of converting tax-free interest into ordinary income on distribution and should be avoided.

The main category of nonallowable investments is collectibles, such as precious metals or stones, antiques, coins, and stamps, except for gold and silver coins minted by the U.S. government or a state. If such investments are made, constructive premature distributions result, along with the consequent taxation and penalties. An IRA cannot borrow, e.g., buy securities on margin, sell short, or use direct leverage. If investing in a limited partnership, which is leveraged, the IRA may be subject to tax on its "debt-financed income." [6]

¶ 1623 DISTRIBUTIONS

A premature distribution (prior to age 59½) is generally fully taxable and subject to a 10% nondeductible penalty tax unless paid in the form of an annuity. A premature distribution of the full account balance results if the participant borrows from the IRA or pledges it as loan collateral. An exception is provided for a loan repaid within 60 days, if treated as a "rollover" on the tax return. Note that the financial institution, e.g., the bank, may impose its own penalties on premature withdrawals of long-term savings certificates.

Once the participant has reached age 59½, becomes disabled, or dies, distributions may be made in full or in part without penalties and without regard to actual retirement. The amounts distributed constitute ordinary income to the recipient, be it the estate, trust, a named beneficiary, or the participant himself. Distributions must start by April in the year after the participant reaches age 70½ to avoid penalties, but may be spread out over the participant's life expectancy and that of a beneficiary, even if younger, if desired.

MISCELLANEOUS

1. Only cash contributions can be made to an IRA.

---

[6] Code Sec. 512.

2. The money needed to fund the IRA may be borrowed without disallowance of the interest deduction.
3. In the event of a divorce, the nonworking spouse keeps any IRA maintained for such spouse.
4. The IRA is not protected from the participant's creditors.
5. The transfer of an IRA in a divorce settlement is tax free, but the zero basis carries over to the transferee.[7]

¶ 1624 ROLLOVERS

Rollovers in connection with a pension plan refer to the portability of the plan, e.g., the ability to reinvest the proceeds from one plan in another within 60 days without paying income tax currently. Twenty percent withholding tax is mandatory, unless a direct trustee-to-trustee transfer takes place. Following are the 10 most frequently encountered rollovers, all of which are permissible:

FROM ONE CORPORATE PLAN TO ANOTHER

The reason for the distribution from one corporate plan to another is largely irrelevant. It could be because of separation from service, e.g., disability, termination or resignation, because of an attained age, or because the plan itself terminates. Any nondeductible contributions made can simply be pocketed free of tax. Of course, both plans must permit the rollover. Thus, an employee who changes jobs may be able to take the pension plan to the new employer. Whether or not the employee can do so is likely to be an important point to cover in preliminary employment negotiations.

FROM A CORPORATE PLAN TO AN INDIVIDUAL RETIREMENT ACCOUNT (IRA), THEN BACK TO A CORPORATE PLAN

This could be useful when going from a corporation with a pension plan to a corporation without one. The IRA can be frozen if the employee does not wish to make additional contributions. In the meantime, it keeps growing tax free.

FROM A CORPORATE PLAN TO A SELF-EMPLOYMENT PLAN (H.R. 10 PLAN)

This makes it possible to defer taxes if the taxpayer leaves a job as an employee to become a consultant, for example. Once in the H.R. 10 plan, the taxpayer can contribute 20% of self-employment income, or $30,000, whichever is less (to a defined contribution plan), or just leave it alone until the taxpayer is ready to retire. Subject to certain restrictions, the H.R. plan may roll the funds back into another corporate plan later.

---

[7] Code Secs. 408(d)(6) and 1041.

FROM A CORPORATE PLAN TO AN IRA, THEN TO AN H.R. 10 PLAN

This is permissible and is applicable in a situation where an employee leaves a corporation with a plan to go to another without a qualified plan, then later becomes self-employed.

FROM A CORPORATE PLAN TO AN IRA

The typical example, again, is the employee who receives a lump-sum distribution when leaving a corporation with a plan and later starts working for a firm without a qualified plan.

FROM AN H.R. 10 PLAN TO AN IRA

This is not recommended. For example, if the client worked as a consultant, established an H.R. 10 plan, then started working for a corporation without a qualified plan, the client *could* roll the H.R. 10 plan money over to an IRA. However, the IRA would not qualify for favorable lump-sum distribution tax treatment, while the H.R. 10 plan would. A better solution would be to freeze the H.R. 10 plan and start a new IRA for future contributions.

FROM AN H.R. 10 PLAN TO A CORPORATE PLAN

By now this should be self-explanatory, but there are possible restrictions to watch for.

FROM ONE H.R. 10 PLAN TO ANOTHER

Subject to certain restrictions, this would cover a situation where an individual was self-employed but later became a partner in a partnership and wished to join the partnership's plan.

FROM AN H.R. 10 PLAN TO AN IRA, THEN BACK TO AN H.R. 10 PLAN

This *may* be permitted. An example includes a consultant with an H.R. 10 plan who joined a corporation without a qualified plan, rolled it over into an IRA, then went back to consulting.

FROM AN H.R. 10 PLAN TO AN IRA, THEN TO A CORPORATE PLAN

This may be permitted, but it is of limited usefulness. Note that the only beneficiary who qualifies for a rollover is the surviving spouse and only to an IRA.[8]

¶ 1625 HIGH COST OF LEAVING

To be vested means to have a present, nonforfeitable right to a future benefit. However, a vested employee who changes jobs three times during a career may very well lose over $100,000 in defined benefits. The projected loss should certainly enter into salary package

[8] Code Sec. 402(a)(7).

negotiations if the move is voluntary. At the minimum, a frank talk with the current pension plan administrator is indicated before the ties are severed.

The reason for the loss of pension benefits is simply that most plans base defined benefits on a formula which favors the highest earning years. Thus, the 65-year-old who quit a job at age 40 will receive a pension from at least one employer based on a salary earned 30 to 40 years ago.

Lump-Sum Distributions

¶ 1630 ANNUITY VS. LUMP-SUM DISTRIBUTIONS

The advantage of an annuity is that the retiree is guaranteed income for life or for the joint lives of the retiree and spouse. The serious disadvantage is that the principal is consumed, i.e., nothing survives the annuitant(s). Therefore, the distributee may consider taking the retirement benefits in a lump sum and investing them, so as to provide for income without forfeiting the principal, assuming the plan permits it. The tax aspects of lump-sum distributions from a qualified plan are quite favorable. Thus, the distributee is eligible for special forward averaging as illustrated below.[9] Lump sums received on separation from service, retirement, disability, or death after age 59½ qualify for averaging if received from a qualified plan, including an H.R. 10 plan (but not from IRAs).[10]

¶ 1631 COMPUTING LUMP-SUM TAXATION

Basically, the recipient has two choices, assuming participation in the plan since before 1974:

1. The whole taxable distribution can be reported as ordinary income under the forward averaging provisions.
2. A fraction of the taxable distribution, equal to *months in the plan prior to 1974* divided by total months in the plan, can be reported as a long-term capital gain and the rest as ordinary income averaged over five years (as in option 1, above).

If it is not obvious which is the most beneficial, both calculations should be made before a decision is arrived at.

Assuming option 1, above, is elected, here are the steps:

1. Determine the taxable amount. This equals the amount distributed less the participant's own, previously nondeductible, contributions.

---

[9] Code Sec. 402(e)(1)(A).

[10] Code Sec. 402(e)(4)(A).

2. Subtract the "minimum distribution allowance," which equals $10,000 – 20% × (Taxable distribution – $20,000). If the taxable distribution is $70,000 or more, none is allowed, i.e., $10,000 – 20% × ($70,000 – $20,000) = 0. But if the taxable distribution is $40,000, for example, the allowance equals $10,000 – 20% × ($40,000 – $20,000), or $6,000.

3. Divide the taxable distribution less the allowance by one-fifth (due to the five-year averaging).

4. Find the tax on this one-fifth in the tax tables for a single person, whether the taxpayer is married or not.

5. Multiply this tax by five to find the tax on the total distribution which would result unless capital gain treatment is elected on a portion of it.

6. Report the resulting tax on Form 4972, Tax on Lump-Sum Distributions. This tax is in addition to the regular tax liability and is independent of it and other taxable income.

In most cases, the tax will be 15% on the first $120,000 or so of the lump-sum distribution and 28% on the excess. Twenty percent withholding is required. If the distribution is under $380,000 (in 1994), 10-year forward averaging using 1986 rates is more favorable and may be elected by plan participants born before 1936.

Of course, no current tax is payable if the lump-sum distribution is rolled over to an IRA. The benefit of tax deferral (including accumulated) income must be weighed against the loss of forward averaging.

¶ 1632 ANNUITY TAXATION

When a plan participant retires and receives an annuity, e.g., a fixed nominal income for life, the annuity is subject to one of two possible taxation rules:

1. *A noncontributory plan.* If the plan participant made no contributions to the plan, the "investment in the contract" is zero. As a result, every dollar received is gross income (Schedule E).

2. *A contributory plan.* A plan participant who made nondeductible contributions to the plan is entitled to recover the sum of these tax free under *the life expectancy rule* through the use of the exclusion ratio.[11] The *exclusion ratio* is equal to

---

[11] Code Sec. 72(b).

$$\frac{\text{investment in contract}}{\text{annuity} \times \text{life expectancy at retirement}}$$

Once computed, the ratio is used each year until the annuitant survives the estimated time of death. If the annuitant dies prematurely, the remaining basis is deductible.

Example: Karen Sims retired with a \$500 a month annuity, in which she had invested \$30,000, when her life expectancy was 20 years. Her exclusion ratio is \$30,000/(\$500 × 12 × 20), or *one-fourth*. If she lives longer than 20 years, she may exclude \$1,500 a year from income (\$125 a month) for the first 20 years and nothing thereafter. However, if she dies after 15 years, her remaining basis, \$7,500, is deductible on her final return.

It should be noted that the 10% penalty (excise tax) on early withdrawal (prior to age 59½) as well as the 20% withholding rule does not apply to annuities.

Fringe Benefits

¶ 1635 INTRODUCTION

Compensation packages, which include fringe benefits, are constructed with an ingenuity limited only by the imagination of compensation specialists and the tax laws. Thus, they run the gamut from an expensive desk to tuition reimbursement plans and quite commonly give the employee an ownership interest in one form or another, based on the employee's or the corporation's performance and/or staying power. The material below summarizes the main forms of the latter incentives.

¶ 1636 SURVEY OF PROVIDED FRINGE BENEFITS

A survey of 1,507 corporations in 1982 conducted by the U.S. Chamber of Commerce revealed the following fringe benefits in order of popularity.

Fringe	*Provided by*	*Cost per employee*
Medical & life insurance	99%	\$ 1,274
Social security	98	1,543
Paid vacation	86	902
Pension plan	83	1,040
Paid holidays	81	553
Paid sick leave	75	244
Paid lunch or rest	67	523
Paid education	63	46
Dental plan	53	83
Disability insurance	50	58
Bonus or award	49	62
Paid thrift plan	26	80
Profit-sharing	23	218

Furnished meals	21	24
Discounts on employer products or services	15	17

¶ 1637 "PURE" FRINGE BENEFITS

A "pure" fringe benefit is one that:

1. pays the employee's personal expenses,
2. does it currently,
3. is not includible in the employee's income, and
4. is deductible to the employer.

Tax-free fringe benefits are divided into five major categories:[12]

1. *No-additional-cost services.* Examples include an empty seat on a corporate jet and an empty hotel room owned by a hotel.
2. *Qualified employee discounts.* The discount must be available to employees on a nondiscriminatory basis, cannot exceed the gross profit percentage or 20%, whichever is less, and is available on items and services except real estate and investment property. Both categories above must be offered in the line of business the employee works, e.g., a conglomerate cannot offer a Disneyland of product and services discounts to *one* employee.
3. *Working condition fringes.* Included are employees provided items or services which would be deductible to the employees if they had to bear the expense themselves. Examples include work clothes and equipment, security, consumer goods for testing purposes, parking, etc.
4. *De minimis fringes.* Included here are incidental services and items so small that it is unreasonable to account for them. Examples include free use of typing pool and photocopier, free coffee, nominal gifts, supplies and subsidized eating facilities. (There are limitations on the latter.)
5. *Qualified tuition discounts* for university employees and dependents. Other "pure" benefits include health, disability, and legal plans. Note that such major fringes as pensions are not pure, because the employees receive no benefits currently and when benefits are paid, perhaps decades later, they are taxed on them.

---

[12] Code Sec. 132.

¶ 1638 PERSONAL FINANCIAL PLANNING AS A FRINGE BENEFIT

An employer may join the growing number of corporations that bring in an outside consulting firm to teach employees to manage their finances. The charge may be $100 to $200 for each employee who attends the seminars or a flat fee per year for defined services, the number of seminars, etc. The services rendered by consulting firms range from merely giving lectures to designing plans for individual executives or any combination thereof.

The basic selling point to the corporation is that executives are busy and pressed for time. If they spend too much time on their personal affairs, they will spend less on corporate business. In addition, not having a decent financial program creates unhappiness, confusion, and wasted resources. The financial planner, in effect, sells the employer the peace of mind of the executives. The advantages to the corporation include the improvement in employer-employee relations that can result from the employer's demonstrated concern about the employee's personal finances. As fringe benefits go, it is relatively cheap. The seminars may be made available to broad classes of employees, but the full individual planning treatment is typically made available only to key executives.

The advantages to the employee hopefully include an improved long-term financial position. This is, however, unlikely to happen after just one seminar. In a one- or two-hour seminar, the advice tends to be a general combination of the unnecessary and the obvious: spend less, save regularly, carry enough insurance, etc. But if the service extends to the development of a detailed plan based on the employee's individual situation, carefully spelled out in a questionnaire, the benefits may be substantial. Many executives who would not themselves take the initiative to hire a financial planner will gladly take the opportunity to consult with one if one is provided as a fringe benefit. The sessions are often called *preretirement seminars* and cover most of the topics in this book, e.g., insurance, housing, investments, estate planning, family tax planning, etc.

Unless and only to the extent the PFP is geared to the participant's unique situation is the value of employer-paid PFP excludible from gross income, according to the IRS.

¶ 1639 GROUP TERM LIFE INSURANCE

Group-term life insurance is a "pure" fringe benefit. If nondiscrimination requirements are met, the cost of up to $50,000 of coverage per employee is deductible with no gross income to the insured. If available, the client should by all means take advantage of it. However, if more than $50,000 of coverage is provided, the excess is gross income to the covered employee in accordance with the following Treasury schedule (without regard to *actual* premiums paid).

Age of employee	*Under 30*	*30-34*	*35-39*	*40-44*	*45-49*	*50-54*	*55-59*	*60 & up*
Cost per $1,000	$ .96	1.08	1.32	2.04	3.48	5.76	9.00	14.04

Since 1988, the taxable portion is wages for Social Security tax purposes.

> ***Example:*** An employee, who turned age 48 during the year, was provided $125,000 of group term life insurance. The employee's gross income is increased by $3.48 × 75, or $261.

¶ 1640 INTEREST-FREE LOANS

An interest-free loan to an employee may also qualify as a "pure" fringe benefit, but only if the imputed interest is deductible to the employee and a compensation deduction is allowed to the employee.

ILLUSTRATIONS:

1. Company X lends $100,000 to Ms. Floss on a demand note the first business day of the year. Since Ms. Floss is not a shareholder the interest *not* charged is clearly compensation. Under Sec. 7872 interest is imputed to both parties at the "applicable federal rate," say 9%. Thus, Company X has interest income of $9,000, offset by salary expense of $9,000. Ms. Floss has salary income of $9,000, but her interest expense is only deductible in full if it is investment interest and only to the extent of net investment income.[13]

2. If Ms. Floss is a shareholder it is possible that the interest not charged is a constructive dividend. If so, Company X has no compensation deduction, just interest income. Also, if the proceeds are used for personal expenditures, Ms. Floss's dividend income is not offset by interest expense deductions, since consumer interest is nondeductible. In any event, her interest is only deductible as an itemized expense.

---

[13] Code Sec. 163(d).

Receiving Property for Services

¶ 1645 GENERAL TAX CONSEQUENCES

The general rule is that the value of any property transferred for services is taxable as compensation, whether the property is defined as goods, common stock, a partnership interest, or any other property.

The property is taxable whenever the right to it is "substantially vested," which means it is either "transferable" or not subject to a "substantial risk of forfeiture." It is to be valued without regard to any such restriction unless it is one which will never lapse.[14] The employer receives a compensation deduction at the same time the transferee has income.[15]

> ***Example:*** If $10,000 of stock is given to an employee for services rendered, the employee has gross income and a basis in the stock of $10,000. The amount of income is reduced by any price paid, even an unsecured promissory note. No income results if there are conditions attached e.g., "substantial risks of forfeiture" (see ¶ 1646 for examples), until the stock may be freely transferred.

¶ 1646 SCOPE OF CODE SECTION 83

The general rule is that compensation results if property is transferred "in connection with" services rendered. Thus, it matters not whether:

1. Services are rendered as an employee or independent contractor;
2. The property was transferred by the employer or another person, such as a shareholder; or
3. Whether the property was transferred to the compensated person or to anyone else, e.g., a beneficiary, a trust, a corporation, or other agent. Any income received, e.g., dividends, before the property is substantially vested is also treated as compensation.

If the property is sold before it is substantially vested, ordinary income results in the amount of the proceeds.[16] This could happen if the property were transferable, but subject to a substantial risk of forfeiture.

SUBSTANTIAL RISKS OF FORFEITURE

The following are examples of *substantial risks:*

1. The property must be returned unless earnings go up.

---

[14] Code Sec. 83.

[15] Code Sec. 83(h).

[16] Reg. § 1.83-1(b)(2).

2. Substantial services must be rendered.
3. A successful completion of "going public" is a condition.

Here are some examples of conditions *not* constituting substantial risks:

1. Being discharged for cause or for committing a crime.
2. Accepting a job with a competitor.
3. The employer must pay the full market value upon return. If the employee will receive 60% of its value, only 40% is subject to a substantial risk of forfeiture.

The property is *transferable* if:

1. the transferee is not subject to a substantial risk of forfeiture, or
2. the transferee can sell, assign, or pledge the property as collateral for a loan.

¶ 1647 ELECTION TO BE TAXED CURRENTLY

If the property transferred is not substantially vested, an election may nevertheless be made to include its value in income.[17] The possible advantage of the election is that any potential future appreciation will qualify as capital gain, which without the election would be plain compensation. But the trap is this: If the property is forfeited before it is substantially vested, no loss is available, notwithstanding the tax paid! The election must be made with the IRS within 30 days of the transfer and a copy of the statement must be included with the next tax return. As a practical matter, the election is irrevocable, unless a mistake of fact was made. The election is unlikely to be made unless the property has excellent appreciation potential and it is likely that the conditions attached will be met.

Clearly, the election is most attractive for taxpayers with capital gains rates substantially lower than ordinary rates. However, the election also postpones the recognition of gain in cases where property is sold after vesting occurs.

¶ 1648 EMPLOYEE STOCK OWNERSHIP PLANS

To provide employees with an ownership interest in American Business, Employee Stock Ownership Plans (ESOPs) have become popular. Through the use of such plans, the employer can deduct the fair market value of its own stock, if transferred to an ESOP. Here is an example of a leveraged ESOP:

1. The employer corporation sets up an independent trust to manage the ESOP.

---

[17] Code Sec. 83(b).

2. The corporation issues $1 million of stock certificates and sells them to the ESOP for a demand note in the amount of $1 million.
3. The ESOP borrows $1 million for a bank, secured by the stock and guaranteed by the corporation.
4. The ESOP pays off the note, resulting in
   (a) the corporation receiving $1 million in tax-free cash,
   (b) the ESOP owning $1 million of stock, and
   (c) the ESOP owing $1 million.
5. The corporation makes tax-deductible payments to the ESOP as contributions to a qualified plan.
6. The ESOP pays off the loan to the bank.
7. Eventually, the ESOP owns the stock free and clear for the exclusive benefit of employees.
8. After the dust settles,
   (a) the corporation gets $1 million of tax-free cash,
   (b) both principal and interest are deducted,
   (c) the ESOP owns the stock, and
   (d) the employees own the beneficial interest in the stock.

Of course, no money need be borrowed. The corporation could just transfer the stock to the ESOP, taking a deduction for the value. In fact, a net operating loss could be created this way, resulting in a refund of taxes paid in previous years. This is because the contribution is based on the wages of the participants, not on the taxable income of the corporation.

¶ 1649 INCENTIVE STOCK OPTION (ISO) PLANS

Under an ISO plan, the tax consequences are as follows:[18]

1. There are none at the time of grant.
2. When the stock is "substantially vested," the excess of the value of the stock over its exercise price is a tax preference item for the purpose of the alternative minimum tax.[19] No gross income results.
3. A long-term capital gain is generated if the stock is sold more than one year after exercise and more than two years after the ISO was granted.[20] No deduction is allowed to the employer. (The one-year requirement may or may not coincide with the general period required for a long-term capital gain.)

---

[18] Code Sec. 422A.
[19] Code Sec. 57(a)(10).
[20] Code Sec. 422A(a)(1).

4. If the holding period requirement is not met, the bargain element (value less exercise price) is ordinary income in the year of sale with an offsetting deduction to the employer. The value on exercise becomes the employee cost basis. A later sale will result in short- or long-term capital gain or loss under the general rules.

¶ 1650 ISO QUALIFICATION REQUIREMENTS

1. The option holder must be an employee from the time of the granting of the option until three months before exercise. Thus, if an employee is fired, resigns, or retires, the employee has three months to exercise (12 months if disabled).[21]
2. The ISO must be offered to an individual employee and must be an option to purchase stock in the employer's corporation, its parent or its subsidiary.
3. The ISO must be exercised within 10 years of grant.
4. The exercise price may be paid in employer stock.
5. The exercise price must at least equal the stock value at the time of grant.
6. The ISO must be nontransferable prior to the employee's death.
7. More than 10% shareholders are generally ineligible.
8. Each employee may be granted options on a maximum $100,000 of stock per year.

With capital gains taxed at rates lower than ordinary income, this and other strategies which convert compensation to capital gains are attractive.

¶ 1651 NONQUALIFIED STOCK OPTIONS

When an employee receives a nonqualified stock option, chances are the exercise price is lower than the market price, resulting in a bargain element. This is immediately taxable as compensation upon exercise, but is deductible to the employer, as well as being part of the cost basis. The exercise period may exceed five years. When the stock is sold, the employee has a capital gain (or loss). The advantages of such an option are several:

1. The discount is income, but is deductible to the employer.
2. There is no waiting period before a sale produces a capital gain.

---

[21] Code Sec. 422A(c)(9).

3. The employer (who deducts the bargain element) also receives the exercise price, making the compensation cost effective.
4. The option is a status symbol. Studies show that in large companies, less than half of one percent of employees are eligible for the plan.

Keep in mind that a client who is an officer or director must hold the stock for at least six months to keep any profit under federal securities laws.[21a]

Most companies do not lend money to exercise their options because of limitations under state law and margin requirements imposed by the Federal Reserve Board. But if they do lend the employee money, the interest rate may be low or nonexistent.

Here is an example of a type of nonqualified stock purchase plan, sometimes referred to as a "yo-yo plan."

> ***Example:*** The exercise price of the option is initially equal to the market price, say $50. If the price goes up, the exercise price is *reduced* $1 for each point the stock moves up. An exercise when the market price is $80 would cost the employee $20 per share ($50 less the price increase of $30 ($80 – $50)).
>
> Thus, the employee receives $2 for each dollar of increase. Upon exercise, the employee has taxable compensation of $60 per share deductible to the employer. The basis equals the full value, i.e., the $20 paid plus the $60 of compensation received. In a 40% tax bracket, for example, the employee is out-of-pocket $44 ($20 paid plus 40% of $60), but the value received is $80. Any future appreciation is capital gain.

¶ 1652 PHANTOM STOCK GRANTS

Under a phantom stock grant (also called stock appreciation right, or SAR), the employee receives units on paper rather than stocks. Each unit is generally equal to the market price for one share of common stock initially. Some years later, typically five, the employee receives the difference between the current price and the initial price in either cash or free shares. In addition, the employee receives the dividends. At the minimum, the employee gets nothing, since a price decline does not cost anything. Therefore, the employee has a riskless incentive without borrowing costs. The problems with phantom stock are these:

1. It is uncertain whether the participant will in fact get a bonus. Someone who has to give up a bird in the hand to get the unpredictable bonus may think twice.

[21a] Section 16(b) of the Securities Exchange Act of 1934.

2. The employer does not know what their reportable compensation expenses are going to be.
3. Any increase in price is taxed as compensation, not as capital gains.

A variation of this theme is *book value phantom grants.* Under this plan, the employee receives the increase in book value. The reasons few companies use this type of plan are:

1. In a normal year, book value increases by earnings less dividends per share. However, since it is an employee who also receives the dividend, the net result is that the employee winds up simply receiving earnings per share.
2. Payments could be due under the plan even if earnings stay the same or go down, limiting the incentive to achieve growth.
3. Numerous changes in book value can occur which are unrelated to performance, such as:
    (a) When the corporation buys back its own shares, book value per share increases if the price paid is less than book value and decreases if the price is higher.
    (b) The same phenomenon occurs if the corporation launches a new issue, acquires another company for shares, or has its convertibles converted to stock.

¶ 1653 BOOK VALUE PLANS

Under a book value plan, the employee may buy a certain number of shares for their current book value. Because the employee actually owns the shares, the employee receives voting rights and dividends. Later, the employee may sell the shares, but only back to the corporation, and again at book value. The advantages are capital gain treatment of any profits and lack of dependence on market prices. But the disadvantages include:

1. Shareholder complaints if the book value is substantially less than market value upon purchase;
2. The employee must raise the money to buy the stock; and
3. The corporation receives no deduction for any gains.

   Additional flexibility can be provided by coupling the plan with stock options. Linking a buy/sell agreement to book values is most common in closely held corporations.

¶ 1654 PERFORMANCE SHARES

There are several disadvantages of linking executive compensation to the market price of the stock:

1. The services rendered by an individual plan participant is unlikely to have more than a negligible impact on the performance of the stock.
2. There is generally no reason to expect an employer's stock to do any better than any other stock investments.
3. The price of the stock will fluctuate with the stock market as a whole, which is a function of the economic outlook, inflation, interest rates, etc.
4. Even if profits go up, there is no guarantee that the price will increase in tandem.
5. When participating in the stock purchase plan, the client's investment in the employer may be an imprudently large share of an overall investment portfolio.

Because of these shortcomings, the plan typically provides "free" shares, options and/or other-than-market price criteria and/or other "sweeteners." Here are some examples:

1. An executive will receive 1,000 shares free in five years provided the executive is still there and earnings grew at an average compounded growth rate of 8% during the five-year period.
2. An executive can buy up to 1,000 shares at the market, putting up only 10% in cash and signing an IOU for the rest. For each year of service, a 5% discount from market will be granted. Additional discounts may be granted by the Board of Directors based on job performance.
3. An executive has a choice of a salary increase of 7% or a 10% increase to be used solely to pay interest on a bank loan guaranteed by the employer to buy company stock on the open market.
4. An executive will receive a package constructed as follows:
   (a) An option to buy 1,000 shares at $50 for two years after five years have lapsed (the current market value).
   (b) One thousand free shares or free shares worth $50,000, whichever is less, after staying with the firm for five years *and* only if certain earnings objectives are met.

   Thus, if the shares sell for $25 after five years, the option is worthless and free shares worth $25,000 will be received. But if the shares sell for $100, 500 free shares will be received, worth $50,000, and the option has an exercise value of $50,000.

5. A variation on number 4 is to pay a bonus in cash or shares regardless of the market price (plus the option) based on length of service and the level of company profit growth. This recognizes that the market "moves in mysterious ways, its wonders to perform." Profits may be up in a bear market, for example.

¶ 1655 LONG-TERM INCENTIVE PLANS IN ORDER OF POPULARITY

Among the 500 largest industrial companies, the most popular ways to compensate executives on a capital accumulation and long-term incentive basis in 1985 were:

	1985	*(1974)*
Incentive and nonqualified (or a combination thereof) stock options	89%	(52%)
Stock appreciation rights	64	(8)
Performance plans	42	(8)
Restricted stocks	27	(3)

While only 5% more companies used long-term incentives in 1985 than in 1974, the average company had 3.2 plans rather than 1.8. In fact, three-quarters of the firms had at least three plans.[21b]

CONCLUSION

Clearly, the rise in maximum tax rates after 1992 increased the interest in deferred compensation, while the taxation of capital gains at the maximum rate of 28% enhanced the attractiveness of "appreciation incentives." The bottom line is that straight cash salaries and bonuses should experience decreased popularity in the future. However, substantial nontax interest should still remain in rewarding employees for performance and providing them with financial security. In addition, deductible fringes not taxable to the beneficiaries will never be out of style.

Seven Stock Incentive Plans Compared

Plan	*Description*	*Tax Consequences*	*Other Factors*
Incentive Stock Option	Option to buy stock for fair market value at time of grant	No tax on grant or exercise capital gain on sale No deduction to employer	Must pay exercise price Must hold two years after grant, one after exercise Risk of loss

[21b] *Journal of Accountancy,* June 1986, p. 28, summarizing a study done by Peat Marwick, a "Big 6" CPA firm.

Plan	*Description*	*Tax Consequences*	*Other Factors*
Nonqualified Stock Option	Option to buy stock at a given price	No gain on grant, gain on bargain element on exercise (deductible to employer). Capital gain on sale	Must pay exercise price No holding period requirement Risk of loss
Stock Appreciation Right	Increase, if any, in price paid in cash after given time	Ordinary income on payment Deduction to employer	No cash necessary No risk of loss
Performance Shares	Stock bonus linked to earnings or other performance	Market value ordinary income upon receipt (deductible to employer). Capital gain on sale	No cash necessary No risk of loss
Phantom Stock	Simulated stock ownership, cash bonus as if owned stock (dividends plus appreciation)	Payment is ordinary income deductible to employer	No cash necessary Some benefit assured
Restricted Stock Grant	Stock bonus, often based on length of service	Value taxed (deductible) on receipt	No cash necessary
Stock Purchase	Purchase of stock from employer	Generally, no tax until sale if full value is paid	No special advantage over other stock purchase unless discount

Social Security

¶ 1660 BACKGROUND—THE SYSTEM

1. The Social Security contribution is a *tax* and is collected and administered as a tax.

2. Social Security benefits received reduce the eligibility for the retirement credit and have an impact on the support test for exemptions, etc.

3. Up to 85% of benefits are taxable to recipients with other income.[22]

---

[22] Code Sec. 86.

4. The average retiree relies on Social Security as the main source of income.

The rules are complex and constantly changing together with dollar amounts. Thus, dollar amounts used are merely for illustrative purposes and only broad principles are covered.

The Federal Insurance Contributions Act (FICA) was passed in 1935 and employees have been covered since 1937 (self-employed from 1951). Contributions are mandatory for both employer and employees, and payments made by the latter come out of after-tax income, i.e., they are nondeductible. Since tax is paid on the amounts contributed, by 1993, a 31% tax-bracket individual had to earn over $6,000 before taxes to pay the employee's share that year. At the same time, up to 85% of benefits received are taxable, unless the recipient has limited income from other sources. In 1978, the maximum old-age benefit for an individual was $459 per month. By 1993, the maximum had risen to $1,128.

Some 30 million Americans collect Social Security each month, of which 10 million are *under* 30 years of age. Three million are disabled or dependents of covered workers. Having a Social Security number is a must, whether seeking employment, paying taxes, applying for credit, or receiving dividend or interest income. The number stays the same if the client moves, changes names, or changes jobs. Unlike the case under private pension plans, a worker receives full credit, regardless of how often the worker changes employers.

Millions of people pay more FICA tax than income tax. This is because there are no exemptions or standard deductions. Thus, a married worker with two children, filing jointly, may pay no federal income tax on up to $15,600 of wages, but the worker *must* pay Social Security taxes of some $1,200.

¶ 1661 COMMON MISBELIEFS

Social Security is often compared to *insurance.* And it is true that Medicare, disability protection, death benefits, and survivor benefits look a lot like insurance. But retirement checks do not. The old-age pension is *not* an insurance scheme whereby the participant makes contributions entitling the payor to future benefits based on payments. Benefits are based *not* only on contributions, but also on "covered wages." If an employee changes jobs, any contributions made by an employer in excess of the annual limit applying to the employee are simply wasted. The "insured" cannot convert the "insurance" into an endowment policy or fixed-term annuity. The worker cannot give it away or leave it to anyone or change the beneficiary. Neither can the worker borrow money against accumulated contributions or use them as collateral. The Supreme Court has held that the "insured" has *no* vested property right in Social Security; the worker has simply paid a federal tax. Overpayments are refunded via the 1040 Form. If the worker is single with no dependents and dies at age 65, nobody will collect anything, even if the worker paid in for 40 years and left property to friends or relatives, or close relatives such as brothers and sisters. This is also true for private annuities and most pensions, however. But, if the worker leaves a widow 62 years of age, who never contributed, *she* can expect to collect for 20 years.

Old-age benefits are *not* related to need. The recipient may be rich or poor, own property, or live abroad, but the benefit check will be the same, generally speaking. A senior citizen can collect a minimum benefit even if the individual never had any covered wages. On the other hand, the worker collects a higher percentage of wages, if past earnings were relatively low. It is not generally true that recipients are uniformly poor and in need of added assistance.

Congress has often stated that benefits are never welfare. The term "insurance" is often used to emphasize that benefits are not "needs related." But many benefits are now based on need, such as:

the minimum benefits,

the "special" minimum benefits for low-income workers,

the disability and survivor benefits, and

the extra 50% for a retired couple.

¶ 1662 COVERED WAGES

A worker is subject to Social Security taxes if earning at least $50 in any one calendar quarter or at least $400 a year as a self-employed person. Historically, the maximum earnings subject to the tax (and on which benefits are computed) were:

1951-54	$3,600	1973	$10,800
1955-58	4,200	1974	13,200
1959-65	4,800	1975	14,100
1966-67	6,600	1976	15,300
1968-71	7,800	1977	16,500
1972	9,000	1978	17,700

These limits are set so that the average wage earner will have to pay tax on *all* earned income.

Example: A 65-year-old man retired in January 1978. He had paid the maximum since the inception of FICA, ranging from $30 on $3,000 of wages in 1937 to $965.25 on $16,000 in 1977. If he had invested these amounts at regular passbook savings rates, he would have had about $28,000. This amount would have purchased an annuity of only $230 a month from an insurance company. Instead, he received $459.80 a month in Social Security, $689.70 if he was married, plus the automatic price level increases. By 1993, his monthly benefit was about $1,000. Social Security is a good deal, based on the above assumptions. In addition, he had disability and survivorship protection.

The trend is towards raising both the tax rate *and* the annual wage limits simultaneously. Legislation passed in 1977 dramatically increased the tax. The need for more funds was a result of bad past estimates of present benefit costs coupled with the expense of automatic cost-of-living increases. Benefits are linked to the Consumer Price Index and go up each time the price level increases at least 3%. In 1986, an exception was granted from the 3% rule when prices rose moderately. Since the system works on a "pay as you go" basis, more money had been going out than in. Even though, in effect, today's workers pay for the retirement of yesterday's workers, the system was going broke. This was further caused by dropping birth rates and increased longevity, leading to a higher percentage of senior citizens in the population. Here are the current tax rates and maximum salaries covered:

Year	*Covered Wages*	*Tax Rate*	*Tax Paid*
1983	$35,700	6.70%	$2,392
1984	37,800	6.70	2,533
1985	39,600	7.05	2,792
1986	42,000	7.15	3,003
1987	43,800	7.15	3,132
1988	45,000	7.51	3,380
1989	48,000	7.51	3,604
1990	51,300	7.65	3,924
1991	53,400	7.65	4,085
1992	55,500	7.65	4,241
1993	57,600	7.65	4,406

For the employees above, the employer also pays a like amount. Self-employed persons pay a higher percentage on the same maximum earnings, since there is no employer's share, but less than twice. Thus, self-employeds paid 7.9% in 1977, 8.1% in 1978-80, 9.3% in 1981, 9.35% in 1982-84, 11.8% in 1985, 12.3% in 1986, 13.02% in 1988 and 15.3% in 1991 and later.

The Social Security Administration works on the assumption that a retired individual will receive about 43% of average lifetime covered earnings when retiring.

¶ 1663 BENEFIT COMPUTATION PROCEDURE

Computing the Social Security retirement benefit under the so-called "new method" (that has been used since 1978) is complex but may be summarized as follows:

1. Find the number of *"elapsed years."* (Workers born before 1930 count the years starting with 1951 and ending with the year before reaching 62. Workers born after 1929 start with the year they attain age 22.)
2. Deduct the number five from the "elapsed years" to arrive at "computation years."
3. Make a list of *"base years"* and *"base year earnings,"* e.g., for each year, beginning with 1951 and ending the year before benefits will begin, covered wages are listed (up to the maximum listed above).
4. Index these earnings to the national averages over the base period (the national average earnings went from $2,800 in 1951 to about $22,000 in 1993, and from 78% to 42% of maximum covered amounts).
5. Eliminate base years with the lowest indexed earnings until base years equal computation years under 2, above.
6. Add up indexed earnings from the remaining base years.
7. Divide this sum by the number of months in the computation years and round off down to the nearest dollar. The result is the *Average Indexed Monthly Earnings* (AIME).
8. Convert the AIME to a *Primary Insurance Amount* (PIA) by applying a formula for the year benefits will start. (For 1993, the PIA was 90% of the first $401 of AIME, plus 32% of the next $2,019, and 15% of the excess.) The PIA is rounded down to the nearest dime.
9. Adjust PIA, if necessary, for:
   (a) Retirement prior to age 65.
   (b) The appropriate fraction for a spouse (one-half) or children and other dependents.
   (c) Delayed retirement up to age 70.
   (d) The reduction for earnings above the exemption amount for retirees under age 70.

   The PIA is adjusted for inflation annually through cost-of-living increases.

SOCIAL SECURITY BENEFITS FOR WORKERS REACHING AGE 65 IN 1993 (Excerpts)

Average Indexed Monthly Earnings	*Benefit for Single Individual*	*Benefit for Spouse Age 65*	*Benefit for Spouse Age 62*	*Survivor Benefit*			*Maximun Family Benefit*
				Child	*Spouse 62*	*Spouse 60*	
$ 500	$412.30	$206.10	$154.50	$309.20	$341.70	$294.70	$ 618.60
750	502.50	251.20	188.40	376.80	416.50	359.20	753.70
1,000	592.50	296.20	222.10	444.30	491.10	423.60	986.80
1,250	682.50	341.20	255.90	511.80	565.70	487.90	1,231.70
1,500	772.60	386.30	289.70	579.40	640.40	552.40	1,429.50
1,750	862.60	431.30	323.40	646.90	715.00	616.70	1,550.20
2,000	952.80	476.40	357.30	714.60	789.80	681.20	1,670.80
2,250	1,022.70	511.30	383.40	767.00	847.80	731.20	1,789.00
2,500	1,064.90	532.40	399.30	798.60	882.80	761.40	1,862.80
2,878*	1,128.80	564.40	423.30	846.60	935.70	807.00	1,974.70

* Maximum for most workers age 65 during 1993.

¶ 1664 WHO QUALIFIES FOR BENEFITS?

To qualify for Social Security, the worker must fall into one of the following categories:

1. *Retired.* Retired workers age 62 or older or a widow or divorcee of such worker age 62 or older. For a widow caring for a child (except a student age 18 or older), age is irrelevant. A child or grandchild of a retired worker under age 18 (22 if a student) or any age (if disabled) is entitled to benefits.

2. *Survivors.* A surviving spouse or divorced person of at least age 60 (or at least age 50, if disabled) is entitled to benefits. Such persons can be any age if caring for a child (except students age 18 or over). In addition, a dependent parent, age 62 or over, and children or grandchildren under age 18 (22 if a student) or any age (if disabled) are covered.

3. *Disabled.* Disabled workers and disabled surviving divorced persons are covered.

4. A lump-sum *death benefit* of $255 is paid upon the death of a covered worker to the surviving spouse or child.

To receive benefits, a qualifying person must file a *claim.* Workers retiring before age 65 receive 20% less than full benefits if they are age 62, more if they are age 63 or 64. By year 2022, the reduction is going to be 30%. A surviving spouse receives full benefits if at retirement age. If not, 75% is received, *if* there is a dependent child under age 16. After age 60 and *after* 1978 a survivor may remarry without loss of benefits. There is a limit on the amount one family can receive in total benefits.

A divorced spouse will receive survivorship benefits if the marriage lasted at least 10 years.

FULLY INSURED

There is a *minimum* pension which is $11.50 multiplied by the number of years the claimant was covered by the law in excess of 10, up to 30. The maximum benefit paid under this rule was $513 in 1993.

To collect full retirement benefits, a worker must be "fully insured." Forty quarters of coverage insures a worker for life. A quarter of coverage (maximum 4) is provided for each $590 of earnings in 1993. Surviving spouses and children get survivorship checks if the deceased was covered at least six quarters of the last 13 quarters ending with retirement, disability, or death.

CURRENTLY INSURED

The worker need only be "currently insured" (have six quarters of coverage in the last 13 quarters) to be eligible for the following benefits:

1. Survivor benefits to surviving spouse or divorced parent of deceased worker's child, caring for a child entitled to benefits.
2. Survivor benefits to child or grandchild under age 18 (over 18 if student, any age if disabled).
3. Lump-sum death benefit.

RETURN TO WORK AFTER DISABILITY

A *disabled* worker may go back to work for up to nine months as a "trial-work period" without worrying about the checks stopping. An individual who continues to work receives three more checks for a total of 12. If the individual cannot work, the checks run uninterrupted. There is a waiting period of six months after becoming disabled, but the worker is paid for the waiting period retroactively. If a second disability occurs within five years of the first, there is no waiting period.

INCAPACITY

A Social Security recipient who becomes unable to function should appoint a "representative payee," a friend or relative who will handle the checks.

DELAYED RETIREMENT CREDITS

If the worker chooses *not* to file a claim until after age 65, benefits will increase 3% per year from age 65 to 70. People born after 1924, however, receive an increase of 3.5 to 8% a year. Thus, someone born in 1925 gets 3.5% a year, but someone born in 1943 or later receives a full

8% a year increase. These "delayed retirement credits" will be passed on to a surviving spouse as well.

MARRIAGE

Under prior law a worker could lose benefits by getting married. This primarily affected surviving spouses who remarried. As mentioned, surviving spouses over age 60 can now (since 1979) remarry without losing benefits. On the other hand, an 18-year-old female student, who receives benefits because of her deceased father, would *lose* them upon marriage.

PRACTICAL HINTS

The worker has a lifetime earnings record with the Social Security Administration, P.O. Box 1756, Baltimore, MD 21203, U.S.A. The Social Security number is the same for life regardless of name, address, and job changes. Someone losing a Social Security card can easily get a duplicate by filling out a form.

A worker should check the balance periodically and get refunds from the employer, if only one and from the IRS on tax Form 1040, if more than one in the same year. When filing a claim, the retiree should obtain a copy of the current booklet and compute the benefit personally to ensure full payment. The Social Security Administration now also gives estimates of future benefits upon request.

The worker will receive nothing unless a claim is filed. It is necessary to have documents, such as the social security card, birth certificate, baptismal certificate, marriage certificate, and if self-employed, the latest tax return (Form SE in particular).

The worker needs to keep the Social Security Administration posted about such things as:

Change of address

Work or self-employment while underage

Changes in citizenship

Becoming disabled or improving or going back to work

Others must report:

The worker's death or incapacity

Spouses, surviving spouses, dependents must report:

Marriage or divorce

Child reaching majority or leaving home

Child's school attendance, attaining age 18, or becoming disabled, etc.

Benefits received may be taxable, but *cannot* be attached by creditors.

The retiree should not cash the checks in lump sums, but keep a checking account, have the checks deposited *directly* to this account, then pay all bills by check.

¶ 1665 WORKING AFTER AGE 65

A person who continues to be employed after age 65 should note the following:

1. Wages are still subject to Social Security taxes (including Medicare), but the worker accumulates the extra annual credit referred to above if filing no claim. Even if no claim is filed, the worker is covered by Medicare.
2. If the worker is *on* Social Security but works, benefits are reduced by one-third of earned income above certain levels until age 70 (one-half if under 65). For 1993, the earned income level was $10,560 for workers over age 65, $7,680 if under age 65 the whole year.
3. Recall that Social Security benefits also reduce the retirement credit for income tax purposes.
4. If the client's work or business is *not* subject to Social Security tax, the client does not qualify for a benefit check for any month during which seven days or more (full- or part-time) of work was performed.
5. Investment income, such as interest, dividends, capital gains, pensions, royalties, etc., does *not* reduce benefits.

LATE RETIREMENT

The age at which a person can retire with full benefits is scheduled to gradually increase from age 65 to age 67 as follows:

If born in	*Reaching age 62 in*	*Retirement age is*
1937 or earlier	1999 or earlier	65
1938	2000	65 and 2 months
1939	2001	65 and 4 months
1940	2002	65 and 6 months
1941	2003	65 and 8 months
1942	2004	65 and 10 months
1943 - 1954	2005 - 2016	66
1955	2017	66 and 2 months
1956	2018	66 and 4 months
1957	2019	66 and 6 months
1958	2020	66 and 8 months
1959	2021	66 and 10 months
1960 or later	2022 or later	67

¶ 1666 FICA AND PRIVATE PENSIONS

Under the new law, FICA payments exceed 15% of total covered payroll. Because private pension plans can "integrate" their coverage with Social Security, i.e., making higher contributions on salaries in excess of covered FICA limits, FICA is becoming *the* national pension plan. The increased FICA payments, coupled with the complex private pension laws since the Employee Retirement Income Security Act of 1974 (ERISA) was enacted, have led to the demise of thousands of small pension plans. When the new pension law became effective on January 1, 1975, some 35,000 plans were scrapped within two years. By 1993, some $500 *billion* was paid in to FICA annually.

¶ 1667 RETIRING ABROAD

Here are some tips for clients who wish to retire abroad:

1. Generally, benefit checks will be mailed to retirees, regardless of where they choose to retire. Many Americans retire abroad to places such as Mexico, Canada and Europe, both because of the change of pace and because the dollar may purchase more. The checks are still dated the third of each month for the previous month (no check is paid for the month of death).
2. The government will *not* send checks to certain countries, such as Cuba, North Korea, North Vietnam, and the People's Republic of China. The worker gets paid for missing checks, however, if and when returning to the U.S.
3. In addition, if the worker becomes a citizen of certain countries, the checks will stop after six months. The Social Security Administration keeps a list of "approved" citizenships.
4. If a worker is deported, no benefits will be paid.
5. Some countries tax benefits as income, and some countries restrict payments to absentee U.S. citizens.
6. All the above rules are subject to change as are all *tax* laws, indeed all laws. For answers to specific questions, contact the nearest Social Security office.

CHAPTER 17

ESTATE, GIFT, AND GENERATION-SKIPPING TRANSFER TAXES

¶ 1701 INTRODUCTION

In this chapter, the main features of the estate tax, i.e., what is includible in the estate and the deductions, are summarized. Next, the gift tax and the generation-skipping tax are discussed at length. The following chapter shows applications, or how to minimize the effect of the wealth transfer taxes, i.e. "estate planning". The main features of estate and gift taxes must be understood before any meaningful estate planning can be done.

The marginal estate and gift tax rates reach the 55% level after $3 million of taxable transfers. This could at first blush seem to discourage savings. A high-bracket individual can be hypothesized who first earns an extra $100,000, leaving $64,000 after income taxes. When leaving the savings to the heirs, they receive $28,800 after estate taxes. This 71% reduction is without regard to state income taxes and administration expenses. Fortunately, the next two chapters show many ways to avoid this extreme result.

¶ 1702 HOW THE ESTATE TAX IS COMPUTED

The key point to remember is that all lifetime gifts and transfers by death are all treated as one big pile and that pile, whether it still exists or not, is taxed using the same unified tax table. In capsule form, what happens is this:

1. Everything the decedent owned, retained a life estate or reversion in, or had a general power of appointment over, constitutes the *gross estate.*
2. From the gross estate is subtracted funeral expenses, administration expenses, debts, and losses during administration.
3. The result is the *adjusted gross estate* (AGE).
4. From this is subtracted items passing to the surviving spouse, up to the full value of the AGE (the marital deduction).
5. Charitable contributions are then deducted.
6. The result is the *taxable estate.*
7. Add *adjusted taxable gift,* i.e., taxable gifts after 1976 not otherwise included in the gross estate.
8. The tentative tax on the sum of 6. and 7. is found in the multipurpose tax table.[1]
9. Gift taxes paid or payable on post-1976 gifts (a tax credit) are subtracted. Otherwise, double taxation would result.
10. The *unified credit* is subtracted ($192,800 after 1986).[2] A 5% surtax is imposed on taxable transfers over $10 million until the tax liability equals a flat 55%. Thus, both the lower brackets and the unified credit are phased out.
11. If any tax liability remains, and if applicable, the following credits, if available, may be subtracted:
    (a) state death taxes paid,
    (b) gift taxes paid on gifts made prior to 1977 included in the gross estate,
    (c) foreign death taxes,
    (d) taxes on prior transfers. This is a credit allowed if property is transferred by death two or more times within a 10-year period. The most typical case is spouses dying within a few years of each other.[3]
12. The net is taxes due and owing.
13. The estate tax return (Form 706) is due nine months after death and is filed by the executor.[4]
14. Extensions to pay can be granted under certain circumstances.[5]

---

[1] Code Sec. 2001.
[2] Code Sec. 2010.
[3] Code Secs. 2011-2014.
[4] Code Sec. 6075(a).
[5] Code Sec. 6081.

ESTATE, GIFT, AND GENERATION-SKIPPING TRANSFER TAX TABLE

Taxable Estate or Cumulative Taxable Gifts or Transfers	*Marginal Tax Bracket*	*Tax Liability After $192,000 of Unified Credit*
$ 600,000 or below	37%	None
750,000	39%	$ 55,500
1,000,000	41%	153,000
1,250,000	43%	255,500
1,500,000	45%	363,000
2,000,000	49%	588,000
2,500,000	53%	833,000
3,000,000	55%	833,000 + 50% of excess over $2,500,000

¶ 1703 PRESENT AND FUTURE INTERESTS IN PROPERTY

Anyone who owns property outright, whether personal or real, can divide up this ownership in several ways. How this can be done and how to identify these interests are crucial to the understanding of estate and gift taxes.

¶ 1704 LIFE ESTATES, REMAINDERS, AND REVERSIONS

Distinctions between life estates, remainders, and reversions can best be illustrated as follows:

Case 1: *The grantor (G) transfers property to A for life.* A has a *life estate* and is a *life tenant*. A can sell the interest to B, but B still has a life estate for the life of A. G has a *reversion* because the property will revert back to G or G's heirs when A dies.

Estate tax consequences: Nothing will be taxed in A's estate because the only interest owned, the life estate, is extinguished upon A's death. But the whole property will be included in G's estate, less the value of A's life estate at G's death, actuarially determined.

Case 2: *G transfers the property to A, but retains the income and/or possession of it for life.* Here G retains a life estate and A receives a *remainder.*

Estate tax consequences: G never gave up the present enjoyment of the property, therefore the full value of it will be included in G's estate. A's estate will also include the property, but if G outlives A, only the remainder will be taxed.

Case 3: *G transfers the property to A for life, then to B.* A has a life estate, B has a vested remainder, G has disposed of all interest. Even if B predeceases A, B's heirs will receive ownership.

Estate tax consequences: Nothing is included in G's estate, but B owns either the remainder or the property, depending on whether B predeceases G. However:

1. All transfers of property, even partial, are subject to gift tax.
2. All adjusted taxable gifts are included in the estate computation, even if not part of the gross estate.
3. Some gifts made within three years of death are includible in the gross estate.

Case 4: *G transfers the property to A for life, and, if B survives A, then to B.* A has a life estate and B has a contingent remainder, because B must survive A to take anything. In addition, G has a reversion, because G or G's heirs will receive the property if B predeceases A.

Estate tax consequences: A's estate is unaffected. B's estate has nothing if B predeceases A. If B survives A, B's estate will include the full value of the property. G's estate has nothing if B survives A prior to G's death. G's estate will include the property, multiplied by the probability of B predeceasing A, less A's life estate if G predeceases A and B.

Case 5: *G transfers the property to A for life, then to B if B survives A, otherwise to C.* A has a life estate, B has a contingent remainder and C has an *executory interest,* a remainder of sorts.

Estate tax consequences: G can never get anything back, so G's gross estate includes nothing. A's estate is unaffected. B's estate will include the property if B survives A, otherwise it will include nothing. C's estate problem is more complex:

1. If A predeceases B, nothing will be included.
2. If C predeceases A and B, there is still a possibility that B will predecease A. Therefore, the property will be included in C's estate multiplied by the probability of this happening, but less A's life estate.

The above transactions are generally done for family members in trust, e.g., life estate to wife, remainder to children.

¶ 1705 PROPERTY OWNED AT DEATH

Everything a person owns at death (or had made an incomplete transfer of) is included in the grantor's gross estate. The property may be real or personal, tangible or intangible, depreciable or nondepreciable. The grantor may have a partial interest in it, e.g., a remainder or an undivided interest, such as being a tenant in common or a joint tenant. The following are examples of includible property:

1. Tax-exempt municipal bonds.[6]
2. Accrued interest on any bonds.
3. Dividends receivable if death occurs on the record date or later.
4. Life insurance policies.
5. Personal effects, such as clothes, bonds, furniture, jewelry, art, bank accounts, securities, and cars.
6. Real estate, such as the home investment property, etc., even if located abroad.
7. Interests in lawsuits brought by the decedent.
8. Promissory notes, even if the debts are forgiven in the will.
9. All property is includible even if subject to the surviving spouse's statutory share, typically one-third.

The following are examples of excluded property:

1. Qualified employment annuities purchased by the employer, if in pay status by 1983.
2. Social Security and workers' compensation death benefits.
3. Proceeds from wrongful death actions.
4. Jointly held property purchased by someone other than the spouse.
5. Life estates, if obtained from another.

As discussed at ¶ 1706, under many circumstances property transferred during life will be included in the gross estate, if certain controls were retained, or certain property was transferred within three years of death.

¶ 1706 LIFE INSURANCE

Almost every working person carries life insurance. The earlier a person dies, the greater the excess of proceeds over premiums paid. In most cases, the full proceeds will be includible in the gross estate unless steps are taken to keep it out more than three years prior to death.[7]

The proceeds are taxable in the estate if

1. the proceeds are payable to the executor,
2. the decedent possessed any "incidents of ownership" in the policy at death, or
3. the decedent made a transfer of the policy within the last three years of life.[8]

---

[6] Reg. § 20.2033-1(a).
[7] Code Secs. 2042 and 2035(d)(2).
[8] Code Sec. 2035(b)(2).

The proceeds are payable to the executor if payable to the estate. Even if they are payable to another, they are deemed to be received by the executor if the beneficiary is under obligation to use the proceeds to pay taxes, debts, or claims of the estate. Following the same line of reasoning, if a trustee collects the proceeds and is authorized to pay such claims, proceeds are taxed to the extent so used.

INCIDENTS OF OWNERSHIP

Even if a named beneficiary, other than the estate, collects the proceeds, they are includible if the decedent possessed any incidents of ownership. It is difficult, but not impossible, to divest the insured of these, because they include the following:

The power to change the beneficiary.

The power to cancel the policy (not just to stop paying premiums).

The power to assign the policy.

The power to revoke an assignment, e.g., transfer the policy to a revocable trust.

The power to pledge the policy for a loan.

The power to borrow the cash value from the insurer.

The power to veto any incident held by another.

A reversion in the policy worth over 5%, e.g., the possibility that the policy or the proceeds will be returned to the insured or the insured's estate.

Not included in the list of incidents of ownership are the following:

The power to receive dividends, i.e., overpayments of premiums.

The power to quit one's job, thereby causing a cancellation of group employee life insurance.

The power to get a divorce, thus terminating the spouse as a beneficiary of death benefits.

Fiduciary powers, if the powers are received from a third party and the insured cannot benefit as a result.[9]

Annuities

¶ 1710 PRIVATE ANNUITIES

If the annuity is paid to the annuitant for life with no survivor feature, nothing will be includible in the estate, since nothing passes from the decedent. Should the annuity continue to the surviving spouse or other beneficiary, the estate will include the present value of the

[9] Rev. Rul. 84-179, 1984-1 CB 111.

future payments, based on the survivor's life expectancy, times the fractional consideration paid by the decedent.[10]

> ***Example:*** G and W sold securities to their child for a private annuity of $5,000 a year for as long as they both live, plus $3,000 a year for the life of the survivor. G had put up 80% of the purchase price of the securities. G died first, and W's age at that time was 60 years. One dollar a year to a 60-year-old woman for life is worth $7.45 at 10%.[11] Therefore, if the discount rate to be used equals 10%, G's estate will include:
>
> .80 × $7.45 × $3,000, or $17,880.

¶ 1711 COMMERCIAL ANNUITIES

By far most annuities are of the commercial kind and are issued by insurance companies. Unlike private annuities, the values of which are found in tables based on assumed interests rates, commercial annuities are valued based on comparable sales. In other words, the issuer is asked: How much would a 60-year-old woman have to pay to get $3,000 a year for life? The answer to that question is the value of the annuity.

Most commercial annuities can be divided in four groups:

1. *Straight-life annuities,* which are paid for the life of one person.
2. *Joint and survivor annuities,* whereby payments are made, typically to a couple, as long as one of them lives.
3. *Self and survivor annuities,* whereby payments continue to be made to a beneficiary after the death of the buyer.
4. *Minimum guarantee annuities,* whereby a refund feature provides for a lump-sum payment, unless the annuitant survives a minimum period of time.

To be an annuity for tax purposes, it is immaterial whether the payments are periodic or sporadic, equal or unequal, conditional or unconditional.

Straight-life annuities will never result in estate taxation, but once a survivor feature exists, the value of the payments due after death will be included in the estate *if the decedent contributed to the purchase price.* A very similar rule applies to joint tenancy property, as will be seen in the following discussion. In formula form, we have

> Estate value = value of annuity at death × decedent contribution/total purchase price.

---

[10] Code Sec. 2039(b).

[11] Reg. § 20.2031-7(f). However, the discount rate varies from month to month.

Contributions made by an employer are considered made by the employee.[11a] Thus, the account balance of *any* deferred compensation plan is includible in the participant's gross estate.

Whether the plan is qualified or nonqualified, a pension or profit-sharing plan, contributory or not, payable to the estate or a named beneficiary, payable in a lump sum or as an annuity, or whether the plan is an individual retirement account, a Keogh plan, or a corporate plan, *all* plans are includible in the gross estate (offset by the marital deduction, discussed below, if the beneficiary is the plan participant's spouse).

Joint Tenancies

¶ 1715 INTRODUCTION

To understand the unique features of joint tenancies with right of survivorship, their four main attributes must first be defined. For example, joint tenancies are treated quite differently from tenancies in common. Despite the incredible propularity of joint tenancies, particularly between spouses, they are not always recommended as an estate planning device.

¶ 1716 JOINT TENANCY DEFINED

A joint tenancy has the following characteristics:

1. Two or more people own an equal undivided share of a piece of real or personal property. If there are two owners, they must own one-half each, if there are *n,* they must own one-*n* th each, etc.
2. The interests must be created at the same time in the same instrument. If someone owns a house, gets married and deeds one-half to the spouse, the couple are tenants in common. Should they wish a joint tenancy, the owner must deed the property to a third party, e.g., a lawyer, who then deeds it back to them as joint tenants.
3. Survivorship is the most typical feature of a joint tenancy. If there are two joint tenants and one dies, the other immediately becomes the sole owner by operation of law, will or no will. Therefore, the property does not go through probate.
4. Each joint tenant can sell an undivided interest, but there is a limited market for partial interests.

Some states have a *tenancy by the entirety,* which is like a joint tenancy with two exceptions:

[11a] Code Sec. 2039(b).

1. It only exists between spouses.
2. Both spouses must join in a transfer to a third party.

¶ 1717 TENANCIES IN COMMON

If the requirements of a joint tenancy are not met, the co-owners are tenants in common. This could happen if their interests are different or were created at different times. Unless it is spelled out that a joint tenancy is created, co-owners are presumed to be tenants in common, even if they meet the requirements of a joint tenancy. Tenants in common do *not* have the right of survivorship. Therefore, a tenant's interest passes by will or the laws of intestate succession.

Community property is like a tenancy in common between spouses only and is forced on couples in the nine community property states: Arizona, California, Idaho, Louisiana, Nevada, New Mexico, Texas, Washington and Wisconsin. Each spouse owns one-half of most income and assets earned and acquired during marriage by operation of law.

¶ 1718 ESTATE TAX CONSEQUENCES OF JOINT TENANCIES

Let us first emphasize the following:

1. Joint tenancies and tenancies by the entirety are treated the same.
2. If survivorship is not present, such as in a tenancy in common or community property, the decedent's undivided share is all that is included in the gross estate. Once a joint tenancy exists, the estate tax consequences are as follows:
    - (a) If the co-owners are married, *one-half* of the property is included in the estate of the first to die.[12]
    - (b) If the co-owners are *not* married, *the full value* of the property is included in the estate of the first to die, *unless* and to the extent the survivor can show a contribution in money or money's worth.[12a] Furthermore, no marital deduction is available, per definition, to offset the inclusion. Since the survivor now becomes the sole owner, the full value will later be includible in the survivor's gross estate as well.

Example 1: Sam bought a house with Hilda, his girlfriend, many years ago for $20,000. They equally contributed to the down payment of $4,000, but Sam paid off the mortgage from his salary. At Sam's death, the house was worth $150,000. If Hilda can *prove* her contribution 40 years ago, only then will one-tenth ($2,000/$20,000) of the value of the property be excluded from his

[12] Code Sec. 2040(b).

[12a] Code Sec. 2040(a).

estate. Even if she contributed but cannot prove it, the full value will be included in Sam's gross estate.

On the other hand, if Hilda dies first, only one-tenth of the house is includible in her estate, *if* Sam can show *his* contribution. Some problems with the survivorship feature are illustrated below:

Example 2: A grandfather wants his savings account to go to his grandson, age 15. His son is 40 and for convenience he puts the account in joint names, his and his son's, because the grandson is so young. He dies and leaves a will stating the bank account is to go to the grandson. Who gets the account? The *son,* because the surviving joint tenant receives the property by operation of law. A will cannot change the nature of a joint tenancy. Good intentions are no substitutions for knowledge or the advice of counsel.

Example 3: H owned a house as joint tenant with W1. They divorced, W1 moved out, and H married W2, who moved in. Many years later H died. Who gets the house? W1, assuming she is still alive. A divorce does not sever a joint tenancy. Imagine W2's emotions upon being kicked out of "her" home after 30 years!

Gifts

¶ 1720 ADVANTAGES OF LIFETIME GIFTS

Due to the unified tax structure *all* gifts made after 1976 will be included in the estate tax computation as "adjusted taxable gifts." It might appear that few advantages of lifetime gifts are left. However, the following benefits still remain:

1. Up to $10,000 a year per donee can be given away without gift or estate tax consequences.[13] This is true even for death-bed gifts.
2. A key consideration is appreciation. The "adjusted taxable gift" comes in at the value at the time of gift. Testamentary gifts come in at *death* value. Thus, lifetime gifts will save estate tax on the appreciation, an important point in these inflationary times.
3. The income generated by gifted property belongs to the donee and will not come back in the estate of the donor.
4. If the gift is made more than three years prior to death, any gift tax paid is not includible in the gross estate, even though a credit for the tax reduces estate taxes payable.
5. Income taxes can be reduced through income splitting, i.e., through gifts of income-producing property.

[13] Code Sec. 2503(b).

6. The donor can experience the joy of giving.
7. The donor may wish to be relieved of the management of the property.

The main disadvantage of lifetime gifts is that the donor gives up property that may later be needed or regretted.

Retained Life Estates

¶ 1725 GENERAL RULES

The estate tax can be avoided on lifetime transfers only if the decedent does not retain control over the property, including being in a position to enjoy some or all of the fruits of ownership until death. If some control was retained, it does not matter how long ago the transfer was made. The grantor has a "retained life estate" if three factors are present:

1. A lifetime transfer was made.
2. It was a gift in whole or in part.
3. At death, the donor had the right to the possession or enjoyment of, or income from, the property or to designate the persons who shall have its possession or enjoyment.[14]

The second point is by far the most important as a practical matter. If the estate can prove that the property was originally sold for its full value, the estate was obviously not reduced by the transaction and the rule does not apply.

Here are some examples of retained control which would *not* remove a gratuitously transferred property from the estate of the transferor:

1. A parent deeds a house to a child, but continues to live there for life. Since the grantor still possesses it, the house will still be in the grantor's estate. Ownership is irrelevant. If the grantor occupies only one-fourth of the house, only one-quarter of the value would be included. Paying a fair rent *may* keep it out. In any event, the transfer would be subject to gift tax (on the remainder).
2. A parent gives away a securities portfolio to the children, but retains the right to the interest and dividends in case of need.
3. The grantor retains possession or income for a given period, such as 10 years, but dies before it expires.

---

[14] Code Sec. 2036.

4. If a grantor transfers property to a trust, the following retained powers will be deemed to constitute a retained life estate:
   (a) the power to determine the amount and timing of income distributions,
   (b) a "sprinkling power," e.g., the right to favor child A over child B or vice versa each year,
   (c) the right to accumulate or distribute income, and
   (d) a power to dip into the capital.

The above applies even if an independent trustee has one or more of these powers *and* the grantor has the right to shop around for a different trustee without cause.[15] Note that the property is includible even if the grantor personally can never benefit directly from the powers.

¶ 1726 STOCKS IN CLOSELY HELD CORPORATIONS

For many years it was unclear whether the retention of voting rights after a transfer of stock would constitute a retained life interest. If stocks are transferred to a trust and voting rights are retained, the stock will be includible in the grantor's estate under current rules if:

1. there was a gift element,
2. the *grantor* retained the voting rights, either alone or in conjunction with another party, and
3. some time during the last three years of the grantor's life, the grantor owned at least 20% of the voting power of the corporation, directly or indirectly (using attribution rules).[16]

The third requirement makes it clear that the rule only is intended to apply to closely held corporations. If any voting rights were relinquished during the last three years prior to death, and the voting control dropped from 20% or more to below 20, the result is deemed a transfer.

The reason why the retention of voting rights is deemed a retained life estate is that, through a voting power, the grantor may be able to control the Board of Directors, which is the body that determines dividend policy.

¶ 1727 FAMILY PARTNERSHIPS

As was seen in the chapter on financial planning with closely held businesses (see ¶ 1726), a family partnership is a typical device to shift income and appreciation to other family members. The grantor-partner

---

[15] Rev. Rul. 81-51, 1981-1 CB 458.

[16] Code Sec. 2036(b).

should be careful not to run afoul of the retained life estate rule by retaining too much control. If the grantor retains a power to control income distributions after the transfer, the rule could apply. But the exercise of traditional managerial powers by the grantor should not invoke the rule. Thus the scope of powers customary in recognized business relationships should not be exceeded. Here are some key factors the IRS looks at:

1. Was the partnership created for business purposes or principally to carry out a desired estate plan?
2. Did the other partners contribute any capital?
3. Did the grantor-partner have the power to accumulate or distribute income?
4. What percentage of profits were in fact distributed to the grantor-partner?

Buy/sell agreements serve a business purpose and should not be a negative factor.

¶ 1728 REVERSIONS

A rule related to the retained life estate rule is the reversion rule. It is made up of three elements:

1. Possession or enjoyment of the property can only be obtained through ownership by surviving the decedent.
2. The decedent retained a reversion.
3. The value of the interest exceeded 5% of the property value just prior to death, using actuarial principles.[17]

Example: G transferred property to W for life, reversion to G if W predeceases him, otherwise to S. G died at age 48, prior to W and S. Although we now know that G or G's estate will never receive the property, the point is that G had a reversion immediately prior to death. S could receive the property if G predeceased W. G died so as to vest S's contingent remainder. This is similar to a testamentary transfer. To measure the value of G's reversion, we disregard his death and ask: What is the probability a man age 48 will survive his wife, given her age? The result is based on the life expectancy of the average 48-year-old male, even though we know that this one died. Since the average male invariably has a more than 5% chance of surviving his wife, the property is included in his estate, reduced only by the value of her life estate, based on *her* life expectancy. The 5% rule applies because S had to survive G to acquire the property.

---

[17] Code Sec. 2037.

Powers

¶ 1730 REVOCABLE TRANSFERS

If a person died with the power to alter, amend, revoke or terminate a gratuitous transfer, all property subject to the power is includible in the estate. It is immaterial whether the decedent could directly benefit from the power. A power to change beneficiaries or to accelerate or increase payments to given beneficiaries would be sufficient. If the power was given up within three years of death, the property is includible as a gift in contemplation of death.[18]

Example: In order to split income G transferred securities to his one-year-old child, S, under the Uniform Transfers to Minors Act, designating himself as custodian. As custodian he had the right to terminate the custodianship any time and distribute the proceeds to the minor. The transfer is subject to gift taxes and is effective to shift the income to the child. Nevertheless, if the grantor-custodian dies before the arrangement is terminated, the full value of the property, including accumulated income, is includible in his estate. This is true even if more than three years have passed.

If the *spouse* was appointed custodian, the property would not be included in the *grantor's* estate, even if the transfer was made within three years of death. (*Reminder: All* taxable gifts are added to the taxable estate, if made after 1976, with a credit for gift taxes payable. The key difference in the result is therefore valuation.) If the spouse dies as custodian, nothing is includible in such spouse's estate. The powers as custodian are not significant enough to warrant inclusion, unless the custodian was the transferor. The mere fact that someone consented to gift-splitting does *not* make that person a transferor for estate tax purposes.

G transfers securities in trust with his two sons as income beneficiaries and his grandchildren as remaindermen. As trustee he has the power to accumulate or distribute the income, to add a beneficiary, to distribute income to one son, but not the other and to invade corpus in favor of either son, or both. Any one of these powers is sufficient to include the trust property in his estate, should he die possessed with one or more of these powers. Also, if the last of these powers was relinquished within three years of death, the gift in contemplation of death rule applies.

The above looks very similar to the retained life estate rule, discussed above, as well as the revocable transfer rule. In fact, there is

[18] Code Sec. 2035(d)(2).

considerable overlap and the IRS will argue whatever rule would cause the greater inclusion.

¶ 1731 POWERS OF APPOINTMENT

If the decedent had transferred property as a gift but retained certain powers of control, such powers could be extremely limited and still cause the property to be included in the decedent's gross estate under the retained life estate, reversion or revocable transfer rules, discussed above. If the decedent simply had been given a power by someone else over property never owned, the power would have to have been a *general power of appointment* to cause inclusion. The expression "general power" does not have to be stated as such.

To constitute a general power of appointment, the instrument creating the power must have given the decedent the power to appoint the property to the decedent, the decedent's estate or the creditors of either, by will and/or during life.[19] The following are *not* general powers:

1. The power to appoint the property to anyone in the world, such as a child or grandchild, except the decedent, the decedent's estate or their creditors.
2. The power to appoint it to anyone, including the decedent, but only with the consent of an adverse party, such as the remainderman or an income beneficiary, whose interest would be extinguished in the process.[20]
3. The power to withdraw from capital an amount equal to 5% of value or $5,000, whichever is greater, once a year.[21]
4. The power to invade capital for expenses related to health, education, support, or maintenance.[22]

Powers which fall short of general powers are called *special* or *limited* powers.

Once a general power exists, the release, lapse, or exercise of it during life creates a taxable gift. Also, if the decedent's will provides for the release, lapse or exercise of a general power in the will or lets it lapse or releases it, the property is includible in the estate.[23]

> ***Example:*** G transfers property in trust to his son, S, for life. S has the power to give the property to any or all of his children and the right to use whatever he wants for himself. The property will be included in S's estate.

---

[19] Code Sec. 2041(b)(1).
[20] Code Sec. 2041(b)(1)(C)(ii).
[21] Code Sec. 2041(b)(2).
[22] Code Sec. 2041(b)(1)(A).
[23] Code Sec. 2041(a)(2).

Expenses

¶ 1735 EXPENSES, DEBTS, AND TAXES

Expenses, debts, and taxes owed are deductible from the gross estate.[24] Note the following:

EXPENSES

These include funeral expenses and administration expenses. The latter can be deducted either from the estate or from the estate's income pursuant to the executor's election.[25] This also applies to losses from casualties and theft. Administration expenses include executor's fees, lawyer's fees, accountant's fees, court costs, and selling expenses when property is sold during administration to pay debts, taxes, and other expenses, or to effect distributions.

DEBTS

To be deductible without limit, the debts must have been enforceable against the decedent personally. Such debts would include charge accounts, car loans, and mortgages, for example. Nonrecourse debts are deductible only to the extent of the value of the property encumbered by the debt.

TAXES

Taxes owed by the decedent are deductible, such as accrued property taxes, unpaid income taxes, and unpaid gift taxes. But note that the last of these is offset by the provision governing a gift made within three years of death, which provides that the tax on such is also included in the gross estate.[26]

Marital Deduction

¶ 1740 COMMUNITY PROPERTY STATES

In a community property state, half of all property acquired during marriage belongs to each spouse. Thus, upon the death of the first spouse, only one-half of the property is included in the estate. This one-half interest qualifies for the marital deduction if willed to the surviving spouse.

COMMON-LAW STATES

Unlike in community property states, in common-law states, the marital deduction works as a deduction from the adjusted gross estate after all the property passing to the surviving spouse is included in the first place.[27] Here is a summary of the rules:

---

[24] Code Sec. 2053.
[25] Code Sec. 642(g).
[26] Code Sec. 2035(c).
[27] Code Sec. 2056.

1. *Amount of deduction.* The maximum marital deduction is 100% of the adjusted gross estate (gross estate less expenses, taxes, debts, and losses). The minimum deduction is whatever is left to the surviving spouse.
2. *Conditions for deduction—*
   (a) There must be a surviving spouse who is a U.S. citizen.
   (b) The surviving spouse must receive a *nonterminable interest* in property.
   (c) The property must be includible in the gross estate.
   (d) The property must pass or have passed to the surviving spouse.

THE MEANING OF "PASS"

Once the property is included in the estate, the surviving spouse can receive or have received the property outright as:

1. heir, devisee, or legatee,
2. surviving joint tenant,
3. beneficiary of life insurance,
4. spousal award (support during probate administration), or
5. beneficiary of a lapse, release, or exercise of a general power of appointment, etc.

Disclaimers by other beneficiaries will often lead to additional amounts passing to the surviving spouse. Only the net value of the property, after deducting any encumbrance on it, counts.

¶ 1741 TERMINABLE INTERESTS

It is not sufficient that property simply pass to the surviving spouse. The interest must also be nonterminable, i.e., it cannot lapse, expire, or terminate with the mere passage of time, or be bound by a contingency. Examples of terminable interests include term interests, life estates, and annuities. The purpose of the rule is to ensure that the surviving spouse receives full, or almost full, ownership of property owned by the decedent.

> ***Example 1:*** G dies, leaving his wife, W, income for life, after which the property goes to the grandchildren. W's life interest does *not* qualify for the marital deduction.

> ***Example 2:*** G dies, leaving W a life interest in his stock portfolio, but the interest goes to his children should she remarry. If she does not remarry, she can leave the stocks to anyone. No marital deduction is available, due to the condition.

One reason for the rule is that estate tax should be paid in at least one spouse's estate. If G's estate is given a deduction for an interest which ceases on W's death, the tax would be avoided for one generation or more. Thus, the marital deduction is designed merely to postpone taxation, not to avoid it altogether. On the other hand, if G leaves W all he has, the marital deduction is allowed.

Example 3: G purchased a joint and survivorship annuity providing for monthly payments to G for life, then to W, should she survive him. Upon G's death, the value of W's annuity is included in his estate and a marital deduction is allowed. Although W's interest expires upon her death, G left her all he had, and no other person may possess or enjoy the property after W's death.

MINIMUM REQUIRED INTEREST OF SURVIVING SPOUSE

The surviving spouse need not be given outright ownership of property in order to qualify for the marital deduction. A *life interest plus a general power of appointment* will suffice, or specifically:

1. The surviving spouse must be entitled to all income from the property for life, to be paid at least annually.

2. The surviving spouse must have a general power of appointment over the whole property, to be exercised alone and in all events.[28] Such power can be exercisable during life and/or by will. As noted above, the holder of a general power is treated as the owner of the property so that the gift or estate tax cannot be avoided.

In addition, the executor may elect to treat a life estate as "qualified terminable interest property."[29] This has the following effects:

1. A marital deduction is allowed for the full value of the property in which the life estate is carved out.

2. The full value of this property is includible in the surviving spouse's estate.[30]

To qualify for "QTIP" treatment all income must be distributed currently (at least once a year) to the surviving spouse and no powers may be held by anyone to appoint the property to someone other than such spouse during the lifetime of the surviving spouse.

---

[28] Code Sec. 2056(b)(5).

[29] Code Sec. 2056(b)(7).

[30] Code Sec. 2044.

¶ 1742 OPTIMAL SIZE OF THE MARITAL DEDUCTION

The "best" size of the marital deduction depends on the wealth, life expectancy, consumption habits, and probability of remarriage of the surviving spouse, as well as income tax brackets, existence of children or grandchildren, etc. At the very least, if there are other recipients of the decedent's bounty, the marital deduction should be reduced by the tax-free amount covered by the unified credit, currently $600,000.

Valuations

¶ 1745 IMPORTANCE OF VALUATION

Both the gift tax and the estate tax are levied on the *value* of property at the time of transfer, the time the gift is made and the date of death, respectively.[31] For income tax purposes, the value on the date of death also becomes the new owner's basis for determining gain or loss but, for gifts, the donor's basis carries over to the donee.[32] Except for listed securities and other fungible assets with quoted prices, valuation is at best a rough estimate, even when qualified appraisers are used.

ILLUSTRATIONS OF HOW PROPERTIES ARE VALUED

1. *Listed securities.* An average is taken between the high and low prices at the date of death (bid and asked prices, if sold over-the-counter). A dividend receivable is a separate asset, as is accrued interest on bonds.
2. *Notes receivable.* Full value equals face value plus accrued interest, unless the estate can establish a lower value based on interest rates, lack of security, or worthlessness.
3. *Insurance policies.* Value equals proceeds, if on the life of the decedent; otherwise, it is the cost of a comparable contract.
4. *Annuities.* Commercial annuities are valued at the price of comparable contracts, while private annuities are valued at the present value of expected payments over the expected life of the annuitant at the appropriate discount rate.[33]
5. *Life estates, terms for years, and remainders.* These are valued like private annuities by reference to standard unisex actuarial and present value tables published in the Treasury Regulations.
6. *Income in respect of a decedent.* This is future income already earned by the decedent, such as an account receivable. Even though the successor in interest must report this as income,

[31] Code Secs. 2033 and 2512.
[32] Code Secs. 1014 and 1015.
[33] Reg. § 20.2031-7 and Code Sec. 7520.

the present value is included in the estate. Some relief is provided by allowing an income tax deduction for the extra estate tax caused by the item.[34]

7. *Business interests.* An appraisal of assets plus the earning power of the business are the most significant factors.

8. *Real estate appraisals.* Real estate appraisals, taking into account comparable sales, would be required. No reduction is permitted for commissions, but they are deductible as administration expenses, if the real property is sold during administration to pay debts or taxes or to effect a distribution.

ALTERNATE VALUATION DATE

If the estate as a whole declines in value the first few months after the decedent's death, there may be an advantage in electing the alternate valuation date six months after the death. Note the following:

1. The alternate valuation can only be elected if a return is required, which is the case for a gross estate of $600,001 or more. Also, an estate tax actually payable, after credits, must be reduced if the election is made.[35]
2. The election covers all property included in the gross estate, and the latter must have declined.
3. The date of valuation is the earlier of six months after death or when the property is disposed of, i.e., sold, exchanged, or distributed.
4. Income generated after death does not influence value.
5. No reductions in value due to the mere lapse of time are allowed. Affected assets include patents and annuities. But if the surviving annuitant dies during the six-month period, only amounts collected are included.
6. If the decedent owned insurance on someone else's life and the insured dies by the alternate valuation date, the full proceeds are includible.
7. The reduced value must be used as the adjusted basis for income tax purposes.

VALUATION PLANNING CONSIDERATIONS

It is never too early to build valuation data. Here are some suggestions:

1. Collect and save comparable sales information.

---

[34] Code Sec. 691(c).

[35] Code Sec. 2032.

2. Choose the right appraiser. Specialized and different training is required to value closely held businesses, art, antiques, mineral deposits, real estate, and so on.
3. Keep a record of acquisition costs and dates of securities and real estate.
4. Keep gift tax returns filed. Remember that, under the unified system, lifetime transfers and transfers at death are looked upon as a continuum.

The Gift Tax

¶ 1750 INTRODUCTION

The preceding material introduced the estate tax. The sections that follow explore the gift and generation-skipping transfer taxes. All three taxes are, in fact, only different aspects of one tax, a tax on transfers of property from one individual, be it during life or at death. This section highlights the main aspects of gift taxes, such as the types of transfers subject to the tax, exclusions, deductions, and gift-splitting. Emphasis is placed on problem areas, such as jointly held property, powers of appointment, and transfers in trust. The new generation-skipping transfer tax is surveyed primarily through the use of examples.

¶ 1751 WHO PAYS THE GIFT TAX?

It may not seem logical at first, but if someone gives away property, that donor is liable for the gift tax.[36] This is because it is a substitute for the estate tax, i.e., if property is given away, it will not be part of the estate later. However, if for some reason the donor does not pay the tax, the donee is liable to the extent of the value of the gift.[37]

A donor can enter into an agreement with the donee that the latter pays the gift tax. The tax is then based on the value of the property less the gift tax. This is called a *net gift.* In a net gift situation the donor realizes a gain if the gift tax actually paid by the donee exceeds the cost basis.

Form 709 is used to report gifts over $10,000 to one donee in any calendar year. It is due April 15. There may not be any gift tax due with the return, but it must be filed even if:

1. The remaining unified credit exceeds any gift tax otherwise due.
2. The gifts are to charity and are fully deductible.

---

[36] Code Sec. 2502(c).

[37] Reg. § 25.2502-2.

3. Two spouses elect gift-splitting and the gifts do not exceed $20,000 per year per donee.

The gift tax is only applicable to gifts *from individuals*. The donee, however, can be anyone. A gift to a closely held corporation may be deemed to be a gift to its shareholders. Similarly, a gift from a small corporation may be attributed to the shareholders. Unless the donor is a resident or citizen of the United States or the property is situated in the United States, the gift tax is not levied.

¶ 1752 SCOPE OF THE GIFT TAX

Under local law a gift only takes place if a competent donor with donative intent delivers property to a competent donee who accepts the property. For gift tax purposes, the only requirement is that an individual transfer property for less than a "full and adequate consideration in money or money's worth." The donation of *services* is tax-free.[38]

Example 1: G, age 58, wishes to marry F, age 23. They enter into a pre-nuptial agreement whereby F promises to marry G and G promises F $350,000. F also waives any property rights upon divorce or G's death. Since love, affection, promises to marry, etc., are not money or money's worth, the $350,000 is a gift. For obvious reasons, the agreement is signed before the ceremony and the money transferred after it. G is entitled to the gift tax marital deduction, discussed below.

Example 2: G divorces W and transfers property to her as a property settlement. This is *not* a gift, since W gives up her marital and support rights, according to Congress.[39]

Example 3: G transfers property in trust to W for life, then to S, but retains the right to revoke the trust. No gift tax is due, because the transfer is incomplete. However, if G ever relinquishes his power to revoke, the transfer is complete at that time and the gift tax is computed on the current value, whether more or less than the value at the time of original transfer.

Example 4: A buys real property from B for $50,000. B was unaware that it was actually worth $60,000. The mere fact that A made a bargain purchase does not create a gift from B to A. However, if they were close family members, a gift is presumed if the consideration was substantially more or less than the value.

Example 5: A sold securities worth $50,000 to his son B for $30,000. There is a gift of $20,000 from A to B. If they were sold for $65,000, B would have given his father a gift of $15,000.

---

[38] Code Sec. 2512(b).

[39] Code Sec. 2516.

Example 6: A gave the above securities to B, but subject to a liability of $40,000. The gift is only $10,000.

Example 7: A lent his daughter $10,000 to go to college. Upon graduation, A tore up the note, resulting in a gift of $10,000. If the "loan" was intended as a gift initially, the gift was complete at that time.

Example 8: Appreciated securities are given to a political organization. No gift tax is imposed on such transfers, but the appreciation is subject to income tax.[40]

Example 9: A shareholder transfers cash and property to a closely held corporation for business reasons. Even though some shares are owned by others, even family members, this will be a contribution to capital, increasing the basis in the shareholder's stock.[41] In general, transfers made in the ordinary course of business are exempt from the gift tax.

Example 10: A purchases U.S. savings bonds registered to A, payable to B upon A's death. B has a mere expectancy. Any time before death, A may cash in the bonds. Therefore, there is no gift.

Example 11: Someone purchases life insurance, naming a son as beneficiary. There is no gift because the insured may change the beneficiary at any time. If the insured irrevocably designates the beneficiary, then there is a gift of the value of the policy, if any, but not of the proceeds.

¶ 1753 MISCELLANEOUS GIFTS

The following transfers constitute taxable gifts:

1. Paying for a daughter's wedding is a taxable gift, even if it is "support" for income tax purposes.
2. Irrevocable transfers to a trust.
3. The cancellation of indebtedness (except in a business setting).
4. The transfer of insurance policies.
5. Payment of life insurance premiums on policies owned by others, unless the payor is a beneficiary.
6. The assignment of a judgment.
7. Nonqualified disclaimers of jointly held property upon the death of the other joint tenant. A qualified disclaimer can be made within nine months of death and be effective for tax purposes. (Tenancy by the entirety property must be disclaimed within nine months of creation.)

---

[40] Code Secs. 84 and 2501(a)(5).

[41] Code Sec. 358.

8. The purchase of U.S. savings bonds in the name of another.
9. The creation of a joint tenancy with someone (other than the spouse) contributing less than an equal share, except for bank accounts.
10. Paying off somebody else's debts.

¶ 1754 ANNUAL EXCLUSION

An individual can give away up to $10,000 a year to any one donee without gift tax consequences.[42] Because of gift-splitting with a spouse (returns must be filed even if no tax is due), this amount may be effectively doubled.[43] The exclusion is only allowed for *present interests,* i.e., interests unrestricted as to immediate use, possession, or enjoyment.

Example 1: A donor gives away securities worth $40,000 to a son and daughter-in-law in joint names. If gift-splitting is elected, no gift tax results. The gifts are deemed made by two people and four times $10,000 is $40,000.

Example 2: A grantor transfers property in trust to A for life, then to B for life, then to C. Only one exclusion is available, because only A has a present interest.

Example 3: A donor transfers property in trust with three sons to share the income equally. Three exclusions are available.

Example 4: In order to split income with a child, age five, a mother transfers securities to herself as custodian for the child under the Uniform Transfers to Minors Act. The exclusion is available if the securities and the income may be expended on the child before age 21, any unexpended portion passes to the child at age 21, and, if the child dies, it all goes to the child's estate.[44] Note that the income can still be accumulated.

Example 5: Sam transfers property to a trust. The trustee may pay the income to his wife or accumulate it. Upon her death, the property plus accumulated income is to be paid to their grandchildren. *No* exclusion is available. The remainder does not qualify and the wife is not guaranteed any present enjoyment either.

There is no real correlation between future interests and terminable interests.

Example 6: A transfer is made to W for life, then to S. The 100% gift tax marital deduction is not available, because W's interest is terminable. However, the $10,000 exclusion is available because it is a present interest.

---

[42] Code Sec. 2503(b).
[43] Code Sec. 2513.
[44] Code Sec. 2503(c).

¶ 1755 GIFT SPLITTING

Gift splitting has the following advantages:

1. Two annual exclusions per donee per year are available instead of one.
2. The spouses' estates can be somewhat equalized because only one-half of the gifts will come back as "adjusted taxable gifts" in the estate tax return of the contributing spouse.
3. The noncontributing spouse may be in a lower gift-tax bracket or even have an unused unified credit, so that no tax is presently payable.

To effect gift splitting, all gifts made during a given year by both spouses must be covered by the election.[45] There is no joint gift tax return. Therefore, both spouses must file either Form 709 or Form 709A (the short form) to elect gift-splitting. They become jointly and severally liable for the gift tax, however.

SPECIAL RULES

Note the following special rules:

1. The couple must be married at the time of the gift, not necessarily at the end of the calendar year during which the gift is made. However, if they are not married at the end of the year, the donor cannot remarry until the following year.
2. Both spouses must be residents or citizens of the U.S. at the time of the gift.
3. If either spouse dies within three years of the gift, the gift tax, if any, paid by such spouse will be included in such spouse's gross estate.
4. If the gift was made by both, e.g., jointly held or community property, gift splitting takes place automatically. No consent is needed, since one-half of the gift was in fact made by each.

¶ 1756 HOW TO COMPUTE THE GIFT TAX

The gift tax is computed on a cumulative basis as follows:

1. Add up all gifts made in excess of $10,000 per donee in the year plus gifts of future interests.
2. Spouses may elect to treat all gifts to third parties as made one-half by each.
3. Deduct the lesser of $10,000 or amount of gifts per donee.

[45] Code Sec. 2513.

4. Deduct the 100% marital deduction on gifts of present interests to spouse. (These are not even reportable.)
5. Deduct gifts to charities.
6. The result is taxable gifts.
7. Add taxable gifts to prior lifetime taxable gifts.
8. Look up the gift tax on the cumulative total in 7, above, in the multipurpose transfer tax table in Code Sec. 2001.
9. Look up the gift tax on previous lifetime gifts.
10. The difference (8 – 9) is the tax imposed.
11. Reduce the unified credit by the tax imposed.
12. Once the unified credit ($192,800 in 1987 or later) is reduced to zero, taxes must be paid currently.

The effect is to tax each gift at a higher marginal tax.

CREATIONS OF CO-OWNERSHIPS

Whenever someone makes another person a co-owner of property, the transferor has made a taxable gift.

> ***Example:*** Two brothers buy a building for $400,000. Of the $80,000 down payment one brother puts up $60,000, but they are both liable on the mortgage. Since one brother paid $20,000 more than half, this constitutes a gift to the other brother. This is true whether they are tenants in common or joint tenants. If they wished to avoid a gift, they might take 3/4-1/4 interests as tenants in common. Paying off more than half the mortgage will result in additional gifts each year, but only principal reductions will count as gifts and most of the payments will be for interest for many years.

¶ 1757 EXCEPTION FOR BANK ACCOUNTS

Someone who puts money in a joint savings or checking account is still free to withdraw part or all of it. Therefore, there is no completed gift until the co-tenant withdraws more than any contribution made. Similar rules apply to brokerage accounts and U.S. savings bonds issued in two names.

¶ 1758 GENERAL POWERS OF APPOINTMENT

General powers of appointment were discussed in connection with estate taxes (see ¶ 1731). If someone possesses a general power of appointment and the power is exercised, released, or simply lapses during the holder's lifetime, there is a gift.[46]

---

[46] Code Sec. 2514.

Example 1: G takes out a $100,000 life insurance policy and transfers all incidents of ownership to his wife, including the right to change the beneficiary. Before G transferred the policy, G named his child as beneficiary. His wife took no action and many years later G died, survived by his wife. Whether she knew it or not, her right to change the beneficiary to anyone, including herself, constitutes a general power of appointment. Up to the date of G's death she could have changed the beneficiary; when G died, her power lapsed and the child received a vested right to the proceeds. The wife is deemed to have made a completed gift to the child on the date of G's death in the amount of $100,000, the proceeds of the policy. She would have to file a gift tax return and pay the tax if her tax liability exceeds her remaining unified credit. The problem could have been avoided by specifying that she could change the beneficiary to anyone except herself or her estate. Had she been able to change the beneficiary with the consent of G, this would have had two consequences:

1. G's right to veto any change would have constituted an incident of ownership, making the proceeds includible in G's estate.[47]

2. The wife's power would not have been a general power, but a limited power, the lapse of which would not have constituted a taxable gift.

Note that a power of appointment only exists if created by another person. When a general power is exercised, released or lapses during the holder's lifetime, the gift tax is levied on the full market value of the property subject to that power, while the estate tax is levied on a testamentary exercise, release or lapse. Special powers are not taxed.

Example 2: G transfers property in trust to his wife, W, for life. W is also given the power to appoint the property to anyone by gift or will. If W exercises the power in favor of anyone, even an unrelated party, a gift tax results.

Example 3: Same as Example 1, except that W has the power to appoint the property to anyone except herself, her estate, or the creditors of either. She exercises the power in favor of her children and grandchildren. Since she only has a special power, no gift tax results. However, under Example 1, G or his estate could claim the marital deduction; in this example, no deduction is available.

Example 4: Same facts as in Example 1, except that W needs G's consent to exercise the power. No gift tax will result, because the

---

[47] Code Sec. 2042.

power is reduced to a special power when the creator's consent is needed.

Example 5: G transfers property to W for life, with the remainder to his children. W can appoint the property to anyone, but only with the consent of the children. An exercise is not taxable because the consent of an adverse party is required.

Example 6: G transferred property in trust for his son, S, for life, then to his grandchildren. S also has the power to appoint up to 10% of the value of the property each year. If S chooses not to do this, the lapse of his power each year will constitute a gift of 10% of the value of the property each year (less the greater of 5% or $5,000). The same result will follow if S exercises his power in favor of an individual, other than himself, each year.

Powers limited to an ascertainable standard, e.g., for the health, education, maintenance and support of the power holder, and powers to appoint up to $5,000 or 5% of the property, whichever is greater, each year on a noncumulative basis, are exempt from gift tax.

The Generation-Skipping Transfer Tax

¶ 1760 GENERATION SKIPPING

Historically, the most effective way to avoid the decimation of large estates through the payment of up to 70% estate taxes in each generation was to skip generations.

Example: At age 70, G sets up a trust to pay income to S, his son, for life, then to SS, his grandson, for life, with the remainder to SSD, his great-granddaughter, then age 5. Two generations would be skipped, since no estate tax will be imposed until the death of the remainderman. Of course, G's transfer would be subject to gift tax.

In fact, the son and the grandson could exercise all of the following powers without estate tax consequences:

1. a life income interest,
2. power to invade corpus for health, education, and support,
3. power to draw the greater of $5,000 or 5% of value each year,
4. limited power to appoint the property to anyone, except themselves, their estates or the creditors of either, and
5. right to become a trustee.

SUMMARY OF THE GENERATION-SKIPPING TRANSFER TAX

The purpose of the GST tax is to subject property to at least one wealth transfer tax once in each generation. Thus, a flat GST tax equal to the maximum estate and gift tax rate is imposed on three types of transfers: *taxable distributions, taxable terminations,* and *direct skips* to someone at least two generations below that of the transferor or donor.[48] A $1 million exemption is allowed each transferor, as well as a $2 million exemption per grandchild for pre-1990 direct skips.

THREE TYPES OF GENERATION-SKIPPING TRANSFERS

Taxable Distributions

A taxable distribution is a distribution out of income or corpus to a beneficiary at least two generations below that of the grantor (unless the beneficiary's parent is deceased and is a linear descendant of the grantor) while an older generation beneficiary has an interest in the trust.

Example: At his death G set up a trust for his daughter for life, with the remainder to his grandson. To the extent the trustee makes distributions to his grandson during the daughter's life, and does so, taxable distributions result. (To reduce the effect of double taxation, the GST tax is deductible to the grandson for income tax purposes.)[48a]

Taxable Terminations

A taxable termination means that by reason of death, expiration of time, or otherwise, the interest of a non-skip person terminates and a skip person becomes the recipient of the trust property or the sole beneficiary.

Example: G set up a trust with income to his daughter for life, with the remainder to his grandson. If, upon the death of the daughter, the trust terminates and the trust property is transferred to the grandson, a taxable termination has occurred.

Direct Skips

A direct skip occurs when one or more generations are bypassed altogether and property is transferred directly to, or in trust for, a skip person.

Example: G makes a transfer in trust for his grandson for 20 years, whereupon the trust fund is to be turned over to the grandson. A direct skip occurs upon the funding of the trust, not when the grandson's mother dies.

Note that beneficiaries of a trust do not "count" for purposes of the GST tax unless they have a present right to a distribution or, at least are permissible distributees.[49]

---

[48] Code Sec. 2612.
[48a] Code Sec. 164(a)(5).
[49] Code Sec. 2652(c).

THE TAX RATE

The GST tax rate is the highest marginal estate and gift tax rate, i.e., 55%. This rate is multiplied by the "inclusion ratio," which equals 1 less the exemption assigned to a transfer divided by the value of the property transferred (less death taxes and charitable contributions). Thus, the "applicable rate" equals

Tax Rate × (1 − GST Exemption Allocated/(Value Transferred − Death Taxes − Charitable Portion).

The effect of the use of the inclusion ratio is to exempt the appreciation allocable to the GST exemption from the GST tax when ultimately imposed.[50]

> ***Example:*** G transfers $4 million in trust for his daughter for life, with the remainder to his grandson, and allocates his $1 million exemption to the transfer. The inclusion ratio equals 1 − $1 million/$4 million. If, at the time the daughter dies the trust fund is worth $8 million, the GST tax is $3.3 million (55% × 75% of $8 million).

EXEMPTIONS

Exemptions from the generation-skipping transfer tax fall into three categories:

1. A $1 million exemption per transferor ($2 million if "gift-splitting" is elected by transferor's spouse).[51]
2. An unlimited number of $2 million grandchild exemptions for pre-1990 direct skips ($4 million with "gift-splitting").
3. An unlimited exemption for direct skips to a grandchild if the grandchild's parent is deceased and was a lineal descendant of the transferor, the transferor's spouse, or former spouse.[52]

GENERATION ASSIGNMENTS

Individuals are assigned along family lines, whether by adoption, whole or half blood.[53] Thus, a spouse is assigned to the same generation as the transferor, as are siblings and first cousins. Similarly, children, nephews and nieces belong to the generation below. Other beneficiaries are assigned to one generation below the transferor if they are more than 12½ years younger, but not more than 37½, two generations below if more than 37½ years younger, etc.

---

[50] Code Secs. 2641 and 2642.

[51] Code Sec. 2631.

[52] Code Sec. 2612(c)(2).

[53] Code Sec. 2651.

¶ 1761 TAX COMPUTATIONS

The following examples regarding the generation-skipping transfer tax assume that exemptions are exhausted and that the tax rate is 50%.

Example 1: *Taxable Distribution.* A taxable distribution of $1 million is made to G's grandson, who must pay $500,000 in GST taxes, retaining the rest.

Example 2: *Taxable Termination.* Upon termination of a trust, $1 million remains in the trust and is subject to the GST tax. The trustee pays the tax of $500,000, remitting the other half to the skip person, the grandson.

Example 3: *Testamentary Direct Skip.* G left $3 million to the grandson, before taxes. After estate taxes, $1.5 million remained. The GST tax is levied on the amount received by the distributee in a direct skip. Thus, $1 million is distributed to the grandson, and the trustee or executor pays a GST tax of $500,000.[54]

Example 4: *Inter Vivos Direct Skip.* G made a gift of $1 million to the grandson. The GST tax is $500,000. For gift tax purposes a gift of $1.5 million was made.[55] Thus, a gift tax of $750,000 is payable as well. Note, however, that it took only $2,250,000 to transfer $1 million to the grandson, as opposed to $3 million in a testamentary transfer.

¶ 1762 MISCELLANEOUS GST TAX RULES

Here are four miscellaneous GST tax rules:

1. *Payment of tax.* The GST tax is paid by the transferor or trustee except that the distributee pays the tax on taxable distributions.[56] The GST tax return is due by the 15th day of the fourth month after the taxable year of the person who pays the tax and during which the transfer takes place, except that in the case of a direct skip, other than from a trust, the return is due at the same time as the estate or gift tax return is due with respect to the transfer.[57]

2. *Credits and deductions.* Up to 5% credit is allowed for state GST taxes imposed on taxable distributions and terminations resulting from death.[58] Expenses, debts and taxes are deductible under the same principles as for estate tax purposes.[59]

3. *Unused exemptions.* Any unused GST tax exemption is first allocated to inter vivos direct skips, then to testamentary

---

[54] Code Sec. 2623.
[55] Code Sec. 2515.
[56] Code Sec. 2603.
[57] Code Sec. 2662.
[58] Code Sec. 2604.
[59] Code Sec. 2622(b).

direct skips, and finally to generation-skipping trusts from which taxable transfers may be made after death.[60]

4. *Basis adjustments.* Special use valuation under Code Sec. 2032A is available for property included in the gross estate, and alternate valuation under Code Sec. 2032 is available in the cases of direct skips of property included in the gross estate and taxable terminations resulting from death.[61]

   Property receives a step-up in basis for GST taxes attributable to appreciation, but if a taxable termination at death has occurred, a fair market value basis generally results.[62]

This concludes coverage of three wealth transfer taxes and their interrelationships. The next chapter will cover planning opportunities and applications, e.g., "estate planning."

---

[60] Code Sec. 2632.
[61] Code Sec. 2624.
[62] Code Sec. 2654.

CHAPTER 18

ESTATE PLANNING

¶ 1801 INTRODUCTION

The first half of this chapter discusses the tools and techniques of estate planning, e.g., housekeeping items, such as legal terminology, the use of wills and trust, the selection and use of fiduciaries, as well as lifetime gifts, and planning for the dead and dying.

The second half is a survey of modern transfer tax reduction strategies. Here, shown in detail, are several proven ways for the planner to reduce or eliminate the client's family's transfer taxes. Techniques discussed include deferred payment sales, charitable lead trusts, and grantor trust annuities.

Tools and Techniques of Estate Planning

¶ 1802 SCOPE OF ESTATE PLANNING

Broadly defined, estate planning comprises the accumulation, conservation, and disposition of capital and income. The most common ways to accumulate wealth and pass it on are:

1. Savings and investments.
2. Inter vivos gifts outright or in trust.
3. Annuities, including joint and survivorship annuities.
4. Jointly held property.
5. Life insurance.
6. Wills.
7. Family businesses, whether partnerships or corporations.

8. Social security benefits, including disability, old age and survivor benefits.
9. Pension and profit-sharing plans, including self-employment plans and individual retirement plans.
10. Trusts created by will (testamentary trusts).
11. Miscellaneous, such as the creation of powers of appointment, life estates, remainders, and reversions.

¶ 1803 USEFUL LEGAL TERMS

Lawyers use expressions like "corpus," "general power of appointment" and "preresidual pecuniary marital deduction formula bequest," not because they want to show off, but because these expressions have precise meanings. These meanings may have evolved over the years through statutes and court decisions and their use protects people. Here are some terms employed in connection with wills.

Administrator/Administratrix: Appointee of a court to administer an estate of an intestate deceased. Duties include the filing of tax returns.

Administration expenses: Costs of managing and settling an estate, such as fees of executors, lawyers, accountants, and appraisers.

Beneficiary: Anyone receiving a benefit under a will or trust.

Bequest: A testamentary gift of personal property.

Codicil: An addition to a will executed with the same formalities as a will.

Corpus: The principal of the estate or a trust as opposed to the income generated. Capital gains are generally allocated to corpus.

Devise: A testamentary gift of real property to a devisee.

Estate: The probate estate is property owned by the decedent at death, but less property passing by operation of law, such as jointly owned property and life insurance paid to a named beneficiary. The gross estate for tax purposes can encompass much more.

Exculpatory clause: A statement in the will which relieves the executor of personal liability except for fraud.

Executor/Executrix: A legal person appointed in the will to administer an estate.

Holographic will: Some states recognize such a will, which must be written entirely by the testator in longhand.

Intestate: To die intestate means to die without a valid will.

Issue: Lineal descendants of the testator, e.g., children, grandchildren, etc.

Legatee: Beneficiary receiving personal property.

Letters testamentary: A certificate issued by a court showing that a will has been admitted to probate and giving the executor the authority to act for the estate.

Per stirpes and per capita: This can best be illustrated by an example.

Example: The testator was survived by one son and five grandchildren. Two grandchildren were the children of the son, the other three were the children of a predeceased daughter.

If the decedent had left the descendants the estate *per capita,* they would each get one-sixth based on a head-count. But if the estate was left to them *per stirpes,* the son would receive one-half, his children nothing at this time, and the other three children would share their deceased mother's half, still winding up with one-sixth.

Probate court: Court having jurisdiction of wills.

Real estate: Land, buildings, condominium units, and the like, distinguished from personal property. But if the client owns real estate indirectly, the stock, partnership interest and beneficial interest in a trust are all personal property.

Testate: The act of dying with a valid will.

Testator/Testatrix: A person who makes and leaves a will.

Trust: Someone transfers property to a trustee during life (inter vivos trust) or through a will (testamentary trust). The trustee, individual or corporate, manages the property and distributes or accumulates income and principal according to the will or trust instrument.

Will or No Will

¶ 1805 THE LAW OF INTESTATE SUCCESSION

A person who dies without a will dies intestate. State law then specifies who inherits the property, whether in accordance with the decedent's wishes or not.

Example: A client, A, dies suddenly, leaving a wife and two minor children. Under many state laws his widow receives one-third of his estate and the children two-thirds. Since they are minors, a guardian has to be appointed. Even if the widow is appointed, she may have to provide a bond, be under court supervision, file annual accountings, etc. These expensive and time-consuming procedures could have been avoided by a properly drawn will.

Even though each state has its own laws of intestate succession, the following results are representative of what typically happens to the estate if A has left no will:

1. If A leaves a wife and children, she gets one-third, the children two-thirds.
2. If A leaves a wife and no children, she gets it all.
3. If A leaves children and no wife, the children get it all.
4. If A leaves grandchildren, they share their parents share if the parents are deceased.
5. If A leaves no wife and no children, A's parents receive it all.
6. If A leaves no wife, children, or parents, A's brothers and sisters share equally, with their children receiving their deceased parents' share.

Dying without a will therefore guarantees the wife and children the property. Even if A leaves a will not mentioning his wife and children, he can generally cut off his children, but *not* his wife. She is typically entitled to one-third, will or no will. However, if there are no children, she generally receives only one-half if the will is contrary, as opposed to all if there is no will. The widow is harder to disinherit than her children. However, even her forced share qualifies for the marital deduction.

OTHER REASONS FOR HAVING A WILL

Here are the main advantages of having a will:

1. The testator can specify who shall receive what and when, and who shall safeguard the assets and in what fashion.
2. The testator can draft the will to minimize estate and inheritance taxes and administration expenses.
3. The survivors are less likely to be involved in court battles.
4. The will can name the executor and the guardian for minor children.
5. Final instructions based on the knowledge of the testator's own property may be invaluable.
6. The testator can forgive debts owed by close friends and family members.

WHY PEOPLE DO NOT HAVE WILLS

Psychologists have determined that youth and a relative lack of property, in addition to the reasons listed below, are factors contributing to intestacy:

1. People are intimidated by lawyers.

2. People subconsciously rebel against "The Law" and the system.
3. Many individuals hate to ask for professional help unless strictly "necessary."
4. It is hard to face one's own mortality.
5. Some people cannot make decisions easily, such as the distribution of their belongings.
6. People avoid confronting their true feelings about their spouses and other family members.
7. To make a will requires an appraisal of "worth," difficult for someone with low self-esteem.
8. Discussions about money are distasteful to some.
9. If people are passive and lack initiative, they keep putting it off until intestacy results.

¶ 1806 JOINT AND MUTUAL WILLS

A joint will is the will of two people, usually spouses, executed on one form. It should not be done. It does not simplify matters and may lead to complications. For one thing, probate on the death of the survivor may become cumbersome.

Mutual wills are executed on separate forms, but are normally reciprocal. Both types of wills are usually employed to ensure the first to die that the property will wind up where wanted when the survivor dies. Consider the following disadvantages of joint and mutual wills:

1. A court may find that the agreement not to revoke is unenforceable, even though the parties intended otherwise.
2. Even though the parties intended to be able to revoke, the survivor may be locked in.
3. A survivor who does not want to be locked in may simply dissipate the property or give it away.
4. Circumstances change over time and flexibility is important.
5. Joint and mutual wills lead to litigation.
6. If there is a binding agreement that the surviving spouse leave the property to a third party, e.g., the children, the marital deduction may be unavailable. The gift tax may also be imposed.

In conclusion, if the client is afraid of what will happen to the property after death, e.g., the surviving spouse may remarry and the new spouse gain access to the funds, the client should use annuities or set up a trust to preclude such a contingency.

¶ 1807 WHEN TO REVIEW A WILL

A will, sensible when made, may lead to insensible results years later. At a minimum the client should review a will at the following times:

1. When the estate may be affected by changes in tax laws. An example is the unlimited marital deduction first made available in 1982.
2. Both parents should review their wills when a child is born.

Example: A leaves everything to his wife, confident that she will take care of his son. After a daughter is born, A dies. The daughter may receive one-third, A's son nothing and the widow two-thirds, unless it is clear from the will that all children, including the afterborn, shall receive nothing.

3. Review the will upon marriage or divorce. Upon marriage, a male client may wish that his wife receives more than her statutory share. Upon divorce he may wish to make sure his ex-wife receives nothing. In most jurisdictions, a divorce revokes any bequest to the ex-spouse, but a decedent may still wish to leave a remembrance.

¶ 1808 THE WILL WHEN MOVING

This is the age of the migratory worker. A client who works for a national or multinational firm is apt to be transferred to another state or another country. Each state has its own laws governing wills, trusts and estates, gifts, disclaimers, charitable contributions, intestate succession, etc. Therefore, the client's will should be reviewed each time the testator moves to another jurisdiction. The age of majority may be 21 in one state and 18 in the next, and the term "children" may or may not include adopted children, to name just two specific problems.

¶ 1809 COMMUNITY PROPERTY

Special problems occur when moving to and from community property jurisdictions (there are nine such states—Arizona, California, Idaho, Louisiana, Nevada, New Mexico, Texas, Washington and Wisconsin). For added complexity, the community property states have different rules. Community property retains its character after a move to a common-law state, sometimes even after a sale and reinvestment. Many such problems can be dealt with through interpersonal agreements and living trusts.

¶ 1810 FOREIGN LOCATIONS

When foreign locations are involved, it is wise to consider two wills, one for property abroad, one for U.S. property. Try to keep property interests outside the U.S. to a minimum, U.S. bank and brokerage accounts and U.S. trusts are helpful. Property abroad will have to go through probate abroad. The U.S. estate tax is levied on all property, wherever situated.[1] If the foreign jurisdiction taxes the property as well, a foreign death tax credit is available.[2]

¶ 1811 LETTERS OF LAST INSTRUCTION

It is advisable to give the executor or lawyer a list of final instructions separate from the will to be opened when the will "becomes effective" (upon death). Here are some examples of final instructions:

1. Listing of all real and personal property owned. (Bank accounts may be especially important since the banks may make no effort to pay beneficiaries unless the latter know about the accounts.)
2. The location of the will and other important papers, such as social security cards, marriage certificates and citizenship papers.
3. Desired funeral arrangements.
4. A list of insurance policies, pension and profit-sharing plans, and the like.
5. If the will contains unusual bequests, disinheritances and the like, special explanations may be furnished.
6. Instructions regarding any business interests.
7. The location of safe-deposit boxes and keys to same.

Use of Trusts

¶ 1815 HOW TO USE TRUSTS

When someone creates a trust, assets are turned over to a trustee to hold and manage for the benefit of a third party. If the grantor gives up control, the trust is treated as a separate taxpayer with the result that either the trust or the beneficiary, but not both, will be taxed on the income. (See the chapter on family tax planning.) A client who sets up a trust should know exactly what is to be accomplished and that the trust instrument reflects just that.

A trust can exist for a few years, a generation, or several generations. It can be funded or unfunded and provide for current distributions or for accumulation of income.

ILLUSTRATIONS OF TRUST OBJECTIVES

The trust objectives are the following:

---

[1] Code Sec. 2033.

[2] Code Sec. 2014.

1. Provide income for life to parents (a support trust), to an ex-spouse until death or remarriage (an alimony trust), or to children.
2. Provide for discretionary invasion of corpus or its outright distribution.
3. Defer payments to children or grandchildren until they reach a certain age.
4. Provide secrecy about the client's financial affairs after death.
5. Prevent a widow from turning the funds over to her new husband.
6. Avoid probate and hasten the distribution of the wealth. Many financial goals are difficult to accomplish without trusts. For example, the client wishes to provide the children with income until age 30 and then provide the grandchildren with income until they are 30. It would be very difficult to hand over the securities to the children and make sure they only touch the income, and then make them turn them over to their children, etc. As a practical matter, only a corporate trustee, such as a commercial bank, can make sure the grantor's wishes are carried out.

¶ 1816 WHEN TRUSTS ARE CREATED

Trusts may be classified by when and how they come into (or go out of) existence.

1. *Testamentary trusts.* These are created at death pursuant to the will to make it unnecessary to liquidate the estate and to carry out testator's wishes for many years.
2. *Inter vivos or living trusts.* These are set up during life to accomplish living objectives, such as asset management, but also to avoid probate. "Pour-over" provisions in the will can provide for additional transfers to the trust after death. If the trust was revocable, it becomes irrevocable when the grantor dies.
3. *Revocable trusts.* These can be "recalled" during the grantor's lifetime. As a result, the transfer is not subject to gift tax, but the grantor still pays income tax on the income. Upon death the trust funds are subject to estate tax. The advantages of such trusts are that management is shifted to the trustee, that probate is avoided, and that the grantor can make changes if desired to streamline an estate plan.

4. *Irrevocable trusts.* The transfer is subject to gift tax, not to estate tax, and the income is shifted. But remember: the client cannot undo the transfer once the transfer is made.
5. *Life insurance trusts.* Making an irrevocable transfer of a life insurance policy to a trust will keep the proceeds out of the estate, providing the insured lives over three years thereafter, keeps no incidents of ownership in the policy, and the proceeds will not be used to pay claims against the estate. The gift tax will be based on the low value of the policy at the time of transfer. If the trust is unfunded the client has two choices:
    (a) The client can pay up the policy, but unless it is a term policy, it will have a high value subject to gift tax.
    (b) The client can continue to pay the premiums after the transfer, each of which will be taxable gifts (to the extent the annual premiums exceed $10,000).

In addition to estate tax avoidance, the trust can protect the beneficiary, authorize the trustee to use the proceeds for support and maintenance of family members and/or to invest the proceeds for long-term growth.

¶ 1817 HOW TO MAXIMIZE ENJOYMENT OF PROPERTY WITHOUT ESTATE INCLUSION

If property is transferred in trust by gift or inheritance, it is almost incredible to what extent the beneficiary can use and enjoy that property *without* that property *being includible in the gross estate.* The beneficiary can have all the following rights and powers:

1. The right to receive all the income from the property for life.
2. The power to draw funds from the trust (invade corpus), as long as the power is subject to an ascertainable standard relating to health, education, support and maintenance.[3]
3. A power to withdraw the greater of 5% of the value of the trust property or $5,000 each year.[4]
4. The power to appoint all or part of the property to anyone, during life or by will, except to the powerholder, the estate, or the creditors of either.[5]
5. The beneficiary can even be the trustee of the trust.

None of the above will subject the property to estate tax, but there may be gift tax, and/or generation-skipping transfer tax consequences (see the previous chapter).

---

[3] Code Sec. 2041(b)(1)(A).
[4] Code Sec. 2041(b)(2).
[5] Code Sec. 2041(b)(1).

¶ 1818 POWER-OF-APPOINTMENT PLANNING

An estate plan can retain desired flexibility through the use of powers of appointment. A trust is necessary to give someone such a power.

> ***Example:*** A male client has accumulated a substantial securities portfolio. Two of his children are minors and his wife has a limited knowledge of investments and money management. One alternative is to simply leave everything to her, confident that she can handle it. Another alternative is to place the property in trust and provide:
>
> 1. An income to the wife for life (or until remarriage),
> 2. the rest to the children upon her death, and
> 3. provide her with a power of appointment.

This type of arrangement makes it unnecessary to guess what the family's future needs will be and reduces the worry about her potential new husband. The power of appointment can be broad or narrow. It may be exercised only in favor of children and grandchildren, for example, or in favor of other relatives, or even in favor of the wife. It can be a lifetime power and/or a testamentary power.

If the power is general, e.g., the wife in the above example can appoint the property to herself or her estate, the transfer qualifies for the marital deduction. A special, or limited, power does *not* qualify for the marital deduction, because her estate will not include the property. If she has a general power and exercises it during life, the transfer is subject to gift tax, but the property is removed from her estate.

The greatest advantages of a limited power are as follows:

1. The wife has an income to live on.
2. She can appoint the principal only to persons designated by the decedent.
3. She cannot appoint the principal to herself.
4. The property will not be taxed in her estate.

Use of Fiduciaries

¶ 1820 FIDUCIARY DEFINED

A fiduciary is a legal person, individual or corporation, who is appointed by the client or a court to handle someone's affairs, personal and/or financial. Such legal person has a duty to act for the benefit of another in matters regarding his appointment. A breach of a fiduciary duty leads to legal sanctions and possibly personal liability.

¶ 1821 TYPES OF FIDUCIARIES

The most common fiduciaries discussed here in connection with the client's affairs are:

Administrator/Administratrix: A person appointed by a court to handle the estate if there is no will or the executor is unable or unwilling to serve.

Conservator: A person appointed by a court to handle the affairs of a living, but mentally incompetent, person, e.g., someone who is insane, too old, or too sick to do it personally.

Executor/Executrix: A person appointed in the will to handle the estate through probate.

Guardian: A person who is appointed to raise minor children and/or handle their financial affairs in the absence of, or death of, the parents.

Trustee: A person who holds legal title to property and manages it for the benefit of beneficiaries.

¶ 1822 WHO SHOULD SERVE AS FIDUCIARY

A fiduciary could be an individual or corporation. People often select individuals in order to have a "friendly trustee," such as a spouse, other relative, or a friend. If the client employs individuals, consider the following:

1. The client may use more than one fiduciary simultaneously. Theoretically, there is no limit to the number. In the interest of family harmony, the client may find that if appointing one brother, the client may also have to appoint the other. Co-fiduciaries may be useful to split up a task, e.g., one makes investment decisions, the other evaluates the needs of beneficiaries, etc. When the client serves as fiduciary, the spouse may be an ideal co-fiduciary. If the client uses more than one fiduciary, consider an odd number, and let majority rule.
2. Individuals are mortal. Therefore, make sure to provide for a successor fiduciary.
3. Do not select an individual merely because of a family tie. A fiduciary must be qualified to represent the interests at stake, be mature, and have integrity. A family member may have a personal touch, but sometimes people hesitate to disclose information to anyone except strangers.

The trend is towards the use of professional fiduciaries, particularly corporations and notably large commercial banks. The reasons are:

1. A bank, unlike a lawyer or other individual, provides continuity. Bank failures happen, but many large banks are already more than 100 years old.
2. A bank can provide investment counseling, tax advice, accounting services, and administration. It has a whole package of services available. The entire bank staff will back up the client when needed.
3. The bank is conservative, unlike many individuals.
4. An individual is more susceptible to the temptation of converting funds to personal use.

The disadvantage in using a bank as a fiduciary is its reluctance to handle trusts and estates below $100,000, unless the funds are pooled in a common trust fund. Even so, the minimum annual fee is likely to be $1,500 or more.

¶ 1823 FIDUCIARY POWERS

Generally, a fiduciary's power to do anything is severely limited by law, unless broader powers are expressly granted. Following are some of the most useful powers the client should at least consider giving to a fiduciary:

INVESTMENT POWERS

1. *Securities.* A fiduciary is limited in securities investments to "legal lists" of approved securities in many states and the "prudent man" rule in all states, unless granted permission. A trustee, in particular, should have broader powers, such as investing in growth stocks, and writing covered calls and "naked" puts, which involves the use of margin accounts, etc.
2. *Real estate.* Broad powers are necessary in order not to tie the hands of the fiduciary. The most useful powers include the powers to sell, deal with, mortgage, and lease property.

BUSINESS DISPOSAL

An executor is often responsible for a closely held family business or business interest. To operate effectively, the executor must have the power to continue the business, converting a sole proprietorship to a partnership or corporation, or to liquidate.

PROPERTY RETENTION

One of the most important powers a fiduciary should have is the power not to sell. A trustee, for example, may have to sell stocks not on the "prudent man" list, unless the trust instrument provides the power to retain securities already held.

BORROWING AND LENDING

Without these powers, the fiduciary cannot invest on margin, mortgage property, lend money to beneficiaries, etc.

TAX-RELATED POWERS

The fiduciary must have the power to pay tax, including paying estate tax with "flower bonds," the right to make elections, such as filing a joint return with the surviving spouse, the ability to consent to prior gifts, etc.

¶ 1824 COMPENSATING THE FIDUCIARY

A trustee generally charges a percentage of assets managed annually subject to a minimum floor. An executor or administrator is entitled to a fee, often fixed by statute or awarded by the court. Often a set fee must simply be split by co-fiduciaries. Management commissions may be charged if extra services are rendered. If a lawyer is involved who is also a fiduciary, the individual wears two hats, and may be entitled to two fees. In most states, a lawyer serving in a dual capacity can charge only one fee, which saves the estate money. Some lawyers also waive the executor's commission and charge only the legal fee.

¶ 1825 THE GUARDIAN

Parents with minor children should make a provision for guardians in their will, in the event their children become orphans prior to reaching majority. A guardian may serve two different functions, as guardian of persons and/or property. A child needs a guardian who

1. has the ability and desire to raise the child,
2. can give the child love, affection and continuity, and
3. will raise the child in accordance with the values and principles held by the parents.

A close relation may be the logical choice for raising the children, but not necessarily for managing property. A financial guardian should have the following attributes:

1. The general ability to handle financial matters.
2. The ability to invest and spend money wisely.
3. The ability to conserve capital.

A guardian is regulated by the court. A court order is necessary to draw any funds and the guardian must regularly account for assets, income, and expenses. It may be appropriate to separate the two functions. In many cases a transfer in trust will be more appropriate than using a financial guardian. This is especially true if the minor acquires property from other sources, such as inheritances, during minority.

¶ 1826 THE TRUSTEE

A trust is a device used to separate legal and equitable (beneficial) ownership of property and to manage the assets. The trustee receives legal title and is responsible for managing the assets in the trust, making investment decisions, and managing the collection and distribution of income or principal. Ideally the trustee would have the following characteristics:

1. Personal liability for breaches of fiduciary duty that can be realistically enforced.
2. Mature judgment and financial responsibility.
3. Experience in handling investments, taxation, and accounting.
4. Continuity over the years.
5. Discretion in evaluating the needs of the beneficiaries.

An executor, responsible for an estate, is typically needed for only a few years. A trustee may have to serve for generations. For a long-term trust, only a corporate trustee, typically a bank, can meet all of the above attributes. But in the case of a short-term trust, an individual may serve equally well. The spouse is often the ideal trustee for a short-term trust, as well as the custodian for an account under the Uniform Transfers to Minors Act. For small amounts (less than $100,000), or short durations, individuals usually charge less, particularly if they are close family members. At the same time the mortality of an individual becomes less crucial. It is best to make provision for successor and contingent trustees, just in case.

¶ 1827 THE EXECUTOR

It is a rare individual who will not need an executor. Theoretically, one might envision an individual client with the following total assets:

1. A home owned in joint tenancy.
2. Savings and securities held in joint tenancy.
3. Life insurance payable to the spouse.

In a simple case like this there will be no probate estate, all assets pass to the beneficiary and joint tenant by operation of law, and not even a will, much less an executor, may be needed. As a practical matter, the client owns numerous items which must be distributed upon death, such as a car, a boat, individually owned savings and securities, books, silverware, etc. Therefore, the client needs a will and should name an executor and contingent executors.

If the client does not have a will naming an executor, or the named executor cannot or will not serve, the court will appoint an *administrator.* The choice is completely impersonal and the spouse and heirs have no control over who it is.

The client is strongly advised to name an executor in the will, regardless of current age or net worth. An executor will accomplish the following broad objectives:

1. Save the estate and the heirs time and settlement costs.
2. Prevent legal complications.
3. Provide advice to the beneficiaries.

In general terms, the role of the executor is to carry out the expressed intent and settle the estate as required under local law. Thus, both the will and the law define duties and obligations. Accordingly, the executor must report to the beneficiaries, as well as the probate court and the IRS.

The duties of the executor include the following:

1. To make funeral arrangements.
2. To collect and safeguard assets, including the compilation of an inventory list of all assets. Assets may be located in several states, in safe-deposit boxes, in the home, or in various bank and brokerage accounts. The assets must also be valued for estate tax purposes and to satisfy pecuniary bequests. A separate bank account should be opened for the estate.
3. To provide for living expenses for the surviving spouse and children. The executor can withdraw funds from bank accounts, collect life insurance, etc. Widows' allowances are typically available through the period of administration.
4. To collect income, pay expenses and taxes.
5. To liquidate assets, e.g., sell marketable assets to the extent not distributed in kind.
6. To pay debts against the estate, claims for which are filed within the statutory period, typically six months.
7. Because the estate is a separate taxpayer, income tax returns must be prepared, as well as the estate tax return, the decedent's final return, etc.
8. To apply for death benefits, such as employee benefits, Social Security, union benefits, etc.
9. To decide on the preliminary distribution of assets to the beneficiaries.

The executor serves until the estate closes. If illiquid assets are involved, such as a closely held business, this may take years. This is often true when settling the estate tax issue in a contested case. The testator has the right to impose duties on the executor, such as requiring the executor to select beneficiaries, choose charitable organizations, distribute personal effects, etc. One duty the client should consider relieving the executor of in the will is posting a bond.

The executor has the right to use professional advisors. At a minimum, a lawyer is usually needed. But it may also become desirable to utilize an accountant, a real estate broker, an investment counselor, etc. An executor who is reckless, imprudent, or grossly negligent is personally liable to the beneficiaries for losses sustained for those reasons. The testator should provide for broad powers, such as the right to retain property, handle real estate, and borrow or lend money.

There are four categories from which an executor is most commonly chosen: relatives, friends, lawyers, and institutions. Keeping in mind that settling an estate can be difficult and time-consuming, the following characteristics of an executor are desirable:

1. Familiarity with the relatives and personal situation.
2. Sound and mature judgment.
3. Ability to get along with the heirs (to minimize disagreements).
4. Availability. The executor should live conveniently close and have the time to do a thorough job.
5. Business expertise.

A nephew or friend of the testator may be close to the people involved, but will not necessarily have the practical ability to make financial decisions. As a result, the executor will most likely hire a lawyer to do the work. The spouse is often a logical choice early in life, unless the estate is complex. The older both the testator and spouse get, the less likely they are to appoint each other.

A lawyer, or at least a law firm, may be a good choice, assuming the firm has experts in estate work. The firm should be large enough to handle a complex estate needing a variety of skills.

The more complex the estate, the more likely it is that the client will name a financial institution, such as a commercial bank, as the executor. The client may in fact wish to change the executor from an individual to an institution as the client accumulates more holdings. In other words, in the earlier years a testator is likely to name the spouse, other relative or friend, in the middle years, as the financial substance grows, a financial institution becomes a more likely choice. The advantage of a bank, for example, is its experience and skill in handling real estate, securities, taxes, estate planning (including postmortem estate planning), etc. On the other hand, trust operations tend to be impersonal. The client may be well advised to visit the trust department of a large commercial bank to get an idea of what the bank can do. Large banks often have business departments with experts to run small businesses after the death of the owner.

Keep in mind that once an executor is actually serving, it is almost impossible to remove the person. Changing the name of the executor in the will, however, is a simple matter.

¶ 1828 ESTATE PLANNING PROCESS

A client who owns or will own property for keeps needs an estate plan. The client alone can decide what will happen to the estate. Chances are a client wishes to accomplish at least two broad objectives:

1. The client's intent should be carried out, i.e., the client wants to make sure that the property winds up in the hands of whomever the client wishes to favor. In extreme situations this may mean disinheriting a child or a spouse, but normally the spouse and children are the "natural objects of the client's bounty."
2. The client wishes this intent to be carried out at the least possible cost, i.e., with minimum estate tax and administration cost consequences.

To formalize and implement an estate plan, the client needs a competent estate lawyer. Ideally, the client should employ an estate planning team consisting of a lawyer, an accountant, a life insurance professional, a trust officer, and an investment counselor. Many major banks feature personal financial planning departments employing experts in all aspects of estate planning. Unless the estate amounts to $2 million or more, it is unlikely that a team is justified.

PREREQUISITES FOR ESTATE PLANNING

In order to implement an estate plan, the planner must know:

1. The client's assets, liabilities, and earning power. If the planner does not have all the facts, the advice will be less useful.
2. The client's needs, objectives, and family situation.
3. What the client *knows* about investments, property law, insurance, etc.

The client's intent is largely determined by any knowledge of alternative ways of transferring property. Obviously, clients are not going to ask for a trust, a reversion, or a general power of appointment, if they have no idea what they are, or even that they exist. Therefore, the estate planner's job may include educating the client about the choices available.

Example: A client wants his estate to use the marital deduction, but he wants his spouse to have the income only during her life while being unable to touch the principal. Upon her death, he wants the property to go to the grandchildren. Also, he wishes the income to be accumulated until her death, should she remarry. It is impossible to guarantee all these results simultaneously, but here is how to get close:

1. If she gets the income for life, with the remainder to the grandchildren, no marital deduction is available. (A QTIP election may be made, but then the income cannot be accumulated).
2. If a testamentary general power of appointment is added, the marital deduction *is* available, but the wife may then appoint the property by will, which may lead to the children or other beneficiaries receiving it at the grandchildren's expense.[6]
3. If the client utilizes an *estate trust,* income can be accumulated during his wife's life at the trustee's discretion without loss of the marital deduction. In other words, the closest we can get is a testamentary transfer to an estate trust with the spouse receiving a life estate plus a general testamentary power of appointment, leading to taxation in her estate.[7]

¶ 1829 COMMON MISCONCEPTIONS IN ESTATE PLANNING

The following is a partial list of oversimplified notions people have about estate planning:

1. *It is always good to avoid probate.* The client can avoid probate if owning only life insurance, jointly held property, and inter vivos trusts, but consider the drawbacks:
   (a) The client winds up paying trustee fees every year rather than one probate fee.
   (b) The client loses flexibility and control over the estate.
2. *The maximum marital deduction should always be utilized.* Under the following circumstances, use of the maximum marital deduction may be unwise:
   (a) The spouse's estate may be in a higher tax bracket than that of the client.

[6] Code Sec. 2056(b)(5).

[7] Code Sec. 2041.

(b) The spouse may consume or give away the property (for example, to a new spouse) at the expense of children and grandchildren.

(c) The first $600,000 is tax free anyway, so only bequests to the spouse above this amount are needed to save taxes.

3. *Giving the spouse the life insurance policies is smart.* A gift of all incidents of ownership in an insurance policy on the client's life more than three years before death keeps the proceeds out of the estate if paid to a named beneficiary. If the donee is the spouse, this could backfire. For example:

(a) If the spouse dies first, the cash value is included in the spouse's estate. Very possibly, the donee spouse is leaving property to the donor spouse, which means the donor spouse has to start all over again.

(b) If the donor spouse dies first, the donee spouse is deemed to have made a gift to the beneficiary at that time. Since the donee has no spouse, gift-splitting is not available.[8]

4. *Joint ownership is the best way to pass on the property.* Joint ownership carries with it unique problems. For example: Since only half the property is includible in the estate of the first to die, the survivor receives a stepped-up basis in only one-half.[9] But since the other joint tenant becomes the sole owner, all of the property is included in the survivor's estate.

Estate Planning with Lifetime Gifts and Sales

¶ 1835 ADVANTAGES AND DISADVANTAGES OF LIFETIME GIFTS

Despite the unified estate and gift-tax system, substantial advantages of lifetime gifts still remain. The client is likely, however, to be torn between the tax advantages and the nontax disadvantages.

The tax *advantages* are:

1. There is no gift tax on $10,000 a year per donee.
2. Gift-splitting with the donor's spouse is available, which effectively doubles the tax-free amounts that can be given.[10]
3. Gifts to a spouse can serve to minimize the estate tax in both estates through equalizing the estates by means of gifts eligible for the unlimited gift-tax marital deduction.[11]
4. Gifts of income-producing properties can result in substantial income tax savings due to income splitting.

---

[8] Code Sec. 2514(e).
[9] Code Sec. 1014(a).
[10] Code Sec. 2513.
[11] Code Sec. 2523.

5. Gift taxes paid on gifts more than three years prior to death are not included in the gross estate, but a credit against the estate tax is still available.[12]
6. Any appreciation on gifted property will be excluded from the estate, since "adjusted taxable gifts" are frozen at their value at the time of transfer.
7. No gift tax is currently payable until the unified credit is exhausted.

The tax *detriments* are:

1. Once the unified credit is exhausted, i.e., once $600,000 in taxable gifts have been made, a gift tax is due with the gift-tax return.
2. Property gratuitously transferred in whole or in part will still be part of the gross estate if the client:
   (a) retained a life estate,
   (b) retained a reversionary interest, or
   (c) had the power to alter, amend, revoke, or terminate (see the estate tax chapter).

The nontax *advantages* are:

1. Donors can experience the joy of giving and see the beneficiaries enjoy and use the property. On the average, people die in their seventies with middle-aged children. Testamentary transfers are, therefore, more likely to go to the grandchildren, with whom the testator may have had little contact. Lifetime transfers should be made to the children while they are still in a position to enjoy the greatest benefit from the gifts, e.g., obtaining a college education, starting a business, or getting married.
2. By transferring property to a trust, for example, the donor, for a fee, can be relieved of property management and investment decisions.

The nontax *disadvantages* are:

1. The property leaves the donor's control. This is probably the greatest impediment to lifetime gifts. Once the gift is complete, the donor cannot revoke it. A time may come when the client may wish not to have favored that particular donee or when the client might need the property. An example would be a transfer to a spouse prior to marital discord and divorce. On the other hand, if strings are attached, such as the right to

[12] Code Secs. 2035(c) and 2012.

revoke, there is no completed gift and the property is still part of the gross estate.

2. It may be too early to make a decision, e.g., the children are not mature enough to handle sizeable gifts. If the gifts are in the will, the will can be revised at any time. Also, the donees may be uncomfortable, feeling—rightly or wrongly—that the donor is looking over their shoulders to see if the gifts were justified.

¶ 1836 HOW TO SELECT GIFT PROPERTY

The following factors should be considered before a property selection is made for gift purposes:

1. *High-income-producing assets.* Securities with a high current yield do not tend to appreciate substantially in value, but are good candidates for income-splitting purposes.
2. *"Difficult" properties.* Some assets are difficult to value, sell or split up, such as stock in closely held businesses. These are attractive gift properties.
3. *Low gift value—high estate value.* Ideally, a gift of low value will reduce the estate by a large value. The classic example is life insurance policies. At the time of gift the value may be negligible, while the estate would include the full proceeds, absent the gift.
4. *Property with appreciation potential.* These tend to be low income-producing properties, such as pieces of real estate. As a result a gift is made almost solely for estate planning purposes, i.e., to get the appreciation out of the estate, rather than to effect income-splitting.
5. *Wasting assets.* Unpopular gift assets include options, patents, leaseholds, and others that tend to shrink in value with the passage of time.
6. *Business interests* can create special problems. If control is retained, the business interest comes back in the estate; if not, the donor may be out of business.

Real estate is probably the most popular gift with appreciation potential, while securities are mostly used for income-splitting. Life insurance is unique in that the estate value is automatically much greater than the cash value, unless the insured lives to a really ripe old age.

¶ 1837 GIFTS OF LIFE INSURANCE TO CHARITY

Several tax, legal, and practical advantages exist when life insurance policies are given to charity:

1. There need be no publicity, which minimizes the risk of family arguments.
2. State laws do not limit the amount which can be given to charity via life insurance, limiting only amounts that are given by will.
3. The donor gives up no current income.
4. It is so simple, no will drafting is needed.
5. If the charity pays the premiums, the donor saves cash currently, and if the insured continues to pay, the premiums are deductible.

The charitable donee also likes life insurance, because:

1. There is no probate delay.
2. The cash value can be reached any time or it can be borrowed at low rates.
3. A windfall gain results whenever the insured meets with an untimely death.
4. The charity can convert the policy to a paid-up policy or an extended term policy.

The tax consequences of a life-time gift of life insurance can be summarized as follows:

1. An income tax deduction is allowed for the value of the policy, i.e., the price that would have to be paid for a comparable policy, plus premiums paid by the donor later.
2. No estate tax inclusion results, unless:
    (a) The transfer took place within three years of death.[13]
    (b) Incidents of ownership or a reversionary interest are retained.[13a]
    (c) The policy is in a revocable trust or one in which the insured has a life interest or reversionary interest.[14]

¶ 1838 ESTATE PLANNING FOR THE DYING

Quite often a well-to-do individual is aware that a short time to live remains, e.g., in terminal cancer cases and the like. The following

---

[13] Code Sec. 2035(d).
[13a] Code Sec. 2042.
[14] Code Secs. 2036 and 2038.

are examples of tax-savings opportunities that are often possible in these circumstances:

1. *Charitable contributions.* The will often provides for considerable amounts of testamentary charitable gifts. If at least some of these gifts are made before death, the tax consequences are quite favorable:
   (a) The taxpayer receives an immediate income tax deduction for the gift (for example, on the final return).
   (b) The gift is not included in the gross estate, with resultant estate tax savings as well.
2. *"Flower" bonds.* Certain U.S. Treasury bonds, issued before March 4, 1971, are usable at par to pay estate taxes. Since these bonds often carry a coupon rate of 3 to 3½% and mature as late as 1998, they sell at a discount. As a result, savings can be made by purchasing these bonds just prior to death. (See below.)
3. *Gifts.* A person can give away $10,000 a year ($20,000 if the spouse consents) to any one individual per year, without gift tax liability.[15] The amounts are removed from the estate permanently, even if made on the deathbed. It does not sound like much, but if $20,000 is given to a number of children, grandchildren, friends, in-laws, etc., several years in a row, it may add up to more than $1 million, which may result in estate tax savings of one-half of the gifts or more.
4. *Medical expenses.* If all possible medical expenses are paid prior to death, they reduce the gross estate in addition to being deductible for income tax purposes. Should they be paid after death, they are still deductible (on either Form 1040 or 706), but the gross estate is not reduced.
5. If the dying person owns property which has decreased in value, a sale should be considered. The losses are deductible, unless the property is purely personal. Securities are the most common candidates. In the absence of a sale, the heir fails to benefit from the loss, receiving a fair market value basis.
6. If the taxpayer has capital loss carryovers, these will expire upon death. It can therefore be a good idea for the spouse to sell some appreciated capital assets to offset these on a joint return before it is too late.
7. The will should be reviewed to make sure it conforms to both the testator's intent and recent tax developments.

---

[15] Code Sec. 2503(b).

8. A dying person who holds any powers of appointment should consider exercising them to prevent lapse, or at least provide for exercise by will, if desired.
9. It should be kept in mind that if a person becomes incompetent prior to death, all powers of attorney may expire under general agency law.
10. If the spouse has income and a joint return is filed, the spouse's income tax liability can be paid without gift tax consequences, even though the estate is reduced.

¶ 1839 "FLOWER" BONDS VS. LIFE INSURANCE

As mentioned above (see ¶ 1043) "flower" bonds are U.S. Treasury bonds redeemable at par to pay estate taxes, even though they sell below par due to the low interest coupon. If the client has a short time to live, it is a wise decision to purchase some. However, before rushing out to buy flower bonds, consider the following comparisons with life insurance:

1. Interest on bonds is taxable, but dividends and build-ups in cash value on insurance are not.
2. Insurance can be purchased on the installment plan; bonds cannot be.
3. Insurance proceeds can be used to pay any expenses of the estate, but bonds can be used only to pay estate taxes.
4. Insurance is often exempt from local inheritance taxes, bonds are not.
5. Life insurance can be purchased with minimal liquidation of securities to avoid loss of growth and capital gains taxes.
6. Bonds must be included in the gross estate, but insurance can be excluded if the decedent had transferred all incidents of ownership more than three years prior to death.
7. Insurance does not pass through probate, while bonds are subject to delay and probate costs.
8. On the other hand, bonds can be purchased on the deathbed when the buyer is uninsurable.

Overall, a combination of life insurance and tax-exempt municipal bonds, for example, will often provide better income tax results during life, and better estate planning consequences on death, than "flower" bonds.

¶ 1840 POSTMORTEM ESTATE PLANNING

Even after a person dies, there are numerous financial decisions which can be made to reduce tax liabilities, improve liquidity, and protect assets. Here is a list of some of the things an executor can do, with help from the beneficiaries:

1. *The decedent's final return.* The final return can be a joint return with the surviving spouse, assuming the surviving spouse is unmarried on December 31. Capital losses sustained by the decedent can be offset against capital gains generated, even after death, by the spouse. Medical expenses on behalf of the decedent can be deducted on either the income tax return or the estate tax return, if paid within 12 months of death.[16]

2. *Waiver of surviving spouse executor commissions.* An executor's commission is taxable income. The surviving spouse should consider waiving the commission by filing a timely disclaimer. This is particularly true if nontaxable bequests are to be received in any event.

3. *Series EE savings bonds.* All accrued interest on EE bonds may be reported on the final income tax return. This is particularly beneficial if the decedent died early in the year and is in a low bracket. Any unpaid income taxes resulting from the election are deductible as a debt on the estate tax return.

4. *Solving liquidity problems.* If the estate consists primarily of illiquid assets, several approaches are possible:

   (a) If a closely held business interest represents more than 35% of the adjusted gross estate, it is possible to pay the estate tax in installments over 15 years.[17]

   (b) The executor typically has the authority to satisfy pecuniary bequests in kind. Thus, if the nephew is favored with a $10,000 bequest in the will, the executor can hand him $10,000 worth of securities, land, or stamps.

   (c) The estate can raise cash by borrowing from a beneficiary or a trust.

   (d) If the estate tax return is filled out competently, taxes will be saved, thereby reducing the need for liquidity.

   (e) Marketable securities can be sold.

---

[16] Code Sec. 213(c).

[17] Code Sec. 6166.

ADMINISTRATION EXPENSES

Administration expenses, such as legal fees, but not funeral expenses, can be deducted either on the estate's income tax return (Form 1041) or on the estate tax return (Form 706). A comparison of estate tax and income tax brackets is therefore necessary. In general, the smaller the estate, the more likely it is that the income tax deduction is best.

DISCLAIMERS

No one has to accept a gift or bequest if one does not want it. Sometimes substantial savings can result from a disclaimer:

1. The surviving spouse may wish to disclaim a portion of the marital bequest. This might save estate taxes in the surviving spouse's estate, and the disclaimed portion would pass directly to the other beneficiaries, typically children or grandchildren. A qualified disclaimer within nine months is not subject to gift tax, and the property is treated as if it had never been transferred to the surviving spouse.[18] The disclaimer should only be made if the surviving spouse would not consume the excess for living expenses in any event.
2. A third party, such as a child, may wish to disclaim a bequest in favor of the surviving parent, so as to increase the marital deduction and save estate taxes immediately. The disclaimer may also be prompted by a concern for the parent's financial needs and the hope that the property will eventually pass to the child anyway, for example through a systematic gift program.
3. In general, a beneficiary may be financially secure and disclaim, if, as a result, the funds will go to someone the beneficiary wants to benefit without incurring any gift tax liability.
4. If one is given a general power of appointment but does not intend to exercise it, by disclaiming the power of appointment, one can avoid estate tax in the estate if one dies possessing the power.
5. Someone receiving an income interest may wish to disclaim it if it goes to a lower-income tax-bracket family member.
6. If a disclaimed interest will go to charity and the charity is one of the beneficiary's favorites, the beneficiary may disclaim the interest and reduce estate taxes. But the estate savings must be compared with the income tax savings resulting from acceptance plus contribution.

---

[18] Code Sec. 2518.

To qualify, the disclaimer must be:

1. made in writing,
2. made within nine months of the transfer or nine months after the beneficiary reaches age 21, and
3. irrevocable and unqualified.

In addition, the disclaimant must not have accepted the bequest or any benefits from it initially. If the disclaimer is tardy, for example, it results in a taxable gift.

STATUTORY SHARES

In most states, a surviving spouse can elect against the will if the late spouse left less than a certain fraction of the net probate estate. Typically, a surviving spouse is entitled to one-third of the estate if there are children or grandchildren, one-half if there are none. Even if this is against the testator's intent, the survivor's forced share qualifies for the marital deduction.

¶ 1841 EFFECTIVE ESTATE TAX SAVINGS TECHNIQUES

With proper planning, practically no family, not even the very wealthy, need pay wealth transfer taxes. The main tools and techniques of sophisticated estate planning are described and illustrated with simple numerical examples at ¶ 1842-1849. The inevitable conclusion is that estate and gift taxes are truly avoidable if proper action is taken.

¶ 1842 UNIFIED CREDIT

Since 1987, the unified credit has been $192,800, which shelters the bottom (not the top) $600,000 of taxable transfers from the unified gift and estate tax.[19]

Example: Hector Crofts transfers $1,240,000, all his worldly goods, to his two daughters, Hope and Charity. His wife, Serena, consents to gift-splitting. Each of the two gift tax returns, Form 709, filed by Hector and Serena will reveal the following:

Gross Gifts	$ 620,000
Exclusions	– 20,000
Taxable Gifts	$ 600,000
Gift Tax	192,800
Unified Credit	192,800
Gift Tax Payable	$ 0

Thus, due to the exclusions and the unified credit, no transfer tax is payable. Furthermore, when Hector dies several years later, his estate tax return, Form 706, will contain the following information:

[19] Code Sec. 2010.

Gross Estate	0
Taxable Estate	0
Adjusted Taxable Gifts	+$600,000
Estate Tax Base	$600,000
Tentative Estate Tax	$192,800
Unified Credit	– 192,800
Estate Tax Payable	$ 0

This illustrates clearly the unified nature of the wealth transfer tax and shows that a married couple can transfer $1,200,000 plus exclusions to any third-party donee they choose.

CONSUMPTION

A simple and enjoyable way to avoid the wealth transfer tax is to consume all personal assets in excess of $600,000. However, this may neither be practical nor desirable, particularly when the estate is large.

¶ 1843 GAINING TIME WITH THE MARITAL DEDUCTION

The unlimited marital deduction has at least one virtue: If no estate planning has been done before the first spouse dies, there is still time to save taxes. Regardless of the size of the estate of the first spouse, no estate tax is due if the unlimited marital deduction is taken.[20] Because of the unified credit, the most popular bequest is the simplest one, e.g., the first $600,000 is left to the children or grandchildren and the excess is left to the surviving spouse in a form that qualifies for the marital deduction. The pressure will then be on the surviving spouse to avoid estate taxes through the use of one or more of the strategies discussed here.

DEDUCTIBLE PROPERTY SETTLEMENTS

Envision the following alternative scenarios:

1. F and M get a divorce. M receives $1 million as a property settlement. 17 years later F dies leaving everything he owns, some $10 million, to the children of F and M. The estate is fully taxable, and the children receive approximately $5 million.
2. Assume the same scenario as in 1 above, except that F in the divorce settlement also agreed to leave the children everything he owns at death. Result: $10 million is deductible under Code Sec. 2053 as a claim against the estate. Consequently, the children receive the full $10 million.

[20] Code Sec. 2056.

Ordinarily, bequests other than to charity and the surviving spouse are nondeductible. However, there are several reasons that the nondeductible bequest in 1 above, was converted into a deductible claim in situation two:

(a) The $10 million effectively became a debt of the estate for which the decedent was presumably liable.

(b) Property transferred in settlement of marital rights for the children's support is considered to have been transferred for consideration by statute under Code Secs. 2043 and 2516.

(c) Property transferred pursuant to a court order, where the court has authority to amend the judgment, is considered transferred for consideration under case law.

¶ 1844 OUTRIGHT TRANSFERS TO CHARITY

For estate and gift tax purposes, the charitable contribution deduction is unlimited and is available for the full fair market value of the property.[21] Thus, if $1 million worth of property is included in the estate and is left to charity, a $1 million deduction is available. However, if the property has been given away during the decedent's lifetime, estate taxes still would not be paid on the $1 million. In addition, $1 million (subject to some limitations) would be *deductible for income tax purposes*. Assuming maximum tax brackets, the combined tax savings could amount to 94.6% (55% + 39.6%) of the value of the property (less the estate tax on the unconsumed portion of the income tax savings). The lesson is clear: to maximize tax savings from charitable gifts, no testamentary bequests should be made.

CHARITABLE REMAINDER TRUSTS

If a trust is set up to distribute income to A for life and then to terminate in favor of B who receives corpus, A has a *life estate,* a present interest, and B has a *remainder,* a future interest. If A is a noncharitable person and B is a charitable organization, a charitable deduction is permitted at the time the interests are created. In other words, a current deduction is permitted for a present transfer of a future interest. However, there are some conditions:

1. The charitable remainder trust must qualify as an annuity trust, unitrust, or pooled income fund.[22]
2. The income interest can run for the life or lives of one or more noncharitable beneficiaries or for a term of 20 years or less.

---

[21] Code Secs. 2055 and 2522.

[22] Code Secs. 170(f)(A), 2055(e)(2)(A), and 2522(c)(2)(A).

3. For an annuity trust the fixed amount of the annuity must equal 5% or more of the initial value of the trust fund. For a unitrust the fixed "adjusted payout rate" must be at least 5% of the annual value of the trust fund.

Example 1: *Inter vivos (living) transfer to an annuity trust.* Harry, age 60, transfers appreciated securities, worth $1 million to an annuity trust for Stanvard University, retaining an annuity of $80,000 (8%) for life. If a 10% rate is applicable, an annuity of $1 a year for the life of a 60-year-old is worth $7.4491. An $80,000 annuity is therefore worth $7.4491 × $80,000, or *$595,928.* An immediate income tax deduction is allowed for the remainder, $1 million less $595,928, or *$404,072.* The appreciation escapes income tax. When Harry dies the value of the trust fund is $1,200,000. The full amount is includible in his gross estate because he had a retained life estate. However, since Stanvard receives the full value, $1,200,000 is deductible as a charitable contribution of the estate.

Example 2: *Testamentary transfer to an annuity trust.* Assume the facts are the same as in Example 1, except that Harry left $1 million to his son, Henry, for life and thereafter to charity. Harry's estate would include $1 million and a charitable deduction of $404,072 would be allowed.

Example 3: *Intervivos transfer to a unitrust.* If the facts are the same as in Example 1, except that Harry retains 8% of the *annual* value of a unitrust, the estate tax result is the same, e.g., the inclusion is offset by the deduction. However, the discount rate used is the adjusted payout rate, 8%, under Reg. § 1.664-4(b)(5). The remainder factor is only .29136, yielding an income tax deduction of *$291,360,* or some $113,000 *less* than with an annuity trust. The lower the discount rate used, the higher the value of the income interest and the lower the value of the remainder. Since a flat rate is used to compute the interests in an annuity trust, this leads to a simple rule of thumb: if the payout rate exceeds the flat rate, a unitrust should be used, and if it is less, an annuity trust should be employed. (In August 1993, the flat rate was 6.6%.)

Example 4: *Inter vivos transfer to an annuity trust with a noncharitable income beneficiary other than the grantor.* Harry transfers $1 million to an annuity trust for his daughter Harriet for life, remainder to Stanvard University. He receives an income tax deduction of $404,072, but has made a gift of $595,928 for gift tax purposes. His gross estate will not include the trust fund, but the estate tax base will include the adjusted taxable gift.

¶ 1845 CHARITABLE LEAD TRUSTS

A charitable lead trust is the opposite of a charitable remainder trust, i.e., the income interest goes to charity and the remainder goes to a noncharitable beneficiary, or is retained by the grantor (a reversion). Unlike in the case of the remainder trust, *an inter vivos transfer does not reduce the estate tax.*

> ***Example:*** Beverly buys $100,000 of par value, 6% municipal bonds ("tax-free" bonds) for $70,000 and transfers them to charity for 10 years, reversion to herself, guaranteeing the charity $6,000 a year. The result is as follows:
>
> 1. Beverly can deduct currently the present value of the guaranteed annuity of $6,000 a year at the prevailing discount rate, e.g., 10%, i.e., $6.1446 × $6,000, or $36,868. The condition is that the trust is a grantor trust.[23] Since income is deemed to be for the "use" of charity, the annual deduction limit is 20% of adjusted gross income.
> 2. Beverly's favorite charity will collect $60,000 over 10 years.
> 3. Beverly will eventually collect the par value of $100,000. Her $30,000 gain will be a long-term capital gain, except to the extent that it is "original issue discount," in which case it is nontaxable.
> 4. Beverly has $6,000 of income each year from the trust, but it is excluded from gross income, although it may be subject to state and local taxes. Clearly, the above arrangement may be desirable for income tax purposes, but it does not remove any property from Beverly's gross estate.

To result in an estate tax charitable contribution deduction, the transfer to charity must be testamentary.

> ***Example:*** Natalie dies, leaving a $1 million bond portfolio to Aardvark University for 25 years, remainder to her grandchildren. Her estate is permitted a charitable deduction for the present value of a 10% income interest for 15 years, or $760,608 assuming a 10% discount rate.

¶ 1846 GRANTOR INCOME TRUSTS

For transfers after November 30, 1983, the IRS used a 10% discount rate to determine the present value of private annuities, term interests, life estates, and remainders. These tables, which are unisex, are found in the estate tax Reg. §§20.2031-7(f) and 25.2512-5. The assumed rate of 10% applied regardless of the actual income earned on

[23] Code Sec. 170(f)(2)(B).

the assets employed, the market rate of interest, and the marginal income tax rates of the parties involved. The Technical and Miscellaneous Revenue Act of 1988 redetermines the discount rate monthly, i.e., the rate is 120% of the "Applicable Federal Midterm Rate."

> ***Example:*** Mrs. Bates transfers $1 million of securities to a trust for her son, Norman, but retains a 10% income interest on the trust funds for 15 years. The present value of a 15-year income interest at 10% is 76.0608% of the asset transferred. Thus, Mrs. Bates is deemed to have retained a term interest worth $760,608 and to have given Norman a remainder worth $239,392. If Mrs. Bates survives the 15-year term, no portion of the trust fund is included in her estate. Should she not survive the term, however, the full value of the trust fund at the time of her death is includible in her estate. This result follows from Code Sec. 2036, which holds that if a retained income interest in property gratuitously transferred has not expired before the grantor dies, the property is includible in the grantor's estate.

The advantages of the grantor income trust are the absence of consideration and recognition of no gain. However, the grantor must survive the term interest. It is, therefore, an all-or-nothing proposition. The longer the term retained, the lower the gift, but the higher the probability that the grantor will not survive the term.

¶ 1847 DEFERRED PAYMENT SALES

The obvious way to transfer property to the younger generation so as to achieve exclusion from an estate without incurring a gift tax liability is to sell it. A deferred payment sale, e.g., a sale for a private annuity or an installment note, offers the following advantages:

1. If the value of the consideration for tax purposes equals the fair market value of the property sold, there is no gift for gift tax purposes. Furthermore, if the sale is "bona fide," the sold property is removed from the estate of the seller.
2. If payments from the buyer are to stop on the seller's death, or earlier, only the unconsumed portion of payments already made will be included in the seller's estate.
3. The seller may make gifts to the buyer by forgiving one or more installments when due.
4. By transferring properties to a grantor trust and selling the beneficial interest *in the trust*, the seller can keep full control over the trust investments. Since no interests in specific properties are transferred the seller may use, sell, replace, and otherwise deal with trust assets, as long as the seller does not

commit waste and takes care to observe the formalities of arm's-length transactions. No income tax advantages or disadvantages are encountered since the income, gain, loss, deduction, or credit available to the trust winds up on the seller's own tax return under the grantor trust rules.

5. Because of the unlimited marital deduction and the step-up in basis to estate tax value under Code Sec. 1014(a), the deferred payment sale should be entered into by the surviving spouse. However, even if there will be little or no gain to the seller, the buyer's basis will be limited to consideration paid.

Possible disadvantages of deferred payment sales in estate planning include possible recognition of income to the seller upon collecting or forgiving payments due and the possibility that the buyer will end up with a cost basis lower than the value of the property purchased. Below, private annuity and installment sales are examined separately.

¶ 1848 PRIVATE ANNUITY SALES

In a private annuity sale, the older generation sells property for a private annuity to the younger generation. The seller thus becomes the annuitant and the buyer the obligor. Tax consequences are as follows:

1. There is no gift tax as long as the present value of the annuity equals the value of the property interest transferred.
2. The sold property is removed from the seller's estate.
3. If the annuity stops on the seller/annuitant's death, no portion of the annuity is includible in the seller's estate.
4. The buyer's unadjusted basis in the property equals the sum of payments actually made.[24] No portion of the payment is deductible as interest.
5. The seller is only taxed as payments are received under the exclusion ratio approach under Code Sec. 72(b) *if the annuity is unsecured.*[25] However, if the annuity is secured, gain is immediately recognized (present value of annuity less basis in sold property) with a resulting increase in the exclusion ratio.[26]

An example that illustrates this is as follows:

Example: *Outright sale of property for unsecured annuity.* Milton Senior, age 67, sells his $1 million farm corporation stock, in which he has a basis of $400,000, to his son Milton Junior for an unsecured private annuity. Assuming a 10% discount rate, the

[24] Rev. Rul. 55-119, 1955-1 CB 352.

[25] Rev. Rul. 69-74, 1969-1 CB 43.

[26] *Lloyd Bell,* 60 TC 469 (1973).

present value of an annuity of $1 for the life of a 67-year-old person is 6.5098. The required annuity is therefore $1 million/6.5098 or $153,615. This may be a prohibitive amount for Milton Junior to pay. Furthermore, if more than $10,000 a year is forgiven ($20,000 if Mrs. Milton Senior consents to gift-splitting), there will be gift tax consequences. Assuming the transaction is entered into, both the stock and the annuity are excluded from Milton Senior's estate without gift tax consequences. Milton Junior's basis in stock equals what he pays for it, but not until he has paid the entire amount. If Milton Senior's life expectancy is 15 years, for income tax purposes he can exclude

$$\frac{\$400{,}000}{\$153{,}615 \times 15}$$

or 17.36% of each payment made to recover his investment in the annuity contract for 15 years until he has recovered the entire amount.

Note that if the annuity is secured, Milton Senior would be taxed immediately on his $600,000 gain with no basis increase to Milton Junior. The exclusion ratio will change to

$$\frac{\$1{,}000{,}000}{\$153{,}615 \times 15} \text{ or } 43.44\%.$$

If a trust is used it is important to avoid the pitfalls of the grantor trust. Under the grantor trust rules,[27] the grantor is taxed on the income from the trust rather than on the gain from the sale of property to the trust under the exclusion ratio approach. The Court of Appeals for the Ninth Circuit has suggested the following guidelines to ensure a "sale for an annuity," as opposed to a "retained income grantor interest," treatment:[28]

1. The arrangement must have economic substance.
2. Proper formalities must be observed in the sale transaction.
3. The trustee should be independent of the grantor.
4. The grantor should not be a beneficiary of, or an "advisor" to, the trust.
5. Annuity payments should not be tied to, or depend on, the income of the trust.

¶ 1849 INSTALLMENT SALES

An outright sale of property by the parent to the child for an installment obligation offers many of the same advantages as a sale for

[27] Code Secs. 671-679.

[28] *Stern*, CA-9, 84-2 USTC ¶ 9949.

a private annuity. Thus, if the consideration paid equals the value of property sold, the property is removed from the seller's estate without gift tax consequences. However, there are several differences:

1. If the seller outlives the note, the buyer's payment obligation is over, i.e., there is a guaranteed maximum purchase price.
2. If the seller dies early, any unpaid portion of the note is an asset of the estate.
3. The buyer immediately receives a basis in the property transferred equal to the face value of the note (assuming sufficient interest is charged).
4. The seller is taxed on the interest and the buyer may deduct it.
5. The seller is taxed on the gain, if any, as payments are collected, if installment reporting is used under Code Sec. 453. Even payments forgiven are deemed to have been collected with the proceeds gifted to the buyer, resulting in recognized gains to the seller or the seller's estate.[29]

Example: Assume the same facts as the example in ¶ 1848. Milton Senior sells his farm corporation stock, worth $1,000,000, with a basis of $400,000 to his son, Milton Junior. The buyer is to pay $100,000 a year for 10 years, plus 10% interest. The tax consequences are as follows:

1. There is no gift for gift tax purposes.
2. The farm stock is not includible in Milton Senior's estate.
3. When the seller dies, his estate includes any collected aftertax and unconsumed proceeds, plus the fair market value of remaining payments, if any.
4. Milton Junior's basis in the stock is $1 million immediately and remains so.
5. Interest paid is income to Milton Senior and interest expense to Milton Junior.
6. Milton Senior must recognize gain upon collection of principal. Since his basis was 40% of the selling price, 60% of each dollar of principal collected is income (the "gross profit percentage").

Due to the income tax consequences of the above example, this method should be employed by the surviving spouse or other heir who has a stepped-up basis, necessitating little or no gain recognition.

---

[29] Code Secs. 435B(f) and 691(a)(5).

If the buyer has limited funds, the seller may, of course, forgive one or more installments and/or couple the arrangement with a long-term gift program.

¶ 1850 SELF-CANCELLING INSTALLMENT NOTES (SCINs)

In brief, a self-cancelling installment note (SCIN) is a note providing, up front, that payments are to stop upon the seller's death. In other words, the life of the note is the lesser of a fixed term or the seller's life. An SCIN falls somewhere between a regular installment note and a private annuity and should be compared to both. It is assumed that the seller's life expectancy exceeds the fixed term of the SCIN.

¶ 1851 SCINs VS. PRIVATE ANNUITIES

1. The seller may survive an SCIN explained in ¶ 1850, but not a private annuity. This may be construed as an advantage to the buyer, but not to the seller.
2. The gross profit percentage method, not the exclusion ratio approach, is used to compute gain under an SCIN.
3. The interest paid an SCIN is deductible.

SCINS VS. REGULAR INSTALLMENT OBLIGATIONS

1. Since the unpaid portion of an SCIN is automatically extinguished at death, these cancelled payments are *not* includible in the seller's gross estate.[30] This results in the same advantage as a private annuity.
2. If unpaid installments on a regular note are forgiven in the seller's will, not only are the payments still includible in the estate, but also the income on the installments forgiven is "income in respect of the decedent" under Code Sec. 691 and is taxed, typically, to the estate. This is also the case with an SCIN even though the decedent *never* had the right to collect postmortem payments.
3. With an SCIN the purchase price and/or the interest rate charged must be higher because of the "risk premium" necessary to pay for the actuarial probability that the seller will die before all payments under the contract are made.

   Note: The IRS position is that, if the fixed term of an SCIN is at least equal to the seller's life expectancy, it is to be taxed as a private annuity, otherwise as an installment note.[31]

---

[30] *John A. Moss,* 74 TC 1239, CCH Dec. 37,230, *acq.,* 1981-1 CB 2.

[31] GCM 39503 and Rev. Rul. 86-71, 1986-1 CB 102.

CONCLUDING REMARKS

Gift and estate taxes are truly avoidable taxes, much more so than the income tax. Due to the annual gift tax exclusion, the unified credit, marital and charitable deductions, as well as transactions between family members, virtually no estate need be subject to estate taxes. However, considerable planning and skill are required to minimize transfer taxes in the estate of the surviving spouse. Each technique comes with some disadvantages. Thus, the grantor annuity trust depends on some degree of luck, but the remainderman needs no funds, while in a deferred payment sale the result is virtually guaranteed, but the buyer needs independent means. A knowledge of available tools of estate planning and their comparative strengths and weaknesses is a prerequisite to effective transfer tax reduction.

CHAPTER 19

PROFESSIONAL ADVISERS

¶ 1901 INTRODUCTION

This chapter surveys professionals who render financial advice, their areas of expertise, when to use them and when not to. Lawyers, tax advisers, accountants, stock brokers, insurance professionals, and personal financial planners are emphasized. The latter is a new, rapidly growing profession, indicating a great need.

¶ 1902 WHEN TO USE LAWYERS

A good lawyer can give a client peace of mind, save time and money, and protect the client's interests over the years. This does not mean that one should automatically be used in trivial cases. Here are some situations that a person should consider handling personally:

1. Investments, but not if substantial.

2. Collection work.
3. Traffic tickets.
4. Routine sales and purchases, including autos.
5. Changing employment.
6. Filing a tax return.

In other words, a lawyer should not be consulted unless the client has a real, honest-to-goodness legal problem. Here are some situations where one invariably needs a lawyer, but not necessarily *any* lawyer:

1. A divorce, separation, prenuptial agreement, adoption, or other family changes.
2. Making or revising a will and setting up a trust.
3. Estate planning, including estate and gift tax matters.
4. Buying, leasing, or selling a home or other expensive property.
5. Drafting legal documents, such as contracts, e.g., partnership agreements, buy/sell agreements, etc.
6. Complicated tax work, unless a CPA can handle it.
7. Any litigation work.
8. Incorporations, mergers and acquisitions, and other corporate reorganizations.
9. Any complicated and technical claim for damages.
10. The foreclosing of a mortgage.
11. Arrests for a crime.

The client should prepare before seeing a lawyer, and anticipate the documents and information needed. The better prepared the client, the less time they will need together, and the less the lawyer will charge.

¶ 1903 HOW TO SELECT LAWYERS

A lawyer is selected on the basis of the client's needs, present and future, but the former's experience and expertise. For routine tasks such as the simple will, the closing, and the uncontested divorce, a general practioner may be employed. Young lawyers should not be overlooked. For routine tasks they will do, and at less cost! A client who has a complicated case should not use a general practitioner, young or old, but should go to an expert. Lawyers specialize in literally hundreds of areas. Here are a select few: immigration, bankruptcy, patents, estate planning, personal injury, criminal law, criminal tax law, labor law, collections, divorce, administrative agencies, real estate, etc.

Here are some sources for obtaining lawyers:

1. *The Yellow Pages.* Lawyers can advertise to a greater extent these days and are permitted to list their specialties and other credentials in the phone directories.
2. *Friends, relatives, and business associates,* as well as the bank, accountant, or the client's employer's legal department.
3. *The Martindale-Hubbell Law Directory* is available at the public library or law library and lists almost all lawyers in the U.S. by age, school, expertise, affiliation, associates, types of clients, etc.
4. *The local bar association* typically runs a "lawyer reference service," but no attempt is made to rate the lawyers by experience or skill. The lawyers merely sign up in the hope of getting some business.

A final note: Whether the client uses a sole practitioner, a small partnership or a giant law firm, the client will have *one* lawyer. Even in a firm, the client will be the responsibility of one person.

¶ 1904 HOW TO USE LAWYERS

First of all, the client should not do everything personally. "How to" books can never be up to date under local law. No lawyer can function without continuous access to a law library. New court cases are decided every day which may have a bearing on the problem at hand. Preparing one's own documents can be dangerous and costly. In some routine cases a realtor, stock broker, accountant, or insurance agent may be a reasonable substitute for a lawyer, but more often a client cannot afford to take a chance when significant issues or sums are involved.

Keep the following in mind when using a lawyer:

1. Make it a lifelong commitment, if possible. Changing a lawyer necessitates starting all over again to bring the new one up to date with the client's overall situation. The new lawyer must be paid to learn what the old lawyer already knows.
2. Everything the client says will be kept in confidence due to the attorney-client privilege. Therefore, the lawyer should be told the truth, the whole truth, and nothing but the the truth. Without all the facts, a lawyer cannot provide the needed advice.
3. A lawyer (or, indeed, any adviser) should be consulted *before* entering into a significant transaction, purchase, sale, or contract. The only time the client must wait until afterwards is

when something unexpected happens; e.g., the client had an accident, was arrested, etc.

4. A lawyer *can* represent both parties to a transaction, but only after disclosure and consent.
5. When someone receives legal advice, it should be taken. The client may not like it, but why pay for advice if the client has already decided what to do?
6. Prepare carefully for a meeting with the lawyer. If necessary, double-check on the phone what is needed at the meeting, from information to documents. Write down an outline of the problem and questions to ask, so as not to waste time and money. The lawyer's time is never wasted because the client will pay for every minute of it.
7. Get a complete, itemized bill. At the minimum the client may deduct the part allocable to tax advice.
8. If the lawyer is incompetent, dishonest, or unfair, the client may file a complaint with the local bar association. Many associations even have funds for clients victimized by dishonest lawyers. Malpractice suits against lawyers, and for that matter accountants, physicians, and other professionals, are on the rise. But note that professional liability insurance does not cover criminal and dishonest behavior. The malpractice carrier will, however, pay for damages caused by negligence and omissions.

This chapter is concerned with many groups of professionals. Lawyers are found in many of these professional groups, notably tax advisers, investment counselors, and fiduciaries, from executors to trustees.

¶ 1905 HOW FEES ARE DETERMINED

According to the Code of Ethics of the American Bar Association, these are the factors to be considered by a lawyer when setting fees:

1. What kind of resources are needed, such as time, labor, expense, novelty, complexity, and special skills?
2. To what extent are other fees lost if the case is accepted, i.e., what does the opportunity cost?
3. What do other lawyers charge for the same service?
4. What is the amount at stake, or what is the potential benefit to the client?
5. Is the payment of the fee contingent or uncertain?

6. Is this likely to be a one-shot deal or is a continuing relationship possible?
7. How experienced, reputable, capable, or specialized is the lawyer?

When all is said and done, the average lawyer will charge what the traffic will bear, like everyone else. And the criteria for billing tend to boil down to three: time, value and contingency.

Hourly fees are most appropriate when routine work is performed, such as drafting legal documents. The most common rate is probably $75 - $150 an hour, but it could be higher.

Fees based on value are common when property changes hands. An example is closing a real estate transaction. Many lawyers charge 1% of the price, but others charge a flat fee for a closing of a principal residence. Expect to have to pay for phone consultations, but do not pay for an initial interview.

RETAINERS

A retainer may mean two different things. It may mean a fixed fee per month or year to ensure having a lawyer "on call" any time one is needed. Such an arrangement makes no sense for most individuals, but may be natural for a business. A retainer may also refer to the down payment. Thus, a lawyer who takes a case may want 50% of the fee up front and the other 50% after the divorce is final, the visa is issued, etc. The client should only pay upon need and receipt of legal help. The old minimum fee schedules published by the American Bar Association were held unconstitutional. Therefore, the client can shop for bargains in routine cases. Legal clinics are springing up, charging low and flat fees for routine services, such as the drawing of a will, real estate closings, or an uncontested divorce.

CONTINGENT FEES

Contingent fees are charged in civil cases for damages, e.g., personal injuries, libel and slander, etc. The advantage is that the client pays nothing, except expenses, unless successful. The disadvantage is that the lawyer collects at least one-third of the settlement. Make sure the expenses come off the top first. The arguments for contingent fees are that the client can afford the best and that the lawyer will work harder when having a piece of the action.

MISCELLANEOUS

Whatever the fee arrangements are, make sure the client knows up front. Too many lawyers wind up suing their clients for their fees. In anything other than a routine, short-term case, a fee contract may be appropriate.

Some lawyers charge a heavy fee to get rid of an undesirable case or client, then sometimes accept the case if the client agrees. Others may charge a nominal fee the first time someone walks in for a will, in the hope of handling all the client's legal affairs later. Standard services will be billed in a rather narrow range, the will, the uncontested divorce, etc. But the fees vary greatly once it comes to lawsuits, extended litigation, and special problems.

¶ 1906 THE ACCOUNTANT

The typical employee with no complex business interests, may only need an accountant as a tax adviser and return preparer. But an accountant can be much more, such as the keeper of financial records and the overseer of the client's continuing financial health. Once someone owns a business or has extensive business holdings, such as partnership interests, the accountant will be needed for bookkeeping services, audits, and the preparation of financial statements, budgets, cash-flow analysis and the like. Note that there is no accountant-client privilege, except in a few state courts. The CPA designation is only granted after passing four rigorous exams and typically only to a person with a college degree and relevant practical experience. But, as usual, the client gets what is paid for. Although there are some 300,000 CPAs in the U.S., the demand so far exceeds the supply by a wide margin. In many cases, a non-CPA accountant will serve the purpose well. (See ¶ 1907 below.)

¶ 1907 THE TAX ADVISER

A tax professional is needed for several reasons:

1. Changes in the statute, regulations, tax forms, procedures, and court cases take place on a daily basis.

2. The taxpayer needs the peace of mind caused by the knowledge that a professional has handled the taxpayer's special situation.

3. Tax practice has emerged as a new, separate, and distinct profession with its own regulations and sanctions.

4. Chances are at least 30% of gross income is spent on taxes, making it the number one expense of most clients' budgets. The taxpayer cannot afford to save the modest fee charged by most tax professionals.

TAX PLANNING

What is the difference between tax avoidance and tax evasion? About five years! In other words, *tax avoidance* is another term for tax planning and is perfectly legal. *Tax evasion* is illegal and has been a felony since 1921. Very little tax planning can be done after the fact. Someone looking for a tax person the first half of April needs only a clerk, a tax return preparer. It is then too late to do any tax planning of much significance. The time to seek tax advice is *before* entering into any significant financial transaction, be it a divorce, the sale of a house, or even the purchase of a new car.

¶ 1908 WHO ARE THE EXPERTS?

LAWYERS

There are some 800,000 lawyers in the U.S. The typical lawyer, not specializing in taxation, is *not* a tax expert. In law school, tax courses are available, but rarely required. The typical law student takes one survey course at the most. In addition, there are no tax questions asked on many, if not most, bar examinations. Even if a lawyer specializes in taxation, does the client really need one? Why use a cannon to kill a fly? A lawyer is *not* needed to file a return or answer routine tax questions. Lawyers hate to file Form 1040s, but many will, and they charge plenty. One disadvantage of having *anyone* do a return is that the preparer will know how much the taxpayer makes and owns and will charge what the traffic will bear based on that information. But unlike unlicensed persons, a lawyer is subject to dual codes of ethics, those of the American and the State Bar Associations.

Here are some situations when the client either should use a lawyer, or winds up using one automatically:

In court. As a practical matter only a licensed lawyer can represent a client in court. A lawyer also must be admitted to practice in the particular forum selected, be it the U.S. Tax Court, U.S. District Court (including the Appellate Court) or the U.S. Court of Federal Claims. The client needs a lawyer who not only has litigation experience, but who also has litigated tax cases.

Criminal tax cases. A client who is visited by a regular IRS agent should call an accountant. But if the visit is from a *special agent,* the taxpayer should keep silent and consult a criminal tax lawyer. This person is not a tax lawyer, nor a criminal lawyer, but a criminal tax lawyer.

Complex financial transactions. The client should not sell a house, obtain a divorce, or incorporate without competent tax advice. A client who is employing a lawyer should make sure the same person, or at least the same firm, can also render expert tax advice.

Estate planning. This has been the almost exclusive domain of the lawyer, but a growing number of accountants and financial planners are now working in this area. A client who has substantial property, needs trusts, or a complex will, etc., should use a lawyer. A lawyer can work with the client's other professional advisors and is needed to draw up the appropriate legal documents.

LAWYERS IN PUBLIC ACCOUNTING

The public may not be aware of this, but not only are a growing number of lawyers CPAs, but they work in public accounting firms as well. Increasingly the large CPA firms employ lawyers, particularly in their tax departments. They work as CPAs, not lawyers, although there is a fine line. They do everything, except litigation, from tax and estate planning to obtaining private rulings from the IRS.

CPAS

There are some 300,000 CPAs in the U.S. The average CPA knows more about taxes than the average lawyer because 20% of the Accounting Practice Exam, which constitutes 40% of the CPA exam, is devoted to taxation on every exam. It is hard to pass the CPA exam without having some tax knowledge. A licensed CPA can represent the client before the IRS, just like a lawyer or an enrolled agent (see below). A Form 2848, Power of Attorney, must be executed and the client does not even have to show up. The average CPA knows more and charges less than the average lawyer and is not above filing the tax return either. But once the client is dealing with leading tax experts, their fees are about the same regardless of degrees or professional designation, say $150 - $300 per hour.

A licensed CPA is subject to sanctions like a lawyer. If in breach of the Code of Ethics or convicted of tax crimes, a CPA stands to lose the license, temporarily (suspension), or permanently (revocation). The American Institute of CPAs in "Statement of Responsibilities in Tax Practice," lays out detailed rules of conduct. Since 1943, a CPA generally cannot practice in any court. Theoretically, anyone *can* practice in the Tax Court, but only if among one of a few dozen people nationwide who has passed a demanding annual Tax Court exam, given in Washington, D.C., in November.

ENROLLED AGENTS

Ex-IRS employees with stated practical experience, or persons who have passed a rather basic Treasury exam, are entitled to cards as *enrolled agents.* Such persons are subject to Treasury rules of conduct and can represent taxpayers before the IRS. Some 20,000 people are enrolled to practice. Many of them, however, are not eligible to sit for the CPA exam or have given up trying.

THE IRS ITSELF

The IRS gives free advice, forms, and publications to the public. They also have phone numbers for instant answers and will even prepare returns for people who do not mind waiting. It should be noted that the IRS is not bound by any oral advice rendered by an employee or by any information printed in their own publications—just as they are not bound by the taxpayer's opinion or that of an adviser. However, advice of counsel or a tax adviser may be a defense in a civil or criminal case, but the client still owes the tax plus interest.

MISCELLANEOUS TAX ADVISERS

There must be some 300,000 return preparers in the U.S., most of whom are seasonal or part-time people. Large chains operate on a national basis, employing housewives and others on a low, hourly pay scale, often only for the season. These people are *not* tax advisers, but clerical return preparers only. They need hardly be more, since on April 15 there is precious little tax planning to be done. They can *accompany the client* to the IRS office, but they *cannot* represent the client.

Anyone can legally prepare a return. It is not a licensed profession. However, since 1976, there are statutory penalties for negligence, fraud, and unauthorized disclosure of information. The preparer must also be identified and give each client a copy of the return.

A word of caution: Taxpayer receives a refund check and is very happy. But a refund is *automatic*. If the return asks for it and there are no mathematical errors, it will be received. The IRS then has three years to select the return for audit and may perhaps collect the refund back with interest and penalties.

WHO CAN REPRESENT THEMSELVES?

Individuals may appear before the IRS on their own behalf and need no enrollment to represent the following legal persons, assuming proper identification:

1. A full-time employee may represent the employer.
2. A full-time employee or a partner may represent a partnership.
3. An individual may represent immediate family (brother, sister, son, daughter, or parent) without compensation.

4. Officers or full-time employees may represent their corporate employers, subsidiaries, brother-sister corporations, unincorporated associations, etc.
5. Trustees, receivers, guardians, administrators, and executors may represent their trusts, receiverships, guardianships, or estates.
6. An officer or employee may represent a government unit, agency or authority, if within the scope of official duties.
7. Any return preparer may appear to explain the particular return prepared.

¶ 1909 LIFE INSURANCE AGENTS

A life insurance salesperson is just that, a salesperson. Obviously, a salesperson is going to sell the product that offers the best commission, invariably a whole life policy, also called ordinary life or straight life. The commission earned is generally 50% of the first year's premium plus 5-10% of each annual premium thereafter. This is not to say that an agent cannot be helpful, such as having to prove a need to purchase a policy, necessitating a look at the client's overall financial situation and estate plan. Life insurance should in many cases be an important facet of a family's financial well-being and protection. Life insurance is covered in a separate chapter, but here is some advice on the choice of an agent:

1. If possible, use a person with considerable experience in gearing an insurance program to the client's unique situation.
2. A CLU, or Chartered Life Underwriter, should be used, if possible, because a CLU has shown, through rigorous examinations, considerable knowledge about insurance, personal finance, taxation, and estate planning. Unfortunately, of the 400,000 licensed insurance agents, only some 30,000 are CLUs.
3. As a general rule, no one should buy insurance from a relative or friend. The client is not likely to buy what is needed and is precluded from doing comparison shopping.
4. Savings and loan associations sometimes have insurance subsidiaries. They tend to specialize in property insurance for their mortgage customers, but they may also offer mortgage life and disability insurance, accident, sickness, car insurance, etc. The advantage of using the mortagee as an insurance adviser is that the client is more likely to obtain insurance coverage designed to fit the family's needs with a minimum of hard sell.

¶ 1910 APPRAISERS

Apraisers are needed in many situations, such as:

1. Estate and gift tax valuations, charitable contributions valuations, etc., for tax purposes.
2. The purchase or sale of a business.
3. Real estate transactions.

The American Society of Appraisers is a multi-disciplinary, professional appraisal society. It is worth checking that the appraiser used is a member, because society members are tested and certified. Appraisers specialize in the following areas, among others:

1. Real property, urban and rural, from farms to city apartment houses.
2. Personal property, such as fine arts, antiques, jewelry, coins, books, etc.
3. Machinery and equipment.
4. Intangibles, such as copyrights, patents, and franchises.
5. Technical valuations, such as cost surveys, investment tax credit properties, building component allocations, etc.

Mortgage granting institutions, such as "savings and loans" frequently start their own valuations subsidiaries when they become large enough. This enables them to offer better quality and/or lower prices than if independent appraisers were used. They may also be available on a project basis even if the client has no other business with the parent company. The services are centered exclusively on real estate, and each appraiser typically specializes in one small geographic area.

¶ 1911 PERSONAL FINANCIAL PLANNERS

Financial planning services are offered through financial institutions, such as banks, insurance companies, brokerage houses, and by individual practitioners and specialized consulting firms. A recent help wanted ad from a major bank, advertising for people to staff their Financial Advisory Service department, revealed the following:

1. The department renders objective and comprehensive financial counseling to executives of large companies.
2. The service includes estate planning, investment counseling, income tax planning, and corporate benefit analysis.
3. A number of individual account executives are employed with the responsibility for the preparation of comprehensive financial plans for executives and continuing counseling for large corporations and high-income individuals.

4. The people they look for are lawyers, MBAs, CPAs, or CFPs, ideally all of the above in one person, and with a few years of experience in sophisticated financial planning, whether in a large CPA firm, financial institutions, or a financial consulting firm. Some major banks only hire CPAs and lawyers in their personal financial planning department; others hire MBAs or anyone with a degree in business or economics plus experience.

The fees vary greatly:

1. Some consultants charge an hourly fee, typically from $50 to $100 and up.
2. Others charge a lump sum, ranging from a few hundred dollars to several thousand dollars, depending on the size and complexity of the task involved.
3. Some brokerage firms charge an initial flat fee, say $600, plus an additional smaller fee for annual follow-up consultations.
4. "Financial planners" who offer "free" plans are going to sell clients something, and whatever it is, mutual funds, life insurance, or tax shelters, this is what they will recommend that the client needs more of. They may even be right, but they are not going to render objective advice. Major financial institutions, such as banks and brokerage firms often manage to separate financial planning from what they sell.

¶ 1912 PROFESSIONAL DESIGNATIONS

Everything else being equal, a person with professional certifications probably knows more than someone without. Here is a brief description of a few professional designations granted only after exams with some financial content.

CPA OR CERTIFIED PUBLIC ACCOUNTANT

Requirements, in addition to passing the exam, vary from state to state, but typically include having reached age 21, not having been convicted of a felony, a college degree, several courses in accounting and one to three years of practical experience. The subject matter includes Accounting Practice (including taxation), Auditing, and Business Law.

CMA OR CERTIFIED MANAGEMENT ACCOUNTANT

The equivalent of an undergraduate degree, as well as two years' experience, is required. The subject matter includes Economics, Business Finance, Organizational Behavior, Financial Accounting, Auditing, Cost Accounting, Decision Models, and Data Processing.

CFA OR CHARTERED FINANCIAL ANALYST

A college degree, including two years of accounting, is required. The exam is in three parts, requiring one, three and five years' experience in a field related to securities investment respectively. Areas covered on the exam include Accounting, Economics, Financial Analysis, and Portfolio Management.

CLU OR CHARTERED LIFE UNDERWRITER

The candidate needs no college, but three years of experience. The designation is standard for life insurance professionals and dates back to 1927. The exam covers Life Insurance, Health Insurance, Pension Planning, Taxation, Investments, Personal Financial Planning, Accounting, Finance, Economics, and Estate Planning.

CPCU OR CHARTERED PROPERTY AND CASUALTY UNDERWRITERS

Requirements are similar to those for the CLU. Coverage includes Property Insurance and Risk Management, Economics, Insurance and Business Law, Management, Accounting, and Finance.

CFP OR CERTIFIED FINANCIAL PLANNER

A CFP is an individual who has passed six examinations after taking in-class or correspondence courses in personal financial planning offered through the College for Financial Planning in Denver. The number of CFPs is growing and totals over 20,000. The subject matter includes investments, taxation, insurance, retirement planning, and estate planning.

ChFC OR CHARTERED FINANCIAL CONSULTANT

The ChFC designation is granted by the American College in Bryn Mawr, Pennsylvania, and is integrated with their CLU program. The exams do double duty for both certifications, except for three extras for each. Courses are optional, but are offered on hundreds of campuses. Three years of relevant experience is required. The candidate may prepare through self-study. It is a close competitor to the CFP designation.

PFS OR PERSONAL FINANCIAL SPECIALIST

To help CPAs compete with CFPs and ChFCs, the American Institute of CPAs started its own program in 1988. The PFS designation may be granted after a one day exam and 250 hours of relevant experience per year for three years. Only a few hundred PFSs exist as yet.

MSFS OR MASTER OF SCIENCE IN FINANCIAL SERVICES

Offered by American College, courses provide in-depth coverage in areas such as taxes, deferred compensation, and estate planning. A few universities offer undergraduate programs in financial planning. The first MBA in financial planning was started by Golden Gate University in San Francisco.

RFP OR REGISTERED FINANCIAL PLANNER

To become a member of the International Association of RFPs, the candidate must be a CFP, ChFC, CPA, or have a law or business degree, have three years of relevant experience, a clean record, and pay an annual fee.

THE REGISTRY OF FINANCIAL PLANNING PRACTITIONERS

To become a member of the International Association for Financial Planners, the requirements are similar to those of an RFP, but the candidate also must pass a full day's exam, as well as subjecting some personally written plans to review by a national panel. No number of letters after a name provide an ironclad guarantee, but most designations are only granted after rigorous exams and usually after relevant experience has been gained.

¶ 1913 EXTENT AND TYPES OF FINANCIAL PLANNERS USED TODAY

In 1986, Independent Insurance Agents of America made a study of the use of financial planners by U.S. adults making in excess of $20,000 a year. A full 80% did not use financial planning services at all. The 20% who did use financial planners used the following categories of advisers:

Accountants	5%
Lawyers	11%
Bankers	12%
Stockbrokers	20%
Independent Financial Advisers	21%
Independent Insurance Agents	31%

Thus, the personal financial planner has already surpassed accountants, lawyers, and bankers in the personal finance field. This is remarkable for a profession that hardly even existed prior to 1978.

APPENDIX

PRESENT VALUE TABLES AND TAX RATES

Present Value Tables

¶ 2001 PRESENT VALUE TABLE: HOW MUCH $1 TO BE PAID IN THE FUTURE IS CURRENTLY WORTH

The table shows how much $1 to be paid at various periods in the future is now worth, with interest at different rates compounded annually. Adding an annual inflation factor to the interest rate will help to compute real present value, i.e., assuming an interest rate of six percent and an annual inflation rate of three percent, the nine percent interest rate would be used to determine present value. See the following pages.

YEAR	4.50%	5.00%	5.50%	6.00%	6.50%	7.00%	7.50%	8.00%
1	0.956938	0.952381	0.947867	0.943396	0.938967	0.934579	0.930233	0.925926
2	0.915730	0.907029	0.898452	0.889996	0.881659	0.873439	0.865333	0.857339
3	0.876297	0.863838	0.851614	0.839619	0.827849	0.816298	0.804961	0.793832
4	0.838561	0.822702	0.807217	0.792094	0.777323	0.762895	0.748801	0.735030
5	0.802451	0.783526	0.765134	0.747258	0.729881	0.712986	0.696559	0.680583
6	0.767896	0.746215	0.725246	0.704961	0.685334	0.666342	0.647962	0.630170
7	0.734828	0.710681	0.687437	0.665057	0.643506	0.622750	0.602755	0.583490
8	0.703185	0.676839	0.651599	0.627412	0.604231	0.582009	0.560702	0.540269
9	0.672904	0.644609	0.617629	0.591898	0.567353	0.543934	0.521583	0.500249
10	0.643928	0.613913	0.585431	0.558395	0.532726	0.508349	0.485194	0.463193
11	0.616199	0.584679	0.554911	0.526788	0.500212	0.475093	0.451343	0.428883
12	0.589664	0.556837	0.525982	0.496969	0.469683	0.444012	0.419854	0.397114
13	0.564272	0.530321	0.498561	0.468839	0.441017	0.414964	0.390562	0.367698
14	0.539973	0.505068	0.472569	0.442301	0.414100	0.387817	0.363313	0.340461
15	0.516720	0.481017	0.447933	0.417265	0.388827	0.362446	0.337966	0.315242
16	0.494469	0.458112	0.424581	0.393646	0.365095	0.388735	0.314387	0.291890
17	0.473176	0.436297	0.402447	0.371364	0.342813	0.316574	0.292453	0.270269
18	0.452800	0.415521	0.381466	0.350344	0.321890	0.295864	0.272049	0.250249
19	0.433302	0.395734	0.361579	0.330513	0.302244	0.276508	0.253069	0.231712
20	0.414643	0.376889	0.342729	0.311805	0.283797	0.258419	0.235413	0.214548
21	0.396787	0.358942	0.324862	0.294155	0.266476	0.241513	0.218989	0.198656
22	0.379701	0.341850	0.307926	0.277505	0.250212	0.225713	0.203711	0.183941
23	0.363350	0.325571	0.291873	0.261797	0.234941	0.210947	0.189498	0.170315
24	0.347703	0.310068	0.276657	0.246979	0.220602	0.197147	0.176277	0.157699
25	0.332731	0.295303	0.262234	0.232999	0.207138	0.184249	0.163979	0.146018

YEAR	8.50%	9.00%	9.50%	10.00%	10.50%	11.00%	11.50%	12.00%
1	0.921659	0.917431	0.913242	0.909091	0.904977	0.900901	0.896861	0.892857
2	0.849455	0.841680	0.834011	0.826446	0.818984	0.811622	0.804360	0.797194
3	0.782908	0.772183	0.761654	0.751315	0.741162	0.731191	0.721399	0.711780
4	0.721574	0.708425	0.695574	0.683013	0.670735	0.658731	0.646994	0.635518
5	0.665045	0.649931	0.635228	0.620921	0.607000	0.593451	0.580264	0.567427
6	0.612945	0.596267	0.580117	0.564474	0.549321	0.534641	0.520416	0.506631
7	0.564926	0.547034	0.529787	0.513158	0.497123	0.481658	0.466741	0.452349
8	0.520669	0.501866	0.483824	0.466507	0.449885	0.433926	0.418602	0.403883
9	0.479880	0.460428	0.441848	0.424098	0.407136	0.390925	0.375428	0.360610
10	0.442285	0.422411	0.403514	0.385543	0.368449	0.352184	0.336706	0.321973
11	0.407636	0.387533	0.368506	0.350494	0.333438	0.317283	0.301979	0.287476
12	0.375702	0.355535	0.336535	0.318631	0.301754	0.285841	0.270833	0.256675
13	0.346269	0.326179	0.307338	0.289664	0.273080	0.257514	0.242900	0.229174
14	0.319142	0.299246	0.280674	0.263331	0.247132	0.231995	0.217847	0.204620
15	0.294140	0.274538	0.256323	0.239392	0.223648	0.209004	0.195379	0.182696
16	0.271097	0.251870	0.234085	0.217629	0.202397	0.188292	0.175227	0.163122
17	0.249859	0.231073	0.213777	0.197845	0.183164	0.169633	0.157155	0.145644
18	0.230285	0.211994	0.195230	0.179859	0.165760	0.152822	0.140946	0.130040
19	0.212244	0.194490	0.178292	0.163508	0.150009	0.137678	0.126409	0.116107
20	0.195616	0.178431	0.162824	0.148644	0.135755	0.124034	0.113371	0.103667
21	0.180292	0.163698	0.148697	0.135131	0.122855	0.111742	0.101678	0.092560
22	0.166167	0.150182	0.135797	0.122846	0.111181	0.100669	0.091191	0.082643
23	0.153150	0.137781	0.124015	0.111678	0.100616	0.090693	0.081786	0.073788
24	0.141152	0.126405	0.113256	0.101526	0.091055	0.081705	0.073351	0.065882
25	0.130094	0.115968	0.103430	0.092296	0.082403	0.073608	0.065785	0.058823

YEAR	12.50%	13.00%	13.50%	14.00%	14.50%	15.00%	15.50%	16.00%
1	0.888889	0.884956	0.881057	0.877193	0.873362	0.869565	0.865801	0.862069
2	0.790123	0.783147	0.776262	0.769468	0.762762	0.756144	0.749611	0.743163
3	0.702332	0.693050	0.683931	0.674972	0.666168	0.657516	0.649014	0.640658
4	0.624295	0.613319	0.602583	0.592080	0.581806	0.571753	0.561917	0.552291
5	0.554929	0.542760	0.530910	0.519369	0.508127	0.497177	0.486508	0.476113
6	0.493270	0.480319	0.467762	0.455587	0.443779	0.432328	0.421219	0.410442
7	0.438462	0.425061	0.412125	0.399637	0.387580	0.375937	0.364692	0.353830
8	0.389744	0.376160	0.363106	0.350559	0.338498	0.326902	0.315751	0.305025
9	0.346439	0.332885	0.319917	0.307508	0.295631	0.284262	0.273377	0.262953
10	0.307946	0.294588	0.281865	0.269744	0.258193	0.247185	0.236690	0.226684
11	0.273730	0.260698	0.248339	0.236617	0.225496	0.214943	0.204927	0.195417
12	0.243315	0.230706	0.218801	0.207559	0.196940	0.186907	0.177426	0.168463
13	0.216280	0.204165	0.192776	0.182069	0.172000	0.162528	0.153615	0.145227
14	0.192249	0.180677	0.169847	0.159710	0.150218	0.141329	0.133000	0.125195
15	0.170888	0.159891	0.149645	0.140096	0.131195	0.122894	0.115152	0.107927
16	0.151901	0.141496	0.131846	0.122892	0.114581	0.106865	0.099698	0.093041
17	0.135023	0.125218	0.116164	0.107800	0.100071	0.092926	0.086319	0.080207
18	0.120020	0.110812	0.102347	0.094561	0.087398	0.080805	0.074735	0.069144
19	0.106685	0.098064	0.090173	0.082948	0.076330	0.070265	0.064706	0.059607
20	0.094831	0.086782	0.079448	0.072762	0.066664	0.061100	0.056022	0.051385
21	0.084294	0.076798	0.069998	0.063826	0.058222	0.053131	0.048504	0.044298
22	0.074928	0.067963	0.061672	0.055988	0.050849	0.046201	0.041995	0.038188
23	0.066603	0.060144	0.054337	0.049112	0.044409	0.040174	0.036359	0.032920
24	0.059202	0.053225	0.047874	0.043081	0.038785	0.034934	0.031480	0.028380
25	0.052624	0.047102	0.042180	0.037790	0.033874	0.030378	0.027255	0.024465

YEAR	16.50%	17.00%	17.50%	18.00%	18.50%	19.00%	19.50%	20.00%
1	0.858369	0.854701	0.851064	0.847458	0.843882	0.840336	0.836820	0.833333
2	0.736798	0.730514	0.724310	0.718184	0.712137	0.706165	0.700268	0.694444
3	0.632444	0.624371	0.616434	0.608631	0.600959	0.593416	0.585998	0.578704
4	0.542871	0.533650	0.524624	0.515789	0.507139	0.498669	0.490375	0.482253
5	0.465983	0.456111	0.446489	0.437109	0.427965	0.419049	0.410356	0.401878
6	0.399986	0.389839	0.379991	0.370432	0.361152	0.352142	0.343394	0.334898
7	0.343335	0.333195	0.323396	0.313925	0.304770	0.295918	0.287359	0.279082
8	0.294708	0.284782	0.275231	0.266038	0.257189	0.248671	0.240468	0.232568
9	0.252969	0.243404	0.234239	0.225456	0.217038	0.208967	0.201228	0.193807
10	0.217140	0.208037	0.199352	0.191064	0.183154	0.175602	0.168392	0.161506
11	0.186387	0.177810	0.169662	0.161919	0.154560	0.147565	0.140914	0.134588
12	0.159989	0.151974	0.144393	0.137220	0.130431	0.124004	0.117919	0.112157
13	0.137329	0.129892	0.122888	0.116288	0.110068	0.104205	0.098677	0.093464
14	0.117879	0.111019	0.104585	0.098549	0.092884	0.087567	0.082575	0.077887
15	0.101184	0.094888	0.089009	0.083516	0.078384	0.073586	0.069101	0.064905
16	0.086853	0.081101	0.075752	0.070776	0.066146	0.061837	0.057825	0.054088
17	0.074552	0.069317	0.064470	0.059980	0.055820	0.051964	0.048389	0.045073
18	0.063993	0.059245	0.054868	0.050830	0.047105	0.043667	0.040493	0.037561
19	0.054930	0.050637	0.046696	0.043077	0.039751	0.036695	0.033885	0.031301
20	0.047150	0.043280	0.039741	0.036506	0.033545	0.030836	0.028356	0.026084
21	0.040472	0.036991	0.033822	0.030937	0.028308	0.025913	0.023729	0.021737
22	0.034740	0.031616	0.028785	0.026218	0.023889	0.021775	0.019857	0.018114
23	0.029820	0.027022	0.024498	0.022218	0.020159	0.018299	0.016616	0.015095
24	0.025596	0.023096	0.020849	0.018829	0.017012	0.015377	0.013905	0.012579
25	0.021971	0.019740	0.017744	0.015957	0.014356	0.012922	0.011636	0.010483

¶ 2002 ANNUITY TABLE

(Present Value of $1 Received at the End of Each Period)

Payout Periods	*6%*	*8%*	*10%*	*12%*	*15%*	*20%*	*30%*
1	.943	.926	.909	.893	.877	.833	.769
2	1.833	1.783	1.736	1.690	1.626	1.528	1.361
3	2.673	2.577	2.487	2.402	2.283	2.106	1.816
4	3.465	3.312	3.170	3.037	2.855	2.589	2.166
5	4.212	3.993	3.791	3.605	3.352	2.991	2.436
6	4.917	4.623	4.355	4.111	3.784	3.326	2.643
7	5.582	5.206	4.868	4.564	4.160	3.605	2.802
8	6.210	5.747	5.335	4.968	4.487	3.837	2.925
9	6.802	6.247	5.759	5.328	4.772	4.031	3.019
10	7.360	6.710	6.145	5.650	5.019	4.192	3.092
11	7.887	7.139	6.495	5.937	5.234	4.327	3.147
12	8.384	7.536	6.814	6.194	5.421	4.439	3.190
13	8.853	7.904	7.103	6.424	5.583	4.533	3.223
14	9.295	8.244	7.367	6.628	5.724	4.611	3.249
15	9.712	8.559	7.606	6.811	5.845	4.675	3.268
16	10.106	8.851	7.824	6.974	5.954	4.730	3.283
17	10.477	9.122	8.022	7.120	6.047	4.775	3.295
18	10.828	9.372	8.201	7.250	6.128	4.813	3.304
19	11.158	9.604	8.365	7.366	6.198	4.844	3.311
20	11.470	9.818	8.514	7.469	6.259	4.870	3.316
25	12.783	10.675	9.077	7.843	6.464	4.948	3.329
30	13.765	11.258	9.427	8.055	6.566	4.979	3.332
40	15.046	11.925	9.779	8.244	6.642	4.997	3.333

¶ 2003 PRESENT WORTH OF LIFE INTERESTS AND REMAINDERS

Table A Single Life, Unisex, 10% Showing the Present Worth of an Annuity, of a Life Interest, and of a Remainder Interest

Age	Annuity	Life Estate	Remainder	Age	Annuity	Life Estate	Remainder
0	9.7188	.97188	.02812	55	8.0046	.80046	.19954
1	9.8988	.98988	.01012	56	7.9006	.79006	.20994
2	9.9017	.99017	.00983	57	7.7931	.77931	.22069
3	9.9008	.99008	.00992	58	7.6822	.76822	.23178
4	9.8981	.98981	.01019	59	7.5675	.75675	.24325
5	9.8938	.98938	.01062	60	7.4491	.74491	.25509
6	9.8884	.98884	.01116	61	7.3267	.73267	.26733
7	9.8822	.98822	.01178	62	7.2002	.72002	.27998
8	9.8748	.98748	.01252	63	7.0696	.70696	.29304
9	9.8663	.98663	.01337	64	6.9352	.69352	.30648
10	9.8565	.98565	.01435	65	6.7970	.67970	.32030
11	9.8453	.98453	.01547	66	6.6551	.66551	.33449
12	9.8329	.98329	.01671	67	6.5098	.65098	.34902
13	9.8198	.98198	.01802	68	6.3610	.63610	.36390
14	9.8066	.98066	.01934	69	6.2086	.62086	.37914
15	9.7937	.97937	.02063	70	6.0522	.60522	.39478
16	9.7815	.97815	.02185	71	5.8914	.58914	.41086
17	9.7700	.97700	.02300	72	5.7261	.57261	.42739
18	9.7590	.97590	.02410	73	5.5571	.55571	.44429
19	9.7480	.97480	.02520	74	5.3862	.53862	.46138
20	9.7365	.97365	.02635	75	5.2149	.52149	.47851
21	9.7245	.97245	.02755	76	5.0441	.50441	.49559
22	9.7120	.97120	.02880	77	4.8742	.48742	.51258
23	9.6986	.96986	.03014	78	4.7049	.47049	.52951
24	9.6841	.96841	.03159	79	4.5357	.45357	.54643
25	9.6678	.96678	.03322	80	4.3659	.43659	.56341
26	9.6495	.96495	.03505	81	4.1967	.41967	.58033
27	9.6290	.96290	.03710	82	4.0295	.40295	.59705
28	9.6062	.96062	.03938	83	3.8642	.38642	.61358
29	9.5813	.95813	.04187	84	3.6998	.36998	.63002
30	9.5543	.95543	.04457	85	3.5359	.35359	.64641
31	9.5254	.95254	.04746	86	3.3764	.33764	.66236
32	9.4942	.94942	.05058	87	3.2262	.32262	.67738
33	9.4608	.94608	.05392	88	3.0859	.30859	.69141
34	9.4250	.94250	.05750	89	2.9526	.29526	.70474
35	9.3868	.93868	.06132	90	2.8221	.28221	.71779
36	9.3460	.93460	.06540	91	2.6955	.26955	.73045
37	9.3026	.93026	.06974	92	2.5771	.25771	.74229
38	9.2567	.92567	.07433	93	2.4692	.24692	.75308
39	9.2083	.92083	.07917	94	2.3728	.23728	.76272
40	9.1571	.91571	.08429	95	2.2887	.22887	.77113
41	9.1030	.91030	.08970	96	2.2181	.22181	.77819
42	9.0457	.90457	.09543	97	2.1550	.21550	.78450
43	8.9855	.89855	.10145	98	2.1000	.21000	.79000
44	8.9221	.89221	.10779	99	2.0486	.20486	.79514
45	8.8558	.88558	.11442	100	1.9975	.19975	.80025
46	8.7863	.87863	.12137	101	1.9532	.19532	.80468
47	8.7137	.87137	.12863	102	1.9054	.19054	.80946
48	8.6374	.86374	.13626	103	1.8437	.18437	.81563
49	8.5578	.85578	.14422	104	1.7856	.17856	.82144
50	8.4743	.84743	.15257	105	1.6962	.16962	.83038
51	8.3874	.83874	.16126	106	1.5488	.15488	.84512
52	8.2969	.82969	.17031	107	1.3409	.13409	.86591
53	8.2028	.82028	.17972	108	1.0068	.10068	.89932
54	8.1054	.81054	.18946	109	.4545	.04545	.95455

Table B Table Showing the Present Worth at 10% of an Annuity for a Term Certain, of an Income Interest for a Term Certain, and of a Remainder Interest Postponed for a Term Certain

Number of Years	*Annuity*	*Term Certain*	*Remainder*	*Number of Years*	*Annuity*	*Term Certain*	*Remainder*
1	.9091	.090909	.909091	31	9.4790	.947901	.052099
2	1.7355	.173554	.826446	32	9.5264	.952638	.047362
3	2.4869	.248685	.751315	33	9.5694	.956943	.043057
4	3.1699	.316987	.683013	34	9.6086	.960857	.039143
5	3.7908	.379079	.620921	35	9.6442	.964416	.035584
6	4.3553	.435526	.564474	36	9.6765	.967651	.032349
7	4.8684	.486842	.513158	37	9.7059	.970592	.029408
8	5.3349	.533493	.466507	38	9.7327	.973265	.026735
9	5.7590	.575902	.424098	39	9.7570	.975686	.024304
10	6.1446	.614457	.385543	40	9.7791	.977905	.022095
11	6.4951	.649506	.350494	41	9.7991	.979914	.020096
12	6.8137	.681369	.318631	42	9.8174	.981740	.018260
13	7.1034	.710336	.289664	43	9.8340	.983400	.016600
14	7.3667	.736669	.263331	44	9.8491	.984909	.015091
15	7.6061	.760608	.239392	45	9.8628	.986281	.013718
16	7.8237	.782371	.217629	46	9.8753	.987528	.012472
17	8.0216	.802155	.197845	47	9.8866	.988662	.011338
18	8.2014	.820141	.179859	48	9.8969	.989693	.010307
19	8.3649	.836492	.163508	49	9.9063	.990630	.009370
20	8.5136	.851356	.148644	50	9.9148	.991481	.008519
21	8.6487	.864869	.135131	51	9.9226	.992256	.007744
22	8.7715	.877154	.122846	52	9.9296	.992960	.007040
23	8.8832	.888322	.111678	53	9.9360	.993600	.006400
24	8.9847	.898474	.101526	54	9.9418	.994182	.005818
25	9.0770	.907704	.092296	55	9.9471	.994711	.005289
26	9.1609	.916095	.083905	56	9.9519	.995191	.004809
27	9.2372	.923722	.076278	57	9.9563	.995629	.004371
28	9.3066	.930657	.069343	58	9.9603	.996026	.003974
29	9.3696	.936961	.063039	59	9.9639	.996387	.003613
30	9.4269	.942691	.057309	60	9.9672	.996716	.003284

Tax Rate Schedules

¶ 2005 TAX RATE SCHEDULES X—Z, ESTATES, AND TRUSTS

1993 SCHEDULE X: Single Individuals—No Dependents

Taxable Income Over	But Not Over	Pay	+ % on Excess	of the amount over—
$ 0	—$ 22,100	$ 0	15%	$ 0
22,100	— 53,500	3,315	28	22,100
53,500	— 115,000	12,107	31	53,500
115,000	— 250,000	31,172	36	115,000
250,000	....	79,772	39.6	250,000

1993 SCHEDULE Y-1: Married Individuals, Joint Returns and Surviving Spouses

Taxable Income Over	But Not Over	Pay	+ % on Excess	of the amount over—
$ 0	—$ 36,900	$ 0	15%	$ 0
36,900	— 89,150	5,535	28	36,900
89,150	— 140,000	20,165	31	89,150
140,000	— 250,000	35,928.50	36	140,100
250,000	....	75,528.50	39.6	250,000

1993 SCHEDULE Y-2: Separate Returns, Married Persons

Taxable Income Over	But Not Over	Pay	+ % on Excess	of the amount over—
$ 0	—$ 18,450	$ 0	15%	$ 0
18,450	— 44,575	2,767.50	28	18,450
44,575	— 70,000	10,082.50	31	44,575
70,000	— 125,000	17,964.25	36	70,000
125,000	....	37,764.25	39.6	125,000

1993 SCHEDULE Z: Heads of Households

Taxable Income Over	But Not Over	Pay	+ % on Excess	of the amount over—
$ 0	—$ 29,600	$ 0	15 %	$ 0
29,600	— 76,400	4,440	28	29,600
76,400	— 127,500	17,544	31	76,400
127,500	— 250,000	33,385	36	127,500
250,000—	......	77,485	39.6%	250,000

1993 INCOME TAX RATE SCHEDULE FOR USE BY ESTATES AND NONGRANTOR TRUSTS

Taxable Income Over	But Not Over	Pay	+ % on Excess	of the amount over—
$ 0—	$ 1,500	$ 0	15 %	$ 0
1,500—	3,500	225	28	1,500
3,500—	5,500	785	31	3,500
5,500—	7,500	1,405	36	5,500
7,500—	.....	2,125	39.6	7,500

AVERAGE ITEMIZED DEDUCTIONS

The following chart of average major itemized deductions is based on preliminary statistics of income for 1990. The chart is provided solely for informational purposes and should not be regarded as indicating properly allowable amounts. Claimed itemized deductions are subject to substantiation. Furthermore, it should be noted that for the 1990 tax year, only 10% of personal interest was deductible. Effective for 1991 and subsequent tax years, interest on personal loans is not deductible.

Preliminary Average Itemized Deductions for 1990 by AGI Ranges

PRELIMINARY AVERAGE ITEMIZED DEDUCTIONS FOR 1990 BY ADJUSTED GROSS INCOME RANGES

Adjusted Gross Income Ranges	*Medical Expenses*	*Taxes*	*Interest*	*Contributions*
$ 15,000 under $ 20,000	$ 4,281	$ 1,520	$ 5,393	$ 1,142
$ 20,000 under $ 25,000	3,812	1,806	4,314	1,249
$ 25,000 under $ 30,000	3,306	2,069	4,662	1,129
$ 30,000 under $ 40,000	3,137	2,477	4,980	1,213
$ 40,000 under $ 50,000	3,612	3,015	5,667	1,315
$ 50,000 under $ 75,000	4,002	4,049	6,595	1,665
$ 75,000 under $ 100,000	6,003	5,888	8,847	2,112
$ 100,000 under $ 200,000	12,087	9,359	13,324	3,442
$ 200,000 under $ 500,000	26,295	20,075	20,831	7,367
$ 500,000 under $1,000,000	58,296	42,609	30,315	16,815
$1,000,000 and over	68,915	140,715	67,440	80,144

Corporation Income Tax Rates

¶ 2006 CORPORATIONS

For tax years beginning on or after January 1, 1993, the corporate tax rates are as follows:

Taxable income over	Not over	Tax rate
$ 0	$ 50,000	15%
50,000	75,000	25
75,000	100,000	34
100,000	......	34 plus 5% of the taxable income in excess of $100,000 or $11,750, whichever is less
10,000,000	......	35

Estate and Gift Taxes

¶ 2007 COMPUTATION OF TAXES

Estate Taxes. Estate taxes are computed by applying the unified rate schedule to the cumulated at death and lifetime transfers and subtracting the gift taxes payable. The unified rate schedule is effective for gifts made after December 31, 1976, and to estates of decedents dying after that date.

Gift Taxes. Gift taxes are computed by applying the unified rate schedule to cumulative lifetime taxable transfers and subtracting the taxes payable for prior taxable periods. There is an annual $10,000 exclusion for gifts, with an annual maximum of $20,000 for spouses for gift-splitting. Additionally, there is an unlimited exclusion for payments of tuition and medical expenses.

Generation-Skipping Transfer Tax. The tax on generation-skipping transfers is computed with reference to a flat rate equal to the product of the maximum estate tax rate (55%) and the inclusion ratio with respect to the transfer.

UNIFIED CREDIT

Subject to phaseout for transfers exceeding $10 million (for estates of decedents dying, and gifts made, after 1987), estates of decedents dying after 1986 qualify for a unified credit of $192,800 (equivalent to an exemption of $600,000). For transfers subject to the phaseout, the tentative tax (computed in arriving at the ultimate tax) is increased by 5% of the excess of the cumulative transfer over $10 million until full recapture of the benefits of both the unified credit and graduated transfer-tax rates. Currently, full phaseout occurs at the $21,040,000 level. The credit is adjustable to shield pre-1988 gifts from the effects of the phaseout. Any part of the credit used to offset gift taxes is not available to offset estate taxes.

Amount of Credit. The unified credit is subtracted from the taxpayer's estate or gift tax liability. However, the amount of the unified credit available at death will be reduced to the extent that any portion of the credit is used to offset gift taxes on lifetime transfers. In addition, the amount of the unified credit will be reduced by 20% of any portion of the $30,000 specific gift tax exemption allowable under pre-1977 law that was used with respect to gifts made after September 8, 1976, but before January 1, 1977. Thus, under this rule, the maximum reduction of the unified credit will be $6,000 (20% of $30,000).

Unified Transfer Tax Rate Schedule *

If the amount is:		Tentative tax ** is:		
Over	But not over	Tax +	%	On excess over
$ 0	$ 10,000	$ 0	18	$ 0
10,000	20,000	1,800	20	10,000
20,000	40,000	3,800	22	20,000
40,000	60,000	8,200	24	40,000
60,000	80,000	13,000	26	60,000
80,000	100,000	18,200	28	80,000
100,000	150,000	23,800	30	100,000
150,000	250,000	38,800	32	150,000
250,000	500,000	70,800	34	250,000
500,000	750,000	155,800	37	500,000
750,000	1,000,000	248,300	39	750,000
1,000,000	1,250,000	345,800	41	1,000,000
1,250,000	1,500,000	448,300	43	1,250,000
1,500,000	2,000,000	555,800	45	1,500,000
2,000,000	2,500,000	780,800	49	2,000,000
2,500,000	....	1,025,800	53	2,500,000
3,000,000	....	1,290,800	55	3,000,000

* This rate schedule applies to estates of decedents dying, and gifts made, after 1987. For estates of decedents dying, and gifts made, in 1984 through 1992, the top tax rate is 55% for transfers in excess of $3,000,000. A 53% rate applies to transfers in the $2,500,000—$3,000,000 range.

** The cumulative transfers to which the tentative tax applies are the sum of (a) the amount of the taxable estate and (b) the amount of the taxable gifts made by the decedent after 1976 other than gifts includible in the gross estate.

CREDIT FOR STATE DEATH TAXES

The table below is to be used in calculating the amount of the credit available for state death taxes paid with respect to property included in a decedent's gross estate.

State Death Tax Credit Table [1, 2]

Estates of Decedents Dying after 1976

Adjusted Taxable Estate [3] At least	But less than	Credit =	+ %	Of Excess Over
$ 0	$ 40,000	$ 0	0	$ 0
40,000	90,000	0	.8	40,000
90,000	140,000	400	1.6	90,000
140,000	240,000	1,200	2.4	140,000
240,000	440,000	3,600	3.2	240,000
440,000	640,000	10,000	4	440,000
640,000	840,000	18,000	4.8	640,000
840,000	1,040,000	27,600	5.6	840,000
1,040,000	1,540,000	38,800	6.4	1,040,000
1,540,000	2,040,000	70,800	7.2	1,540,000
2,040,000	2,540,000	106,800	8	2,040,000
2,540,000	3,040,000	146,800	8.8	2,540,000
3,040,000	3,540,000	190,800	9.6	3,040,000
3,540,000	4,040,000	238,800	10.4	3,540,000
4,040,000	5,040,000	290,800	11.2	4,040,000
5,040,000	6,040,000	402,800	12	5,040,000
6,040,000	7,040,000	522,800	12.8	6,040,000
7,040,000	8,040,000	650,800	13.6	7,040,000
8,040,000	9,040,000	786,800	14.4	8,040,000
9,040,000	10,040,000	930,800	15.2	9,040,000
10,040,000	....	1,082,800	16	10,040,000

[1] There is a limitation on the credit in estates of nonresident aliens dying after November 13, 1966. See Code Sec. 2102.

[2] The above table may not be used in computing taxes on estates of certain members of the Armed Forces.

[3] The adjusted taxable estate is the taxable estate reduced by $60,000.

¶ 2008 NONRESIDENT ALIENS

For the estates of decedents dying after November 10, 1988, estate and gift tax rates presently applicable to U.S. citizens are also applicable to estates of nonresident aliens. The amount of estate and gift tax is determined by applying the rate schedule set forth in Code Sec. 2001(c) to the cumulative lifetime and deathtime transfers subject to U.S. transfer taxes and then subtracting gift taxes payable on post-1976 lifetime transfers. Because the estate of a nonresident noncitizen generally does not (except where permitted by treaty) receive the $192,800 unified credit available to U.S. citizens, the additional 5% rate applies to the taxable transfers of nonresident noncitizens in excess of $10 million only to the extent necessary to phase out the benefit of the graduated rates and unified credit actually allowed by statute or treaty.

If the amount with respect to which the tentative tax to be computed is:	The tentative tax is:
Not over $10,000	18 percent of such amount.
Over $10,000 but not over $20,000	$1,800, plus 20 percent of the excess of such amount over $10,000.
Over $20,000 but not over $40,000	$3,800, plus 22 percent of the excess of such amount over $20,000.
Over $40,000 but not over $60,000	$8,200, plus 24 percent of the excess of such amount over $40,000.
Over $60,000 but not over $80,000	$13,000, plus 26 percent of the excess of such amount over $60,000.
Over $80,000 but not over $100,000	$18,200, plus 28 percent of the excess of such amount over $80,000.
Over $100,000 but not over $150,000	$23,800, plus 30 percent of the excess of such amount over $100,000.
Over $150,000 but not over $250,000	$38,800, plus 32 percent of the excess of such amount over $150,000.
Over $250,000 but not over $500,000	$70,800, plus 34 percent of the excess of such amount over $250,000.
Over $500,000 but not over $750,000	$155,800, plus 37 percent of the excess of such amount over $500,000.
Over $750,000 but not over $1,000,000	$248,300, plus 39 percent of the excess of such amount over $750,000.
Over $1,000,000 but not over $1,250,000	$345,800, plus 41 percent of the excess of such amount over $1,000,000.
Over $1,250,000 but not over $1,500,000	$448,300, plus 43 percent of the excess of such amount over $1,250,000.
Over $1,500,000 but not over $2,000,000	$555,800, plus 45 percent of the excess of such amount over $1,500,000.
Over $2,000,000 but not over $2,500,000	$780,800, plus 49 percent of the excess of such amount over $2,000,000.
Over $2,500,000 but not over $3,000,000	$1,025,800, plus 53% of the excess over $2,500,000.
Over $3,000,000	$1,290,800, plus 55% of the excess over $3,000,000

For the estates of decedents dying after November 10, 1988, where permitted by treaty, the estate of a nonresident alien is allowed the same unified credit as a U.S. citizen multiplied by the proportion of the total gross estate situated in the U.S. In other cases, the estate of a nonresident alien is allowed a unified credit of $13,000 (which exempts the first $60,000 of the estate from estate tax). Residents of possessions are entitled to a unified credit equal to the greater of $13,000 or $46,800 multiplied by the proportion of the decedent's gross estate situated in the United States.

Pursuant to treaty obligations, a nonresident alien who is a domiciliary of Australia, Finland, Greece, Italy, Japan, Norway, or Switzerland are allowed a unified credit equal to $192,800 multiplied by the proportion of the decedent's gross estate which is situated in the United States at the time of his or her death.

Any amount that had been allowed as a unified credit against the gift tax for any gift made by a decedent will reduce, dollar-for-dollar, the unified credit allowed to the estate.

In the case of the estate tax provisions relating to expatriation to avoid estate tax (Code Sec. 2107), the allowable unified credit is $13,000.

TOPICAL INDEX

References are to paragraph (¶) numbers.